Second Edition

ISRAEL

On Your Own

by Harriet Greenberg

Arnold Greenberg
Series Editor

Special Essay by
Kate Simon

Published by Passport Books in conjunction with
Alive Publications

Printed on recyclable paper

PASSPORT BOOKS
a division of *NTC Publishing Group*
Lincolnwood, Illinois USA

Note: As this edition goes to press, a peace agreement has been signed between Israel and the Palestine Liberation Organization. Under the terms of this agreement, the Gaza Strip (not of interest to tourists) and the West Bank town of Jericho will be administered by a new Palestinian government. Other parts of the West Bank will continue to be administered by Israel. Other changes will surely take place during the life of this edition. Since these are impossible to predict, the reader should stay abreast of current poltical conditions. The Israel Government Tourist Office is a good source of information.

Cover photo: Courtesy of the Israel Government Tourist Office, Chicago.

Greenberg, Harriet.
  Israel on your own/by Harriet Greenberg; special essay by Kate Simon. — 2nd ed.
      p.   cm.
    Includes index.
    ISBN 0-8442-9643-0: $14.95
    1. Israel — Guidebooks. I. Title.
DS103.G69   1993   93-35685
915.69404'54 — dc20   CIP

1996 Printing

Published by Passport Books, a division of NTC Publishing Group,
4255 West Touhy Avenue,
Lincolnwood (Chicago), Illinois 60646-1975
© 1994, 1988 by NTC Publishing Group and Alive Publications Ltd.
All rights reserved. No part of this book may be reproduced,
stored in a retrieval system, or transmitted in any form,
or by any means, electronic, mechanical, photocopying or otherwise,
without the prior written permission of NTC Publishing Group.
Manufactured in the United States of America.

6 7 8 9 ML 9 8 7 6 5 4 3 2

Acknowledgments

To Linda Tristin, for her help in researching and writing the first edition of this guide, and to Susan Brushaber, for all her help in writing this second edition—thank you. To Arnold, Michael, and Douglas, who've made me laugh a lot in my life— "Guys, remind me, the next time we're in Tijada, there's a chicken sandwich...."

Dedication

*To my mother, Lillian Pinchoff,
and the memory of my father, Joseph,
with love*

Contents

The "On Your Own" Travel Guides

In a series of essays written in 1597, Francis Bacon penned, "When a traveller returneth home, let him not leave the countries where he hath travelled altogether behind him." Although we might phrase it rather differently, we wholeheartedly second that sentiment, and with it in mind, we have launched the "On Your Own" travel series.

These unique guides were created for the traveler who wants to be immersed in a different culture for a length of time. And for the adventurous independent traveler, curious and open minded, young and not "as young as they feel," who is eager to explore new travel horizons or yearns for a fresh approach to visiting those beloved familiar places.

For the individualistic traveler, a guidebook can be the key ingredient in a delightful travel experience. The "On Your Own" guides were designed to increase your knowledge of the destination before you depart by offering detailed information about the country today, the faces and faiths of the people, their foods and mores. Because the "past is prologue" we offer a concise glimpse into the country's history.

Travel has become a vital part of peoples' lives, but for most of us, travel time is limited by work or family commitments. We must make each vacation minute count. We have kept this firmly in mind when preparing these guides. Each author visited scores of places that are not included in the guide. Rather than merely offering a list of hundreds of sights or an alphabetical, dispassionate report about a site, we have focused on those with unique features. We have visited each site, hotel, restaurant, and shop personally. Our choices are subjective, but recognizing that a person should "travel to his own drummer," we offer many options. These allow you to plan a trip to fit your style, interests, pace, and pocketbook.

The heart of the "On Your Own" guides is the designation of "base cities" — each interesting in its own right, located in an area of major tourist interest, and offering the region's best accommodations, restaurants, and nightlife. From the base, we offer exciting excursions that allow you to explore the surrounding area at your leisure and return to a comfortable bed, hot bath, and delicious dinner each night. A time saver, base cities permit you to spend your precious time seeing and experiencing –rather than packing and unpacking.

The guides are designed to be carried with you each day as every base city and major excursion is explored in depth and detailed walking tours lead you through the most important sights.

Aren't there plenty of guidebooks available already? Yes there are, but those old familiar names are just that–old and familiar. Having carved out comfortable niches for themselves thirty or more years ago, they have merely added new destinations while maintaining a pre-set format.

How can identical guidebooks work for destinations as disparate as Paris and Bali? Just as destinations vary so does our coverage, in an effort to present the information in the way it will work best for you. Guides with the most detailed sightseeing have inevitably been written for the low-budget backpacker who has several months to roam the destination's backroads.

Why do most guides assume that more affluent travelers require only superficial information? Other guides have remained static while American travelers, more of whom traveled abroad in recent years than ever before, have become increasingly confident, adventuresome, eager to explore, and involved. Travel is a hands-on experience.

If travel is your passion and you are curious, open-minded, and willing to strike out on your own, you are an "On Your Own" Traveler. Welcome aboard!

Harriet & Arnold Greenberg

Introduction

There's something extraordinary about a vacation that in one stay offers an opportunity to visit historical sites and holy places with names familiar since your childhood, an authentic flavor of two ancient heritages, a tropical swimming and diving resort, a pristine mountain lake, and, at the center of it all, bustling cosmopolitan cities with deluxe hotels, restaurants that make dining a definite pleasure, hundreds of interesting shops, and a surprising range of nightlife. Oh yes, there is a very salty sea encircled by a stark desert—and a snowcapped mountain as well.

Israel in effect offers many vacations in one and, while they intertwine and mesh, each is quite different.

The historical and religious aspects of any trip to Israel are paramount of course, for this fertile land strip in which Jews have lived and died since the days of the Old Testament, where Jesus was born, where he preached and was crucified, and from which the prophet Mohammed ascended to heaven on his white horse, has been at the core of history since the beginning of human kind.

The stunning ruins of ancient civilizations that flourished here, the hidden desert caves which gave shelter to parchment scrolls and the remains of the prophets, the mute stone wall of a beloved temple, and magnificent churches and mosques built on the sites of miracles are thrilling to see, to touch, to climb, and to explore—no matter your religion, the marginality or depth of your faith, or whether you have an established faith or not.

Jerusalem, at the heart of it all, is unique. Physically beautiful, it is actually three cities in one. The ancient holy one, its thick walls striving to keep the history and legend intact, is encircled by a modern Jewish city to the south and west and a picturesque, slower-paced Arab one to the north and east. In its narrow labyrinth of streets, two ancient cultures meet in an uneasy peace. The Hassidic Jew, his long silk coat tightly buttoned, his curled side locks flapping wildly beneath his fur-rimmed hat, rushes along barely glancing at his Arab neighbor, patterned headscarf flowing, skillfully arranging his multicolored ceramic bowls, woven rugs, and aromatic spices as his family has done for generations. The city is dominated by the gilt cupola on the Dome of the Rock, which stands on the Temple Mount and is the holiest Moslem site in Israel.

To the north, the Sea of Galilee and the villages surrounding it played a vital part in the life of Christ. Since Jesus was born, lived, and died within the borders of modern Israel, virtually every sacred Christian site lies within its boundaries.

But unless you are like the pilgrims who have journeyed here for thousands of years (Christian, Orthodox Jew, devout Moslem) you will want to balance your vacation, and that is why the diversity of Israel will delight you.

Brash Tel Aviv, one hour from Jerusalem, on the Mediterranean Sea, and the stunning trilevel seaport of Haifa, just two hours north, are twentieth-century cities with all the amenities a vacationer enjoys and the necessities a business traveler requires. When you consider that until the end of the nineteenth century a visitor to this land stayed in a *khan* (a roadside caravanserai set up to accommodate merchants and their wares, be they gems or goats), you'll be amazed at the luxurious hotels with pools, health clubs, and spas that abound here. The sheer number and diversity of restaurants will add to your pleasure.

Leisure-lovers will enjoy sunning on Elat's sandy beaches, skimming over the stunning coral reef in its bay, and dancing till dawn at one of the discotheques that keep this hedonistic city alive at night. A revitalizing dip in the salty Dead Sea, where you absolutely cannot sink, will do wonders for your skin and for your photo album. Active sports enthusiasts can enjoy horseback riding in the Galilee and in the Arava desert, play eighteen holes of golf and unlimited tennis, or rappel down sheer desert cliffs.

Slightly tamer pleasures await the bargain hunter at frenetic flea markets in Jaffa and Akko, the Arab market in Old Jerusalem, and the Bedouin market in Beersheba.

If you are concerned about the environment, you will appreciate the steps Israel has taken to preserve unique aspects of its environment with the development of nature park reserves. Biblical animals, ancient copper mines, a desert spring where ibex drink, and a wadi as full of craters as the moon is, are all parts of the protective parks system.

As a nation, Israel is an infant, but the Hebrew identification with this land can be traced back to the day Abraham, his wife Sarah, and his nephew Lot left the city of Ur in Chaldea (now Iraq), ventured forth toward the Holyland, and multiplied. After thousands of years in exile, scattered over different parts of the world, on each Passover firmly renewing their vow, "Next year in Jerusalem," Jews returned to this land in 1948 and set about building a modern nation with an urgency born out of unspeakable suffering.

When my parents returned from their first visit to Israel, I asked what had impressed them and my mother replied, "Harriet, you should see the flowers and trees everywhere." I was too young to appreciate what that meant until years later when I too visited Israel.

The fabulous flowers and trees sprouting in the cities and in the deserts are the outward manifestations of the pride and love the Israelis have for this land. Again and again, in a variety of contexts, you'll hear "Finally, our own country!" To me, nothing illustrates these emotions better than the juxtaposition of Memorial Day on May 13 and Independence Day on May 14. The former, a somber day, is dominated by visits to military cemeteries, where virtually every family has a son, husband, or father to mourn, and a two-minute silent tribute when the entire nation literally comes to an absolute halt. The latter, immediately following, is celebrated each year with an unrestrained joy that spills over into the streets and skies. By linking these two days forever, the Israelis never forget that the freedom of their young nation rests on the sacrifice of young lives. It is my favorite time to be in Israel. Israelis can be abrupt and challenging and often are infuriating, but they are a vital and unique people. You'll find your visit with them a richly rewarding one.

By any standard, Israel represents an ideal vacation destination. All that is required of you now is to follow the words of the Bible, "Get thee out unto the land that I will show thee" (Genesis) and ours, "Have a wonderful trip."

Harriet Greenberg

Israel

by *Kate Simon*

James Joyce once said of Roman ruins that they served Italians to show off the bones of their grandmothers. It cannot be said, even by a latter-day Joyce, that Israel, a land resting on a deep meshwork of ruins incessantly explored by professional and amateur archeologists, is a pile of distasteful bones. Her ruins are the living spine, the limbs, the braincase, that still carry the memories and passions which shaped the country and even now determine its unique character. The burdens of its history create a monumental, many-voiced symphony; a vast, majestic tapestry rich in colors and textures. The startling density of sounds and tones dazzle and move the visitor rarely ready for the riches that pour out of this small vessel—the whole of Israel is about the size of America's New Jersey.

Even the earth's early myths, before the time of records, attached themselves to this welcoming soil, readying it for earth-shaking events—from drives of early imperialists, the strife of religious fervors, to desperation for shelter and the avid search for Utopias. The pleasant playground that is Jaffa, for instance, points to a rock in its fishing harbor and explains that it was here that Andromeda, chained by her father as a sacrifice to Poseidon, was rescued by Perseus on his winged horse. The frustrated dragon who was to eat her became, after many transfigurations, the dragon ultimately killed by St. George. A myth that may have been as old and reshaped also rises from these waters (claimed to be the earliest of Mediterranean ports) as the ordeal of Jonah, held in the belly of a whale for three days and nights and then spilled onto Jaffa's shore.

Jaffa might also be used as an exemplar of the later vicissitudes which made, unmade, and remade Israel. Joshua, who conquered Jericho, was less successful here; he was stopped by the Philistines, a triumphant people whose large lands bore their name, "Palestine," through the centuries. Around 1000 B.C. King David conquered Jaffa, and in Solomon's time it became the region's prime port, through which the King imported the cedars of Lebanon for his great temple. (Mystics have said that King Solomon's legendary wealth was yielded to him by the sea at Jaffa and that immense watery treasures were still to be expected, those to be apportioned to the devout and just by the Messiah when he arrives.) In the fourth century, B.C., Alexander the Great took the port, later retrieved by the Hebrew Simon Maccabee. Then came the Romans, who ceded the town to their energetic, bestial, partial-Jew friend, Herod. In the Jewish rebellion against the Romans of A.D. 70, the sea raised huge black teeth and drowned many of the rebels. Leaping centuries, we come to a period of Moslem rule. Christianity, which had earlier marked Jaffa with its miracles, returned with the Crusaders who were, in turn, ousted by Egyptian Mamelukes. The Turks took over in comparatively recent times when the port was already a neglected backwater which, however, the young Napoleon found worth despoiling, killing a large number of Christians and Moslems during his short stay. The depleted town became an Arab stronghold and stayed such until it reverted to the Israelis in 1949 to become the bright village we know now.

Although the Israeli sky has covered many interactions of Jaffa's history, each place and city has its own distinctive mood and tones, its own deep sorrows and beauties. Zefat sits high, mysterious, evocative as a meshwork of curving, narrow streets through which howling winds occasionally barrel and scream, possibly echoing old conflicts and desperate prayer. One of the four sacred cities of Judaism, Zefat became a center of rabbinical learning as early as the first and second centuries and later the font of Cabbalistic mysticism. After the depredations of the Crusaders—who did not always bother to differentiate between Jews and Moslems—and of the conquering armies of Islam, the Jewish population dwindled, to grow again in the sixteenth century as a singular place of Hebrew learning, producing the first Hebrew book. Later disasters reduced the colony of Jewish families who stayed as a small minority under the Arabs until it was retaken by Israeli forces in 1948. Now it is a Jewish city of painters and their studios and a still intensely religious community that maintains a cluster of extraordinarily decorated synagogues, the loveliest and poorest recently painted in primitive flower designs by a beadle and his son. One senses the mystic, religious flavor almost before actually entering the city, that sense justified by the fact that a woman about to ask directions of a young man in the long back coat, the wide black hat, and the sidelocks of the Orthodox first ascertains whether he is one of the religious a woman might address; some will not respond since it is an abomination to talk to a strange woman. He will—if he will—lead one to a synagogue which has a small enclosure, like a low cell, in which only rabbis prayed, or he may direct the visitor to inventive new housing whose pinnacles might have been touched by the Spanish Gaudi.

There are towns whose history stopped early, leaving astonishing extents and depths of ruins. By way of the appealing, picturesque town of Rosh Pinna one reaches the nearby kibbutz called Ayelet Hashahar. It was founded in 1916 and had developed a variety of activities, including the care of a modest, elegant museum of finds from the nearby excavations of venerable Hazor. A walk past mirrors of fisheries, through clusters of yellow blossoms and thistle, to the hum of a small plane dusting growing fields, one approaches the vast ruined city which requires decades—some say centuries—to explore thoroughly. So far twenty-one layers of communities have been uncovered, dating from not quite 3000 B.C. to the time of the Greeks. It was, in its time, a major Canaanite city, the capital of numerous pre-Israelite kingdoms which Joshua destroyed in the thirteenth century B.C., burning the city to the ground. Two centuries later the Israelite colony that had settled in was fortified by King Solomon and additionally expanded and strengthened by King Ahab. It became a significant city until in the 700s B.C. the Assyrians destroyed much of it and closed its history. Archeologists have brought to view vestiges and ornaments of a Canaanite temple and small houses, one still accompanied by its grindstone. The most extraordinary find so far is a masterwork of engineering devised in King Ahab's time—a water storage system that one can actually explore. By walking down modern steps built over the ancient, one sees the deep cut that leads to a tunnel and a pool that served as a reservoir in times of drought or siege. (If you are lucky, there will be a bird or two singing and endlessly circling the higher levels, where sunlight still strikes the shaft to the pool.)

Moving back to the music of living cities, one hears the Cabbalistic whispers of Zefat outshouted by the raucous trumpet tones and roll of martial drums over Caesarea, through endless time the goal of marching armies, tearing through marshes and woods. The Phoenicians used its seafront as their local harbor, as did the Greeks after Alexander the Great took the area and settled in soldiers, gods, and their temples. When the Romans arrived, the larger-than-life Herod, Rome's good friend (except for short intervals when he sought favor of the Jews) built them a fine city and dedicated it to Augustus. He thus created the font of Roman power: Pontius Pilate kept his official residence in the city which Herod embellished with a theater, racing grounds, a temple dedicated to Augustus—all for the use of Roman officials —and for himself, a magnificent residence. In spite of Herod and the Romans, Christianity was, as we know, setting down strong roots. St. Paul was kept imprisoned in Caesarea for two years and St. Peter converted a centurion, the first known act of baptism, here. After the Romans left, Christian powers built an impressive library and produced the first history of the early Church.

As local history frequently goes, Caesarea had also been the scene of Jewish dedication, expressed as revolts against the Romans, which lost them great heroes and dragged them into slavery. When, centuries later, the Crusaders marched in to displace the resident Arabs, the decayed city took on Christian luster with a fortress built by St. Louis of France and the purported discovery of the Holy Grail by Christian soldiers from Genoa. The sojourn of the Crusaders was brief and Herod's proud city dissolved as wilderness, to be reclaimed by the Israelis as a kibbutz, Sedot Yam, established in 1940. Around the settlement there grew a resort city of rangy, gardened houses, the retirement place of a number of famous and prosperous Israelis who share, along with the ghost of Herod, the marble pillars and headless gods that sit at the edges of their gardens and beaches.

As Caesarea was indelibly marked by Rome, Akko still bears the large, heavy stamp of the Crusades, driving with intense religious fervor to counter the frightening advances of the Arabs in new territories. Through endless time Akko was an important port, used successively by the Canaanites, by the Phoenicians, and by the long following litany of invaders to come to rest under the control of the Arab caliphs of Damascus. The armies of the Crusades took the city in 1104, renamed it St. Jean d'Acre, and filled it with palaces, fortresses, and trading centers, each under the control of different knightly orders who together created a flourishing center. For four years the city was under the majestic hand of the famous Saladin, but it was taken back by the equally majestic hand of Richard the Lion-Hearted. The infinitely more gentle hand of St. Francis of Assisi worked here at establishing a nunnery for the Poor Clares who, it is said, scarred and deformed their faces to repel the Arabs.

When Jerusalem fell to the Arabs in 1187, Akko became the capital city of the Christian kingdom, a troubled city torn by contention between two major orders who killed not only each other but thousands of Moslems. A year later the avenging Mameluke sultan of the area put an end to the Crusader kingdom which had existed for not quite two hundred years. After gathering silt and decay for three hundred years, the port was rebuilt by a Druze leader and later a Turkish pasha. In 1918 Akko came under the control of the British, who had a diminished town to guard against the Jewish underground, who entered in 1920. Those captured were held in the black cells of the Crusaders' immense citadel, as were the Jewish prisoners taken during World War II. In May of 1948, Israeli soldiers took Akko and soon helped in the placing and acculturation of newly arrived Romanian and Russian Jews, who were followed by an international flow which mingled with the remaining Arabs. They have built new housing and shopping areas but kept the immense stand of Crusader walls and the vibrant Arab souks of fish and spice stalls and souvenirs whose vendors have good English, replete with phrases like "Look here, you beautiful American rose!" Below the flattering merchants, there is a gaiety of fishing boats and excursion boats that ply between Akko and Haifa and Nahariya. In spite of the present ebullience, however, Akko is still overshadowed by the enormous enclave built by the Knights of St. John. Most of it lies under a great mound, but recent excavations have cleared large sections of the twelfth-and thirteenth-century buildings. One area, which is referred to as the crypt, is actually a vast refectory whose beams bear the coat of arms, ornamented with the fleur-de-lis, of Louis VII of France, who stayed here in 1148. In this refectory there is a deep opening that leads to a subterranean passage that may have existed long before the Crusaders but must have been useful to them in reaching the sea and marauding ships unseen in the dark of night.

While the lances and the scimitars of the Crusaders and the Arabs, the representatives of two monotheistic religions, became strongly rooted in this bloodied earth, where was the third great root, planted by Abraham, Isaac, and Jacob? Passive, speaking in low voices in threatening times, at times driven to heroic rebellion, sometimes borrowing invaders' mannerisms, cleansing itself to essential purity at others, Judaism persisted and insisted on persisting. Bet Shearim, for one, is an entirely Jewish ruin though it is touched by symbols imposed by a controlling civilization. A curiously moving witness of a noble time, Bet Shearim is a necropolis, now attractively sheltered by broad trees and flowering bushes of the venerable learned in Jewish history. The story begins with the defeat of the Bar Kochba rebellion against the Romans in 135. A leading religious academy decided to move from its center south of what is now Tel Aviv, vulnerable to avenging Romans, to this obscure place, where it would establish the Sanhedrin (religious court) under the leadership of the "Prince" Judah ha-Nassi, the court's patriarch. Here he died as did his sons, one of whom had followed him as ruler of the community. Other religious Jews came to be buried here among the holy and learned when their cemetery on the Mount of Olives in Jerusalem was taken from them. The endless imposing catacombs and their large sarcophagi are marked with names in Hebrew and Greek (a witness of the Hellenized Romans) while among the pagan ornaments—a gazelle, lions, an eagle, a bull—one finds a menorah. An odd place, free of bones and other objects that through the centuries were taken by grave robbers, it lacks any of the morbidity of mausoleums; the easy, confident mood of these dead devout and learned is expressed in an inscription, in Greek, said to mean, "Good luck in your Resurrection."

Resounding names of Hebrew learning are also commemorated in Tiberias, the town named for the emperor Tiberius, as singularly abandoned and perverted a man as its Hebrew holy men were disciplined and moral. In the expected mélange of Crusader castle, Roman vestiges, and Christian church sit the tombs of great scholars and teachers, resting, as they should be, in yet another of the four sacred Jewish cities. One tomb is dedicated to the great scholar Akiba, who was killed by the Romans for his vigorous support of the Jewish rebel Simon Bar

Kochba. Here, too, is the tomb of Yohanan Ben Zakkai, the founder of a noted rabbinical school, set among a group of tombs that hold the remains of miracle rabbis and rabbis who were saints. In the center of town appears the most radiant name, that of the Spanish-born Maimonides, who died in 1204, leaving a cherished, vivid memory of wide learning and keen intellect, as well-versed in medicine—he was a physician—as he was in Greek philosophy and Hebrew thought. To accompany the tombs, the city holds two antique synagogues melded as one. A pavement of the older unit (third to fourth centuries) bears a marvel of mosaics that conspicuously depict a Torah shrine flanked by two seven-branched candelabra and Shofar horns.

Two of the three religious voices that dominate the rich music that sings "Israel" rise above Capernaum on the north bank of the Sea of Galilee. It was in and about Capernaum that Jesus gathered his fishermen disciples, taught his parables, performed his several miracles, including that of the five loaves and two fishes that fed thousands, and preached in a local synagogue. Among the flower-hung ruins there is an imposing stretch of synagogue remains in pure white stone shaped as fluted columns and ornate Corinthian capitals. Among the fine carvings still discernible, one finds vine clusters and olive branches surrounding a design that might be the Star of David and a version of the Ark of the Covenant. The original design of the synagogue can be traced out in the aisles and the stone benches and also by sections of structure that suggest a women's gallery. As is the myth- and miracle-making habit in Israel, pilgrims who visit the Octagon of St. Peter, a church that stands on a cluster of humble houses of Peter's time, insist on believing that the spectacular Capernaum synagogue is the one in which Christ preached, not historically possible since the temple postdates the man by three to four hundred years.

The varied music sounds as dulcet voices from the north—Cana, the Mount of the Sermon—and from the south the keening of despair and the heroic calls that rise from the brutal, rusty hill of Massada, where 960 Jews arranged their own deaths by killing each other, ten men putting the others to the sword, they to succumb to one and the last to die on his own sword, a defiant act that denied the Romans the final victory over the long-besieged fortress. Younger, fresher voices sing out of the many kibbutzim busy at their miscellany of tasks—growing fruits, feeding herds of cattle, entertaining and housing vacationers, experimenting in improved optics, manufacturing clothing and furniture, staging theater and music festivals.

The heart of this singular symphony, its grand finale, is "Jerusalem the golden, with milk and honey blessed," the Jerusalem so cherished that one psalm calls out, "If I forget thee, O Jerusalem, let my right hand forget her cunning." All the multitongued voices gather here—Abraham, David, Solomon, Jesus Christ, Herod, Pontius Pilate, Mohammed, Saladin, Richard the Lion-Hearted—and soaring above them the profound emotions that emerge from the mosques, the stones of ancient synagogues, and the churches which keep as their trust the religions that guide the lives of millions of people in every corner of the earth.

No important name is muted; there are no ghosts in Jerusalem. Jesus Christ still sits with his apostles at the Last Supper here and carries his heavy cross through the narrow streets of the Old City. The Dome of the Rock, which glistens above the city, is a goal of devout Moslems second only to Mecca. They come to worship at the place of the Moriah Rock, from which Mohammed rose to the seven Heavens on his way to Mecca, the same Rock to which Abraham brought his son Isaac to perform the sacrifice that would assert his faith. Below is another object of ancient and present awe, the Western Wall of the Great Temple first built by Solomon, destroyed and then rebuilt by tireless Herod. As the Wailing Wall, it lamented the irreparable loss of Scrolls and the Ark centuries ago; as the present-day Western Wall, it is a place for dedications along with prayers. David still lives, as testified to by the vast excavations of the city he conquered and from whose halls he consolidated an empire. His son, Solomon, lives as one who strengthened and enriched the city which became the center of his faith and that of his kingdom.

Historically a crossroads city, a polyglot receptacle of many peoples, Jerusalem has returned fully to its colorful old role. The small city of golden-white stone and verdant parklets displays in its lively streets the faces and speech of people from over one hundred different provenances. Much of the dazzling variety can be experienced at one of Jerusalem's favorite meeting places, the shops and cafés of the pedestrian mall called Ben Yehudah

Street, burbling and laughing in Russian, Afghan, several kinds of English, the lilts and falls of Hungarian and Romanian, of Bulgarian, of Ashkenazi Yiddish and Sephardic Ladino. A few streets away, an Italian synagogue and a kosher pasta house and again nearby, in another direction, small obscure streets into which have settled, each in his own minute community, Jews from Syria, Jews from Greece, devout Jews from central Europe who, trusting no one else to observe the stringent requirements that rule the making of matzo, bake their own.

Always the city of the "People of the Book," Jerusalem supports universities and other esteemed centers of learning, maintains theater and concerts and a number of museums, some large and significant, some smaller and appealing, all in their individual ways learning centers.

When its working day is over, the city turns to its essential venerable symbols and their quiet tunes—the gentle call of church bells, the chanting of the mosques, and the humming of prayers in the synagogues—a pause in the immortal Israeli music of strife, of woe, of faith, of hope, of fulfillment.

Israel— The Country Today

The word Palestine always brought to mind a vague suggestion of a country as large as the U.S. I don't know why, but I suppose it was because I could not conceive of such a small country having so large a history.

Mark Twain, The Innocents Abroad, 1869

I srael, a very new country and a very old one, has always been a very small one. Yet, for all six thousand years of its existence its affairs have been prominent on the world's stage. And never more so than in the last forty-five years, since that momentous day in May 1948 when David Ben-Gurion declared the formation of a modern Jewish state. In our history section, we will recount some of the events that led to that day.

For the next twenty years, the fledgling nation struggled to secure its hard-won borders. Immigrants from Diaspora countries throughout the world arrived, encouraged by the new nation's Law of Return, which promised immediate citizenship to any Jew wanting it. Many immigrants arrived, however, without the skills necessary to earn a living. With food scarce, the new nation turned for help to its brethren abroad, particularly to those in the U.S., and to other friendly nations as well. Ironically, reparation money paid by the German government for the atrocities of the Nazis aided the country in those perilous times.

Realistically, it is more accurate to measure today's Israel from June 1967, when in six days the map and the psyche of the country were changed forever. Faced with an increasing number of sniping, rocket, and sabotage attacks from its hostile Arab neighbors, on June 5 Israel forces struck back in a series of perfectly executed attacks and, incredibly, six days later, on June 10, they had captured the Sinai region from Egypt (since returned), the Golan Heights from Syria, and, of primary importance, the old city of Jerusalem and the territory on the western side of the Jordan River, previously held by Jordan (now called the West Bank/Judea-Samaria). Their triumph, a tremendous psychological boost for the struggling state, gave Israelis renewed confidence in their leadership and assurance that they would prevail as a nation. It also changed the face of the entire Middle East.

But, as frequently happens in this violent region, new, even more threatening problems arose—both from within the country and from without. In the waning months of the British Mandate before the War of Independence, the Arab nations urged the Arabs of Palestine to flee their homes, promising that they'd return quickly when the Jews had been driven into the sea. Many did so, while others abandoned their homes during the fighting as their villages came under attack. These houses and villages were then occupied by Jewish settlers, for Ben-Gurion's orders were to occupy and hold every inch of ground. When the Jews prevailed, the Arabs could not return to their homes and instead were placed in refugee camps in Lebanon, Syria, and parts of Israel. Angry and embittered, living under the worst possible conditions, young Palestinians turned to terror as a weapon to achieve their goals—the return of their lost homes and the establishment of a Palestinian state. In Israel, groups of right-wing, ultrareligious nationalists pressured the government to allow Jewish settlements in the West Bank. In December 1988 the Palestinian struggle took on a new face, the *intifada* (uprising). Beginning in the Gaza Strip and spreading rapidly to the occupied regions of the West Bank, the intifada primarily consists of young Palestinians throwing rocks at cars, burning tires to block off streets, and constantly attacking Israeli patrols. This has escalated into greater violence in which both Israelis and Palestinians have lost their lives.

The euphoria of 1967 came to a screeching halt on Yom Kippur 1973. Israel was attacked by its Arab neighbors once again. Caught unaware on the holiest day of the Jewish calendar, it took days for the Israelis to mobilize. Although they "won," it was a hollow victory, leaving 2,500 young men lying dead. During the more recent invasion of Lebanon, Israelis openly questioned the actions taken by their government. This was a first and it was obvious that a period of soul-searching had set in.

In the Persian Gulf War, Iraq showered Scud missiles on Israeli cities, and images of Israelis wearing gas masks appeared on television screens around the world. When the war ended, the United States and the Soviet Union, using their enormous influence, convinced the Israelis and their still-hostile Arab neighbors to attend a peace conference. For the first time, Israelis, Syrians, Jordanians, Lebanese, and Palestinians met in a series of talks. Disappointingly, these talks made very little progress and were frequently suspended as positions staked out over long years of strife appeared to be fixed and immutable. So, it seemed to be a miracle that secret talks, mediated by a Norwegian diplomat, resulted in a peace treaty between Israel and the Palestine Liberation Organization (PLO). This new agreement, signed by Israel's Foreign Minister Shimon Peres and the PLO's Yasser Arafat in Washington, D.C., allowed for limited self-rule for Palestinians living in the Gaza Strip and in the oasis town of Jericho, in the West Bank. Of course, signing the treaty is only the first step, and many aspects of the agreement still need to be worked out. A tentative agreement has also been reached with Jordan and talks with Syria continue.

Israel is a parliamentary democracy. Its chief governing body, the Knesset, is a 120-member parliament, chosen by nationwide election. Under this system, votes are cast for a party slate rather than for an individual. The Prime Minister is selected by the majority party. Israel has two major parties: Labor (socialist, left of center) and Herut (conservative, right of center). Neither ever gains a clear majority, forcing them to assemble a coalition. The additional votes come from small splinter parties that often represent narrow interests. These groups therefore wield power disproportionate to their actual numbers. In the next scheduled national election (1996), Israel will switch to direct elections such as those held in the United States. This will have a dramatic effect on Israeli politics. Jockeying for position by the parties has already begun.

The Labor party, that of Ben-Gurion and Golda Meir, governed for almost twenty years. Forced to utilize votes from ultra-orthodox groups, Labor's concessions sowed seeds of discontent in the secular community. One highly unpopular concession exempts ultraorthodox youth from army service on the grounds that they are Talmudic scholars. All others must serve for three years at age 18. In 1977, in a stunning upset, Menachem Begin, leader of Herut and best known for his Irgun activities, fashioned a coalition called the Likud Bloc and became prime minister. His coalition included members representing the growing Oriental (North African) community, which felt overlooked by Labor, and also included ultranationalists. In a short time, settlements started in the West Bank, a source of friction to the Arabs living there and disconcerting to many Israelis as well.

Mr. Begin resigned after the invasion of Lebanon and was replaced as the leader of Likud and as prime minister by Yitzhak Shamir. Mr. Shamir remained prime minister until the 1992 election, when Likud was defeated by the Labor Party. Yitzhak Rabin, a former general and short-lived prime minister, became prime minister once again and vowed to press forward with the peace process. He signaled the Israelis' willingness to make territorial concessions to garner a true peace.

Rabin was tested by a rise in terrorism in the West Bank and Gaza instigated by fundamentalists seeking to derail the talks, as well as increased opposition from Likud and Israeli settlers on the West Bank, but he would not allow these activities to impede the peace process. The new agreement was an acknowledgment by Israel that a more creative answer to the Palestinian "question" was needed, and by the PLO that they would have to accept less than the entire West Bank as a start if their goal of a Palestinian state was ever to be realized. These astonishing events continue to unfold as we go to press. What effect, if any, they may have on your visit to Israel and West Bank destinations are unknown. Stay abreast of current political situations and check with the IGTO.

Israel is a democracy, with a vibrant free press and a people who love a good argument. Only a day or two of reading the editorials, articles, and letters in the *Jerusalem Post* will alert you to her concerns. Obviously, a serious rift exists between the secular community and the orthodox one, led by the vocal and increasingly militant Hassidim. For years, this clannish, highly observant group closed its neighborhoods to traffic on the Sabbath, even stoning offending cars that wandered by. Now, moving into the larger community, they are burning and vandalizing bus shelters whose ads feature a model clad in a bathing suit, picketing cinemas that open on Friday night, and shrilly warning a young female tourist not to expose her body when she removes her shoes for an instant to rest her weary feet. The war of words is on. An infant nation, Israel is at the "terrible twos" stage, seemingly going in several directions at once. How these differences are resolved will in large measure determine how the state grows into adulthood.

The constant need to maintain a high military profile plays havoc with the Israeli economy, which at one point had the "distinction" of having the world's highest inflation rate—1,000 percent annually against the dollar. Since prices are pegged to the dollar (prices are often quoted in dollars), this had little effect on tourists, but for Israeli citizens it was a terrifying period. Recently, using stringent controls, the government has managed to control the rate.

Samuel Johnson once said, "The use of traveling is to regulate imagination by reality, and instead of thinking how things may be, to see them as they are." When you travel in Israel, the timeless images of the past and the unforgettable experiences of each day blend and become a wonderful reality.

The Safety Issue

Is Israel a safe place to travel? We've been asked this question hundreds of times, and our answer is "yes." You will feel more comfortable in Israel than in any large city in the United States or Europe. There is virtually no street crime in Israel, and intifada activities are usually organized in the West Bank and Gaza Strip. However, you must exercise the same common sense you would use at home. Stay abreast of the current political climate. Read the *Jerusalem Post* and check with the Israeli Government Tourist Office (IGTO). If you are planning to visit West Bank towns, such as Jericho and Bethlehem, stay on major roads and do not wander off the beaten track. Avoid walking through the walled city's deserted alleys late at night. Don't hitchhike and don't pick up riders—even those dressed as soldiers.

Faces and Faiths

Eighty-five percent of Israel's population is Jewish with the other 15 percent composed of Moslems, Christians, and Druze. If this leads you to believe that the population is homogeneous, forget it! Israelis come in all sizes, different shapes, and an assortment of colors as well. You'll see Israelis with a Mediterranean look— olive complexions, dark eyes, and curly black hair—while others are blondes and redheads with blue eyes and freckles. Still others have the Semitic facial structure and profiles dating back to antiquity when these people crossed the Euphrates (the word *Hebrew* comes from "Ivrit," an alteration of the river's name) and started a quest that would last for centuries.

Religious practices within the Jewish community differ greatly as well, with some people being only marginally observant and others extremely devout. Israel, much like the United States, is a melting pot, albeit a narrower melting pot, since virtually all newcomers are Jewish. In the years before Independence, most Jewish Palestinians were of Eastern European descent. However, since Israel became a nation, it has encouraged and, in fact, has taken active steps to bring Jews from all countries of the Diaspora to Israel. With few Jews left alive in Europe after the Second World War, the largest immigrations came from neighboring Arab countries, such as Egypt, Morocco, and Iraq. In fact, virtually every Jew in Yemen was airlifted into Israel in 1949. These "newcomers" now account for over 60 percent of the Jewish population.

When Mikhail Gorbachev came to power in the Soviet Union, he permitted Russian Jews to emigrate to Israel, something that previously had been highly restricted. Thousands of Jews left the Soviet Union to live in the makeshift settlements previously occupied by Yemenites and Ethiopians.

Over the two thousand years of the Diaspora, each of these Jewish communities had adapted the outer trappings of their lives to the demands of the country in which they lived, while discreetly observing the basic tenets of their religion. They arrived in Israel with varying traditions, customs, clothing, and foods. Many of these have been integrated into Israeli life. One example of this is the Mimouna Feast Day, on the day following the final day of Passover. It originated in Morocco, where gentiles offered bread to their Jewish neighbors who had observed the holiday and thus the ban on bread. In Israel, it is marked by large picnics and lots of food. A visit to the ethnographic collection at the Israel Museum in Jerusalem provides a fascinating glimpse of Jewish life in several Diaspora countries.

Israel's Jewish Community

The Jewish community can be classified into three large groups. **Ashkenazi Jews** originated in Central and Eastern Europe or are descended from Ashkenazim who had previously immigrated to the United States, Latin America, and South Africa. Speaking Yiddish, a combination of Hebrew and medieval German, they came to Palestine in large numbers in the sixteenth century to escape the pogroms (murderous raids by non-Jews). They settled in the four sacred Jewish cities—Jerusalem, Hebron, Tiberias, and Zefat. Among them were many Hassidim, members of an ultraorthodox mystical sect. The Hassidim stand out in their style of dress and grooming. The silk brocade waistcoats, black-brimmed hats (trimmed with fur for special occasions), their *peyot* (sidecurls), and *tzitzim* (long prayer shirts which serve to remind the wearer of his obligations) are all holdovers of a tradition that began in Poland several centuries ago. In the heat of Jerusalem, these clothes seem out of place. The women of the sect shave their heads immediately after marriage and from that moment cover their heads with wigs or handkerchiefs. The little girls are dressed primly, and the young boys wear the *peyot* and *kippeh* (yarmulke) at all times. The Hassidim are viewed by many as being iconoclastic or rather reluctant Israelis. Most are exempt from military service and many do not even acknowledge the modern state. They will not accept a state formed by the people —only the Messiah, for whom they are waiting, can proclaim this land as *Ha-Eretz Yisrael*, the Land of Israel. Their rigidly structured lives leave little time for fun and games, and their children learn from a tender age the meaning of study and duty. A stroll through the Hassidic community, Mea She'arim, in Jerusalem will provide you with an intimate glimpse into the life of this unique sect. Ashkenazi Jews started the kibbutz movement, and most of Israel's founding fathers were Ashkenazi.

Sephardic Jews fled to Palestine in large numbers in 1492, when they were expelled from Spain. They spoke Ladino, a mixture of Spanish and Hebrew. Sephardic traditions differ in many respects from those of Ashkenazim. Part of the fleeing community settled in North African countries rather than in Palestine. Called the *Ma'Aravim*, many completed their immigration to Palestine in the late 1800s.

The Askenazi and Sephardic Jews constituted the Jewish population of Palestine before 1948. The newest immigrants arriving after statehood are classified as **Oriental Jews,** which is a confusing term since they are not from the Far East, but are primarily remnants of the Ma'Aravim communities in various Arab nations. Yemenites, Iraqis, Kurds, Persians, and Cochin Jews from India, together with the secretly airlifted Black Ethiopians, now constitute a majority of Israeli Jews.

Many Yemenites continue to wear their traditional long dresses, which are highly embroidered and fetch quite a price when you try to buy an authentic one from the *souk* (market). The women wear a lot of silver and brass (gold if they can afford it) filigree jewelry, which they make and sell as well. Some Moroccan and Indian Jews wear the djellabas and saris of their former lands, while Ethiopians can be seen in the tie-dyed fabrics they drape around themselves. Soon they too will assimilate, fold up the saris, and put on the jeans and T-shirts popular here.

Most young Israelis do not wear the *kippeh* on a daily basis (Israel is a secular state) and restrict its use to the Sabbath and holy days. When they go to synagogue, diversity disappears. Men wearing *kippehs* and *tallis'* (prayer shawls) join in the worship of one God, while the women, secluded in a separate section of the temple, do the same. Only the Orthodox ritual is accepted here. The *tallis* is traditionally blue and white; the Israeli flag bears these same colors.

Israeli life has become increasingly influenced by the *Halacha*, Jewish religious law. The founding fathers, only marginally religious themselves, realized that religious belief and practice were the glue that bound the Jews of the world together and so, when the laws of the new nation were written, they worked out an agreement with Orthodox leaders called "keeping the status quo." The Sabbath (Saturday) and all religious holidays are strictly observed. This means that at sundown on Friday (holidays begin at sundown of the previous day), all public transportation comes to a complete halt. This means intercity buses as well as local ones. Most restaurants, shops, museums, cinemas, and theaters are closed until sundown on Saturday. Even El Al, the national airline, does not fly on the Sabbath. Because this agreement stated that each municipality could continue to function as it had done prior to statehood, confusion reigns. In Haifa, some buses run but the Carmelit subway and cable car do not. In Tel Aviv, some cinemas open while others stay closed. The unobservant head to Little Tel Aviv, where everything is open. In Jerusalem, most things shut down, but scores of restaurants and clubs near Zion Square, in the German Colony, and in Talpiot now stay open on Friday evenings. Unless you are observant yourself, this can be confusing and frustrating. However, with good planning you can work around the confusion.

The Arab Community

There are 700,000 Arab Israelis, 80 percent of whom are Moslems belonging to the Sunni sect. State schools in Arab towns, conducted in Arabic, are administered by Arabs and follow Arab customs. There are Arabic newspapers and radio and TV programs. Most Arabs live in villages and are involved in agriculture. Many young Arabs attend Israeli universities and live in their own neighborhoods in the large cities. Haifa has a large Arab community. **Bedouins** are nomadic Arabs who move across the desert setting up their black tents near grazing lands for their herds of sheep, goats, and camels. The Israeli government has encouraged them to settle permanently in small adobe houses but only a few have done so. The male Bedouins wear the *kaffiyeh* (checkered head scarf) and long white *gelabeyyas* (robes) of the desert while the women, in their black, heavily embroidered robes, head scarves, chunky jewelry, and facial tattoos, are interesting-looking.

The holiest Moslem site in Israel is the Temple Mount in Jerusalem. According to Moslem tradition, it was from a rock on this site (over which the stunning Dome of the Rock mosque was built) that Mohammed ascended to heaven on his horse. Ramadan, the month during which an observant Moslem may not eat or drink from sunrise to sunset, is a cornerstone of the faith.

Over one million Arabs live on the West Bank, an area administered by Jordan until 1967; virtually the same number live in the Gaza Strip. The new peace agreement between Israel and the PLO means that Gaza and the town of Jericho (see Dead Sea) will be under Palestinian authority, while other parts of the West Bank continue to be administered by Israel.

The Christian Community

The Christian population of Israel has remained static, consisting primarily of clergy who are charged with the care of the Christian sacred sites. Nazareth and Bethlehem do have large Arab Christian communities. The holiest sites of the Christian religion lie within Israel's borders, since Jesus was born, lived, and died here. Churches, convents, and monasteries mark the most prominent sites. Sharp disagreements between various Christian sects with regard to traditions and rites have caused an unusual arrangement in the Church of the Holy Sepulchre. Lines on the floor and even down the center of some pillars separate the areas administered and decorated by each sect. Greek Orthodox, Roman Catholics, Armenians, Copts, Syrians, and Ethiopian Abyssinians each have an area unto themselves.

The Druze Community

There are approximately fifty thousand Arabic-speaking Druze in Israel, with most living in their own villages in the Galilee. Their religion, a secret one, was named for Ismail Darazi, who preached in the eleventh century. Druze serve in the Israeli army and are represented in the Knesset. Their most holy site, the tomb of Nebi Shueib, the prophet, is found in a valley near Tiberias. The Druze, a very attractive people, can be discerned by the dashing bushy mustaches worn by the men and the pure white scarves worn on the women's heads.

The Bahais

The spiritual center of the humanistic Bahai faith in Haifa is marked by magnificently sculptured gardens and a hushed tomb that is the final resting place of one of its prophets, farther north on the road to Akko.

The Samaritans

Samaritans, a Jewish-related sect, have lived in the Holy Land for centuries. Once occupying the biblical city of Shechem, they now number a scant 550 souls and live in Tel Aviv and nearby Holon. Mount Gerizim (near Nablus), which they believe to be Mount Sinai, is the site of a ritual sacrifice each Passover eve. Sheep, slaughtered amid chanting, dancing, and clapping, are then roasted and eaten at midnight with matzo and bitter herbs.

If you bring to Israel a fascination for people and their diversity, you'll be amply rewarded.

The Taste of Israel

Israel, a sun-blessed land that straddles the western edge of the Middle East and the eastern edge of the Mediterranean, is the homeland for people from at least thirty countries. You have every right to expect widely varied fare: exotic, nouvelle, sometimes *haimishe*—and you won't be disappointed. But keep in mind that there is no indigenous Israeli cuisine nor a real Israeli way of cooking.

North African and Argentinian Jews brought with them a talent for grilling meats which has become a mainstay in Israeli restaurants. Steaming grain dishes, like couscous and kubbeh, remind the eater of Rabat and Tunis, while blintzes and cholent were favorites in the shtetls of Eastern Europe. This amalgam of cultures makes for some amusing vignettes. Whether it's a group of Ethiopian Jews wolfing down kreplach or Cochins from India munching on falafels, the fact remains that Israel is no culinary melting pot, but rather a buffet piled high with the diverse and beloved dishes of people from every corner of the world.

For the sake of simplicity, Israeli cuisine can be loosely classified into three groups: Eastern European (which most closely resembles American Jewish food), Middle Eastern/Arab, and Western European (authentically prepared or altered for the kosher palate).

Jews from Russia, Hungary, Romania, Poland, and Germany are responsible for the dishes most Americans associate with Jewish cuisine. Pickled (marinated) and smoked fish (salmon and whitefish) prevail at every Israeli breakfast, often accompanied by a thick chunk of challah (eggy bread) or a bagel (needs no explanation). Borscht (beet soup), blintzes (thin rolled crêpes filled with soft, sweet cheese and baked), and potato latkes (ground potatoes and onions, fried and served with applesauce) are often served at dairy restaurants where they are lunch and late-afternoon treats. The dinner hour frequently brings either that brown paste, which when badly prepared can double as cement, chopped liver, or kreplach (triangles of dough filled with meat). Kneidlach (matzohball dumplings served in chicken soup) are eaten as appetizers, while such traditional favorites as boiled beef or schnitzel (usually veal but sometimes turkey) are pleasing entrées. Sample some gefilte fish (a ground mixture of several types of fish formed into oval patties, then poached and served with horseradish) or a cholent, the stick-to-your-ribs beef, potato, and barley stew traditionally prepared on Friday afternoon and left to warm over a small flame till Sabbath lunch. You won't have to eat again for days.

Jews from North Africa share a cuisine similar to those of their Arab neighbors. Many of these foods are part of the country's consciousness by now, and restaurants serving Middle Eastern kosher food form the majority of moderately priced eateries in Israel, while Arab restaurants are very popular in East Jerusalem. Falafels (small fried balls of ground chickpeas) served in a pita (pocket bread) garnished with raw vegetables and tehina sauce, and shwarma (sliced lamb or beef served inside a pita) are sold by sidewalk vendors and at fast-food counters everywhere. Hummus (a thick dip made from ground chickpeas and olive oil) and tehina (a thin paste made of ground sesame seeds) are often served as appetizers, while kebabs (chopped lamb or beef) and shishliks (chunks of beef or lamb broiled on skewers) are popular as main courses. Turkish salad (minced tomato with pungent spices in olive oil), eggplant salad, marinated mushrooms, and a colorful array of meat- and rice-stuffed vegetables are served as part of a mezze, assorted salads served in tiny bowls as hors d'oeuvres. The origin of most of these dishes can be traced back to a particular town or country, but the origin of the falafel arouses controversy. The mystery remains unsolved!

When eating at French or Continental restaurants, which are the most elegant and the most expensive in the country, keep in mind that in most cases dishes have been adapted to conform to kosher dietetic law. While they are delicious, the spicing and preparation (without butter) do alter the taste from the one you may be used to. Our French and Continental restaurant selections (kosher and nonkosher) are limited to those we ate in ourselves and found to be exceptional. When in doubt, stick to Eastern European and Middle Eastern restaurants where the dishes, although lacking some imagination, are made with the freshest ingredients. The result is infinitely superior to a French concoction that has been fussed over by an Egyptian cook who has never been to France and must rely on canned or frozen items to complete the dish.

One of the high-calorie joys of Israel noshing is a late-afternoon or midnight stop on Dizengoff Street (Tel Aviv) or Ben Yehuda Street (Jerusalem), where the konditoreis vie with one another over who can produce the most tantalizing array of baked confections. We are talking here about the best strudels, layers cakes, linzer tortes, and Napoleons this side of Vienna. You'll find these European-style cafés in all of Israel's larger cities. Not to be overlooked are the Middle Eastern pastries and sweets which are drenched in honey or sugar syrup and taste great even after you've eaten far too many. Exceptional baklava (honey, walnuts, and cinnamon layered with phyllo dough), kadaifi (shredded wheat, pistachios, and honey baked in a nest shape), and halva with nuts and wrapped in foil are sold by vendors on the streets of East Jerusalem and in the Moslem quarter of the Old City.

Learning which foods are naturally grown in Israel will help you order wisely. The oranges, bananas, dates, tomatoes, avocados, olives, melons, cucumbers, grapes, and the most delightful surprise of all—fresh, sweet kumquats—are all excellent.

Israel's dairy products are also of the highest quality (the sweetest milk is said to come from the kibbutz at Yotvata, in the south) and the yogurt, which is best eaten plain, is a most refreshing snack on a hot day. The labaneh, which is a soft white cheese made from yogurt (traditionally goat's or sheep's milk) with the whey removed, is a tangy appetizer, served with a drizzle of olive oil and warm pita bread to "spoon" it up with.

Because Jewish orthodoxy prohibits the consumption of meat and dairy dishes at the same meal or on the same plates, restaurants serve either dairy foods or meats. Beware of dishes that seem to contain milk or cream that appear on meat restaurant menus. The ubiquitous Bavarian cream, for instance, a gluey concoction of custard and gelatin topped with chocolate sauce and "whipped cream," will be made with a soya milk substitute or a chemical dairy impostor in a meat-only eatery. Your first swallow will undoubtedly be your last.

Israeli-made alcoholic beverages are not up to snuff, so if you take your drinking seriously or want to enjoy a predinner cocktail, specify imported brands of liquor. On the other hand, Israeli wines are very good and rapidly becoming in vogue abroad. The country's leading producers are the Carmel cooperative, which you can visit in Zikhron Ya'akov (near Haifa), and Montfort. Cabernet Sauvignon and Carignan are the red wines most often served by the glass or carafe, while the very dry Sauvignon and sweeter Chenin Blanc are white-wine choices. Stop and sample the wines made by the Trappist monks at the Latrun Monastery (near Jerusalem). These monks have taken a vow of silence, but the one in the shop does speak and will even show you around on a slow day.

Geography

Topography

The modern state of Israel, tucked in the southwest corner of Asia, occupies a sliver of land just 320 miles long and 50 miles wide to the Jordan River. Hundreds of pages in our ancient-history textbooks record the fierce battles fought for control of this fertile strip, known as the Levant, Canaan, and Palestine. Its location, part of a vital caravan route, the Via Maris, formed the sole land bridge between the lush lands of Egypt and Mesopotamia to the south and the weathy empires of Europe and Asia to the north and east.

Numerous invasions by Assyrians, Persians, Romans, and Crusaders, to name but a few, caused vast migrations by the natives, who returned after each conquest. Cities, built as ports near major water sources or as strategic points, were often destroyed by one invader and rebuilt by the next on the very same site and for exactly the same purpose. Tels, huge, gumdrop-shaped mounds of earth, can be found throughout Israel. They are clues that layers of destroyed civilizations lie buried below. Many tels have been partially excavated, so you can explore them. Even more astonishing than ancient tels is the fact that several modern cities in Israel—cities that you will visit, such as Jerusalem, Jericho, and Haifa—existed in exactly the same locations in ancient times. These, because they were built near major water sources or as vital seaports, remained continuously settled, while those built for strategic purposes and fortified against long-vanquished foes were abandoned.

Israel's ten thousand square miles offer tremendous contrasts. Its major regions vary enormously in topography, landscape, and climate, and one trip will encompass a variety of experiences. These fantastic contrasts create stunning views and eerie natural phenomena. Five geological formations are responsible for the uneven topography. Moving eastward from the ***Mediterranean Sea***, Israel's western border, in vertical lines are a ***coastal plain***, a ***vast mountain range***, a ***desert***, a ***rift***, and a ***smaller mountain range***.

The ***coastal plain***, consisting of wide sand dunes in the south, narrows as it moves northward in almost a straight line till it curves in a graceful arc at the Bay of Haifa. North of Haifa to the Lebanese border, the coastline zigzags at scores of inlets and coves. The plain, divided into three sections, is the country's citrus-growing region, known for its mild, frost-free winters. The most important region, the Sharon, lies between Tel Aviv and Haifa.

The ***western mountain range***, a single mountain chain that changes its name frequently, dominates the country. In the far north, from the Lebanese border to the Jezreel Valley (near Nazareth), the peaks are highest. The range and the region is called the ***Upper***, or ***Northern***, ***Galilee***. Adjoining it to the south is the lower-in-altitude range known as the ***Lower Galilee***. Moving southward, we find the ***Samarian Hills*** and then the rolling hills of ***Judea***, which surround the capital city of Jerusalem. The mountain range continues southward into the Negev Desert.

The ***Negev***, a triangular price of land, has Elat as its southern tip and its wide base just to the north of Beersheba. The Negev Desert encompasses one half of the country's land, but only a tiny fraction of its population lives there.

The ***Jordanian Rift*** forms Israel's eastern belt. An unusual phenomenon, it is an enormous crack in the earth's surface, and in it lies the ***Dead Sea***, known in Israel as the ***Salt Sea (Yam Hamelach)***. The sea is the lowest point on earth of 1,312 feet below sea level.

The ***Golan Heights***, part of the eastern mountain range (in Jordan), were held by Syria until 1967. Mount Hermon, at 7,400 feet the highest point in Israel, is often snow-capped and used as a ski facility in the winter.

As you drive through Israel you cannot help but be impressed by the works of the Jewish National Fund (Keren Kayemet). Even before Israel became an independent state, the fund financed vast irrigation and reforestation projects. Settlements were organized in desolate areas and trees planted where only sand dunes lay. As you drive through the parched Negev you will suddenly turn a bend in the road and see a green patch, a settlement, surrounded by barren desert. It's absolutely breathtaking.

Israel's Major Tourist Regions

On the Coastal Plain

The coastal plain is the most populated region of the country, with large cities and excellent beach areas. From the south: *Ashqelon*, a beach community with some areas of archeological importance; *Ashdod*, a growing commercial area with Israel's most modern harbor facilities; and *Bat Yam*, a lovely beach area just to the south of Jaffa. *Tel Aviv/Jaffa*, Israel's largest city, lies on the Mediterranean Sea at the midpoint of the coastal plain. *Herzliya*, only ten miles north of Tel Aviv, is a wealthy bedroom community for foreign diplomats and the site of posh resort hotels. *Netanya*, twenty miles north, is a less affluent beach area and center of Israel's growing diamond industry. *Caesarea* is home to one of the country's most spectacular archeological sites and its only golf course. *Haifa*, on the coast and the country's major port, is dominated by Mount Carmel, on which the city stands. *Akko*, just to the north of Haifa, has a fascinating old Moslem city to explore and an active marina. *Rosh Hanikra*, which adjoins the Lebanese border, is known for its grottoes (like those of Capri), which are reached by cable car.

The Upper Galilee/Golan Heights

There are no large cities in this area of the country, but it has some of Israel's most beautiful towns and natural sites. *Zefat*, a quiet, ultrareligious small city, now a resort area with a large artist colony, housed Jewish intellectuals who fled there in the sixteenth century. They completed the part of the Talmud known as the *Mishna* and a mystical interpretation of the Old Testament known as the *Cabbala*. Zefat is a good base from which to explore the **Hula Valley**, the **Golan**, and **Banias Waterfall**.

The Lower Galilee

This is another physically beautiful area with a mélange of Arab and Israeli towns side by side. Many of the important sites in the area are associated with the life and teachings of Jesus. **Tiberias**, an ancient town and one of Israel's leading winter resorts, sits on the shores of the **Sea of Galilee (Lake Kinneret)**. **Nazareth**, the town where Jesus grew to manhood, houses Israel's largest Christian Arab community and many churches, convents, and monasteries and is also known for its lively market.

The Samarian Hills

This region lies in the West Bank, the area that was part of Jordan until 1967. Israelis refer to it by its biblical name, **Judea and Samaria**. The status of this region, unlike East Jerusalem and the Golan (which were annexed to Israel), is uncertain, and therefore it is best to check on local political conditions before visiting the area. The major towns in the region are **Nablus**, a commercial center, and **Ramallah**, a lovely mountain retreat that was a winter resort for wealthy Jordanians. In biblical times, the city of **Shechem** stood not far from present-day Nablus. Shechem, where Abraham first entered the land of Canaan, was populated by a small Jewish-related sect called Samaritans. Still in existence, they believe that nearby Mount Gerizim is actually Mount Sinai. Each year, on Passover eve, the five hundred remaining adherents gather at the mountain's base to hold a sacrificial ceremony. Open to the public, it is rather gory but fascinating.

Judean Hills

The uneven distribution of rainfall and underground water sources has made the western portion of Israel, the heart of the country and site of its capital, green and habitable while the eastern slopes are russet-brown desert. *Jerusalem*, perched upon rolling hills, is physically beautiful and historically fascinating. *Bethlehem*, seven miles south, the birthplace of Jesus, is a picturesque Arab village which houses the Church of the Nativity. A new Israeli settlement is located here, *Kiryat Arba*. *Hebron*, one of four ancient Jewish holy cities, is an Arab West Bank town. It is often a site of continuing conflict, so stick to major tourist tracks when visiting. The Cave of Machpelah, which contains the Tomb of the Patriarchs, is nearby.

The Jordanian Rift

Much of this region is below sea level and it is very hot year-round. *Jericho*, one of the world's oldest cities, thought to have been inhabited for eleven thousand years, has several interesting excavated ruins and a monastery that clings to the side of the mountain. The *Dead Sea*, the lowest place on earth, is well known for its sulphur and mineral baths, which aid victims of psoriasis and rheumatic diseases. The *Massada*, on a mountaintop overlooking the Dead Sea, was the last refuge of a Jewish community against the Roman army. It has become a rallying symbol for the nation.

The Negev

An arid region with few natural oases, the Negev is very mountainous. *Beersheba*, capital of the area, modern and growing quickly, is best known for its lively Bedouin market and the Bedouin encampments nearby. *Elat*, at Israel's southern tip, is a booming resort town which attracts young Israelis and Europeans with its deluxe hotels, topless beaches, and lively nightspots. The southern portion of the Negev, near Elat, is called the *Arava*.

History

Early History—to 1917

The history and mystery of Israel and the Holy Land is so vast a topic that it could fill volumes. It starts six thousand centuries ago in 600,000 B.C., when scientists believe human beings first began to inhabit the area, but since this is a guidebook and not an ancient-history text, we've chosen only a few of the more important events to give you a feel for the incredible past of this land known as Canaan, Palestine, and now Israel. For a more complete picture, we recommend reading *The Holy Land* by Jerome Murphy-O'Connor (Oxford University Press). You might also enjoy reading the Bible, for if you open to the tenth chapter of the Book of Genesis, you can follow Abraham, Isaac, and Jacob as they "toured" the Holy Land. Don't scoff! It seems impossible, yet archeological finds here have consistently supplied evidence that confirms biblical accounts.

Six thousand centuries ago, during the Old Stone Age, cave dwellers roamed the area, and your conjecture and imagination are as reliable as anyone else's about what their lives were like. However, as the human race evolved, farming methods were developed, and by 12,000 B.C., there is evidence of advanced tools and cultivated grains. The early signs of what we would call "industralization" are found by 7000 B.C., when the first villages were built, and soon thereafter irrigation was started.

The Early Bronze Age (3200 B.C.) finds temples and palaces erected and advanced tools leading to towns being formed and fortified.

The Middle Bronze Age (2000 B.C.) marks the appearance of Abraham and the other Israelite patriarchs. Of Mesopotamian origin, they headed typical nomadic clans who migrated into the land of Canaan. Mount Moriah, where Abraham prepared to sacrifice his son Isaac, is now believed to be the Temple Mount in Jerusalem. The Hebrews became slaves in Egypt, where they remained until their Exodus under the leadership of Moses. Perhaps one can pinpoint the moment that Moses received the Ten Commandments on Mount Sinai as the event that crystallized the Hebrew nation. The Commandments form the foundation of both religious and ethical conduct. By the way, the location of Mount Sinai is not identified in Jewish tradition; the event is considered more important than the locale.

After wandering in the desert for forty years, the Hebrews returned to this land and conquered it, but their triumph was short-lived as they were invaded by the Philistines. Led by their first king, Saul, the Hebrews fought valiantly, but Saul and his sons were killed. The country in turmoil turned to David, who with his slingshot conquered the giant Goliath and with him, the Philistines. David united the nation and named Jerusalem at its political and religious capital. The Golden Age of Israelite culture and power was ushered in by King Solomon, who built the first Temple on Mount Moriah. The Temple was a symbol of national unity, hence the grief as its destruction. When Solomon died, his kingdom fell apart as various empires and dynasties carved it up. First Babylonians, then Assyrians, then Persians and Greeks controlled the area. The Hebrews, led by Judah Maccabee, wrested control for a short time, only to lose it to the Romans, who ruled for the next four hundred years. It was during the Roman reign that Jesus was born, preached, and was crucified, both the second Temple and Jerusalem were destroyed, and a heroic band of Hebrews committed suicide rather than surrender their last refuge on a mountaintop called Massada. Many of the magnificent churches were constructed during the rule of Emperor Constantine, the first Christian monarch.

In A.D. 620, Mohammed preached a new religion, Islam, which swept Arabia. The Arabs conquered the entire Middle East, which they controlled until 1099, when armies of the First Crusade arrived, determined to free the Holy Land from Moslem control. For the next two hundred years, four Crusades arrived in the Holy Land (the third led by King Richard the Lion-Hearted of Robin Hood fame). On the ruins of the Arab cities they conquered, they built their own. Ruins of Crusader cities (Caesarea) and castles are found throughout Israel.

The Ottomans captured the Holy Land and ruled it for 450 years until the end of World War I, in 1917.

The Modern Zionist Era

The modern Zionist era began in the mid-nineteenth century, as the quality of life for Jews in Eastern Europe deteriorated. Groups of young people seeking to escape the pogroms (murderous raids by non-Jews) formed the First Aliyah (immigration), establishing agricultural villages in the Galilee. With financial and technical aid provided by Baron Edmond de Rothschild, the settlements prevailed. The movement picked up momentum in 1896, when Theodor Herzl, an Austrian newspaperman, published his book, *The Jewish State*. His work, the result of his shock at the open anti-Semitism voiced at the Dreyfus trial, spurred the Aliyah movement and the formation of a Zionist organization which held its first congress in 1897.

The vibrant newcomers to Palestine soon outnumbered the docile Orthodox who had lived there in poverty for generations. It was only a matter of time until the Turks tried to ban new Jewish immigrants. Herzl died in 1904, but his dream did not. As more Jews arrived, usually entering illegally on ships into Haifa, their settlements grew in strength and number. They began to organize a defense force, formed unions, and started the Jewish Agency, which operated as a governing body. World War I, with the Turks fighting on the side of the Axis powers, provided the opening that the Zionist movement needed. Even before General Allenby's British army forced the Turks to leave Palestine, political maneuvering by Zionist organizations prodded the British government to announce its intention to create a Jewish homeland in Palestine. This, the Balfour Declaration, became the hope of the Jewish people and the focus of Arab anger.

The British Mandate period, from 1917 to 1948, was marked by increasing violence between the Arabs and the Jews of Palestine. As the British tried to back away from the Balfour Declaration, riots, general strikes, and attacks by the Arabs created increased tension. When it became apparent that the Jews of Europe were being exterminated during the Nazi era, pressure on the British to allow more Jews to enter Palestine increased. Many illegal immigrants were caught and kept in detention camps on Cyprus. The Jewish underground movement, led by the Irgun, started a series of sabotage raids on British facilities, the most notorious being the bombing of the King David Hotel, which served as British headquarters in Jerusalem. As the situation spun out of control, Britain announced that they would return the mandate of Palestine to the United Nations. The newly formed international organization formally recommended partition of Palestine into a Jewish state and an Arab one in November 1947. When the mandate officially ended on May 14, 1948, David Ben-Gurion formally proclaimed the State of Israel. Dancing in the streets lasted till the next morning, when the fledging state was attacked by the armies of its Arab neighbors. Much to everyone's surprise, the Israelis not only held their own, but increased the amount of land they were to control until the Six Day War in 1967.

Accommodations

Travelers to Israel are in luck when it comes to accommodations. There are lodgings to suit a variety of tastes and pocketbooks. They run a wide gamut from luxurious resort-type hostelries to small simple ones, including kibbutz guest houses, holiday villages, campgrounds, youth hostels, and religious hospices.

Hotels

Hotels, supervised by the Ministry of Tourism and the Israel Hotel Association, are no longer graded with a star system. Rather, they are grouped according to the facilities they offer. Don't be confused by the stars listed next to our hotel recommendations. We have assigned these ratings ourselves to give you a quick fix on the hotels.

Five-star hotels are luxurious, with swimming pools (some heated), a variety of restaurants, health club facilities, business traveler centers, shops, and tennis courts. Four-star hotels are less opulent, but often have pools, saunas, and shopping arcades. Three-star stops, small and functional, are nevertheless well maintained with air conditioning/heating and private baths. Hotels recommended in this guide are all five-star to three-star rated.

Most, but not all, hotels include a huge "kibbutz breakfast" with your room rate. Comparable to a delightful serve-yourself brunch, it includes eggs (to your taste), cheeses, cereals, fresh or canned fruit, fresh vegetables, baked goods, herring, lox, and a variety of cheese spreads. You can request a rate without breakfast. Most Israelis and many European visitors opt for half or full board. They then eat virtually all their meals in the hotel dining room, where there is a fixed daily menu and dining hour and service is hurried and family-style. Avoid this! Israel in general (and our base cities in particular), has an endless variety of restaurants, and you will enjoy sampling them. You can always pay per meal if you are too tired to venture out one evening. Virtually all hotel restaurants, with the exception of East Jerusalem and

West Bank Arab towns, are kosher. A 15 percent service charge is added to all hotel bills. Hotel rates and services such as laundry and food charged to your room are exempt from the additional 18 percent VAT.

Kibbutz Guest Houses

We strongly encourage you to make at least one stop at a kibbutz guest house. There are over two hundred kibbutzim in Israel; twenty-eight of them operate guest houses or holiday villages. Scattered throughout the country, where the kibbutz was often the first line of defense against attack, the guest houses offer comfortable three-star accommodations (two have four-star ratings), excellent kosher dining rooms, swimming pools, large open areas for sunning and strolling, educational lectures, museums, and most of all, a chance to see the kibbutz and its members up close. The Kibbutz Inn and Guest House Association is located at 90 Ben Yehuda Street in Tel Aviv and is open Sunday through Thursday from 9 A.M. to 1 P.M. and 4 to 7 P.M. (Friday till 1 P.M.), closed on Saturday. The guest houses are small, and the popular ones are often booked solid, so it's best to reserve in advance. We'll detail the better ones in their appropriate locations.

Holiday Villages

Somewhat less attractive, holiday villages offer accommodations in mobile homes. Their best selling point is their location, often on stunning Sea of Galilee beaches or in the heart of the Arava Desert near Elat. Not bad if you are traveling with young children.

Youth Hostels

Israel's thirty-two hostels offer comfortable accommodations at rock-bottom prices, regardless of age or membership in a youth hostel group. Located on main streets in large cities and off-beat locations throughout Israel, hostels have kosher kitchens and cooking facilities and some are even air-conditioned. Many limit your stay to three days. The Israel Youth Hostel Association offers members bargain rates at hostels, discounts on buses and trains, and reduced fees at historical sites and museums. For up-to-the-minute news, write to The Israel Youth Hostels Association at 3 Dorot Rishonim Street (Box 1075), Jerusalem or 32 Bnei Dan Street (Box 22078), Tel Aviv. Your local youth hostel organization can give you information as well.

Campgrounds

Weather conditions are usually good enough to permit camping nine months a year. Scattered throughout the country, often near lovely beaches, archeological sites, or national parks, the campgrounds are well planned. They offer tents as well as huts with electricity, kiosks for food shopping, and showers. Public transportation makes them accessible even if you do not have a car. Several campgrounds operate only seasonally. July and August are popular months, as are the Jewish High Holy Days (September and October), so reserve in advance. Write to Israel Camping Union, Box 53, Nahariya 22100, for the latest information. (See Appendix A for a complete list.)

Religious Hospices

Thirty Christian hospices, near Jerusalem or in the Galilee, offer clean, spartan accommodations at extremely low rates on a nonsectarian basis. Usually filled with visiting pilgrim groups, they are very quiet and secluded. Information is available through the Christian Information Center at Jaffa Gate, Jerusalem. Write to it at Ibn Omar Khattab Square, Jerusalem.

Hotel Rates

Hotel prices are usually quoted in dollars and there is no VAT added if you pay by credit card, traveler's check, or dollars. A 15 percent service charge is added to each bill. Most hotels include breakfast in their basic rate, although some deluxe stops do not. You can request a rate that excludes breakfast.

We have described each hotel and its facilities in a concise paragraph and have assigned our own star rating. After each write-up you will see our price scale. This scale is designed to give you a ballpark figure to play with. Obviously rates fluctuate because of holidays, high and low seasons, and other factors.

These categories are based solely on price for double occupancy. Solo travelers can generally figure on a rate of more than half the double rate.

Deluxe—$150 and above per night
Expensive—$90–$150 per night
Moderate—$50–$90 per night
Inexpensive—under $50

Restaurants

Israel has a wonderful assortment of restaurants. The amalgam of people from at least thirty different countries, each arriving with grandma's favorite recipe or two, has resulted in restaurants that cater to a multitude of palates. So, whether your palate tingles to paprika-spiced dishes from Hungary, charcoal-grilled meats from Brazil, or stuffed vegetables from Turkey, you'll find a restaurant —in fact, you'll find several—to satisfy you.

Moderately priced restaurants serving delicious if not creative foods are scattered throughout the country, but the country's finest, most elegant dining rooms are in Tel Aviv and Jerusalem. Tiberias has only a few restaurants, but these serve fresh local foods in charming settings. Elat, on the other hand, has a great many pretentious restaurants, but only a few serve quality fare.

Israeli restaurants are small and it isn't unusual to find an eatery with only a half dozen tables. Most restaurants augment their space by adding a sidewalk café, either open-air or glass-enclosed. These tables are the most sought after and usually fill up first.

Casual dress is *de rigueur* here and that extends to the informal atmosphere in restaurants. A typical man's outfit consists of an open-throated shirt, sans tie, and a sport jacket, while women's outfits run the gamut from trendy to decidedly matronly. Exceptions are the elegant restaurants serving French and Continental food, where people do tend to be more dressed up.

Food is the focus of attention in Israeli restaurants, with ambience seemingly a distant second. One helpful feature is the menu posted near the front door of many restaurants. This gives you an idea of what is served and the price range before you go in. Most of our dinner selections accept major credit cards, but you will notice that smaller cafés and restaurants do not.

You should be aware that the Kashruth (Jewish Dietary Law) has an important influence on dining habits here. The law forbids eating certain foods, such as shellfish and pork, and observant Jews do not ingest a meat product and a dairy one at the same meal. No milk with your roast beef sandwich and no cappuccino if you have just finished a juicy steak. You might not even notice these things, but you will notice that restaurants serve either dairy or meat. All hotel restaurants are kosher and so are most other restaurants. These establishments prominently display their rabbinical certificate and they are closed for the Sabbath. Shrimp and lobster are often found on nonkosher restaurant menus, but pork is rare because Moslems are forbidden to eat it as well. It is sometimes listed as a "white steak."

Dining hours are 11:30 A.M. to 3 P.M. for lunch and 6 to 11 P.M. for dinner, but the most popular dining hours are noon and 8 P.M. Reservations are a must at the few elegant spots in town but are usually unnecessary elsewhere (this is not true in resort areas). Israelis eat out frequently, taking the entire family with them, so booster seats and high chairs are commonplace.

Many restaurants add a 10 or 15 percent service charge to your bill. If they do so, it will be noted on the menu. Israelis rarely leave more of a tip.

Dining choices include fast-food stops serving falafel, shwarma, hamburgers (MacDavid and Burger Ranch are the two favorites), and pizza. Because hotel breakfasts are usually enormous smorgasbords, lunch is often a light meal with blintzes, deli sandwiches, and a variety of salads scooped up with pita at the top of the list.

Restaurant Prices

Most restaurants in Israel are moderately priced and only in Tel Aviv, Jerusalem, and Elat will you find truly elegant dining with prices comparable to those in the U.S. and Paris. You can eat well in Israel inexpensively and that does not mean existing on fast foods. Obviously, eating in Israel's finer restaurants will add to the pleasure of your trip and you will sometimes want to do so. On other nights, you might prefer dining in a setting that is more casual.

We have not attempted to rate restaurants, for that is risky. We have in every instance listed only restaurants we visited personally—and a weight gain of (*deleted*) pounds attests to all the noshing.

In Tel Aviv and Jerusalem, cities with vast numbers of restaurants, we listed them by type of food served, but you will notice that in Tiberias, which has few restaurants, we listed them in the order we liked them, and in Haifa, a trilevel city, we listed them by area. This guidebook is not written according to a formula but hopefully by what will work best for you.

To give you an idea of price before you set out, we have devised this price scale based on three courses (appetizer, entrée, dessert), excluding drinks.

Expensive—$30 plus per person
Moderate—$15 to $30 per person
Inexpensive—under $15 per person

Shopping in Israel

If shopping is your favorite sport, then get ready for an energetic workout. Whether you are looking for a little gift for your Aunt Sadye, want to treat yourself or the special person in your life to a uniquely designed 18-carat gold bauble, or need a battered old copper samovar as the finishing touch in your living room, you'll find it for sale here.

Whether you are an indefatigable shopper or a casual one, you'll be pleased by the diversity both in goods and in atmosphere. A shopping foray in Israel can mean a visit to an elegant fur salon where your mink jacket will be made to order, or a stroll along a bustling street while you ferret out musty antique shops hidden in narrow alleyways. The most fun of all is shopping in the frenetic markets—be they Arab, flea, or Bedouin. Bargaining is a way of life there, so if you hone your skills before you get here and treat it seriously but with a sense of humor and lightness, you'll arrive home with things you'll enjoy for years to come.

Shopping Hours

This is one instance where the diversity can be very frustrating, for Israel does not have set working hours. Every city, every shop, every shopping center seems to set it own hours—which are rarely posted. As a general rule, shops open for business at 9:30 or 10 A.M. and stay open till 1 P.M. They close for a siesta and re-open from 4 to 7:30 P.M. These are Sunday through Thursday hours and do not take into account shops that close one additional day each week. On Fridays or holiday eves, shops close at 2 P.M. and stay closed for the Sabbath. Some then reopen after sundown on Saturday but most do not. Shops in shopping centers do not close for siestas but do keep early-Friday and Sabbath closings. The Arab Sabbath on Friday keeps many stalls in the market and many shops in East Jerusalem shuttered, but they reopen on Saturday. Since old-city shops owned by Jews will close early, avoid a Friday shopping expedition there. If you think it is confusing to read this, just wait till you go shopping. Try to get an early morning start and be prepared to come back another day if necessary.

Languages

If you have a facility for languages, Israel is the place to put it to use. In shops, the languages of business (after Hebrew, of course) are English and French, but in the markets you'll hear haggling in Arabic, Yiddish, and Spanish as well.

Tourist Discounts

Many shops have been authorized by the Ministry of Tourism as "tourist shops." They display a blue-and-white certificate and offer a tourist discount, which can be anything from 12 to 17 percent. It seemed to me that the prices in these shops were higher than elsewhere, bringing the discounted price back into line. Check it out. On the other hand, if you buy expensive jewelry, leather goods, or furs, some shops are authorized to deliver your purchase to the airport when you leave. They need not charge you the 18 percent VAT. If you are charged the VAT on any purchase over $50, save your receipt and get a cash refund at the airport.

Credit Cards

Large, elegant shops accept major credit cards, but many small ones do not. These do however take American and British currency (working the exchange out on minicalculators), and some, surprisingly, take checks.

Where to Shop

Do all your serious shopping in Tel Aviv and Jerusalem. The better shops have branches in each city and except for handicrafts and copper/brass-type antiques, there is little of interest elsewhere. Although Elat is a duty-free port and prices are slightly lower, there is little beyond swimwear to interest the serious shopper. Taste is such a personal thing that I hesitate to make the following statements, but here goes. I prefer to shop for leather goods, jewelry, furs, sportswear, and modern art in Tel Aviv and for antiques, Judaica, sculptures and paintings with religious themes, and handicrafts when I am in Jerusalem. Although well-known Israeli companies such as Beged Or Leathers have shops in each city, styles will vary and Jerusalem, being less cosmopolitan, will have more conservative styles. Don't take this to mean that if you find a necklace you adore in the H. Stern shop in Jerusalem that there will be a nicer one in their Tel Aviv shop. Don't pass up something you really like expecting to find it or something better elsewhere. By the way, many hotels have excellent shopping arcades with branch stores of well-known concerns. Prices are comparable.

Israel's Best Buys

Handicrafts

These make great gifts, come in the widest price range, and are constant reminders of your trip. Israel's craftspeople—Jewish, Arab, and Druze—work with a variety of media and in styles from the avant-garde to the highly traditional. Ceramics (both tile and pottery) are beautiful, with Armenian pottery at the top of the line. Glassware, hammered copper and brass, metal sculptures, batiks and silk screening, woven rugs, and native dresses (Yemenite and Bedouin) are the items most often sold in the markets. Very popular too, particularly in Jerusalem, are olivewood carvings of religious figures and sturdy camels. To get an idea of the scope and price of Israeli handicrafts, head to the nearest Maskit or WIZO shop (listed by us in each city). These shops, featuring items made by immigrants and the needy, have a potpourri of crafts and all are of the highest quality. No bargaining here.

Jewelry

Fine jewelry, in 18-carat gold, is less costly in Israel than in the United States but not inexpensive. H. Stern, an internationally known Brazilian jeweler, has several branches here. The jewelry features multicolored stones set in interesting, one-of-a-kind pieces by skilled Israeli goldsmiths. Israel has a growing diamond industry, with one center in Netanya and another in Haifa. The diamonds are of fine quality but it is the expert cutting by old-world cutters that makes them exceptional. Yemenite jewelry, usually in silver but occasionally in gold, is uniquely fashioned, using a filigree technique. It looks as if the strands have been crocheted together. Most pieces are large and ornate —nothing understated here. Less expensive jewelry, made by Bedouins, Arabs, and Druze, utilizes tin and copper wire along with old coins, chunky, colored rough stones, and polished beads. Sporty and fun to wear! Elat jewelry features the distinctive blue stones mined nearby in King Solomon's mines. These range from light to dark blue and have green, pink, and purple lines. The jewelry is modern in design.

Leathers, Furs, and Knitwear

Israel's reputation for fine leather and suede suits, jackets, and pants for both men and women is well deserved. Quality leather called ''nappa,'' soft and supple, comes in assorted colors, and styles vary enormously. Prices, while not low, are far less than you would pay for comparable items back home, if you could find them. Israel's fur industry is growing by word of mouth as more visitors arrive home sporting a well-fitted mink, raccoon, or Persian lamb coat. The tailoring is superb, the styles chic (you can even bring a photo if you like). You will need two or three fittings and your garment can be shipped home. A problem? Ship it back and they'll take care of it. Prices are far lower than in the United States.

Knitted dresses, suits, and coats are often sold in Maskit and WIZO shops and in fine boutiques. They are comfortably styled and made in upbeat, lively colors.

Antiques and Judaica

Many antique shops stock family heirlooms brought to Israel by immigrants who want to make a total break with the past, or who, because they need money, sell to dealers. Some look exactly like the things I urged my grandmother to discard when she moved. Silver, inlaid wooden boxes, crystal, colored glassware, and carved pieces predominate. Many of the items have religious significance and it isn't unusual to find ornate Passover plates or ceremonial cups and mezuzot for sale. Copper/brass "antiques" are most frequently sold in the markets and may or may not be old. Copper is very heavy so if the piece isn't, it probably is copper-plated. Try rubbing it and see if the color is rusty. Good luck!

Art and Sculpture

Art galleries feature works by modern stylists as well as very traditional ones. Primitive-style paintings and screen prints of Hassidim or with biblical themes are highly collectible. Posters and lithos of works by Shalom of Safed, a favorite Israeli artist, are colorful and typical.

Bathing Suits and Sportswear

Attire by Gottex, an Israeli bathing-suit company whose fashions are sold internationally, is also sold here. There is a larger selection of styles and lower prices too. Gideon Oberson, a local swimwear company, is equally popular here. Styles are slightly more youthful and sexier. Both labels are sold in boutiques, have their own shops, and have discount shops at factory outlets in Ramat Gan, a Tel Aviv suburb. Rosh Indiani is a moderate-priced sportswear company with shops throughout Israel.

Getting There

By Air

From North America

Israel is six thousand nautical miles and ten and a half nonstop flying hours from the east coast of the United States. If you fly on El Al, the Israeli national carrier, you get a ten-hour headstart on your Israel experience. Never was an airline more an extension of its home-base than El Al is of Israel. From the unending bagels and lox at breakfast, to the small clusters of the devout bobbing up and down, lost in prayer, to the joyful singing of folksongs by your fellow passengers as the coast of Israel is sighted, El Al is Israel. You should be aware, however, that El Al does not fly on the Sabbath (Friday sunset to Saturday sunset) or on religious holidays. Because the sun does not set everywhere at the same time, this can get confusing. Make sure to check for exact schedules.

El Al offers more nonstop flights to Israel than any other airline, and has offices in Chicago, Los Angeles, Miami, New York, Dallas–Fort Worth, and Baltimore/Washington, D.C. Passengers traveling from the Philadelphia area can take advantage of the airline's shuttle service to New York's John F. Kennedy airport for only $15. For up-to-the-minute flight information, El Al passengers can call the airline's toll-free number, 1-800-El AL 747, twenty-four hours a day, seven days a week. Reconfirming a return flight is easy. Passengers simply fill out a form on their outbound flight to reconfirm their return flight.

El Al offers escorted and unescorted "Milk and Honey" tour packages ranging from twelve to twenty-two days, and a nine-day/seven-night "Holy Land Experience" tour. Extensions to London, Cairo, Istanbul, and Athens are available. Perfect if you're on a tight schedule or a limited budget. For more information, contact the airline at 1-800-EL AL SUN.

In addition to flying paying passengers, the airline has made a pledge to the Israeli government that it will organize and operate a flight to carry immigrants to Israel from anywhere in the world within twelve hours of notice. Recipients of El Al's aid have included thousands of Soviet immigrants as well as Ethiopian Jews who were rescued as part of "Operation Solomon" in May 1991.

TWA and Delta, the other major carriers on the United States–Israel route, fly nonstop flights several days a week, with other flights making one stop in Europe. Tower Air, not as well known here, is highly regarded in Israel and flights are solidly booked. Canadian Pacific flies from Toronto and Montreal with stops en route. Check with them for schedules.

From Europe

If you live in Europe or are combining a trip to Europe with your trip to Israel, you have far greater options. Fourteen airlines fly to Israel from European cities, including such South American carriers as Varig and Aerolineas Argentina. El Al, TWA, British Airways, Swissair, Lufthansa, and KLM all have scheduled flights to Ben Gurion Airport. Flying time from London is four and a half hours; three hours from Rome and Geneva.

Safety

All airlines flying to Israel (and indeed throughout Europe) have instituted stringent security measures and all airports have upgraded their safety procedures as well. Expect a thorough check-in process at all the airlines, with bag searches and in-depth questioning the norm. El Al requires you to check in two hours before flight time, while the others ask you to arrive one and a half hours early. This is not just lip service; you may actually miss your flight if you allow less time. Travelers, rather than being annoyed by these measures, have been extremely co-operative and appreciative.

Business Class Travel

In an effort to woo business travelers, El Al has remodeled its business class section on the 747 aircraft that make the New York/Tel Aviv run. Changes include a separate section with wider leather seats and extra legroom. A special menu and unlimited bar are also part of the deal. Those who want to take advantage of this option can upgrade for $399 additional each way from New York, Baltimore/Washington, Boston, Chicago, Dallas/Fort Worth, and Miami, and for $429 additional each way from Los Angeles.

Fares

Deregulation, the variance of oil prices, and a host of special package tours, charters, excursions, youth fares, frequent flyer programs, and the like keep air fares in a constant state of flux. Anything specific we described would be out of date before the ink dried. Here, you will have to do your homework or get a top-notch travel agent to do it for you. There are high season rates and low ones. El Al, TWA, Delta, and British Airways often have terrific package tours that include inexpensive car rentals.

El Al offers discounts to passengers over 60 years old as well as special reduced fares for younger passengers. With El Al's family fares, parents traveling with children under twelve years old save 25 percent on their first child, 50 percent on their second, and 75 percent on each additional child.

By Sea

The lucky few with an extended time frame might consider sailing from southern Europe to Haifa. The most popular trip comes from Piraeus, Greece, with stops at Rhodes and Cyprus. Other ships arrive regularly from Venice, Genoa, Istanbul, and Marseilles. Your best contact is Jacob Caspi, Ltd., Natan Kaiserman Street, Haifa. In England, write Sol Maritime, c/o Cyprus Travel London, Ltd., 42 Hampstead Road, London NW. Many cruise ships make day stops at Haifa or Ashdod, but they allow only one day in Israel and are therefore cruise vacations, rather than Israeli ones.

Ground Travel Between Israel and Egypt

Since the Camp David treaty between Egypt and Israel, travel between the two neighbors is commonplace. You are probably best off going from Israel to Egypt, because arrangements are easier to make. Get your visa before leaving the United States. If you only want to visit the Sinai, you can get a special entry permit (see Sinai in the Elat chapter). You cannot drive a rental car into Egypt, but you can go by bus. Your best bet is to fly from Ben Gurion to Cairo. El Al has several flights a week, as does Air Sinai. Tour companies advertise inexpensive bus trips from Israel to Cairo and Luxor. You might investigate these when you get to Israel. The Egyptian Embassy is at 2310 Decatur Place NW, Washington, DC 20008.

Ground Travel Between Israel and Jordan

This is harder to do since technically the two countries are at war. You cannot enter Jordan if your passport is stamped with an Israeli entry, so make sure to inform the Israeli immigration official of your plans. He or she will then stamp only your entry form. Get a Jordanian visa before leaving home, since there are no diplomatic services between the countries. The entry into Jordan usually takes place over the Allenby Bridge (King Hussein Bridge in Jordan). Cab drivers and minibus operators leaving from the Damascus Gate will take you to the Israeli checkpoint (open till 1 P.M. daily; closed Saturday). Cabs need a special permit from the Israeli military to approach the checkpoint. A bus takes you from the Israeli checkpoint to the Jordanian one. Notice the heavy fortifications on both sides of the border. After passport inspection, you can get a taxi to Amman. Once in Jordan, it is very difficult to retrace your steps into Israeli; special permits are required. It's best to plan to fly to Europe from Jordan. The Jordanian Embassy is at 1701 K Street NW, Washington, DC 20006.

Getting Ready

Documents

To enter Israel, American, Canadian, and British citizens need only a current passport. Upon their arrival they will be given a tourist visa. The visa is valid for three months and can be renewed for an additional three months at any office of the Ministry of the Interior.

Vaccinations Required

No special vaccinations are required, but a word about individual medicines is in order. Israel has many pharmacies, at which virtually every over-the-counter item you use is available. You should, however, make sure to travel with a sufficient amount of any prescription medicines you use, a note from your doctor explaining the medicine in generic terms, plus an extra prescription for your eyeglasses or contact lenses should you leave them somewhere.

Driver's License

You can drive in Israel with a valid United States, British, or Canadian driver's license, but having an international license is not a bad idea.

Money Matters

Local Currency

The shekel, a name rooted in ancient Jewish history, is the currency of Israel. The shekel is divided into 100 agorot. The l-shekel piece is a small silver coin, and the 5-shekel piece, also silver, is larger. Bills are 10 shekalim (orange), 50 shekalim (purple), and 100 shekalim (blue). These shekels, referred to as new shekels, were put into circulation in September 1985, replacing the existing shekel coins and bills. The two were used concurrently until September 1986, when the older currency was taken out of circulation.

Exchanging Money

You will notice a minute fluctuation of the shekel's value against the dollar and the pound almost daily. It is no longer a large jump. Money can be exchanged at banks if you are lucky enough to find one open. Banks are easily found in all parts of the country; however, the term *banker's hours* must have originated here. Banks frequently close for a siesta from 1 till 4 P.M. and are closed on Wednesday afternoons, as well as on Friday afternoons and all day Saturday. You can also exchange money at your hotel (some will not do so on Friday or Saturday). The exhange rate will be a few percentage points less for the service. By the way, the rate does vary from city to city, with a less favorable exchange rate in smaller areas.

Credit Cards

Credit cards are alive and well in Israel. American Express, Visa, and Diner's Club are accepted throughout the country, with individual places setting their own policy. Eurocard or Isracard, the international or Israeli MasterCards, are also accepted here.

Traveler's Checks

You get a slightly better rate of exchange for traveler's checks than for cash in Israel. American Express, Cooks, Barclay's, and large United States bank checks are universally accepted.

Tipping

My Israeli friends tell me that tipping was once frowned upon here but that is no longer the case. In fact, hotels add a 15 percent service charge to your bill and many restaurants add 10 to 15 percent to the cost of your meal. Check the bottom of the menu to see if that is the case. You can always leave a bit extra if you care to. Taxi drivers do not expect to be tipped; however, beauticians do. Basically, while tipping is a personal matter, you should tip as you would at home.

VAT

In common with many other countries, Israel has instituted a Value Added Tax (VAT) which is 18 percent for tourists. This tax is added to any shekel purchase, often incorporated right into the price. Hotel bills paid in dollars, traveler's checks, or credit cards are VAT-exempt as are hotel meals and services charged to your bill. Cars with guides, car rentals, and purchases over $50 are also exempt if paid for in the above manner. If you buy an expensive item and are charged VAT, ask for an exemption certificate to present at the airport on departure.

Customs Regulations

Entering the Country

Israeli customs follows the red light-green light system. If you have nothing to declare, line up on a green aisle. You'll either be waved through or your bags will be examined. This is done randomly. You need not declare cigarettes or alcohol for your personal use or cameras, bicycles, camping equipment, or foreign of Israeli money. If you have extra shekels when you leave you can reconvert them. If you exchange large amounts of currency, make sure you keep your conversion receipt for proof.

Leaving the Country

Your bags will be checked upon leaving for security purposes. There is an airport tax of $10 or the shekel equivalent upon departure. By the way, if you are leaving on El Al, you can check your bags through earlier in the day. The service is in effect in Tel Aviv, Jerusalem, and Haifa. Bring your passport, ticket, and money for the departure tax with you to the appropriate El Al office:

Tel Aviv: Arlozerov Street near the Central Railway Terminal, 4 P.M.–midnight, phone (03) 217188 (there is another office, in the Tel Aviv Hilton Hotel.)

Jerusalem: Center One, 49 Yermiahu St., 6:45 P.M.–11P.M., Phone (02) 383166

Haifa: 6 Ha-Namel St., 6:30–10P.M., phone (04) 677036

Returning Home

United States   As of this writing, each United States citizen is allowed to return with $400 worth of foreign merchandise, duty-free. Several costly items are classified as customs-exempt; these include original works of art, furs, and 18-carat gold jewelry.

Canada   Canadian citizens are allowed a $300 exemption each calendar year and reasonable amounts of cigarettes, alcohol, and cigars. Pick up a brochure (''I Declare'') which details regulations for you.

Europe   All European Economic Community countries allow furs, jewelry, and original works of art to be brought home duty-free.

Getting Around in Israel

From the Airport to Major Destinations

Chances are you'll arrive in Israel by air; international flights land (except for a very few in Elat) at David Ben Gurion Airport in the town of Lod, not far from Tel Aviv. In-airport services include a money exchange counter, an Israeli Government Tourist office, and a hotel referral desk. If you have arranged for a rental car pickup at the airport, offices of all international companies are just outside the exit. Several local companies will arrange to pick you up here. Taxis are lined up and waiting. These are regulated and a comptroller will hand you a card listing your cab's ID number and a number to call if you feel you have been overcharged. The fare from the airport is fixed and meters are not used. United Tours shuttle bus (#222) will whisk you to Tel Aviv (to the Central Bus Station and along the major hotel strip) for four dollars. It leaves on the hour and is fine if you have very little luggage. Egged Bus has service from the airport to Tel Aviv, Haifa, and Jerusalem. You might like to try a *sherut* (a jitney taxi) to Jerusalem. Large limos (usually Mercedes) that seat eight, sheruts are very popular. They'll wait till they fill up (but they do quickly) and off you go—directly to your hotel! Make sure to ask an Israeli what the fare is or you'll surely overpay—we learned this the hard way. There is no sherut from the airport to Tel Aviv.

Car Rentals

The best way to see Israel is to drive yourself. You'll find that the roads are very good (but are unlit), distances between stops are short, and there will be lots of interesting ministops en route. Direction signs are in English, and international traffic signs are used. Major roads (four lanes) run from Tel Aviv to Haifa, Jerusalem, and Beersheba. Most other roads are paved, two lanes, and easy to drive, although Negev roads have hairpin turns and you should avoid them at night.

A word or two about Israeli drivers seems in order at this point. Contrary to what you may have heard, they are not the worst drivers in the world. New York cabbies and those in Rio are certainly worse, but Israelis do drive aggressively and they are highly uncautious. They pass whenever the whim strikes: going uphill, on a blind curve, or when a huge truck is rumbling toward them. They often squeeze back into the lane directly in front of you. To research this guide, we drove 3,500 kilometers throughout Israel. We were passed by trucks, buses, cars, taxis, and camels. You will not feel uncomfortable, for Israelis do not honk their horns incessantly. The speed limit is 90 KPH (55 MPH) and you can drive at your own pace.

Rental Agencies

Every major international rental agency has offices in Israel. Hertz, Avis, Budget, and National (called Eurocar) are in all the large cities, at the airport, and at major hotels as well. Cars of varying sizes are available, with air conditioning, automatic drive, or five-speed stick shifts. Car rental prices are far higher than those in the United States because cars are far more expensive to buy in Israel. We offer two money-saving suggestions. Suggestion #1: Rent your car from an international agency before you leave home. Gather all the information available (type of car, how equipped, mileage regulations) and reserve at least a week in advance of pickup. All these agencies have international desks. Prices are far lower than if you make arrangements in Israel (in fact, almost half), and your chances of getting exactly what you want are far greater.

Through El Al's "Sensational Car" package, travelers can rent a car through Hertz for as low as $15 a day with unlimited mileage for seven days. The airline's "Arrive and Drive: Israel Program," designed for independent travelers, includes a Hertz rental car with unlimited mileage in addition to deluxe accommodations. Suggestion #2: Rent from a local agency. There are a great many of them and prices seem far lower (read all the fine print). Obviously, if you rent from Honest Sam's you can get stuck, so here are some of the larger reputable Israeli agencies:

Autorent: Jerusalem (02) 244222; Tel Aviv (03) 5271333

Eldan Rent-A-Car: Jerusalem (02) 513030 (Hilton Hotel); Tel Aviv (03) 5371122. To reserve prior to your departure call toll-free (in the US) 1-800-938-5000 or 212-629-6090 in New York

Eurodollar: Jerusalem (02) 611122; Tel Aviv (03) 5271122

Driving Incidentals:

1. Minimum age for rental varies from twenty-one (Budget) to twenty-three (Avis). Insurance costs rise for drivers under twenty-three as well.

2. You'll need your passport and driver's license plus a major credit card.

3. There are no tolls on roads, but there are occasional military roadblocks to pass through. Most just wave you on, but others will talk to you.

4. Gas stations are plentiful, but be cautious in the Negev and fill up before the Sabbath.

5. Most hotels offer free parking.

6. Avoid driving in Tel Aviv, Haifa, and Jerusalem, which have rush hours and parking problems. Cars are sometimes parked on sidewalks.

7. Don't park illegally. The Denver Boot, an orange tire clamp, may be placed on the car and a fine must be paid to get it off.

8. Israel is very serious about its seat-belt law. Wear yours or chances are you will be stopped on the highway. There is a heavy fine.

9. Israel's automobile club, MEMSI, has an office at 19 Petach Tikva Road in Tel Aviv. AAA members can use their emergency assistance program and get touring information too.

Domestic Airlines

Arkia, the domestic carrier, has a regular schedule of flights that connect major destinations in the north with Elat in the south. Arkia does not fly on the Sabbath. Flights link Tel Aviv and Jerusalem with Elat and Rosh Pinna (near Zefat). There are also flights between Haifa and Elat. Arkia has offices in these cities, but your best bet is to drop in at the nearest IGTO and ask about the latest schedules and fares. You can also take Arkia tours into the Sinai.

Intercity Travel

Buses

Egged, a bus cooperative, is ubiquitous. Buses run to virtually every part of the country, and in the Negev it is a common sight to see a lone passenger waiting patiently at a bus stop where nothing else is visible for miles in either direction. The buses we used were fairly new, air-conditioned, and quite clean; however, we were told by fellow passengers that some routes have older, less attractive buses. It seems to be the luck of the draw. There are usually several buses between stops each day and fares are very low. One of the drawbacks to touring by bus is that their stops are not always convenient to the sites you'd like to visit. Intercity buses do not operate on the Sabbath.

Israbus

Egged offers special-fare tickets good for unlimited travel on any Egged bus anywhere in the country for a specified length of time. For information, call Egged's toll-free number from anywhere in Israel: 177-022-5555.

Trains

Israel's train system is not extensive and trains tend to be old and slow-moving. The route between Tel Aviv and Jerusalem is picturesque because it goes through the Judean Hills. It's fun for children as well. Trains connect Jerusalem, Tel Aviv, Haifa, Beersheba, Dimona, and Nahariya. All make local stops. You can reserve seats. The tracks were laid during the British Mandate period.

Taxis and Sheruts

Taxis will take you from one city to another. Fares are fixed (ask to see the rate chart) and are rather expensive. Sheruts, which run along fixed routes, link most cities and large towns. These large limousines can hold eight people and a lot of luggage. If you want to travel on the Sabbath, a sherut may be your only option. Rates are higher at night and children receive a discount. Reserve a seat in advance for long trips. You can get a sherut phone number from your hotel concierge. Sheruts' fares are a bit higher than those for a bus on the same route. It's a great deal.

Within Cities

Buses

Local buses start to run at 5 A.M. and run until 11:30 P.M. They stop on Friday nights at 5 P.M. and do not run until after sundown on Saturday. The exceptions are Haifa, which has limited bus service on Saturday, East Jerusalem, and the West Bank towns. Bus fares are very low or are calculated by distance traveled. Multifare cards can be purchased from bus drivers.

Subway

Haifa has an underground train called the Carmelit, which runs in a straight line and connects the three levels of the city. It does not operate on the Sabbath, nor does the city's cable car.

Taxis

Taxis are equipped with meters; occasionally you will have to ask for them to be turned on. Fares are lower than those in the United States for a similar trip.

Traveling with Children

Having traveled extensively with both my children from the time they were infants, I speak from experience when I say that Israel is one of the best places to visit with children of all ages.

Accommodations

Hotels offer a 50 percent discount on the extra-person rate for children under six (staying in the same room as parents) and a 30 percent discount for children from six to twelve. Large hotels will arrange for babysitters (ask early in the day), but even in small hotels, the desk clerk usually has a sister or a friend who can use the extra money. You can stay in homey kibbutz guest houses or holiday villages, both of which draw families with children, serve family-style meals, and usually have playgrounds.

Food

Israelis frequently have large families and even young children eat out often. Many restaurants have high chairs or booster seats. There are middle-priced, informal restaurants throughout the country. Best of all, water is safe to drink anywhere, dairy products are pasteurized, and all foods are safe as well.

Sightseeing

Driving your own car allows you to avoid the anxiety of meeting bus, train, or plane schedules. You can easily plan your trip so that you alternate sightseeing in a big city with a trip to a beach or nature park or a horseback ride. Keep car trips under three hours and ask for a car seat (in advance) if you need one.

Other Children

Many Israeli and European families vacation in Elat and Tiberias and at holiday villages. There will be other children to play with and play is an international language. If you are traveling with teenagers, they will be glad to see that there are many foreign students traveling in Israel as well.

Disposable Diapers

Pampers® and local brands of disposable diapers are sold in supermarkets and pharmacies. Pampers® cost more, but being long past that stage, I cannot attest to the quality of local brands.

The Disabled Traveler

The IGTO told us about a nifty 120-page guide called *Access in Israel*, published by Pauline Hephaistos Survey Projects, 30 Bradley Gardens, West Ealing, London, England. We sent for a copy. Published by a charitable organization, it was sent free; however, a contribution of two pounds or the U.S. equivalent is appreciated. The guide includes information about access at hotels and kibbutz guest houses throughout Israel, as well as detailed maps of major cities with best access routes delineated. Wheelchairs can be obtained free of charge from Yad Sarah, 49 Hanevim Street, Jerusalem, phone (02) 244242. Again, a contribution is welcomed.

Women Traveling Solo

Congratulations! If you have opened to this section, you are at least contemplating taking a trip to Israel on your own or with a female companion. It also means that you have confidence in yourself, a healthy curiosity, and a get-up-and-go attitude. Too many women, timid about being on their own, join a tour. In exchange for constant companionship, they give up the freedom to explore the places that most interest them at their own pace and the options of sleeping late one morning, staying an extra night in Tiberias, or meeting a dozen interesting people.

Your authors, two women, spent a considerable amount of time in Israel researching this guide. Each of us traveled alone for part of the time, then we joined forces at other points. It is our firm belief that no country is safer, more relaxed, and less judgmental than Israel. You can make lifelong friends and add a fresh collection of lovely memories to your mental travel bag. However, as a woman traveling alone, there are certain things you must keep firmly in mind (whatever the destination). Some are common-sense precautions, while others are peculiar to the culture you visit.

A few common-sense observations, if you please: Avoid walking in commercial areas at night when the streets are empty. Although street crime in Israel is negligible, don't carry a lot of money or your passport. (Check them at the hotel.) If you plan to dine at an out-of-the-way restaurant (we try not to select too many of them), take a taxi from the front of your hotel and ask to have a taxi called to pick you up after your meal. Although hitchhiking is extremely common here (called tramping), never accept a ride from strangers. More often than not, the chap will be a perfect gentleman—but why have to think about it? Israel's bus system is excellent and there are more than enough taxis and sheruts around. When you sightsee in the old city of Jerusalem, you will be approached by young, well-dressed Arab men, who will offer to act as your guide—a firm "no, thanks" may need to be repeated several times, but will eventually work. Do not walk on the rampart walls alone. Wait for others to sign up and join them. You won't have to wait long.

Italian men have long held the gold medal for being "on the make." However, if they glance over their shoulders, they will find young Israeli men, toothy grin and macho swagger firmly set, moving up fast. Obviously, the media and the open lifestyles of Western European visitors have awakened a dormant Latin temperament here. On the other hand, you did come here to meet people and to have a good time, so feel free to accept those invitations you feel comfortable with. Israeli women enjoy a great deal of respect and so will you. How the evening turns out will depend in large measure on you. In general, avoid talking to strangers in Arab sections or towns. This statement is not meant to cast aspersions on Arabs, but it is a fact that in their culture, young women are not free to talk to men they do not know, and for you to do so may place you in an unfavorable light.

In Israel, modesty is still a virtue, and in certain places it is an absolute necessity. It can get unbearably hot and your cotton tank top and running shorts may be the coolest clothes you have —but don't wear them in cities or in areas with a large population of Hassidim or Arabs, or when visiting places of worship (whatever the denomination)—it's in bad taste. You will not only be stared at and reprimanded, but you will not be admitted into any of the holy places—and there goes your day. Observing a dress code is a small price to pay for the benefits of seeing all the wonderful things there are to see.

You can explore, experience, and have the time of your life— and you will—if you undertake your journey wisely and with a modicum of caution and common sense. Mazel tov!

Business Travelers

Since a business traveler's time in a foreign country is often limited and because time is money, it becomes essential that your hotel be centrally located, that you don't arrive just before a major holiday, and that any special requirements you have are available and waiting for your arrival. Israel's business centers, Tel Aviv, Jerusalem, and Haifa (with Ashdod and Elat involved in shipping), have hotels that cater to the special needs of business travelers. The Hilton Hotels in Tel Aviv and Jerusalem and the Dans (King David, Jerusalem, Dan Carmel, Haifa, and Tel Aviv) have well-organized departments to expedite your trip. With Hilton's Executive Business Service or the Dan's King David Club, you'll receive priority reservation service and special rates for deluxe accommodations. Plans to reduce long-distance phone charges are available, as are conference rooms, multilingual secretaries, and telex and cable services. For information, contact Hilton International Executive Business Service and the Dan King David Club in the United States at 1-800-223-7773/4 (in New York, call 212-752-6120) and in the United Kingdom at (071) 439-9893.

The Israeli Sabbath (Saturday) and holidays (religious and national) begin at sundown of the previous day, so business slows down by 3 P.M. on Friday. Plan early Friday meetings and keep in mind that public transportation stops, many restaurants close (since cooking is forbidden), and shops close as well. Avoid these holidays: Pesach (Passover) in March or April, Shavuot in June, and the two-week period from Rosh Hashana (Jewish New Year) in September or October to Sukkoth.

Many hotels in these cities have health club facilities to help you wind down, and hotel restaurants and lounge areas are commonly used for business lunches, dinners, and late-afternoon cocktails.

Banks are closed on Monday and Wednesday afternoons, but most hotels have minibranches in their shopping arcades. All banks are closed from Friday at 2 P.M. to Saturday sundown, when hotel branches sometimes reopen.

Although you will probably conduct your business in English (translators are available if necessary), it is courteous to learn a few Hebrew or Arabic phrases, so pick up a phrase book with or without a cassette and give it your best shot.

Traveler's Potpourri

Archeological Sites

You can purchase a fourteen-day pass for entry to all of Israel's archeological sites. Located in all parts of the country, many of these are places you will definitely visit, and you can't beat the price. Tickets are for sale at National Parks Authority, 3 Het Street, Hakirya, Tel Aviv, phone (03) GQ52281.

Book Suggestions

Following is a reading list designed to add to your knowledge and enjoyment of Israel.

Hardcovers

The Holy Land, Jerome Murphy-O'Connor (Oxford University Press, N.Y.). Concise guide to history and archeology from Stone Age to 1700.

Arab and Jew: Wounded Spirits in a Promised Land, David K. Shipler (Times Book). A balanced, revealing examination of Arabs and Jews as they dwell together under Israeli control.

The Arabs: Journeys beyond the Mirage, David Lamb (Random House). Arabs are little understood in the West; this book presents their culture and the Islamic religion as it was and is.

The High Walls of Jerusalem, Ronald Sanders (Holt, Rinehart and Winston). History of the Balfour Declaration and the British Mandate period.

Paperbacks

Exodus, Leon Uris. The clandestine movement to bring Jews to Palestine.

O Jerusalem, Collins and La Pierre. The city from the time of the U.N. partition vote to its capture by the Arab Legion.

The Source, James Michener.

To Jerusalem and Back, Saul Bellow.

Climate

Israel, a year-round vacation destination, has a fabulous climate. Temperatures are recorded here in Celsius numbers, which are lower than those in Fahrenheit, which is used in the United States. The formula for converting Celsius to Fahrenheit is to multiply the Celsius number by 9, divide that sum by 5, and add 32.

Winter in Israel (November–February) can mean rain and even an occasional mini-snowfall in the Jerusalem area, Upper Galilee, and the Golan (where you can ski). If you visit at that time of year, come prepared with a warm sweater, raincoat, and boots to keep your feet dry. It will not be very cold, however; temperatures rarely go below 40°F. Of course, Elat and the Dead Sea area are hot and sunny year round, so don't forget to pack beach gear.

From March through October, it hardly rains and the country is bathed in sunlight virtually every day. July and August are the hottest months. A hot, dry desert wind called *hamseen* (an Arabic word for *fifty*—as in "blows for fifty days") sometimes strikes in early spring and late summer. It can make things uncomfortable, but in spite of its name it lasts for only two or three days. Some general temperatures (in Fahrenheit) follow to aid your planning and packing:

	January	*May*	*July*	*October*
Jerusalem	43–55	59–80	65–84	58–77
Tel Aviv	48–65	63–79	70–87	60–83
Haifa	45–63	60–76	69–86	59–81
Tiberias	50–69	62–89	73–97	65–89
Elat	50–73	70–96	77–103	68–96
Zefat	37–50	58–76	65–84	58–75

Dial a Guide

Israeli guides, licensed by the Ministry of Tourism after a stiff exam, are well trained and extremely knowledgeable. If you are a history buff or have a particular interest in the religious sites, you might consider a guide for one day of your Jerusalem stay. You will get a lot of historical detail and a quick overview of the city, permitting you to explore individual sights at your own pace later. There are several drawbacks. One is the price, which at this writing is $135 to $150 a day with the guide's car and $75 to $90 without a car. Another drawback is that the guide, being the authority, often takes you on his or her standard tour without asking if you have particular interests. It can be difficult to ask for changes. If you want a guide and did not come to Israel with a friend's recommendation, call Dial a Guide, (02) 813817, a co-op operating out of Jerusalem. Make sure to explain exactly what you want and tell them of any special interests you have. You just might get lucky.

Dig Israel

Let the amateur archeologist in you out for a day and have a terrific time digging for artifacts at a valid government-designated excavation site. Digs are under the supervision of the Ministry of Antiquities, but were the brainchild of an American-born Israeli couple. Contact Fran and Bernie Alpert, Dig for a Day, 10 Misgav

Ladach, Jewish Quarter, Box 14002, Jaffa Gate, Jerusalem, Israel, or better still, you can call when you get there (02) 272660.

Electricity

Israel's current is 220 volts, so you will need a converter for your appliances. Sockets are three-pronged, so you will need an adapter as well. You can purchase them in Israel, but it's best to bring them with you.

Embassies

Although Jerusalem is the country's capital, political considerations keep most embassies in Tel Aviv. Consulate offices are in Jerusalem, however.

> *United States Embassy:* 71 Hayarkon Street, Tel Aviv (03) 650015. U.S. consulate in Jerusalem: (02) 255755.

> *Canadian Embassy:* 220 Hayarkon Street, Tel Aviv (03) 448147.

> *British Embassy:* 192 Hayarkon Street, Tel Aviv (03) 5249171. British consulate in Jerusalem: (02) 828281.

Holidays

No lip-service holidays here. Religious and national holidays are celebrated passionately and will inevitably affect your vacation. A source of added pleasure, holidays are festive events with parades, fireworks, dancing in the streets, and speeches; they are also sources of frustration. Israelis do not work on holidays and you will find your sightseeing, shopping, and eating options limited. Try to avoid the long-term holidays (such as Passover) and plan around the Sabbath, a holiday that falls each Saturday.

Add to that the fact that Israel operates on two calendars. The Jewish calendar dates from the Creation and is now 5,740-plus years old. According to the Jewish calendar, 1993 is the year 5752. It is a lunar calendar with twelve months of twenty-eight days and a series of leap years to make up the extra days. The other calendar, the Gregorian one, is in use in other parts of the world, including the United States. The Jewish year starts on the holiday of Rosh Hashana.

Moslems also follow a lunar calendar and alternate months have twenty-nine or thirty days. There are only 354 days a year, which makes Moslem holidays fall on different dates each year.

Jewish Holidays (Based on the Gregorian Calendar)

Note: Holidays that require a shutdown of services are marked with an *X*.

X The Sabbath, which commences at sundown on Friday and lasts till sunset on Saturday, is the most important Jewish holiday. We have discussed its ramifications several times elsewhere, and will discuss only annual holidays here.

January–March

Tu B'Shevat, Israel's Arbor Day, occurs in late January or February. Trees are planted by schoolchildren and if you like you can join in.

Purim, a happy holiday, commemorates Queen Esther, who saved her people from the bad Persian king in the fifth century B.C. *Hamantaschen*, tricornered pastries, are eaten, and there are costume parties and parades. Purim usually falls in March.

April–June

X Passover (Pesach), which usually falls in early April, is the festival that marks the Jews' Exodus from Egypt. It lasts eight days, during which time observant Jews eat *matzoh*, an unleavened bread. Many foods are prohibited at this time and rather than change their kitchen utensils, many restaurants close down for the entire holiday. On the first night of the festival, the *Seder*, a traditional supper is held, during which the story of the Exodus is retold. Christ's last supper was a Seder.

Holocaust Day (May 6) and *Memorial Day* (May 13) are dominated by visits to the country's cemeteries and to the Yad Vashem Memorial.

Independence Day (May 14) is cause for tremendous celebration; parties and parades are held throughout the country.

Lag b'Omer, which falls thirty-three days after Passover eve, is primarily a Hassidic tradition. On this holiday Hassidim journey to Meron (Upper Galilee), where candlelit processions, bonfires, and lusty singing and dancing pay tribute to their sage, Rabbi Bar Yochai.

X Shavuot (Pentecost), which falls seven weeks after Passover (in May or early June), is a harvest festival and is an exciting time on the kibbutzes and moshavs. It also marks the bringing of the "first fruits" to the Temple and therefore is observed as a religious holiday.

July–September

Tish B'av, which falls in midsummer, is a day of fasting; it commemorates the destruction of the Temples (in 587 B.C. and 70 A.D.).

X Rosh Hashana is the Jewish New Year. It usually falls in September and is celebrated for two days. Not a festive occasion, it is marked by prayer. The traditional blowing of the *shofar* (ram's horn) ushers in the New Year.

October–December

X Yom Kippur (Day of Atonement) is the most solemn day in the Jewish year. It falls ten days after Rosh Hashana and is a day of fasting and prayer. Services are held in hotels. Hotel restaurants operate on a limited schedule if at all. On this day, Jews ask God to forgive their sins and to inscribe their names in the Book of Life for another year.

X Sukkoth (Feast of the Tabernacles) starts five days after Yom Kippur. A week-long harvest festival, it also remembers how Moses and the Israelites wandered through the desert, living in simple huts. Small leaf-covered huts are constructed in gardens and backyards and meals are eaten in them. This is a happy time. Restrictions apply only on the first day. *Simhat Torah* is the last day of Sukkoth. It marks the completion of the reading of the Torah (the five books of Moses) for the year and the beginning of the reading for the next year. The Torah scrolls are carried aloft around the synagogue in a parade-like fashion.

Hanukkah (Feast of Lights) is an eight-day festival that celebrates the victory of the Maccabees over the Greek rulers who had forced the Jews to become pagans once again and had desecrated the Temple. The oil for the candles seemed enough to last just one night, but it lasted eight. Candles are lit progressively for eight nights in the Menorah, which is the symbol of this holiday and of Israel.

Moslem Holidays

Moslems follow the Hegira calendar, which starts with the year that Mohammed fled from Mecca to Medina in A.D. 622. Because the year is thirteen days shorter than that of the Gregorian calendar, it is difficult to pinpoint the holidays. The Moslem Sabbath is Friday and you will notice that stalls in the markets and shops in Arab areas are shut. *Ramadan* is the holy month of fasting, when devout Moslems do not eat, drink, or smoke from sunrise to sunset. In Jerusalem, a cannon blast marks the end of the feast and special foods are sold in the streets. *Eid el Adha* celebrates the end of the Haj (pilgrimage to Mecca) and Abraham's offering of his son to God. It lasts for three days. *Muharram I* is the Moslem New Year.

Christian Holidays

Christmas and Easter are the most important Christian holidays and the celebrations are magnificent–opulent, yet touchingly simple. Christmas is particularly memorable in Bethlehem where on Christmas Eve, choirs from the world over sing in Manger Square. Midnight Mass is celebrated and services are held in churches in Jerusalem. (The Greek Orthodox celebrate on January 6, Armenians on January 17.)

Easter celebrations start on Palm Sunday with processions from the Mount of Olives. Most interesting is the Procession of the Cross along the Via Dolorosa on Good Friday. The Greek Orthodox ceremony of the Holy Fire takes place in the Church of the Holy Sepulchre on Holy Saturday. Black-clad pilgrims from all over the world take part in these ceremonies.

How Far Is It to ______ *?*

A handy checklist of driving distances between base cities follows. Distances are listed in kilometers, for your car will register kilometers rather than miles.

From Jerusalem to:		**From Tel Aviv to:**	
Tel Aviv	61	Haifa	97
Haifa	161	Elat	348
Airport	46	Zefat	164
Tiberias	188	Tiberias	134
Beersheba	122	Airport	22
Elat	370	Beersheba	107

Israel Government Tourist Office (IGTO)

Your major source of information within Israel, the IGTO has local offices throughout the country. Each locality stocks maps and brochures about other tourist areas as well as its own. Each publishes a monthly schedule of events that you should pick up at each stop. The Israel Ministry of Tourism is well organized and runs a tight ship. Hotels are inspected, guides are licensed, stores are designated as tourist shops for special discounting, and the people working in the offices are well trained and speak many languages. Look for the ministry symbol on store windows and restaurants. It is a picture of two men carrying a pole from which is suspended a huge bunch of grapes. This, from the Bible, refers to the time Moses sent two spies to Canaan to see if it was fertile. They returned with this huge bunch of grapes. Enough said. We have listed IGTO offices in their appropriate chapters. The IGTO also has offices abroad, and they can offer some pretrip assistance. Here are some locations:

United Kingdom 18 Great Marlborough Street, London WIV 1AF, (01) 434–3651

United States 350 Fifth Avenue, 19th Floor, New York, NY 10118, (212) 560–0620

5 S. Wabash Ave. Chicago, Illinois 60603. (312) 782–4306

6380 Wilshire Blvd., Los Angeles, CA 90048, (213) 658–7462

25 SE Second Avenue, Ste. 745 Miami Beach, FL 33131, (305) 539–1919

Canada 180 Bloor Street West, Suite 700, Toronto, Ontario M5S 2VS, (416) 964–3784

Kibbutz (Kibbutzim)

Kibbutz means "group" and it is unique to Israel. A kibbutz is a communal community where the land, the properties, the industries, and the products are owned collectively and administered as such. The first kibbutz was founded in 1909. The founders, part of the Second Aliyah (immigration) from Europe, wanted to reclaim the land, but realized that they could not do so individually, nor could they as individuals defend themselves. This was an important consideration, for many kibbutzim started as *nahal* (defense) outposts. They grew rapidly in popularity and there are over two hundred today, with approximately 150,000 people. This 4 percent of Israel's population is responsible for 35 percent of the country's agricultural output. Most kibbutzim have diversified a bit and many have a light industry in addition to the agriculture. These include guest houses, candy factories, and carpentry shops making synagogue furniture for export. Not as well known are the moshavim, which are cooperative villages where property is individually owned but the means of production are communal.

Languages

Hebrew, a language that was "dead" for hundreds of years, replaced by the many languages of the Diaspora, is one of Israel's official languages. The other official language is Arabic. English, a compulsory language, is taught in elementary school. Many young Israelis speak English flawlessly. Arabic is spoken in East Jerusalem, the Old City, and in the West Bank. Many Israelis speak Arabic as well. Hassidim, who reserve Hebrew for prayer, converse with each other in Yiddish, but also speak English. North African immigrants often speak French or Spanish as well. You will hear Russian in Beersheba and in Haifa too.

Mail

Post offices are located in every major city and in towns through-out the country. Main post offices are open from 8 A.M. to 6 P.M. Sunday through Thursday, and till 2 P.M. on Friday. Branches are open from 8 A.M. to 12:30 P.M. and 3:30 to 6 P.M. Though the system is seemingly well-organized, it surprisingly takes three weeks (if you are lucky) for your air-mail letter to reach the U.S. Allow turnaround time when writing for reservations or for information. Stamps are very beautiful and can be bought at hotel bookstores and some newsstands, as well as at the post office. You can leave your letters at the hotel and they will mail them for you. Telegrams and telegraphs can be sent from the post office too.

Medical Care

If you should fall ill during your trip, fret not. Israel has excellent medical care. Your hotel will call an English-speaking doctor for you. If you need a hospital, they will handle that too. The *Jerusalem Post* lists pharmacies that stay open twenty-four hours a day. Additionally, Tel Aviv-based INS-Care Ltd. provides medical services to sick or injured tourists nationwide. For assistance, call (03) 5171611 or (03) 997191 in the evening. In an emergency, dial 101 for the Magen David Adom (Israeli Red Cross).

Newspapers

Israel's English-language daily is the *Jerusalem Post*, published every day except Saturday. Friday's edition is the weekend edition and it contains a listing of weekend and the following week's events throughout the country. There is a magazine pullout with interesting articles and a special "In Jerusalem" section as well. You will also find the *International Herald Tribune*, *USA Today*, British dailies, and *Time* and *Newsweek*. Newspapers are sold in hotels and at newsstands.

Packing Tips

Hotels have one-day laundry service (not on Friday or Saturday) and it is not outrageously expensive. It is better, though, to bring clothes that pack well and are washable. What type of clothes you pack will depend on your style and the places you plan to visit. Make sure to bring at least one modest outfit, covering both knees and shoulders, for visiting the sacred sights, and don't forget comfortable walking shoes. Travel light—don't become a walking drugstore. You can easily buy all the essentials in Israel if you forget something.

Plant a Tree

A unique experience! Even before statehood, the Jewish National Fund (Keren Kayemet) was busily greening the Holy Land. You can be part of this wonderful concept by planting a tree or two in a JNF planting center. These, located in various parts of the country, are open from 8 A.M. to 2 P.M. (12:30 on Friday) and you pay only a small fee for the privilege. You receive a tree-planting certificate and pin. Call K.K. Le Israel at (02) 241781, Jerusalem; (03) 234449 in Tel Aviv.

Public Bathrooms

You won't find any signs that say "Restrooms for patrons only" in Israel as you do in New York. Public bathrooms are available at hotels, restaurants, gas stations, campgrounds, nature parks, and archeological sites. They say *WC* or *OO* and have male/female symbols. They sometimes lack toilet tissue, so it's a good idea to tuck some tissues in your pocket or purse.

Radio/TV

Kol Israel, the Voice of Israel, broadcasts in English several times each day. At this writing you can pick them up for news at 7 A.M., 1 P.M., 5 P.M., and 8 P.M. Better still, you can pick up the BBC virtually all day long and get news, sports, and feature items. The **Voice of Peace**, from Abie Nathan's ship in the Mediterranean, also broadcasts in English. Television is mired in the 1960s and 1970s with Donny and Marie stars of the tube here. Sitcoms are often dubbed or have subtitles. Some hotels have in-house channels and show newer films.

Society for the Protection of Nature in Israel

This organization offers very interesting and adventurous tours. A bicycle tour of Jericho, a moonlight tour of the Judean Desert, and a kayak tour of the Sea of Galilee are just a few. You might like to investigate further. Write to the society at 13 Heleni Hamalka Street, Jerusalem, or phone (02) 227682 or (03) 375063.

Spelling

Elat-Eilat, Zefat-Safed, Jaffa-Yafo, Akko-Acre—you get the picture, I'm sure. Names of places here are spelled in many ways and often places have two names in everyday use. For example, the Sea of Galilee is also called Lake Kinneret. There seems to be no definitive reason for the spelling differences, but in 600,000 years there's lots of room for variations. What to do when driving? Relax—sound the word you see phonetically, and if it sounds rather like the one you want, it's probably so. Hopefully you haven't been circling it for the last half hour. Just kidding! You'll get the knack quickly.

Telephones

Long Distance   Many hotels are equipped with direct-dial facilities; in others the operator will place your call for you. Calls are placed quickly and it is rare to wait more than a few minutes. For an AT & T operator, dial the AT & T access code: 177-1002727

Local   Local calls (from a street phone) require tokens which are sold at hotel desks and at newsstands. Israel has an area code system. You must dial the area code first if calling from outside the area. Codes are not used for in-area calls.

Codes for Base Cities:		Tiberias	06
Jerusalem	02	Elat	059
Tel Aviv	03	Zefat	06
Haifa	04	Beersheba	057

Time Zones

Israel time is seven hours ahead of Eastern Standard Time. When it is 10 A.M. in New York, it is 5 P.M. in Tel Aviv. When New York switches to daylight saving time, the difference becomes six hours. Israel switches to daylight saving time in mid-May and the difference then reverts to seven hours.

Volunteer Tourist Service

This organization operates in major hotels throughout Israel and at Ben Gurion Airport. Look for their desk in the lobby. There is usually a volunteer there after 6 P.M. They will put you in touch with an Israeli family if you would like to visit an Israeli home or attend a Seder. They will answer any questions you might have too. Very nice people work in this organization.

Jerusalem/ Yerusha-layim

srael has many faces. Jerusalem's is the loveliest. The old walled city—called Jebus until King David conquered it, renamed it Jerusalem, and made it the capital of his kingdom—sits serenely atop a Judean hill. From the higher peaks of nearby Mount Scopus and the Mount of Olives, the city's skyline—punctuated by church spires, bell towers, golden domes, and minarets—is stunning, particularly at sunset when the golden stones of the buildings and walls glisten. If you listen carefully you'll hear the church bells chime, the muezzins' call to the faithful, and the murmur of prayer at the Western Wall.

Jerusalem has been considered sacred to the three monotheistic religions for centuries, and that has been both a blessing and a curse. It has made the city a magnet for diverse peoples. Many have come as pilgrims eager to build the city, while other have come as conquerors determined to destroy it and reshape it in their own image.

The Canaanites, Israelites, Greeks, Romans, Byzantines, Arabs, and Mamelukes have all come here with contrasting cultures and customs. The city has absorbed them, yet each has left its traces for all to see. That is what makes Jerusalem wondrous.

The coexistence of the ancient and the modern and of different religions and cultures is, after all the trauma the city has gone through, a testimonial to its will to survive and flourish. As you walk through the narrow, crooked streets, the thought will come to you that you are in the city where Solomon dwelt, where Abraham spoke to God, where walls still stand that witnessed both the Crucifixion and Mohammed's ascent to heaven.

These sites will vie for your attention with the modern facets of this twentieth-century city, a symbol of strength and unity for

Diaspora Jews for 2,000 years. Signs throughout the city echo the words of King David: Yerushalayim—city of peace.

Orientation

Getting There

International flights land at Ben Gurion Airport in Lod, forty-six kilometers away. In-airport services include a minibank for money exchange, a hotel reservation service, and a desk of the Israeli Government Tourist Office (IGTO), where you can pick up city maps and touring information. Car rental offices are located just beyond the exit. If you are not picking up a car here, you have several options. Taxis are plentiful and the forty-five minute ride to Jerusalem will cost about $30; a sherut (jitney cab) will run less than half that amount, and your driver is required to drop you at your hotel at no extra charge—check the going rate with an Israeli or ask to see the rate sheet; and there is bus service between the airport and Jerusalem's bus stations.

As you approach the city (you are climbing) on a modern four-lane highway, you'll notice wrecked tanks and overturned trucks at roadside. These were left as memorials to those who died here in the heroic but futile attempt to keep Jerusalem's supply lines open in 1948. Jerusalem is at the heart of this country and is easily accessible from everywhere.

Getting Around Town

Public transportation is excellent and all parts of the city are linked by well-maintained buses running on frequent schedules. Buses do not operate on the Sabbath and usually stop at about 5 P.M. on Friday, resuming service after sundown on Saturday.

Many hotels in Givat Ram offer shuttle bus service to their guests.

Taxis are plentiful and can be flagged or called.

The #99 Egged bus is a special line that stops at all the major sites. You will find details on this line in the "Sunup to Sundown" section of this chapter.

Major Areas

Jerusalem, a physically beautiful city, spreads over the Judean Hills and plunges into the valleys in between. Streets are winding and upgrades are the norm, so walking can be tiring. In spite of the city's sprawling appearance, it is easy to orient yourself, for Jerusalem has three principal areas: the *Old City*, *West Jerusalem*, and *East Jerusalem*. Each area has a distinctive beat and each has sights you'll enjoy. Following is a rundown of these sections.

The Old City

The Old City was until 1860 the only city; it was Jerusalem in toto. Encircled by massive stone walls constructed by Sultan Suleiman the Magnificent in the sixteenth century, it remains a virtual world unto itself. The walls, which you can walk on, are punctuated by eight immense gates, seven of which provide access to and from the modern parts of the city. Of most interest to you are *Jaffa Gate* (entrance from West Jerusalem), *Damascus Gate* (entrance from East Jerusalem), and *Dung Gate* (closest to the Western Wall and Temple Mount).

David Street leads from Jaffa Gate through the market and after a few zigzags becomes Bab el-Silsileh Road (Chain Street Road) and heads to the Western Wall.

Historically, the Old City has been divided into quarters where people of like religions clustered to be near their holy sites. A brief description of the quarters follows.

The Armenian Quarter, in the southwest part of the city, is to your right as you enter Jaffa Gate. The most important street here is *Armenian Orthodox Patriarchate Road*, which leads through the quarter to *Zion Gate*. Beyond this gate is *Mount Zion*, traditional site of King David's tomb and of Jesus' Last Supper. This quarter was the only one walled in and locked by key each night.

The Jewish Quarter adjoins the Armenian Quarter to the southeast. The Jewish quarter was virtually destroyed during the 1948 fighting and the years of Jordanian control. Its synagogues and historic buildings have been faithfully restored. *The Cardo*, a reconstructed Roman road, now houses good shops and restaurants. Although not in the traditional Jewish Quarter, the *Western Wall* is Judaism's most sacred site, for it is the last remnant of the Temple. It is adjacent to Temple Mount.

The Moslem Quarter fills the northeast portion of the Old City and is the most densely populated area. It encompasses the majestic *Temple Mount*, upon which stands the *Dome of the Rock*. From this site Mohammed ascended to heaven. It is Islam's third most important site. Direct access to this quarter is through *Damascus Gate* and *Herod's Gate*.

The Christian Quarter, in the northwest, was established in the fourth century, when the *Church of the Holy Sepulchre* was built. The area is crowded with churches and monasteries of many Christian sects. Follow the *Via Dolorosa* from the Moslem Quarter through the Christian Quarter. It delineates Christ's path on the day of his Crucifixion, and the fourteen stations of the cross are marked. Direct entrance to this quarter is through *New Gate*.

The quarters do have fixed boundaries, but as you walk through them, they all blend into a whole. Narrow, winding cobblestoned streets, the various sections of the Arab market, and the kaleidoscope of people make a colorful tableau.

West Jerusalem

A modern Israeli city, West Jerusalem has wide thoroughfares, high-rise buildings, luxurious hotels, and fabulous museums, restaurants, and shops. West Jerusalem is where the action is. The heart of West Jerusalem is *Zion Square* and the streets radiating from it. It is a ten-minute walk from Jaffa Gate along Jaffa Road. Here are the major streets and neighborhoods:

Jaffa Road: a heavily trafficked street which leads from Jaffa Gate to the city's newer urban areas. Look for the city market, *Mahane Yehuda*, en route.

Ben Yehuda Mall: a lovely pedestrian walk with outdoor cafés and shops. The mall starts at Zion Square.

King George V Avenue: a wide boulevard that has seen better days—lots of fast-food stops here.

Yemen Moshe: the first settlement outside the city walls, across the Hinnon Valley from Jaffa Gate, now an artists' colony. Look for the windmill.

Qiryat Ben Gurion/Givat Ram: adjoining urban areas in the western part of the city. The Israel Museum, the Knesset, a campus of Hebrew University, and hotels are in these areas.

Mea She'arim: an in-city enclave peopled by Hassidic Jews, an ultraorthodox sect, easily identifiable by their traditional garb and grooming. Wear modest dress in this area.

German Colony: originally settled by the Templars, a German Christian sect, in the nineteenth century. This bustling, southern neighborhood boasts very trendy shops and restaurants along its main street, Emek Rafa 'im. The Khan Theater is located here.

Talpiot: southwest of the German Colony. This former industrial center is now home to fine restaurants and popular nightspots (many open on Fridays). The "Tayelet," commonly referred to as the "Gabriel Sherover Haas Promenade," links modern East Talpiot (Armon HaNaziv) with Talpiot. It offers a spectacular view of Jerusalem and is not to be missed.

Mount Herzl/Yad Vashem: two memorial sites on the city's western fringe. Yad Vashem is the memorial for Holocaust victims.

Other key points will be covered in the "Sunup to Sundown" section later in this chapter.

East Jerusalem

Smaller in size and with fewer sights, East Jerusalem, which lies north of the Old City, is languid. Not as modern in appearance as the western part of town, the area is undergoing a construction boom which will alter the skyline but hopefully not the Arab flavor. Hotels in this part of town are Arab-owned, as are restaurants and shops. East Jerusalem has two major streets:

Nablus Road (Derekh Shechem in Hebrew): leads north from Damascus Gate.

Saladin Street: leads north from Herod's Gate.

East Jerusalem's most interesting sight is the *Rockefeller Museum*, which houses a fine archeological collection.

Other Parts of Town

The Mount of Olives   Across the Kidron Valley from the walled city, the Mount of Olives has a score of beautiful churches, including the Chapel of the Ascension, marking the spot where Jesus ascended to heaven. Here too is the world's oldest Jewish cemetery. Fantastic views of the Old City.

Mount Scopus   Northeast of the walled city, Mount Scopus remained in Israeli hands after the War of Independence. The Hebrew University campus (founded in 1925) and Hadassah Hospital (1925) were unusable for the twenty years that the Old City was in Jordanian hands, but were restored after 1967. Both are in operation today. Virtually all of Jerusalem is visible from here.

Hotels

Accommodations in Jerusalem offer a multitude of options. Hotels are scattered throughout the city, so you can opt for a deluxe room within walking distance of the Old City or one in a newer urban area, a ten-minute ride away. Hotels have outdoor pools, health clubs, and outstanding restaurants. You can choose a hotel in East Jerusalem or on the Mount of Olives and savor Arab hospitality at its best.

Be aware that all hotels in West Jerusalem are kosher and those in East Jerusalem are not.

We have selected five-star to three-star hotels but none are in the Old City. Old City hotels are rather basic and most accommodations inside the walls are hospices.

Peak seasons here are Christmas, Easter, and Passover, and the weeks preceding and following them, plus the period straddling the Jewish High Holy Days (Rosh Hashana—Yom Kippur). Rates rise at these times and space is tight, so reserve for these periods long in advance. All hotels listed here are air-conditioned/heated and accept major credit cards.

West Jerusalem Hotels

Hotels near the Old City

If you select one of these downtown hotels, you will be in the heart of West Jerusalem. You can walk to the Old City or Zion Square, to restaurants and shops. No major drawbacks except for traffic noises at rush hours.

KING DAVID HOTEL 5★

23 King David Street	Phone (02) 251111
	Fax (02) 232303

The understated King David, a 258-room hotel, is the most elegant stop in town. The impeccable lobby, furnished with plush leather couches and chairs, is filled with multicolored flowers arranged in huge copper pots. You can take your shoes off and relax with a magazine or newspaper in the wood-paneled reading room adjoining the lobby. The large grassy area beyond the outdoor terrace is perfect for sunning, and there are tennis courts and a good-sized pool. The hotel has several restaurants but none is memorable. There is a terrific shopping arcade and a tasteful piano bar. The King David radiates its long tradition and very good taste. *Deluxe.*

LAROMME JERUSALEM 5★

Liberty Bell Park	Phone (02) 697777
3 Jabotinsky Street	Fax (02) 697268

Larger, with over three hundred rooms, and glitzy where the King David is understated, the low, angular Laromme is housed in a contemporary building. The outer façade, in traditional pink limestone, covers a modern wood-paneled interior with a small front lobby and larger sitting area to the left of the entrance. A nice touch is the inner courtyard, which serves as a sunning area and snack shop. Tables can be shaded with umbrellas. The Laromme has several restaurants and dining rooms, but none is special. The pool, which is covered by a plastic bubble, is heated for winter use. The Laromme has a great location near Yemin Moshe and several parks and is within walking distance of the Old City. A delightful choice. *Deluxe*.

SHERATON JERUSALEM PLAZA 5★

47 King George Street	Phone (02) 259111
	Fax (02) 231667

The 400-room Sheraton Jerusalem Plaza is an excellent choice if you enjoy being in the heart of things. Although the 22-story hotel is recessed from the street (which removes it from traffic noise) and overlooks the city's largest park, Independence, it is actually a five-minute walk to Ben Yehuda Mall, Zion Square, and Yemin Moshe.

The blue velvet couches in the spacious lobby are set off by the modern paintings on the walls. A wide circular staircase leads to the lower lobby, where the restaurants, a video game room, and shops are located. The swimming pool, on a terrace off the lobby, is surrounded by shade trees. The outstanding nouvelle restaurant, Cow on the Roof, is in the lower lobby. *Deluxe*.

KING SOLOMON 5★

32 King David Street	Phone (02) 241433
	Fax (02) 241774
	In U.S.: 1-800-345-8569
	In New York: 718-651-8777

The white marble King Solomon, well located near Yemin Moshe and several delightful parks, is a luxurious stop. The lobby, which has comfortable couches and a small lounge, is dominated by Frank Meisler's acclaimed sculpture, *Jerusalem*, set in a fountain. The hotel's 150 rooms are spread over fourteen floors and many have a view of the Old City. The pool, on the fourth floor, is small and there is a small sunning area as well. *Deluxe*.

MORIAH PLAZA JERUSALEM 5*

39 Keren Hayesod Street	Phone (02) 232232
	Fax (02) 232411

The Moriah is an excellent five-star stop. It has a lively, upbeat feeling with its white-washed stucco walls studded with bright yellow-framed windows. There are several small sitting areas in the lobby, usually filled with guests who just walked back from the Old City. Rooms are large with a sitting area and private bath with tub. The pool is on the roof and there are deck chairs for sunning as well. The Moriah is a very good choice. *Expensive*.

KINGS HOTEL 4*

60 King George Street	Phone (02) 247133
Box 7581	Fax (02) 232303

Kings is a four-star hotel, with two hundred rooms spread over four floors. The hotel does not have many of the amenities associated with four-star hotels. There is no pool or sun area. Rooms are good-sized and adequately furnished. TV sets can be rented for $3 a day. Kings Hotel, across the street from the Jerusalem Plaza and Independence Park, is a mixed bag. *Moderate*.

JERUSALEM INTERNATIONAL YMCA 3*

26 King David Street	Phone (02) 257111
Box 294,	*Visa & MasterCard accepted*
Jerusalem 91002	Fax (02) 253438

West Jerusalem's YMCA, built by New Jersey millionaire James Jarvie in 1928, fills one of the city's most valuable pieces of real estate. It looks like a huge castle, and from its bell tower (take the elevator) you have a marvelous view of the Old City and the new one. The rooms, recently renovated, are still strictly functional. There are thirty-two doubles and sixteen singles with private baths, and six family units which can accommodate four. Economy units have no bathrooms. It's the facilities that make this Y a standout: an indoor swimming pool, tennis and squash courts, a snack bar, and a library, plus a small archeological museum. The Y has concerts and folk dancing and it's a nice place to meet other visitors. Rates include breakfast. *Moderate*.

WINDMILL HOTEL 3*

3 Mendele Street   Phone (02) 663111
                                    Fax (02) 690964

On a small side street, the Windmill is just a block away from the King Solomon Hotel and Yemin Moshe. Three-star rated, rooms at the Windmill are furnished with light Scandinavian-style furniture, which gives them a spacious, clean look. All are carpeted and have private baths. The lobby is small and often crowded with guests waiting for service in the dining room. No pool, but there is a small sun deck. Helpful, friendly staff. *Moderate*.

Hotels in Givat Ram

Givat Ram, a hilly area in the newer western part of Jerusalem, is a delightful place to stay. It has wide boulevards, beautiful parks, and the city zoo. A stop here puts you ten minutes from downtown by bus, and within walking distance of the Knesset, the Israel Museum, and the old campus of the Hebrew University.

JERUSALEM HILTON 5*

Givat Ram   Phone (02) 581414
                                    Fax (02) 514555

A stay at the Hilton will give you a resort hotel in a city atmosphere. A sleek tower on the city's highest hill, the 400-room Hilton is visible from most parts of the city, and from your balcony you will have unobstructed views of the area. Rooms are small but very comfortable with sitting areas, mini-refrigerators, and TVs with in-house videos. The lobby is large, with a popular piano bar, a dairy restaurant, and a large shopping arcade. The lower lobby has an exclusive French restaurant, the Kerem, and a very nice coffee shop. Behind the hotel, you'll find a large pool, a grassy sunning area, tennis courts, and a mini-golf course. The health club has Nautilus equipment, a sauna, and a whirlpool. Hilton's Executive Business Service is available to guests who need secretaries, translators, or conference facilities. An excellent stop. *Deluxe*.

RAMADA RENAISSANCE 5★

6 Wolfson Street   Phone (02) 528111
                                            Fax (02) 511824

The Ramada, a luxurious hotel on a quiet street, is another resort-style hostelry. Its four hundred rooms are large and very comfortable, with modern tweed chairs and bright colors. The lobby is huge and has a lounge area for drinks and light fare and many sitting areas. Plants on the floor and on the tables give the lobby an open, spacious air. The Ramada has a health club and indoor and outdoor swimming pools, as well as tennis courts. *Deluxe*.

SONESTA JERUSALEM 3★

2 Wolfson Street   Phone (02) 528221
                                            Fax (02) 528423

A smaller hotel near the Ramada, the Sonesta is not luxurious, but all 172 rooms are carpeted and have writing areas and private baths. There is no pool, but there is a sun deck. The lively blue-and-green dining room serves all meals and room service as well. The Sonesta is a modern, upscale choice. *Moderate*.

KNESSET TOWER 4★

4 Wolfson Street   Phone (02) 511111
                                            Fax (02) 512266

Another new hotel on the street, the Knesset Tower is more luxurious, with a plush lobby, a bar, an outdoor swimming pool, and a tennis court. Its 219 rooms all have balconies, but because this is not an elevated area, the view is unimpressive. Part of an Israeli hotel chain, the Knesset Tower is run well and has a friendly, informative, well-trained staff. *Expensive*.

East Jerusalem Hotels

The sights and sounds of East Jerusalem are different from those in the western part of the city, and hotels here are an eclectic lot. They stand in the downtown area, within an easy walk of the Old City, and on the Mount of Olives, where the views are striking. While East Jerusalem is not as bustling or modern as the western part, it is nonetheless a busy commercial area, so if you are dreaming of a quiet pastoral setting, you'll be in for a rude shock. Arab hospitality is legendary and hoteliers in East Jerusalem are no exception. They honed their skills during the years that ancient Jerusalem was under Jordanian control and virtually every visitor to the Old City stayed here. Note: No hearty kibbutz breakfast, but you will often get a continental breakfast with your room. All hotels in this area have nonkosher kitchens.

SEVEN ARCHES HOTEL 5*

Mt. of Olives	Phone (02) 894455
Box 19585	Fax (02) 285384
	Major Credit Cards

Built during the period of Jordanian control, and part of the Intercontinental chain for many years, the Seven Arches Hotel fell into disfavor when Israel took the city 1967. It has a nonkosher kitchen, orthodoxy fears that the hotel is atop an ancient cemetery, and it's likely the Israelis were dismayed that the hotel was built during that time frame. All this adds up to a plus for you if you choose the Seven Arches, for it is the least expensive deluxe stop here. This sumptuous hotel sits atop the Mount of Olives, and the views of the Old City at dusk are unreal. It is modern with white walls and huge windows, and the grounds are a labyrinth of flagstone paths and blooming shrubs. The hotel's two hundred rooms are spacious and comfortable, with TV and direct-dial phones. No pool, but there are tennis courts. There are several dining choices. *Expensive*.

AMERICAN COLONY HOTEL 4*

Box 19215	Phone (02) 285171
Nablus Road	Fax (02) 283557
	Major Credit Cards

When the British reminisce about the last great days of the Raj, they think of the Lake Palace Hotel in Udaipur, but if they ever recall the last days of the Mandate, they think of the American Colony Hotel. Splendor, pomp, and a lot of circumstance are part of the ambience of the American Colony. Anybody who was anybody stayed here: sheikhs, sultans, and oil magnates. This palazzo was the home of a Turkish pasha, and his ornamental taste is reflected in the decor. Saturday afternoon buffets in the American Colony Garden (11 A.M. till 3 P.M.) are legendary. The swimming pool is set amid palm trees, and the 102 rooms are in a main building and the smaller buildings that surround the inner courtyard. *Expensive*.

HOTEL ST. GEORGE INTERNATIONAL 5★

Box 19548	Phone (02) 282571/5
Salah-ed-din Street	Fax (02) 282575
	Major Credit Cards

Bringing a touch of class to East Jerusalem, the neo-Moorish St. George was the area's class act, but is slightly faded and could use a sprucing up. The 150 guest rooms are tastefully furnished and color-coordinated, but furnishings are well worn. The public rooms are exotic with fountains and tile. There is a swimming pool and a quiet garden with umbrella-covered tables and aromatic roses, where you can escape the din of local traffic. *Moderate*.

NATIONAL PALACE 4★

4 Az-Zahara Street	Phone (02) 273273
(a.k.a. Port Said)	Fax (02) 282139
Box 19152	*Major Credit Cards*

This hotel is one of the oldest and newest in town, for it has undergone a total facelift and the results are positive. There are seventy-five double rooms and thirty singles, all with private baths. All rooms have balconies, and you should ask for one facing the Mount of Olives. There is a bar and an in-house dining room, but the National Palace Roof Garden Restaurant is famous for its Middle Eastern fare, including grilled pigeon. There is an outdoor pool. *Moderate*.

CAPITOL HOTEL 4★

17 Salah-ed-din Street	Phone (02) 282561/2
Box 19-459	Fax (02) 894352
	Major Credit Cards

Not a glamorous stop, the six-tiered Capitol is nonetheless a fine choice, for its fifty-four rooms are large, comfortably furnished, and impeccably maintained. An additional plus—all have full baths and balconies from which you can survey the scene below. The Capitol bar is usually crowded and the imbibers, speaking a slew of languages, are a lively bunch. *Moderate*.

HOLYLAND EAST 3★

6 Rashid Street	Phone (02) 284841/2
Box 19700	Fax (02) 280265
	Major Credit Cards

The Holyland East is a 99-room stop and most rooms have balconies; ask for one facing the Mount of Olives. The decor isn't fancy, nor is it very Middle Eastern. The lobby looks like those in West Jerusalem, with comfortable club-chair arrangements. You'll like your room; it has a full bath and is always spotless. The Holyland East has an enchanting roof garden. *Moderate*.

YMCA EAST (A.K.A. AELIA CAPITOLINA HOTEL) 3★

29 Nablus Road	Phone (02) 282375
Box 19023	*No Credit Cards*

Here again, the Y, opulent and hidden away, is a real find—it must be the name that keeps this place overlooked. The lounge is Baghdad Moderne with beaten-copper pots, brass lamps, and low couches. You'll feel like a museum piece if you stay here, and the fifty-seven rooms are spic and span. There's a pool in the basement and squash and tennis courts on the grounds. *Moderate*.

Staying on Mount Scopus

HYATT REGENCY JERUSALEM 5★

32 Lehi Street	Phone (02) 821333
	Fax (02) 815947

Situated on the slopes of Mount Scopus, the magnificent Hyatt Regency takes full advantage of its spectacular location. The three-tiered sunlight-filled atrium lobby, replete with plush leather couches, graceful waterfalls, and hanging plants, is a fitting introduction to this magnificent hostelry. Not a detail has been overlooked in the 503 guest rooms and suites, all luxuriously appointed to provide nothing less than total comfort. Whatever your dining pleasure, you'll find it at one of the Hyatt's kosher restaurants and cafés. Northern Italian cuisine is served in elegant surroundings at Valentino's, while the Pavillion, over-looking the pool area, offers a variety of Mediterranean and Continental dishes along with a children's menu. Regional fare is featured at Shamayim. Recreational facilities include indoor and outdoor swimming pools; a full-service health spa staffed by beauty, fitness, and health professionals; two lighted tennis courts; a children's playground and nursery; and the Orient Express Nightclub for after dark. A fully equipped business center, state-of-the-art conference facilities, shopping arcade, limousine and car rental services, baby-sitting, currency exchange, and same-day laundry and dry cleaning round out the list of the Hyatt's five-star services and facilities. *Deluxe.*

MOUNT SCOPUS HOTEL 4★

Sheikh Jarrah Street	Phone (02) 828891
Box 19702	Fax (02) 828825
	Major Credit Cards

The staid, traditional Mount Scopus overlooks East Jerusalem and the Old City. It has sixty-five rooms (all are balconied) and the hotel offers such four-star amenities as one-day laundry service and a beauty salon. Mount Scopus gets the late-afternoon breezes, and it's rather peaceful here. Meals are served on a terrace overlooking the garden, and there is a pool. *Expensive.*

Kibbutz Guest Houses near Jerusalem

MITZPEH RACHEL

Kibbutz Ramat Rachel	Phone (02) 702555
Box 98	Fax (02) 733155
Jerusalem	

Mitzpeh Rachel, with only thirty rooms, is small, but its location is excellent. Atop a hill south of the city, it offers views of

Jerusalem and Bethlehem. Rooms are comfortable with showers only and there is a swimming pool. The kibbutz has an interesting history and was founded (in a different location) in 1926. *Moderate*.

The following guest houses are located in the hills to the west of Jerusalem, near the Arab town Abu Ghosh. All are within twenty minutes of the city.

QIRYAT ANAVIM 3*

Esther Guest House	Phone (02) 348999
Judean Hills	Fax (02) 348848

Closest to the city, Qiryat Anavim houses its guests in a six-story building built on a mountain slope. The fifty-two rooms do not all have private baths, but they are air-conditioned. The Kibbutz has a swimming pool and a fabulous library with over 25,000 books in several languages. *Moderate*.

MA'ALE HACHAMISHA 3*

Judean Hills	Phone (02) 342591
	Fax (02) 342144

Named for five young pioneers who were killed in an Arab attack in 1938, Ma'Ale Hachamisha (Ascent of the Five) is built on a hill high above Qiryat Anavim, and from the peak you can see Jerusalem. A large guest house (seven buildings) with 146 rooms, all with baths or showers, is set on lovely grounds. Known for its Carmit candy factory, the kibbutz has an active foreign volunteer program. There is a swimming pool. *Moderate*.

NEVE ILAN 3*

Judean Hills	Phone (02) 341241
	Fax (02) 348197

An eighty-room house, looking rather like a motel, is the primary guest facility here, but the kibbutz also has several fully furnished cottages. There is a large reception hall with a sunken lounge area and fireplace, a swimming pool, tennis courts, and a convention center. The pool is covered for winter use. Unlike other kibbutzim, the members here mingle freely with guests and are very hospitable. *Moderate*.

SHORESH 3*

Judean Hills   Phone (02) 341171/5
                                               Fax (02) 340262

Shoresh is a moshav, rather than a kibbutz. It has several types of accommodations, including a hotel with seventy double rooms, twenty-four one-story guest houses, and twenty two-story bungalows. The Shoresh is atop a mountain, and both Jerusalem and Tel Aviv are visible from it. The complex has spacious green lawns, gardens, a swimming pool, tennis courts, and a soccer field. *Moderate*.

Restaurants

To write *fini* to an exhilarating day, you can dine in any number of exceptional restaurants in all parts of Jerusalem. You will be pleasantly surprised to find that there is great diversity available in cuisine and in ambience as well. Jerusalem has a score of restaurants where the first-rate food, intimate atmosphere, and impeccable service make dining a definite pleasure. You can enjoy Continental, Italian, Chinese, and Kosher Nouvelle cuisine in elegant surroundings. But on those evenings when your mood is far more casual, you'll find an even larger number of informal eateries where you can enjoy delicious food in unconventional surroundings. You'll discover eating spots that are intimate and dimly lit, have music, are on hotel terraces or in gardens, and even some with sensational views.

West Jerusalem has the greatest number of eating spots and the greatest diversity of cuisine. Chinese restaurants, delis, dairy stops, and steak houses vie for customers with those eateries serving Eastern European dishes and the newest rage, Tex-Mex. Most restaurants here are kosher, but there is a growing number that use Kosher ingredients but cannot be certified since they are open on the Sabbath.

Restaurants in East Jerusalem and those in the Old City serve Middle Eastern fare and are particularly known for their excellent seafood dishes. Only restaurants in the Jewish Quarter of the Old City are kosher. Middle Eastern restaurants are rarely elegant (although some of our selections are very attractive), but their foods are interesting and different from those you are used to eating.

A number of fine restaurants have opened on Nachalat Shiva, a lovely new pedestrian mall that runs along Salomon and Rivlin streets, not far from Zion Square. This area is especially popular after dark, when it is filled with street artists and strollers patronizing the many new cafés, restaurants, and nightclubs that have opened there.

Fast-food stands serving falafel, shwarma, pizza, burgers, and hot dogs are alive and well in Jerusalem. (One note—in Jerusalem, MacDavid is kosher and does not serve cheeseburgers, while this is not true elsewhere.) There is a *Wendy's* on King George Street near Ben Yehuda.

Jerusalem's equivalent to the food courts common to most North American shopping malls these days can be found on Rehov Lunz, just off the Ben Yehuda Mall. Young people congregate at the indoor and outdoor tables of the many small eateries here, whose fare ranges from pizza, hamburgers, and frozen yogurt to falafels and shish kebobs.

Sabbath Dining

Previously, virtually all restaurants in West Jerusalem and in the Jewish Quarter of the Old City closed for dinner Friday evening and remained closed until sundown Saturday, in strict observance of the Sabbath. Unobservant diners would flock to East Jerusalem. Nowadays, however, Israelis don't feel as comfortable going there and most East Jerusalem restaurants have been closed Friday evenings by intifada. On Friday evenings, diners now head to the various new restaurants that have opened in West Jerusalem that are not Sabbath-observant.

West Jerusalem Restaurants

French Cuisine

MISHKENOT SHA'ANANIM

Yemin Moshe (below the windmill)   Phone 251042
                                                    Lunch and Dinner
                                                    Major Credit Cards

Any listing of Jerusalem's top dining spots would have to rate Mishkenot at the very top or close to it. Both the food, which is French and superbly prepared, and the ambience, which includes an up-close view of Mount Zion and the Old City, are first-rate. Owned by Moise Peer, a personable Moroccan Jew who has lived here for twenty-six years, the restaurant reflects his good taste and passions for gourmet food, fine wines, and works of art. The menu features duck as a specialty of the house, served with orange, cherry, or peach sauce. The "Moroccan cigars" are filled with goose liver, and the flaky pastels have ground veal, pine nuts, and Benedictine flavoring. If Moise is there (he travels a lot, collecting art), ask to see his bottle of Chateaux Cheval Blanc. A 1911 vintage, it is worth $3,500. Say hello from us. *Expensive*.

KAMIN

4 Rabbi Akiva Road   Phone 256428
                                                    Lunch and Dinner
                            Diner's Club, Visa, MasterCard, Isracard

Kamin's relaxed and friendly atmosphere makes it a favorite of local artists and writers. Country-style French cuisine is served in a charming old home with whitewashed walls and a beautiful garden. The extensive menu features an interesting assortment of French and international dishes, including entrecôte, chicken in tarragon sauce, sole in mustard and artichoke sauce, and other fish dishes, assorted pastas, and salads. *Moderate*.

French-Moroccan Food

HAHOMA

128 Hayehudim Street
(Jewish Quarter)

Phone 271332
Kosher Lunch and Dinner
(closed Friday)
American Express, Visa

An attractive Old City dining spot, Hahoma serves Moroccan-French foods and prepares them very well. There is only one large dining room, and the tables are rather close together, but the Hahoma also has a bar area. Try some Moroccan cigars or artichokes Greek style. Couscous, osso bucco, Normandy duck, and sole meunière are good entrées. Have some Moroccan pastry —it's very sweet—for dessert. *Expensive.*

LA GUTA

16 Rivlin Street

Phone 232322
Lunch and Dinner
(closed for Sabbath) Kosher

Gourmet French and Moroccan cuisine is served in elegant surroundings at La Guta. Caesar salad, smoked salmon crêpes, or the mixed salad platters is a delightful way to start a meal here. Entrées include steak au poivre, filet mignon, veal chops, or Moroccan dishes including salmon Morocco and couscous prepared with chicken or meat. Crêpes Suzette, assorted fruit, and those ever-so-sweet Moroccan pastries provide a fitting end to your meal. *Expensive.*

Kosher-French Nouvelle Cuisine

COW ON THE ROOF

Jerusalem Sheraton Plaza (lower lobby)

Dinner Only
Phone 259111, ext. 3129
(closed Friday)
Major Credit Cards

A pioneer in the preparation of gourmet kosher food, the Cow on the Roof has been awarded several medals at culinary art exhibits. This dining spot is very attractive, and care has been taken to give you a feeling of privacy, for wicker screens separate the tables. If your table isn't ready when you arrive, have a cocktail in the small sitting area near the bar. The avocado cocktail—chunks of soft avocado and fish with walnut bits in a vinaigrette sauce—was so delicious we wanted to skip everything else and just keep eating it. But the main course, sliced pigeon breast with goose liver, was also fabulous, as was the thinly sliced marinated lamb served with a cassis sauce. Portions are good-sized—not enormous—so you might even sample one of the desserts. Reservations required. *Expensive*.

KESHET

2 Tiferet Yisrael Street	Phone 282232
(Jewish Quarter)	(closed Fridays and Saturday lunch)
	Kosher
	No Credit Cards

A beautiful restaurant with clean lines and wide spacing between the tables, Keshet has a fabulous location in the Jewish Quarter of the Old City. Eggplant salad, Lebanese style, was very chunky and so was the chicken salad, served as an appetizer with a delightful sauce. Both meat and fish dishes are prepared beautifully and taste delicious. We sampled the sea bass sautéed with wine and garlic and the steak filets with morel mushrooms in the sauce. Both were terrific. As is common here, desserts were just fair. I'd stick to fresh fruit salad or, better still, I'd have dessert later in the evening—elsewhere. *Expensive*.

Continental

CHEZ SIMON

15 Shamai Street	Phone 255602
(near Zion Square)	Noon to midnight
	Nonkosher
	American Express, Visa

Chez Simon is among Jerusalem's most elegant dining spots, and photos on the walls show the well-known people who've dined here. There are two dining rooms; the first is done in deep red velvet with matching cloths. Golden platters await your order.

The back room is in pastel pink with crystal chandeliers. Whichever room you sit in, the menu is Continental, but many of the dishes are prepared in French style. Caesar or Roquefort salads are mixed at your table. Mushrooms vinaigrette or stuffed artichokes are served with a delicate sauce. Broiled veal chops, sweet and sour chicken, and veal piccata are very nicely prepared. The bar at Chez Simon serves a mighty potent martini. After the second, it won't matter what you eat. Reserve on Saturday night. *Expensive.*

Eastern European

FEFFERBERG'S

53 Jaffa Road   Phone 254841
(corner King George Street)   Lunch and Dinner
                                                              Kosher
                                                 No Credit Cards

Fefferberg's can feed 150 people in its two large dining rooms and often does, for it is one of the most popular eating spots in town. Opened in 1939, it has been serving its Polish-style Eastern European food ever since. Matjes herring, stuffed derma with gravy, and chopped liver with chunks of onion are always just right, and the featured main courses are the boiled beef, pot roast, and chicken. Fefferberg's also has delicious delicatessen specialties, including the capital's best corned beef. It does an enormous take-out business on weekends. Not an elegant dining spot, Fefferberg's looks "clubby," with wood-paneled walls and paintings of Jerusalem its major decor. *Moderate.*

EUROPA

42 Jaffa Road (Zion Square)   Phone 258953
                                                    Noon to 9:30 P.M.
                                               (closed for Sabbath)
                                                   Visa, Isracard

A second-floor restaurant overlooking Zion Square, Europa's food is Hungarian-style. The restaurant is comfortable but there is little ambience. Portions are enormous, so be cautious when you order—although it is very tempting to try the stuffed cabbage or kishke or goulash soup. Chicken goulash, roast goose, or *gou-*

lash szekely (pot roast with onions) are deliciously spiced and have tasty gravies. Apple strudel is homemade. *Moderate.*

Steak Houses

STEAKHOUSE WHITE HALL

8 Rabbi Akiva Street
Phone 248408
Lunch and Dinner
Visa, American Express

Steakhouse White Hall should be your first choice if you crave a thick, charcoal-grilled steak. The menu features generous portions of aged beef, including entrecôte sirloin, T-bone, prime rib, and New York cut, all grilled to perfection. At lunchtime, steaks come with free salad bar, bread, potato, a soft drink or beer, and coffee or tea. If you have room, desserts include hot chocolate cake, chestnut mousse, nut parfait, and hot apple pie. *Expensive.*

GILLY'S

33 Hillel Street
Phone 255955
Lunch and Dinner
(Dinner only Friday and Saturday)

Gilly's specializes in meat dishes at very popular prices. Hence it's always crowded, and well worth the wait. Juicy steaks are the norm here and the beef stroganoff is a personal favorite. The lamb chops are also quite good. All meals come with salad and potatoes. *Moderate.*

EL GAUCHO

22 Rivlin Street
Phone 256665
Lunch and Dinner
(closed for Sabbath)
Kosher
Major Credit Cards

El Gaucho is an authentic (and kosher) Argentine restaurant in the heart of Jerusalem. The decor is reminiscent of a ranch on the Argentine pampas, with stone floors and walls, arched doorways, hanging lanterns, wine racks, and wagon wheels. Succulent cuts of beef are slowly grilled to perfection *parrillada*-style and served with a delicious avocado and hearts of palm salad. *Moderate.*

OFF THE SQUARE

17 Yoel Salomon Street   Phone 257719
Lunch and Dinner
(closed for Sabbath)
Kosher
Major Credit Cards

Just a few doors down from its vegetarian counterpart, this Off the Square serves only fresh meats. While the decor is nothing to write home about, the menu is extensive and includes beef and poultry, lamb, pot pies, a large selection, of fish, and an extensive dessert menu. All entrées are served with pita and hummus, a salad, and potatoes, and everything is homemade. *Moderate.*

Vegetarian/Dairy

ETNACHTA

12 Yoel Salomon Street   Phone 256584
Breakfast, Lunch, and Dinner
(closed for Sabbath)
Kosher
Visa, Isracard, MasterCard

A fine dairy choice, Etnachta is run by an enthusiastic group of young people who want to make sure their guests come back again and again. The extensive menu includes assorted omelettes, quiches, soups and salads, baked potatoes, crêpes, and pancakes. Spaghetti dishes, pizza, and lasagna are the house specialties. A friendly atmosphere with both indoor and outdoor seating and background music add to the pleasure of a meal here. *Inexpensive.*

OFF THE SQUARE

6 Yoel Salomon Street

Phone 242549
Lunch and Dinner
(closed for Sabbath)
Kosher
Major Credit Cards

In a peaceful courtyard near frenetic Zion Square, Off the Square is owned by two Australians. Wait for a table in the yard, which is shaded by trees and colorful umbrellas. Everything here is homemade, including the rolls and the rich cheesecake. The menu is an interesting one, with mushroom, artichoke, and spinach pot pies, cheese fondues, eggplant parmigiana, crêpes, and salads. A freshly grilled deboned trout was served with potatoes and salad. Fruit drinks as well as alcoholic beverages are available. *Inexpensive*.

NARGILA

3 Hyrcanos Street, 2nd floor

Open 24 hours
Diner's Club, MasterCard, Visa

This large restaurant with several dining rooms is part of a national chain specializing in Yemenite food. High on the menu are *melawach* (a phyllo dough pastry stuffed with a wide range of fillings including pureed tomatoes, cheese, and mushrooms) and *ziva* (a long, tortilla-like pastry stuffed with cheese, mushrooms, and onions). Additional offerings include eggplant, tahini, hummus, meatballs, kebobs, and other traditional fare. *Inexpensive*.

THE YEMENITE STEP

10 Salomon Street (near Zion Square)

Phone 240477
Lunch and Dinner
(closed for Sabbath)
Kosher
No credit cards

This very lovely restaurant is the oldest and most authentic Yemenite restaurant in town. Located in an old stone house, you'll have a choice of indoor and outdoor dining with friendly service provided by Yemenite waitresses. The menu features traditional dishes including *Shaweeya* (meatballs with zucchini and chicken breast in honey and rosemary); salads, including hummus with mushrooms and eggplant salad; soups served with Yemenite pita "saluf and hilbe"; and an extensive selection of *melawach*. All delicious. Yemenite tea and coffee as well as ordinary teas and coffees, fruit juices, and beer and wine are served. *Inexpensive*.

BAVLY-FOUR SEASONS

54 Hanevim Street
Phone 244220
Breakfast, Lunch, and Dinner
(closed for Sabbath)
Kosher
Isracard and Visa

A leisurely lunch in the Four Seasons outdoor courtyard is a great way to spend a sunny afternoon. The all-you-can-eat salad bar (served with soup of your choice) from noon to 4 P.M. is another reason to stop here for lunch. The à la carte menu is extensive and includes house specialities such as zucchini or artichokes filled with cheese, pasta dishes, and blintzes filled with mushrooms and nuts, as well as assorted vegetable pies and quiches, fish dishes, omelettes, and salads. *Moderate*.

CHEESECAKE

23 Yoel Salomon Street, 2nd Floor
Phone 245082
Breakfast, Lunch, and Dinner
(closed for Sabbath)
Kosher
Major Credit Cards

Breakfast at Cheesecake (with *The New York Times*) is a terrific way to start a day in Jerusalem, either outdoors in the lovely courtyard garden or at an indoor table. Breakfast fare includes three-egg omelettes with all the trimmings, granola, fruit salad, muffins, pancakes, and french toast. Lunch and dinner are equally delicious with menus featuring quiche, onion soup, huge salads, spicy vegetarian chili, stuffed potatoes, and assorted sandwiches. Just as the name suggests, you'll want to save room for dessert—cheesecake or a sinfully rich mud pie. *Inexpensive*.

TAVLIN

16 Yoel Salomon Street

Phone 243847
Breakfast, Lunch, and Dinner
(closed for Sabbath)
Kosher

Rustic decor creates a very homey ambience at this lovely dairy restaurant. The salads here are especially good, and when combined with french onion or any of Tavlin's other soups, make a complete meal. Omelettes, crêpes, vegetable pies, pasta, and fish dishes round out the menu. Dessert offerings include blintzes as well as pecan and applie pies. *Moderate*.

Chinese

MANDY TACHI

3 Horkinos Street

Phone 248433
Lunch and Dinner
Visa

Mandy Tachi is a delightful restaurant to eat in. It's colorful, with red-and-white walls and paintings of China. There are Chinese umbrellas and nice lighting in the large dining room, with blue-and-white cloths. This nonkosher eating spot has an enormous menu, which offers bird's nest and shark fin soup, shrimp with coconut and sesame, and beef with black mushrooms or chilis. Good food, nice atmoshpere. *Moderate*.

THE CITADEL

14 Hativat Yerushalaim Street
(Khutzot Hayotzer)

Lunch and Dinner
Open 7 days a week
Diner's Club

If wandering through the artists' studios in Khutzot Hayotzer gives you a craving for Chinese food (or if you just happen to like it), no doubt you'll wind up at The Citadel. This very lovely Chinese restaurant features Szechwan cuisine, including won ton and egg drop soups, chow mein, and fried mushrooms with bamboo shoots, as well as an assortment of beef and chicken dishes. *Moderate*.

Middle Eastern

Agrippas Street

IMA

---

189 Agrippas Street

Phone 246860
Lunch and Dinner
(closed for Sabbath)
Kosher
Visa, Diner's Club

Middle Eastern cuisine is the specialty at this very warm and homey restaurant located in a large stone house at the intersection of Agrippas and Sderot Ben Zvi. The prix fixe menu includes a main course such as beef or chicken shishlik, mixed grill, or meatballs, and two salads, hummus, eggplant, cabbage, or vegetable. Also on the menu are grapevine leaves, kibbe, and stuffed cabbage, peppers, or eggplant. *Inexpensive*.

SAMMIE

---

80 Agrippas Street

Lunch and Dinner
(closed for Sabbath)

Middle Eastern dishes similar to those at Ima are served at Sammie. This large and somewhat austerely decorated restaurant features grilled kebobs and other meats, along with assorted salads.

SHIPUDEY HAGAFEN

---

74 Agrippas Street

Phone 222367
(closed for Sabbath)
Kosher
Diner's Club, MasterCard, Visa

The aroma of grilling meats wafts throughout the large bi-level dining room at the Middle Eastern Shipudey Hagafen. The source: a large open grill, adjacent to the bar area. Grilled entrées include brochettes, chicken, steaks, lamb, and cutlets. The spicy mushroom-and-artichoke salad is very good, as are the Moroccan cigars, fried kibbe, and the bean-and-meat soup. *Moderate*.

SHEMESH

21 Ben Yehuda Street

Phone 252418
Kosher
No Credit Cards

Shemesh is a typical Middle Eastern eatery, serving a tasty mezze with hummus, tehina, and Greek and eggplant salads. Roast lamb and sinia (ground lamb) are the house specialties, and the shishliks and kebabs are perfectly done. Very popular for lunch and for businesspeople, the Shemesh is quieter at the dinner hour. A pitcher of fresh orange or grapefruit juice will be on your table if you like, and there are some comfortable booths in the rear. *Moderate.*

Italian

LA PASTA

16 Rivlin Street
2nd floor

Phone 257687
(closed for Sabbath)
Kosher
Visa, MasterCard

White tablecloths, red cloth napkins, and flowers on the table lend an air of refinement to this charming Italian restaurant. The reasonably priced daily luncheon special includes an appetizer and soup, main course (fish or pasta), dessert, and wine. The à la carte menu features a fine selection of appetizers, such as eggplant parmesan, smoked salmon, or avocado au gratin; fish dishes, including trout in butter and pine nuts and grilled St. Peter's with herbs; and various pizza and pasta dishes, including an excellent vegetable lasagna. A fine choice. *Moderate.*

ALLA GONDOLA

14 King George Street

Phone 255944
Lunch and Dinner
(except Saturday lunch)
Nonkosher
Visa

On the second floor of an office building, Alla Gondola has an authentic Italian kitchen, wood paneling, crystal chandeliers, and scenes of Venice on the wall. It also has shrimp marinara and squid Sicilian style, lasagna, ravioli, and spaghetti bolognese. Osso buco and chicken cacciatore are spicy, with a rich tomato sauce. *Expensive*.

OSTERIA PAPAS

16 Yoel Salomon Street (Nahlat Shiva)   Phone 256738

8 A.M. to midnight

Meat and meatless Italian dishes such as canneloni, lasagna, ravioli, and pizza are prepared fresh every day at this quaint trattoria. The scallopini and chicken dishes are delightful. Breakfast is served daily until noon and features eggs, fruit salad, fresh bread, juice, and coffee.

PEPPERONIS

4 Rabbi Akiva Street   Phone 257829

Lunch and Dinner

The menu changes daily at this gaily decorated Italian trattoria, so rest assured that everything is fresh (and delicious). Whitewashed walls are adorned with the unexpected, including burlap bags, beans, and pasta, to create a very fun ambience. Antipasti and salads include eggplant, peppers, beets, carrots, and assorted cheeses. Then you'll have a wide range of entrées to choose from—fish, chicken, beef, or homemade pasta with a variety of sauces, depending on what looked best at the market. A really terrific nonkosher choice. *Moderate*.

LITTLE ITALY

38 Keren Hayesod Street   Phone 617638

Lunch and Dinner

(closed for Sabbath)

Kosher

Major Credit Cards

Red-and-white checked tablecloths will make you reminisce about the old Italian restaurant in your neighborhood back

home. The pizza here is rumored to be the best in town. A large
selection of fish and pasta dishes are also on the menu, along
with some mouth-watering appetizers, including baked eggplant
stuffed with ricotta cheese, kosher shrimp sautéed in garlic
sauce, and sautéed fresh mushrooms with garlic, lemon, and
herbs. Bring your appetite. *Moderate*.

MAMMA MIA

38 King George Street   Phone 248080
                                              Lunch and Dinner
                                            (closed for Sabbath)
                                                       Kosher

Originally the Tsafta Theater, the lovely old stone house which is
now home to Mama Mia boasts a beautiful outdoor courtyard
overflowing with fountains and greenery. Dine outdoors if you
can. There are also two delightful dining rooms indoors with
ceiling fans and Israeli prints along the walls. Pastas—regular,
spinach, and whole wheat—are homemade, and served with several different sauces. Be sure to order the focaccia bread as a
starter, along with the insalata alla Siciliana Caprese, a delicious
tomato and feta cheese salad. Pizza lovers have several varieties
to choose from. *Moderate*.

DA PIERO

7 Hama'alot Street   Phone 251975
                                              Lunch and Dinner
                                            (closed for Sabbath)
                                                       Kosher
                                             Visa, MasterCard

Homestyle French and Italian cooking is featured at this lovely
little kosher dairy restaurant. Crêpes and homemade pasta are
the mainstays on the menu, along with pizza and *crostinos*
(toasted baguettes topped with mozzarella cheese and anchovy
sauce, fresh mushrooms, or tomatoes). Salad options include an
all-vegetable health salad, salad Roquefort, and Greek salad.
Soups include onion soup with cheese and croutons, minestrone, tomato, lentil, and mushroom. Dine indoors or on the intimate outdoor terrace. *Inexpensive*.

LUIGI

12 Yoel Salomon Street | Phone 232524
Lunch and Dinner
(closed for Sabbath)
Kosher

The pasta is made fresh every day at this charming Italian trattoria featuring both indoor and outdoor seating. Spaghetti, fettucine, gnocchi are served with a variety of sauces including salmon and cream sauce, pesto, Alfredo, and, of course, Napolitana (tomato). The antipasto, featuring eggplant, peppers in olive oil and garlic, and zucchini is a great beginning to a meal here. The thin-crust pizza is also a good choice; our favorite is the four seasons pizza with mushrooms, olives, onion, and anchovies. *Inexpensive.*

All in a Pie

LE TSRIFF (PIE HOUSE)

5 Horkinos Street | Phone 255488
(near Zion Square) | Nonkosher
American Express,
Diner's Club, Visa

Le Tsriff is a delightfully informal restaurant that stays open till 2 A.M., unusual for Jerusalem. Its outdoor garden is shaded and the glass-enclosed porch is also comfortable. Baked "pies" are the specialties, and they are filled with potato, cauliflower, mushrooms, curried chicken with pineapple, or cheese and onion. Greek and Caesar salads are large and delicious, and the hot apple pie and fruit tarts are home-baked. Alcoholic beverages and cappuccino are also available. *Inexpensive.*

LE TSRIFF (PIE HOUSE)

YMCA | Phone 246521
26 King David Street | Lunch and Dinner
Major Credit Cards

Much more elegant that its counterpart at 5 Horkinos Street, this newer Le Tsriff boasts the same great "pies"—filled with potato, cheese and onion, spinach, beef and chicken curry—that the restaurant is known and loved for. This branch also offers a complete meal, including hors d'oeuvres such as salmon or beef carpaccio and foie gras goose liver terrine; soups including salmon bisque and Moroccan harira; and entrées ranging from fresh salmon to goose liver with apples and Calvados. Freshly prepared pastries and profiteroles follow, so save room for dessert. *Expensive*.

A Legendary Watering Hole

FINK'S

2 Histadrut Street	Phone 234523
(corner King George)	Nonkosher
	(closed Friday)

Fink's has been an institution in Jerusalem since its founding during the British Mandate period. A popular watering hole for British officers, who liked its pub-like atmosphere, it was also the hangout for clandestine Haganah officers. Now its famous bar, still serving the best drinks in town, caters to visiting politicos, newspeople, and local celebrities. The walls, a history of the decades that the restaurant has been around, are covered with photos, posters, and plaques. Reserve to eat in the restaurant, which serves shrimp cocktail, veal cutlets, sweetbreads, and goulash. Even if you don't eat here, drop in at Fink's for a drink—it's a Jerusalem tradition. *Moderate*.

Delicatessen

NEW YORK DELI

28 King David Street	Phone 258157
	Lunch and Dinner
	(closed for Sabbath)
	Kosher
	Diner's Club, MasterCard, Visa, Isracard

It seems almost fitting that Jerusalem should boast an authentic New York kosher deli. Sandwiches remind us of home with names like Statue of Liberty (pastrami, tongue, and salami), Wall Street (roast beef and turkey with lettuce and tomato), and the Park Avenue Burger. Main dishes include grilled steaks, a corn beef platter, and roast chicken, all accompanied by baked beans, potato salad, and coleslaw. You'll have a choice of dining indoors or in the outdor courtyard (weather permitting). *Inexpensive.*

Lunch in the Old City

ST. MICHEL

38 David Street
(Old City Market)
A long, narrow restaurant that opens at 7 A.M. and doesn't close till 9 P.M., St. Michel is in the heart of the market. Many Arab merchants drop in for black coffee and the couscous, moussaka, and grilled meats. Eggplant dishes are popular too. No alcoholic beverages here. *Moderate.*

QUARTER CAFÉ

Above Bazaar,   Phone 287770
Tiferet Yisrael Street
Jewish Quarter
I'm partial to this café, which is really rather basic. Dairy foods, served family-style (actually not even served—you take them yourself), are very good but there isn't anything unusual about them. It's the view from the outdoor terrace (wait for a table here if necessary) that's spectacular. I almost have to pinch myself to believe that I am eating my potato latkes while overlooking the Western Wall, with a close-up view of the Dome of the Rock and the Mount of Olives just beyond. It's unreal!

East Jerusalem Restaurants

Our restaurant choices are top of the line and you will enjoy eating in them. All serve Middle Eastern food and excellent seafood, and the service is always courtly. Reserve for Friday night. If you are uneasy about being in the area after dark, these restaurants are open for lunch.

Petra Restaurant

11 El Rashid Street | Phone 283655
Noon to midnight
No Credit Cards

Petra is one of the area's jewels. The interior is all wood, and crimson napkins mark each place setting. But you should ask for a table in the back room, which has stone walls that look at least as old as the Western Wall. The service is purely Levantine—gracious and eager to please. The mezze, a glorious assortment of salads, is set on a large table, so you can pick your favorites. Jumbo shrimp, mixed meat grills, and steaks are on the menu as well. Music Monday, Wednesday, and Thursday. *Moderate.*

Sea Dolphin

21 Al Rashadiah Street | Phone 282788
No Credit Cards

A very popular seafood restaurant, the Sea Dolphin has the typical fishing net on the ceiling and crabs and turtle shells on the walls. There is nothing typical about the food, however, for the Sea Dolphin has an unusual menu. The fish and seafood are prepared in a variety of sauces and styles. Try the shrimp provençal or the snapper poached in white wine. Both are delicious, as is the St. Peter's fish. *Moderate.*

Philadelphia Restaurant

9 Azzahara Street | Phone 289770
Noon to midnight
Visa

Philadelphia is East Jerusalem's most posh eating spot. Done in light woods, with indirect lighting giving it an intimate look, the comfortable Philadelphia serves superior Middle Eastern foods and is best known for its mezze table, which has an uncountable number of salads and tidbits. Try to keep your sampling down so you still have room for the delicious lamb and seafood dishes. *Moderate.*

ARABESQUE

American Colony Hotel | Phone 285171
Nablus Road | Reservation Required
Major Credit Cards

Many Israelis still head to the American Colony for dinner on Friday night. The Arabesque serves a seven-course dinner on Fridays and an à la carte dinner other nights. Most popular is Saturday's buffet lunch, served in the garden. Dinner at Arabesque is accompanied by jazz or piano. *Moderate.*

MASSWADEH

Al Masoudi Street | Phone 284048
| *Visa*

Hatem Masswadeh and his family run this restaurant, and while the decor, which runs to flocked paper and brass shields, may be a bit garish, the mensaf, shish kebab, and shishliks are delicious. *Moderate.*

HASSAN EFFENDI

Rashed Street | Phone 283599
| *American Express, Visa*

Another exotic stop, Hassan Effendi's is less well known than many of our other choices, but the food here certainly matches up favorably. *Moderate.*

Cafés

Jerusalem does not have as many sidewalk cafés as Tel Aviv has, but the Ben Yehuda Mall has a few and they offer a good mix of fare. We have found a few others as well. First, on the mall:

Atara, at 7 Ben Yehuda Street, features a daily breakfast menu with specials such as American waffles and blintzes. The cheese and fish platters are very good, as are the soups. Atara is also popular for its ice cream menu.

Liber Vegetarian Restaurant, across the street from Atara, is not as attractive, but the food is better. Dairy choices here include fried fish, mushroom omelets, and cheese blintzes.

Bagel Nosh serves ten kinds of freshly baked bagels with lots of cheeses, fish spreads, and eggs on them.

Café Max is famous for its smoked fish platters and terrific pastries.

Other Cafés, Not the Sidewalk Variety

Of Course! An attractive café in the Zionist Confederation House in Yemin Moshe, serving home-baked cakes and pies, sandwiches, and cheese platters. Open 11 A.M. to 11 P.M. daily except for Sabbath—reopens Saturday night until 11:30 P.M. (Enter from Botta Street, near the King David Hotel.)

Ticho House, on Abraham Ticho Street off Haravkook (near Zion Square), is part of the Israel Museum, for it was the home of the artist Anna Ticho. Concerts are held here, and there is a nice coffee shop and garden area.

Ye Olde English Tea Room is located at 9 Dorot Rishonim Street (phone 232368). The tea room is open Monday through Thursday from 11 A.M. to 11 P.M. and Friday from 10 A.M. to 3 P.M. It is closed for the Sabbath.

A cup of tea at Ye Olde English Tea Room is a delightful way to rest your weary feet after a day of exploring Jerusalem. Coffee, tea (of course) and espresso are served, along with date-nut and cranberry breads, Welsh rarebit, New England corn chowder, devon cream tea, cinnamon rolls, milk shakes, and other treats. Pamper yourself.

Ice Cream

Ben & Jerry's ice cream is available at a shop at 5 Hillel Street. It is open Sunday–Thursday, 9:30 A.M. to midnight; Friday, 9:30 A.M. to 1 P.M., and Saturday after Shabbat.

Virtually all your Ben & Jerry's favorites are here, along with strudels and cakes. Take-out and table service are offered. If cookies and doughnuts are what you're hungry for, try the Cookie Man next door at 3 Hillel Street.

Sunup to Sundown

Jerusalem has scores of fascinating historical sites to visit, and you should plan your sightseeing meticulously—and in advance. But don't lose sight of the fact that Jerusalem is also a vital twentieth-century city. Allow time to savor today's Jerusalem. A walk through the Old City's Arab market or a stop at the Friday morning sheep market at Herod's gate are as important to your enjoyment and understanding as any ancient synagogue or church.

Don't be concerned if you cannot visit all the sights in this guide—no one sight is crucial. Don't try to do Jerusalem in a day or even two—instead, read this section carefully and select the stops that interest you most. Plan your time to include historical sights and contemporary ones, and don't forget to leave time for a cappuccino on Ben Yehuda Mall and for shopping. Don't force yourself into an "It's 11 o'clock—this must be Mount Zion" situation. Relax and enjoy this delightful city—then plan to come back again next year.

Important Advice

1. Get an early-morning start when you visit the Old City. Remember: Be cautious.
2. Dress modestly (no shorts, tank tops, or sleeveless dresses). Tuck a scarf into your pocket.
3. You must remove your shoes to enter a mosque. If you feel uncomfortable walking barefooted, bring a pair of socks along.
4. If you drive downtown, park in the lot near Jaffa Gate (or near Zion Gate).

Sightseeing

Organization

To help you plan your time, we have organized the historical sightseeing into geographical areas. Within each area, we will detail the most interesting sights, but we'll alert you to others within the area as well.

Because you should plan your sightseeing according to your interests, you'll notice that the Old City walking tours are self-contained and not linked. This permits you to walk a specific tour if and when you desire.

Detailed maps of the Old City and of the modern one are imperative. IGTO maps aren't sufficient; you will have to buy a good one. Streets in the Old City are winding, have both Hebrew and Arabic names and a variety of spellings, and are often omitted from even the best maps. We will give you a street name whenever we can, and when we can't we will use a landmark to guide you.

We have organized the sightseeing as follows:

1. The Old City

2. West Jerusalem Sights

3. East Jerusalem Sights

4. Mounts and Valleys

5. Scattered Sites

Unique Ways to Explore Jerusalem

Bus #99

Egged operates a special bus called #99, or the round line, which links the city's major sites and hotels. Pick up the bus, which leaves on the hour from the Egged Terminal opposite Jaffa Gate, either at the terminal or near your hotel. The first bus leaves at 9 A.M. and the last at 5 P.M. (2 P.M. on Friday). Pick up a schedule at the terminal or at the IGTO. Stops include Damascus Gate, Tourjeman Post Museum, Mount Scopus, Mount of Olives, Dung Gate, Knesset, Israel Museum, Mount Herzl, and Yad Vashem. You can't beat the price. A single tour ticket (ride lasts about one and a half hours) will run about $4, while a one or two-day tickets (you can get on and off repeatedly) will cost $7 to $9.

Walk on the Ramparts (City Walls)

One of the best ways to "feel" the Old City is to walk on the sixteenth-century walls that encircle it. The walkways are paved (but can get slick) and at times are steep, but the scenes and views are unparalleled. The wall cannot be walked around the entire city, but you can walk two miles if you choose. The ramparts are open from 9 A.M. to 5 P.M. (till 3 P.M. on Friday). The walk is divided into four routes (from Lion's Gate to Damascus Gate; from Damascus Gate to Jaffa Gate; from Jaffa Gate to Zion Gate; and from Zion Gate to Dung Gate). You can, of course, walk any portion you choose. The portion from Jaffa Gate to Zion Gate is open till 9:30 P.M., but it is not advisable to walk on the ramparts after dark, nor should a woman do so alone at any time. Your ticket allows for four entries over a two-day period. Buy tickets in advance for Saturdays and holidays. Very inexpensive and a lot of fun.

Join a Group

Jerusalem has been welcoming visitors for thousands of years. Many of the city's most interesting sights have developed their own in-house tours. The local tourist office organizes walking tours to different parts of the city, as do several hotels. Local tour operators also have an interesting schedule of walking tours, as well as out-of-town trips. Many are free or are inexpensive, and the guides speak English well and are well prepared. You can have a lot of fun and see things you'll enjoy.

In-House Tours Israel Museum (different sections), phone 619211; Hebrew University, phone 882819; Rockefeller Museum, phone 285151 (Fridays,); the Knesset (bring passport), Thursdays and Sundays; Italian Jewish Art Museum, phone 241610.

The Jewish National Fund Plant a tree at a center near the city and visit the stalagmite cave and scrolls of fire. Phone 241781. Modest fee.

Jerusalem Sheraton Plaza Hotel 47 King George V Avenue. The hotel organizes tours to various parts of the city. Free to nonguests too. Check at the hotel for itineraries. Tours begin at 8:50 A.M. Phone 259111.

King Solomon Hotel 32 King David Street. Evening strolls through the Yemin Moshe area. 8:15 P.M. Wednesdays (check on schedules). Phone 241433.

Shabbat Walking Tours Organized by the Jerusalem Municipality Tourist Office, Saturday mornings at 10 A.M. Led by guides to a different destination each week. Meet at 32 Jaffa Road at the entrance to the Russian Compound. Wear modest dress. Phone 228844 for specifics.

Religious Walking Tours   Sponsored by the Young Israel of the Old City, these two-hour tours visit the Jewish Quarter and Moslem Quarter and the slant is from the Orthodox Jewish perspective. Meet at Jewish Quarter Post Office, Tiferet Yisrael Street. Tours start on Sunday, Monday, Thursday, and Friday at 10:30 A.M. Wear modest dress. Phone 287065.

Archeological Seminars Walking Tours   All the Archeological Seminar tours are preceded by a slide presentation. Each lasts approximately three and a half hours. Tours are well-organized and very informative. Meet at 34 Habad Street, Jewish Quarter (above the Cardo). At this writing, there are several tours daily; among the sites toured are the Jewish Quarter, the Temple Mount, Walls and Gates, City of David, and the Christian and Moslem Quarters. Check on exact schedules at office above or at IGTO.

Walking Tours Ltd.   Excellent insights into the history of Jerusalem are afforded by the Four Quarters tour, offered twice daily—at 9 A.M. and 2 P.M. Also highly worthwhile is the all-day anthropological tour offered Thursdays at 9 A.M. and the tour of archeological sites given on Sunday and Wednesday afternoons. All tours leave from the Citadel. The office is located at 26 Alkavez Street, phone 522568. Tickets should be purchased in advance.

Society for the Protection of Nature in Israel   Interesting, adventurous tours led by English-speaking guides. In-city tours as well as those farther afield. Riding, bicycling, and moonlight tours of the desert. The office is located at 13 Heleni Hamalka Street, phone 252357.

Archeological Seminars Bus Tours   Half-day and full-day tours to areas near Jerusalem. Massada, Jericho, and Hebron are destinations. Check at United Tours at the King David Hotel, phone 222187.

Ateret Cahanim Old City Tours   This group sponsors educational tours of the old and new Jewish sites throughout the Old

City, including the Kotel Tunnel Excavations and restored synagogues. Call 895101 for schedule information. Tours are free of charge.

Zion Walking Tours   Eight different tours cover everything from the four quarters, historic synagogues, and Mount Scopus to archeological sites around the city. The office is located inside the Jaffa Gate, opposite the police station. Advance reservations are required (phone 287866), and transportation from your hotel will be provided.

Photographic Walk   This tour is held every Wednesday at 9 A.M. For details, call 699499.

Dig for a Day   A full-day seminar and excavation program is held at various sites near Jerusalem. For information, contact Bernard and Fran Alpert, Archeological Seminars, P.O. Box 14002, Jaffa Gate, Jerusalem, phone 273515.

Desert Tours   If you aren't going down to Elat, you can still explore the Negev and Judean Deserts. Both *Neot Hakikar* (36 Keren Heyesod Street, phone 636494) and *Metzoke Dragot*, (02 964501), will pick you up at your hotel.

Before you set out to explore this historic and beautiful city, a bit of background about its history seems in order.

A Capsule History

The living Jerusalem was a settled town in the Canaanite period when Abraham left the city of Ur in search of a land he had seen in holy visions.

The flourishing of Jerusalem is tied to geological factors. The Kidron and Hinnon valleys caught precious rainwater that was necessary for mass inhabitation. The Gihon, or Shiloh, spring also was an important water source in the area, which was close to the arid Judean desert and had a scant average yearly rainfall.

Jerusalem is never mentioned in the first five books of the Bible. History is shady before the period of David and Solomon's reigns. It was Mount Moriah—Temple Mount—that figured strongly in the city's evolution, for David conquered the Mount that Solomon subsequently built his Temple upon, and the area became the capital of Judea.

For Christians, Jerusalem represents the original spiritual center of the universe. The Byzantines built the first churches and made this a Christian city. Pilgrimages became commonplace. The Moslems followed suit, and by the seventh century A.D., Jerusalem had achieved an importance third only to Mecca and Medina. Mohammed's night journey (described in the Koran) ended here, at the El-Aqsa Mosque. The angel Gabriel, who brought him here on the winged horse Buraq, left Mohammed at the holy rock on Mount Moriah, from which he ascended to Heaven. This rock is quite a sacred spot; in fact, this is where, according to Jewish tradition, Abraham was about to sacrifice Isaac, and where the inner chamber of the Temple was built, a chamber so awesome that it could be entered only once a year by the High Priest, expressly to ask forgiveness from God for the sins of Israel.

The First Temple, built by Solomon in the first millennium B.C., forged Jerusalem's role as a seat of religious authority and the cultural and scholastic capital.

Subsequent invasions took a dreadful toll on the bright promise of this city. The town, which was mentioned as early as 1900 B.C. in Egyptian texts, was torn asunder. David had managed to thwart the assault of the Philistines (a non-Semitic tribe of uncertain origin), and even made allies of a number of the would-be conquerors. But Solomon, whose kingdom benefited from the fruits of David's labor, could not avert the chaos that ensued upon his death. As in a game of chess, kingdoms went back and forth, dividing and uniting, among the successive Jewish kings of the Davidic Dynasty.

When these machinations finally came to an abrupt end in 586 B.C. with the victory of the Assyrians (with Nebuchadnezzar at the forefront), the glorious period of Jewish history ended too.

The Second Temple was built with the permission of the Persian king, Cyrus, but it had a precarious existence. Alexander the Great brought his beloved Hellenism to Jerusalem in 332 B.C., and the people submitted quite peacefully. The townspeople venerated the learned aspects of this Grecian culture, and the upper classes emulated it and even took to learning Greek as the language of court. The men who ruled in Alexander's wake were not so just, however, and the Temple was desecrated again.

The Maccabean revolt followed, and the victory of Judas Maccabeus and his brothers in overthrowing the Hellenistic

Seleucid rulers is the reason for the celebration of the festive holiday Hanukkah. The Temple was rededicated and worship resumed, with Herod expanding the Temple area and building a new structure of unsurpassed magnificence (he built the Antonia fortress around the Temple, naming it for Marc Antony).

Herod's unfortunate admiration for the Romans backfired terribly when the emperor Vespasian, taking advantage of the death of King Agrippa (Herod's grandson), entered Jerusalem in A.D. 67 with a Roman horde. The Romans destroyed the Temple and the town, binding the Jews into slavery. The tragic events at Massada record the last desperate attempts of the Jews to withstand the Roman horde. Most Jews fled Jerusalem, going to safer havens. Pockets of stalwart Jews remained in the city and built modest little places of worship—but Emperor Hadrian put an end to this when he arrived in the devastated city with a grand design in mind. The Old City as it appears today is greatly due to the work of Hadrian, who rebuilt Jerusalem on the Roman scale. He renamed it Aelia Capitolina and thus it remained until the emergence of the Byzantines.

The importance of this period (A.D. 380) as it affected the Christian association with Jerusalem cannot be underestimated. The Emperor Constantine and his mother, Helena, abolished all forms of worship except Christianity from the town. Helena proceeded, through divine inspiration, for lack of a better explanation, to reveal or determine the crucial places in Jerusalem where Christ's passions occurred. She determined the place of the Church of the Holy Sepulchre upon the Crucifixion site. This started a wave of church-building; Christians with money descended upon Jerusalem, erecting monuments and edifices in the name of their religious belief.

The Persians conquered Jerusalem again (with the help of the Jews) and destroyed most of the Byzantine structures. The Arabs drove the Persians and Byzantines out. From A.D. 638, Jerusalem answered to the khalif. What followed, for the next four centuries or so, was a tug-of-war, the participants being Moslems from different areas fighting for predominance; the Egyptian, Syrian, and Persian Moslems were contenders in the power play. The greatest thing to come out of this contentious period was the building of the Dome of the Rock and the El-Aqsa Mosque.

The Moslem stronghold had collapsed from within, so it was no great feat when the Crusaders, anxious to save the Holy Land from the infidels, took the city in A.D. 1099. The Crusaders installed their own kings.

French law and Latin ritual were adopted, and French and Latin became the state languages. The Crusaders massacred a great many Jews, Byzantines, and Moslems, building and rebuilding churches and shrines in their paradoxical zeal. The Crusaders' time was limited; they had but two hundred years to prove their point, whose meaning was lost on the Arab invaders.

The Mamelukes, Turks, and other Moslem invaders fought for the rights to Jerusalem. The Turkish rulers were actually not as intolerant toward other faiths as the Moslems who had come before them. In fact, under Suleiman the Magnificent, Christians and Jews were allowed to re-enter Jerusalem and to worship. The Sultan improved living conditions considerably, cleaned the water supply, and built some impressive structures that beautified the city. He even had the area near the Western Wall cleaned up—it had become a refuse dump—and allowed Jews to pray at their most revered spot. Suleiman did not prohibit immigration by non-Moslems and under his rule, thousands of Turkish Jews and Sephardim from Spain resettled in the city. Later, Ashkenazi Jews from Poland came and built several synagogues with money borrowed from the Moslems. When they couldn't repay their debts, the synagogues were destroyed.

Suleiman's benevolence died along with him, and the Egyptians made yet another attempt to control Jerusalem. But now the European powers stepped into the picture, and by the 1840s Jerusalem was fair game for the British and French—and, in fact, for any nation with political aspirations that exceeded their own turf. Missionary work spread throughout the city; Anglicans and Protestants anxiously tried to convert the ''misguided'' Jews and Christians of Eastern sects. Russians, Prussians, and Jews were allowed to build and resettle. Sir Moses Montefiore financed pro-Jewish humanitarian projects.

This period is marked by the first expansion from inside the Old City walls—Mishkenat Sha'ananim and Mea She'arim were among the first Jewish communities to appear on the outskirts of what was then Jerusalem.

By the turn of the century, European forces were staking out their bits of the Middle Eastern map, and a movement called Zionism was fermenting in the mind of a brilliant Jew of the Diaspora, Theodor Herzl. He was the figurehead and most eloquent spokesman of the movement, but the desire and idea to restore Judaism to a position of importance in this area was already taking hold in the 1880s in Jerusalem. By 1912, Jerusalem had over 70,000 people, more than half of them Jewish. History had another stab at destroying the city when World War I broke out. The war took its toll. Thousands had died of wounds, starvation, or disease by the time the Moslem government surrendered to the British, who occupied the city until 1948. Troubles increased throughout this occupation, with Arabs and Jews living uneasily beside each other.

The British Mandate could not withstand the political atmosphere generated by the atrocities of World War II. Jews, who had been restricted from immigrating here in 1939, started to arrive illegally. The Jewish Agency, which acted as a quasigovernment, led the political fight for a Jewish state. When the British threw up their hands, they handed the problem to the fledgling United Nations, which voted to partition the area into Jewish and Palestinian states. From that point, in November 1947, to the declaration of Israel's independence in May 1948, the Old City of Jerusalem came under siege. Random bombings and sniping were everyday events and soon the Jewish Quarter, surrounded by Arab communities, was stranded without food or water. Fierce fighting to keep the supply lines open failed, and the Jewish Quarter surrendered to the Arab Legion just two weeks later.

When the cease-fire was arranged, the Old City of Jerusalem and East Jerusalem were under Jordanian control. Jews were not permitted to enter the Old City nor to worship at their holiest sites until 1967, when they captured the city during the Six Day War. During the twenty years of Jordanian control, much of the Jewish Quarter was destroyed. The Israelis used those years to build up West Jerusalem, which became a modern cosmopolitan area with deluxe hotels, restaurants, and museums.

Exploring the Old City

The City Gates

You enter the Old City through one of the seven massive gates in the encircling wall. The wall was built by Sultan Suleiman the Magnificent between 1538 and 1541 and it remains virtually unchanged. Suleiman's architects (whom he had put to death for neglecting to include Mount Zion within the walls) built six gates; a seventh—New Gate—was built in 1889. An older gate behind the Temple Mount is sealed, as are three smaller gates (single, double, and triple) on the Mount's southern flank.

Following is a capsule comment on each gate from Jaffa Gate (west wall), moving counterclockwise.

Jaffa Gate   The main entry from West Jerusalem, it leads into the Armenian Quarter. Built in 1538, it was the start of the trade route from Jerusalem to Jaffa. The opening in the wall beside Jaffa Gate was made to accommodate Kaiser Wilhelm II, when he visited in 1898.

Zion Gate   Located in the south wall, it leads from the Armenian Quarter to Mount Zion.

Dung Gate   The smallest and least attractive gate, it is in the southeast wall near the Temple Mount. (The gate was so named because the city's waste was placed outside this wall.) Widened by Jordan to permit vehicular traffic, it has lost its original design.

Golden Gate (Mercy Gate)   In the eastern wall behind the Temple Mount, this gate was built in the fifth century over the traditional site of the entrance to Solomon's Temple. It is very beautiful; the best view of it is from the Mount of Olives. Jewish tradition says that when the Messiah comes, he will enter Jerusalem from the Mount of Olives through this gate. To prevent this, the Moslems sealed the gate centuries ago.

Lions's Gate (St. Stephen's)   It is named for the lions carved on either side of the gate. Suleiman dreamed he would be eaten by lions if he didn't build the walls. The Israelis breached this gate when they attacked in 1967.

Herold's Gate (Flowers)   A major entry point from East Jerusalem and the site of a Friday morning sheep market, this gate was named by medieval pilgrims because they erroneously believed Herod Antipas' house was nearby.

Damascus Gate   By far the most interesting of all the gates, it is called Shechem Gate by the Jews, for it led to the ancient city of that name. Solomon's quarry was below and it was here that he got stones to build the Temple. Several earlier structures stood here, and they have been excavated. The oldest is a gate tower from the first century B.C., but the most interesting is the gate built by Emperor Hadrian in the second century A.D. It had three openings, two guard towers, and an interior plaza in which stood a huge column with Hadrian's statue atop it. In Arabic, the gate is called Bab-el-Amud, "Gate of the Column." Excavated now are the two guard towers, one gate, and some of the plaza. Suleiman's gate was built over this one. A small bridge leads over the open artifacts, and a small museum is nearby with a hologram of the Roman Gate. Open 9 A.M. to 5 P.M.

New Gate   This gate was built in 1889 to allow direct access from the Chrisitan Quarter to Notre Dame de France Hospice right beyond the wall. The Jordanians sealed it.

The Citadel (to the right of Jaffa Gate)

It is best to enter from the kiosk in Omar Ibn al Khattab Square. The Citadel dates from Herodian times and marks the location of his magnificent palace. This strategic site had been fortified by every Jerusalem ruler since the second century B.C. When Herod took over, he strengthened the older fortifications and added three huge towers. He named the towers Hippicus, Phasael, and Mariamne. The one that stands today, which is erroneously called David's Tower, is Phasael. Other parts of Herod's Palace stand as well, even though the palace was forcibly taken by the Romans, was burned by Jewish resistance fighters during the Bar Kochba revolt, and was later damaged and rebuilt by the Crusaders and Mamelukes. Suleiman the Magnificent gave the Citadel its final form, even adding a jaunty minaret. The ruins within the Citadel, as well as the museum in the tower (which displays a mosaic map of Israel from the time of Alexander the Great), are explained with English signs and placards. You'll see Crusader gates, a Mameluke mosque, an Ottoman wall, and Herodian blocks.

Walk to the top of Phasael for a fabulous view of the city and the Mount of Olives. Take a peek at the exhibit of tiny mannequins, each dressed with the traditional garb of Jerusalemites. Then glance at the people in the hall and you'll see the same costumes lifesize.

There is a multiscreen show that tells the story of Jerusalem and its importance for the three monotheistic religions. The show (in English) is screened several times daily.

Better still is the Sound and Light presentation which brings the Citadel to life from April through November. Check for schedules at the kiosk. Citadel hours are Sunday through Thursday, 10 A.M. to 4 P.M., Friday and Saturday till 2 P.M. Take bus #1, #3, #19, #20, #23, or #38.

The Souk (from Jaffa Gate)

As you leave Khattab Square along David Street (the narrow street on the square's left), you enter the world of Aladdin and his lamp. The souk, the Arab market, has remained essentially unchanged for centuries. In Crusader times, the market was defined with an area for goldsmiths, another for spice merchants, and still another for the butchers. This has blurred quite a bit, although as you roam around, you will notice concentrations of certain items in a small area. The streets, in reality narrow cobblestoned or dirt alleyways, are crowded with shops and stalls and with an amalgam of people from every walk of life and from all parts of the world.

Goods are displayed on shelves within the shops, on stands outside the shops, and on the sidewalks, making the passageway even narrower. The merchandise varies enormously, but the biggest sellers are ceramic plates, bowls, and bells; olivewood carvings; colorful glass; camel-hair carpets; and brass and copper. Of course, you'll also see the full range of T-shirts with typical phrases imprinted upon them, rock cassettes, and denim jeans. The older merchants, attired in traditional dress, are smooth and courtly. Standing in the doorways, they cry "Welcome, welcome" or "Have a look." They describe their "genuine" antiques—the brass pots, mirrors, and samovars—and show you that camel-hair carpets don't burn by holding lighted matches to them. Younger merchants, in western garb, are more vocal and try to speak in your language while they cajole you to come in. In any case, they anticipate that you will bargain—and you must, or you will over-pay badly. You will likely overpay anyway, but at least you'll have had some fun.

As you stroll around (there is no special route), notice your fellow shoppers, for this is twentieth-century Jerusalem in action. You will see young backpackers from Northern Europe; groups of Italian-speaking pilgrims, many in black dresses to their ankles; fur-hatted Hassidim with their peyots flapping as they scurry through the market; veiled Arab women, in dark em-broidered dresses, bowed under heavy loads; brown-robed monks and others in black with pointed hoods; and sabras in open-throated shirts sans ties. The sounds of many languages, the aromas of foods, spices, and coffee, and the colorful costumes make for constantly changing images. A final obser-vation point is at the corner of Habad Street and St. Mark (near the Cardo). Look for metal steps (on the right), and when you climb them you'll find yourself above the market. You can see the roofs, hear the sounds, and discern the various parts of the city. When you descend, you'll be near the Cardo and the historic Jewish Quarter.

The Armenian Quarter (from Jaffa Gate)

The Armenian Quarter is to the right of Khattab Square. In this plaza you'll see *The Christian Information Center*, which offers information about Christian sites here and throughout Israel. Helpful people work here. Before setting out, stop at *Abu Seif's* (in the square) for a cool drink.

The main street of the Armenian Quarter is *Armenian Ortho-dox Patriarch Road*, which leads through the quarter and to Zion Gate. Avoid this street at peak rush hours, for cars speed through it on their way home.

Armenian Christians have lived in Jerusalem since the fourth century. Their nation, then independent, was converted to Christianity in A.D. 300. Just three hundred years later, seventy Armenian churches stood in Palestine. Their kingdom was divvied up by Rome and Persia and what survived was absorbed by Russia in 1801.

Their quarter, quiet and residential, has many churches and libraries and a small museum. A problem exists for sightseers, for the churches only permit visitors during services.

The Armenian Compound

Many of the important sites in the quarter are within the high stone walls of the Deir al Arman Monastery. This was traditionally locked each night, and it houses churches, a women's convent, and the residences and administrative buildings of the Patriarchate. Most are not open to the public; but you should visit the *Cathedral of St. James*, which is entered through a well-worn porch on the left of Patriarch Road.

This cathedral is the quarter's most important sight. In the courtyard you'll see a beautiful fountain, and in front of the church you'll notice an ancient wooden board. Called a *Nakus*, it was struck to call the faithful, for the Ottomans did not permit bells till 1840. The church is built on the site where the Apostle James the Less was killed. A monastery was built here in the seventh century, and this building dates to the twelfth century. The floors are boldly carpeted in vivid colors, and there are Spanish tiles on the pillars. There is a large dome with a hexagonal star-shaped tower. One shrine has an inlaid door of tortoiseshell and mother-of-pearl. A small chapel off the main church has three rocks: from Mount Tabor, the Jordan River, and Mount Sinai. These are kissed by pilgrims, for they were brought to the Virgin Mary when she could no longer visit the places she held dear.

You can attend the services here from 3 to 3:30 P.M. Monday through Friday and 2:30 to 3 P.M. on Saturday and Sunday. Notice the pointed headdresses that the priestswear. These are symbolic of Mount Ararat, the mountain that is the Armenians' spiritual symbol.

Follow Patriarch Road to the city wall, and through a narrow passage you'll find the *House of Annas Church* and, adjacent to it, the *Monastery of the Olive Tree*. The church, built in 1300, marks the site of the house of Annas, the high priest before whom Jesus was taken after his capture. Here he was beaten and left tied to a tree overnight. The tree stands in the monastery. Jesus was then taken before the High Priest Caiaphas (Annas' son-in-law). The Armenian church that marks Caiaphas' house is on Mount Zion nearby.

The Armenian Museum

Also called the Helen and Edward Mardigian Museum of Armenian Art and History, it is entered from Chabad Street (near Zion Gate).

A small entrance fee is collected by a grizzled Armenian gent who speaks almost no English. Inside this two-story museum with a weedy and charmingly wild flower garden in the court-yard, you'll encounter relics and reminders of what was once a proud and glorious Armenian kingdom. When you realize that the Armenians were the first nation to embrace Christianity, you can understand their sense of belonging here in Jerusalem, even if their numbers are small. Most interesting in the museum is a Byzantine floor of an intricate pastel design; it is partly damaged but retains its delicacy. The ecumenical splendor of the Armenian religion can be seen in the intricate vestments and chalices worn and used by the Patriarchs. There are many examples of brass, gilt, and silver vessels; oil lamps; pottery; and Armenian tile work. The elderly chap who guards the museum will be happy to show you the creaky printing press, one of the oldest in Jerusalem and the first one ever to print the Bible in the Armenian language. The only hitch is that the caretaker speaks only Armenian, but watch his gestures and you'll actually under-stand. It's all self-explanatory. Museum hours are 10 A.M. to 3 P.M. daily (closed Sunday). Take bus #1, #2, #3, #9, #13, #19, #20, #30, #41, or #99.

The Syrian Orthodox Monastery of St. Mark

The black-robed monks speak and pray in Syriac, a language spoken during the time of the Patriarchs. This ornate twelfth-century church stands on the site of the house of Mary, mother of Mark the evangelist. The church is open from 3 to 4 P.M. only. On Patriarch Road, look for El Malek street. Turn left off Habab and then right onto Ararat Road.

The Jewish Quarter

Jerusalem has been sacred to three faiths for thousands of years. For most of these years, the most pious adherents have chosen to live here to be near their holy sites. Over many generations, their communities were established in specific parts of the city. In classical times, this elevated region in the southeast part of the city was called "upper city" and housed the wealthy. But since the fifteenth century, it has been known as the Jewish Quarter.

Unlike European ghettos, the quarter was never walled in and it increased in size with the influx of Jews in the nineteenth century. By 1914, fifteen thousand Jews lived in the quarter, which was terribly overcrowded. The *yishuv* (community) started to buy homes and land in the adjoining Moslem Quarter, where they lived peacefully till the Arab riots in the 1930s. Finally, the crowded conditions overwhelmed the city's sanitation capabilities and by 1860, sewage and garbage disposal presented horrendous problems. Montefiore's idea to build neighborhoods outside the city walls was unpopular at first, but then the idea gathered steam and many Jews from within the city walls and virtually all the newcomers settled outside the walls.

For centuries, Jewish scholars and sages had lived within this inner city quarter near Judaism's most sacred site, the Wailing Wall. They had built twenty-seven synagogues as monuments to their dispersed nation. The synagogues were the anchors of the quarter and dominated its life. Some were built below ground, for the Old Testament says, "from the depths you will call to God," while others were built on higher ground.

During the Mandate period, an uneasy peace hovered over the city, punctuated by Arab riots. By the time the Mandate drew to a close, only two thousand Jews lived within the quarter, which was in disrepair, and most of them were elderly Orthodox scholars living in poverty. From the day the U.N. voted for partition to Ben-Gurion's proclamation of a state six months later, fierce fighting raged in this part of the city. Encircled by hostile Arabs, the Haganah struggled to keep the quarter's supply lines open. Over a thousand people died in this vain effort, and two weeks after the declaration, the Jewish Quarter and its two hundred defenders surrendered. The area was taken by the Jordanian Arab Legion and held till 1967. Most of the public buildings were razed and others were looted. Refugees flooded into the buildings and, uncared for, the quarter became a slum.

When the Old City was retaken by the Israelis, they determined to restore the quarter to its glory days. The restoration process uncovered many archeological sites which had been unknown. The quarter that you are about to explore is historically accurate but includes many new houses, shops, and restaurants. Obviously it does not have the exotic, ancient flavor of the other quarters; however, it does have a lot of litter. If nothing is done, the quarter will soon have the same unsanitary conditions it had in 1860. Take bus #1, #38, or #99 to the Jewish Quarter.

The Cardo

This entrance to the quarter is a reconstruction of a main street from Byzantine and Roman times. The reconstruction was based on plans from the ancient Madaba mosaic map of Jerusalem, now in a Jordanian museum. While unearthing the rubble, workers found parts of the original Cardo and ruins from the First Temple period. These have been left exposed. Today the street has some fine shops that specializ in Judaica, and two dairy eateries. The nicer, *Richie's Cardo Café*, is an L-shaped eatery on the second floor. Good for omelets and salads, Richie's is open 9 A.M. to 7 P.M. daily (till 2 P.M. on Friday). It is closed Saturday. Mid-block *The Cardo Café* is a cafeteria with virtually the same menu. The streets adjoining the Cardo (on either side) have the quarter's best shops. These specialize in Judaica and antiques. Take a peek at *Old City Art Gallery* at 33 Ha-Yehudim Street and *Cardo Antiquities* and *Victoria Antiques* on Habab Street.

The Quartercentre

Before you head into the quarter, stop into the Quartercentre, which is on the Ha-Yehudim Street, adjoining the Cardo. You should see the audiovisual show, which covers the history of the quarter from biblical times to the present, and the photographs taken during the war of 1948. There is also a memorial site for those who died defending the quarter. Hours are 9 A.M. to 5 P.M. daily, 9 A.M. to 1 P.M. Friday. The English shows are at 10:30, 12:30, 2:30, and 4:30. There is a modest fee.

Yishuv Court Museum (take a right up the steps from Cardo)

The steps at the end of the Cardo lead to Habab Street, which has reconstructed houses. Notice the courtyards around which they were built. Directly ahead at 6 Or Ha-Hayim Street is the *Old Settlement (Yishuv) Court Museum*. A typical house of the quarter, it was a famous Sephardic Teaching Center and housed a Sephardic synagogue. Later it was joined by an Ashkenazi synagogue, and so the museum, which illustrates life in the quarter from the mid-nineteenth century to the First World War, blends both strains of Judaism. Impetus for the museum, which opened in 1970, came from descendants of the family who owned the house prior to 1948. Hours are Sunday through Thursday, 9 A.M. to 4 P.M. There is a modest fee. Buy the English pamphlet.

Nearby, a lovely shop, the *Rothschild Craft Center*, has a fine selection of local handicrafts. It's open from 2 till 6 P.M. Sunday through Thursday.

Three Restored Synagogues

Heading left from the Cardo steps, you will enter a large plaza. Just before the spraying fountain, you'll see on your left the partially restored synagogues that were the center of Ashkenazi life in the quarter. The synagogues are quite low, as was customary to avoid drawing the Arab's ire, and towering above them is an ancient mosque.

The first, the *Ramban Synagogue*, was built in 1267 when Nachmanides, one of Judaism's greatest teachers, arrived from Spain to find that the Jews had fled the city and were living on Mount Zion. He convinced them to return and they built a synagogue in which both Ashkenazim and Sephardim worshiped. The adjoining mosque, built by a converted Jew, caused friction between the communities, and the Ramban was burnt. Rebuilt, it again became a center of controversy in the sixteenth century and was closed to worshipers for four hundred years.

Just beyond the Ramban synagogue stands the *Hurva (Ruins) Complex*. In this complex the city's Ashkenazi community lived in small houses around a courtyard. They built a small synagogue which they called Hurva. In 1700, a very large group arrived and rented more land in the area from the Arabs who owned it. When the Askenazim were unable to pay their rent, the Arabs burned the new homes and the synagogues to the ground. In 1837, the Ashkenazim returned and constructed a new community on the site, as well as a tiny synagogue called *Menachem Zion* (the third building).

The settlers of this community were Prushims, a sect that was violently opposed to the Hassidim who had previously emigrated here. Soon the Prushim community outgrew Menachem Zion and constructed a new synagogue on the site where the previous one had stood. Also called the *Huerva* (Hurva), it was the city's tallest synagogue and as you look at its ruined arch, you can see that it was as high as the mosque. These synagogues and the building complex behind them were blown up by the Arab Legion in 1948. The reconstruction efforts are explained in English at the site, but read them from right to left.

The Sephardic Synagogues (follow Mishmerat Ha Kehuna across the Plaza)

Until the mid-nineteenth century, Sephardim far outnumbered Ashkenazim in Jerusalem. They were Judaism's most notable scholars, and it was their leadership that was recognized by the ruling Turks. Sephardic life centered on four synagogues on Mishmerat Ha Kehuna Street.

The entrance is through a sunken courtyard and you'll immediately be struck by the fact that the synagogues are below street level. Although they were built low to avoid controversy with the Arab community, they were not below sixteenth-century street level.

The entrance leads into *Yohanan Ben Zakkai* Synagogue, but to be historically correct, walk through it to *Prophet Elijah's* Synagogue, which was built earlier. It was to Prophet Elijah's that the quarter's Ashkenazim came to worship when the Ramban synagogue was closed to them. It was named for an early legend in which the Prophet Elijah appeared as the tenth man, forming the required *minyan* (quorum) needed for prayer. Elijah's Chair, kept here for his return, was looted, as was the synagogue's famous ancient bridegroom's chair.

Return now to *Yohanan Ben Zakkai*, built in the early seventeenth century in traditional Sephardic style. You can tell by the arrangement of the seats around the wall. The iron rings in the ceiling overhead held oil lamps. In the large window, an oil jug and a *shofar* (ram's horn) were kept for use by the Messiah. These were looted and their replacements are behind a glass case. All the ceremonial objects here were brought from old Italian synagogues.

The *Central Synagogue*, quite small, was actually the courtyard where the women worshiped at the services held at Ben Zakkai.

The fourth synagogue, *Istanbuli*, was built in 1764 and served as the synagogue for those Jews who were neither Sephardim nor Ashkenazim, but were primarily from North Africa. They were called Westerners. Istanbuli also stored damaged sacred texts. Once a year, the members marched from the synagogue by candlelight to bury these ritually and to guarantee a year's rainfall for Palestine. During the final days of the 1948 siege, many of the quarter's Jews gathered here. These synagogues were not destroyed, but they were totally looted and used as refuse dumps.

Galed Road (follow Mishmerat Ha Kehuna toward the parking lot and turn left on Ha Hazorot)

Although Jewish tradition forbids burial within eighty feet of an inhabited area, this became impossible in the final days of the 1948 siege. At first, the dead were taken outside the city walls, under British protection, for burial on the Mount of Olives. But soon snipers made this impossible and rabbis permitted temporary burial in this small alley. Over thirty defenders were buried here in a communal funeral. After the quarter fell, Jordan buried fourteen others. The dead remained here under a layer of rubble till 1976, when they were removed to the ancient cemetery on the Mount of Olives. Look for the sign that marks this area.

Batei Mahse Shelter Houses (on German Square)

The Jewish community of the quarter was very large by the mid-nineteenth century and the area was overcrowded. These houses were built on a large empty plot where once lepers lived and ritual slaughterhouses stood. The low-cost housing, conceived by an association of German and Dutch Jews, provided shelter for over a hundred families. Designed so the families would move out after they were established, the idea failed, for no one moved on and generations of families lived here. In the basements of these houses, the last defenders lived in the final days of May 1948. They surrendered in the plaza out front. Not destroyed but in terrible disrepair, Batei Mahse was the first area to be renovated, permitting residents to return to the quarter.

Ruins of NEA Church (across Plaza where city wall expands)

Once a grand church, built in the sixth century by Emperor Justinian, the ruins of the NEA Church and those all around it were uncovered during the renovation. Other finds include a Crusader building and Byzantine streets.

Tiferet Yisrael Street (follow Midsag Ladach from Plaza to German Hostel)

The quarter's most interesting street is Tiferet Yisrael. It houses two restored synagogues (*Tiferet Yisrael* and *Karaite*), a terrific little museum (*The Burnt House*), and a *bazaar* (with good shops and several eateries). The streat ends at the ancient *German Hostel.*

Tiferet Yisrael Synagogue, which existed for seventy-six years, was the largest Hassidic synagogue in Jerusalem. A tall building capped by a dome, it served as an observation post during the 1948 fighting and was blown up. Part of the façade, bullet holes intact, remains, as does the *mikveh*, but the restoration did not include the lovely dome.

Directly across the street stands the restored *Karaite* synagogue. If you go up the metal steps, you can read about the synagogue, but it is actually below street level. Karaites are members of a Judaic sect that started in Persia in the eighth century. They follow the basic tenets of Judaism as described in the Bible, but do not recognize any of the rabbinical interpretations (Mishnah, the Talmud, the Cabbala) that followed. Their community was established here in A.D. 900, but was destroyed by the Crusaders. They didn't return till 1400. Because the synagogue is in the basement (look for the iron gate in the courtyard), it wasn't destroyed, only looted. Near the entrance you'll see two inscriptions in Hebrew. Before 1948, there were twenty-six.

Burnt House Museum

A delightful museum has opened in the remains of a luxurious Second Temple period house. Called the Burnt House because the Romans torched it, it has been restored and the uncovered artifacts are on display. The audiovisual show describes what the house was like and what life must have been like then. The hours are Sunday through Thursday 9 A.M. to 5 P.M., Friday till 1 P.M. English shows are 9:30, 11:30, 1:30 and 3:30. There is a moderate fee. Take buses #1, #2, #38, #99, or a bus to Jaffa Gate.

The Bazaar

A bustling area with snack shops, souvenir stands, and rest rooms, the bazaar also has three very nice shops. Above it stands the basic but delightful Quarter Café (mentioned previously). The shops, which adjoin one another, are *Ye Burnt House Shoppe*, which sells antiques as well as ceramics and jewelry; *Nicole's*, which has very attractive old and new jewelry; and *Turnowsky's*, which has a variety of handicrafts.

The bazaar area existed in the Crusader period, but no one knows what it was. Houses that were built over the Crusader buildings were badly damaged in the fighting. When they were removed, the beautiful arches appeared and they were left. It looks great.

German Hostel (near the Bazaar)

A former Byzantine church was converted into a hostel for German pilgrims in the twelfth century.

Synagogue of the Westerners (follow Tiferet Yisrael back to the Plaza and bear right on Plugat HaKotel)

The westerners are the Jews of North Africa, many of whom came to Palestine in the mid-nineteenth century. They initially worshiped at the Istanbuli Sephardic synagogue, but finally built this one in 1860. Restored, the building now houses a yeshiva.

The Israelite Tower (near the Synagogue of the Westerners)

Don't try to find the tower by looking skyward, for it is below ground—fifty-five steps down. The Tower is the ruins of a gate tower from the last days of the first kingdom, when it stood on the city's northern wall. There is another tower nearby from the Hasmonean Period.

The Western Wall (HaKotel Hama'aravi)

For a person of the Jewish faith, the Western Wall is the emotional high of a trip to Israel, and even visitors of other faiths will be caught up in the drama—the urgency of the prayer and the obvious depth of the feeling.

The most dramatic time to see the wall is at night, when it is beautifully illuminated. You will see tiers of enormous pale-yellow boulders that stand sixty feet high and stretch for 150-plus feet. At the wall's base, in a vast open plaza, you'll see people lost in prayer: men at the long portion to the left and women at the far smaller area on the right. Men in long black silk coats and fur-trimmed hats alongside those in shirt sleeves and yarmulkes face the wall, prayerbooks in hand, prayer shawls tightly wrapped around their shoulders, rocking gently or spiritedly back and forth while murmuring inaudible prayers. Women of all ages in ankle-length dresses, hair covered with kerchiefs, are also praying, straining to touch the wall, often in tears. You'll also notice tiny scraps of paper in the crevices of the rocks. These represent the hopes and dreams of the writers. Take buses #1 or #38 to the Western Wall.

On Friday night, hundreds of Hassidic men gather at the wall to joyously welcome another Sabbath with prayer, song, and dance.

What is the Western Wall? Till 1967, it was called the Wailing Wall, for it is said that the wall wailed along with the Jews who over the centuries overcame the most arduous obstacles to stand here and pray for the return of their nation. It is actually the western wall of the Temple Mount support, and it dates from the Second Temple period. From behind the wall, at Wilson's Arch, you can see how much deeper the wall is. With the accumulated rubble of several centuries covering it, it is possible that stones from Solomon's Temple still lie below.

The exposed wall (which is only a fraction of the actual wall) has seven tiers of huge stones, piled one atop the other, which have stood without cement for two thousand years. Atop that portion are four tiers of smaller stones, probably added by the Moslems in the seventh century.

Until 1948, Jews were permitted to pray at the wall, ofttimes begrudgingly, but weren't allowed to bring altars, Torahs, or other ceremonial objects. The wall was in a narrow plaza, only big enough for a small crowd, and was surrounded by a Moroccan neighborhood. Things went downhill from there, for from 1948 until 1967, no Jew was permitted to pray at the wall at all — this in spite of the fact that the armistice treaty with Jordan did allow for prayer. On the third day of the 1967 war, Israeli defense forces breached Lions' Gate and raised the Star of David over the wall. The photograph of that moment is as memorable as that of the Marines planting the American flag on Iwo Jima.

The Moroccan neighborhood was razed and a huge open plaza now fronts the wall. It, and all the holy sites in the city, are open to all worshipers and visitors. On Mondays and Thursdays, bar and bat mitzvahs are held at the wall. Since this marks a young person's passage into adulthood and the responsibilities of this religion, I can't think of a more appropriate site for the ceremony.

At night the stones are covered with drops of dew, and legend says it is the wall weeping with the Jews — but obviously now they are tears of joy.

Wilson's Arch To see just how deep the wall is, you have to go behind the men's portion through a series of caves and tunnels and peer down *Warren's Shaft*, which was dug by a British archeological team. You can see down the square shaft to the rock far below — there seem to be fourteen levels below ground level. Women are permitted in this area, but must enter from the door to the left of the wall. It's marked by a blue sign. Open Sunday to Thursday from 9 A.M. to 5 P.M., and Friday from 9 A.M. to 5 P.M. Closed Saturday.

The Western Wall is not in the traditional Jewish Quarter, but in the lower (in altitude) Moslem Quarter. You can enter this area directly from Dung Gate, from the Jewish Quarter, using the staircase alongside the German Hostel, or through the bazaar from David Street to Chain Street. A vast area to the south of the Western Wall/Temple Mount is being excavated, and fantastic things have been uncovered. Not open at this writing, it may be when you are there. If you like ruins, stop at the kiosk alongside Dung Gate and inquire.

The Moslem Quarter

The Moslem Quarter, the city's most densely populated area, is home to fourteen thousand people. Before the Crusader period, this was a Jewish area, for it was nearest to the Western Wall. By the twelfth century it had become Moslem and has remained so. The quarter sits north and west of Islam's most important Holy Land site, the Temple Mount. The quarter itself does not have specific sights of particular interest, but it does have local color, which is reason enough to explore the noisy, crowded streets within this seventy-six-acre area. Take either bus #23 or #27 to the quarter.

Direct access to the Moslem quarter is from Damascus, Herod's, and Lion's gates. The streets are filled with shops and cafés, crowded side by side. Arab merchants courteously welcome you to their shops while others wile away the hours playing dominoes and a game that looks like backgammon (*Shaish Baish*). You'll notice men smoking hookah pipes. These are glass jars, filled halfway with water, with a hot coal and tobacco on the top. The water bubbles as the tobacco smoke is drawn through it. The market here is quieter, not so much for tourists as for locals. You'll see spice merchants, fruit and grain stalls, beans, and straw products as you wander around.

Two of the quarter's most appealing sites are more a part of the Christian tradition than the Moslem one. These are the

Church of St. Anne and the *Pools of Bethesda.* (A description of the Stations of the Cross, located within this quarter, appears under Via Dolorosa in the section on the Christian Quarter that follows.) The *Pools of Bethesda* were the site of one of Jesus' miracles. It was here that Jesus cured a crippled man. The waters of *Bethesda* (Hebrew for "place of mercy") were known in pre-Christian times when people came here to be healed. The pools were a main source of water to the Temple. Nearby *St. Anne's* takes its name from the mother of Mary, whom the Byzantines believed lived here with Mary's father, Joachim. Crusaders built the church we see today in Romanesque style. The hours are 8 A.M. to noon and 2 to 5 P.M. Since this church stands on a site where older structures stood, excavations have yielded bits and pieces of older buildings. These are all marked.

What is of interest within the Moslem Quarter are the architecturally unique buildings built by the Mamelukes. Who were the Mamelukes? They weren't North African Moslems who rose to a speedy ascendancy, nor were they Arabs spreading the words of Mohammed. The Mamelukes were slaves. Originally purchased by wealthy Moslem rulers in slave markets in Turkey as bonded servants, they eventually overthrew their masters. They were converts to Islam. Their buildings are marked by fanciful recessed doorways flanked by two smaller doorways, one on each side. The use of stone-pattern design in beige, black, and red distinguishes their architecture.

The small palace, *Serai es sitt Tunshuq*, was built by a Mongol woman in the fourteenth century. Across the street is the domed tomb she had erected for her passing, *Turbat es sitt Tunshuq*. To find them, follow Bab el-Wad Road (from Damascus Gate) and turn left at Aquabet el Asseileh, one street before Via Dolorosa. On Bab el-Wad you'll see *Ribat Bayram Janish* and the *Tariq Bab en Nazia.*

On Tariq Bab el-Hadid, you will see a *madrasa*, which means "school" or "college." This one, *Jawharizza*, was founded in 1440 by an Abyssinian eunuch, who went on to greater fame by becoming the Superintendent of the Royal Harem in Cairo. The *Arghuniyya* was built in 1350 by an unfortunate scholar who, in his short but illustrious career, was a governor of Damascus and Aleppo and died before his thirtieth birthday. The madrasa *Muzhiriyya* was built in 1480 by a man named Ibu Muzhir, who tried in vain to ward off the attacking Ottomans, who were fear-less and victorious.

Tariq Bab es Silsila (Street of the Gate of the Chain) is a prime spot for viewing Mameluke architecture.

The madrasa *Tashtimuriyya* was built in 1382 by an emir who built this structure to double as a tomb. The windows and the balcony, as well as the door niche, demand special attention.

At the end of the road near the Western Wall is the *Turba Turkan Khatun*, built in 1352 for a Mongol princess who died while on a pilgrimage to Mecca. You will recognize this building by its gray-tone stone and the delicate arabesque designs on the façade. It is an exceptional specimen of Mameluke construction.

The madrasa *Tankiziyya* is right across the road and was an il-lustrious college in the fourteenth century. The Emir Tankiz, who rose from a mere cup-bearer to great wealth (and was later executed on grounds of corruption), built the structure in 1328.

As you approach the Western Wall plaza, you will see the Temple Mount, the must-see site in the Moslem Quarter.

The Temple Mount

The most impressive site in the Moslem Quarter and perhaps in Jerusalem is *Haram esh-Sharif*, the Temple Mount. This is where the *Dome of the Rock* and *El-Aqsa Mosque* are located, along with other important landmarks of Jerusalem's long Moslem as-sociation. The Mount is Islam's third holiest site, after Mecca and Medina.

Use the staircase just right of the Western Wall, called Moors' Gate. Notice the signs from the Chief Rabbinate, forbidding entry to Jews. This is because the exact location of the Temple is un-known, and Orthodox Jews fear walking on it.

As Mount Moriah, this is a supremely sacred spot for Jews, for when David arrived in Jerusalem he purchased this parcel of land from the Jebusites; later his son, Solomon, built the first great Temple on the Mount. Repeatedly plundered, it was finally de-stroyed by Nebuchadnezzar in the sixth century B.C. In 36 B.C., Herod, who had been appointed King of the Jews by Rome, started construction of a Second Temple, more elaborate and magnificent than the first.

Haram esh-Sharif, which means "noble sanctuary," and the wide, flat expanse (thirty acres) of stone pavement rising above the daily concerns of the workaday world, is a place of reflection, sanctity, and immeasurable beauty. Herod was the man responsible for the overall layout of the mount. He had the sides of the hill bolstered by walls on every side, and the land within the walls was filled with additional earth so it would be even more elevated. He then flattened the surface and built a complete Jewish compound, where Gentiles were prohibited entry upon the threat of death. Byzantine Christians avoided the area, for it was considered accursed. When the second Temple was destroyed, the area was left abandoned and neglected, soon becoming the town dump. So it remained till the advent of the Moslems in the seventh century A.D. Omar and the Ummayed Caliphs had the area cleaned up and built the Dome of the Rock (691 A.D.) and El-Aqsa (705–715 A.D.). When the Crusaders came to Jerusalem and installed their own king here, he used the Dome of the Rock as his personal residence. Eventually it was given to a group of soldier-knights, who became known as Templars. Saladin restored the structure to its status as a mosque.

Entrance to the mount is free but there is a fee to enter the buildings. Entrances for non-Moslems are on the west side of the mount and only certain gates can be used. Your best bet is Gate of the Moors (*Babel Magharibeh*), alongside the Western Wall, or *Bab en Nazir* from Alladin Road, Moslem Quarter. The hours are 8 to 11 A.M., 12:15 to 2:15 P.M., and 3:45 to 4:30 P.M.. At other times and on Friday, the mount is open to Moslems only. You must remove your shoes to enter the mosques.

As you enter Moors' Gate, you'll notice three buildings to your right. The first is the *Islamic Museum*, which houses a collection of Islamic art, medieval manuscripts of the Koran, and glazed tiles inscribed with verses from the Koran. The next, *Qubbat Yusef* (Dome of Joseph), was built by Saladin in 1191, and the last, near El-Aqsa, is the women's mosque. Entry is restricted to Moslem women. Decorated in shades of blue, it used to be a dining area for the Knights Templar.

El-Aqsa Mosque was built here in 1033 on the site of an earlier mosque built in 670. On the southern side of the mount, it is the largest mosque here and it faces Mecca. It can hold five thousand people and gets its name from the Koran. It means "farthest point" and signifies that it was the farthest point Mohammed reached when his horse *Baruk* (Lightning) brought him from Medina to Mount Moriah, where he ascended to Heaven.

Its entrance porch has seven arches, and the mosaic work on the cupola is stunning. The frosty marble on the columns was a gift from Benito Mussolini; the ceiling was a donation from King Farouk.

It was in El-Aqsa that King Abdullah of Jordan, King Hussein's grandfather, was assassinated by an extremist in 1951. The prayer niche on the right wall is flanked by small columns; a carved pulpit, which was destroyed in a fire set by a lunatic in 1969, has been rebuilt. (The man believed that the Temple Mount had to be cleansed of infidels before the Messiah would come.)

To the right of El-Aqsa, a small building marks the entrance to Solomon's stables. Built long after Solomon's time, the structure was actually where the Crusaders stabled their horses.

Between El-Aqsa and the Dome of the Rock is a fountain, *El Kas* (the cup). Moslems sit on the stone seats and cleanse themselves before entering the mosques to pray.

As you approach the magnificent Dome of the Rock, you'll notice a miniversion of it nearby. This is *Qubbat es-Silsila* (Chain Dome) and it occupies the exact center of the Temple Mount. The front is marked by a double colonnade of fifteen columns. No one is sure why it was built — perhaps as a treasury — but it would appear that it was built by the same caliph who built the Dome of the Rock. The Crusaders used it as a chapel.

Saving the best for last, you now enter the *Dome of the Rock*, an absolutely stunning, perfectly symmetrical octagonal sanctuary.

Legend says that the original cupola was covered with real gold until it collapsed in 1016. It was replaced by lead until 1963, when gilded sheets were attached as part of a general restoration financed by nearby Arab countries. The mosaic on the cupola, done by Syrian Christians, is fabulous. Since Islam prohibits the representation of the human form in art, only botanical and geometric designs are incorporated into the mosaics. The floor is strewn with brightly colored Oriental carpets, and the colors of the tiles are vivid. The light filters through the arched windows, and every inch of the place is decorated.

The basis for this sanctuary's name is the Holy Rock in the floor, now surrounded by a golden-yellow carved railing. This was the altar where Abraham was ready to sacrifice his son, Isaac, and was the summit of Mount Moriah, where the Jewish Temples were built and from which the Prophet Mohammed ascended to Heaven. Beside the rock is a reliquary which contains a few strands of Mohammed's hair. There is a stairway here that descends to a point below (*Birel Arwah*), where pilgrims go to rub the rock. Over the centuries so many pieces have been chipped off the rock that glass enclosures had to be installed. The Dome of the Rock will be extensively renovated. The cost of the renovation will be paid by King Hussein of Jordan.

There are several other smaller mosques that you can also visit.

The Christian Quarter (from Jaffa Gate)

We will start at Jaffa Gate, which, during the rule of Saladin, was the only point of entry and exit for Christians, who had to pay a fee for the privilege. The Armenian (Christian) Quarter is to the right, while the traditional Christian Quarter is found by following *David Street* into the *souk* and then making a left at *Christian Quarter Road*. Note: For information on those sites of particular interest to Christians, stop at the *Christian Information Center* in the square before you head into the bazaar. It is run by Franciscans and they dispense advice, information, maps, and lists of sites, all free.

It's interesting to note that this portion of the bazaar sells the appropriate merchandise for pilgrim consumption: rosary beads, painted icons that look ancient but are made in present-day workshops in Bethlehem and Hebron, crosses in every style, olivewood statuettes, candlesticks, incense, and lots of other religious handicrafts. The holiest site in the Christian Quarter is the *Church of the Holy Sepulchre*, which is on Christian Quarter Road. But before you get there, nestled between market stalls and postcard stands is the entrance to *St. John's Convent*.

St. John's Convent
The wrought-iron gate is usually open, but it is reminiscent of those days when the compound had to be locked, with a sentry

on guard admitting people one at a time. Things are certainly more easygoing today. Once inside, you'll see that the convent is like a covered maze of low-vaulted ceilings and tidy courtyards. Around the courtyards are spartan-style dwellings for the Greek Orthodox monks who live here as they did in the past. Nothing disturbs the calm except for the soft patter of black-robed priests hurrying along to evening services. The church within the compound is called the *Church of the Prodromos* (the forerunner) or *Church of St. John the Baptist.*

The church is usually tightly locked up but there is a crypt below the structure, dating back to about A.D. 475, making this one of the oldest Byzantine sites in Jerusalem. It's a widely accepted belief that a fragment of the True Cross was discovered here and that the bone that is preserved within the church actually belonged to John the Baptist. The church enclosure is large enough to provide shelter for several hundred people, and it has always been a Greek Orthodox enclave.

To the left of the convent, walled in by buildings, is *Hezeikiah's Pool,* which was a reservoir for Herod's palace at the Citadel. From the Citadel Tower, you have a view of the pool.

As you continue along Christian Quarter Road, you'll notice signs of family life in the quarter—lines hung with the day's washing, small bowls of milk in front of doorways for the hundreds of strays cats in the city, and flowerpots ablaze with geraniums. The distinctive gold-toned Jerusalem stone that gives the city its special beauty was at first used because there were no timber forests nearby. In modern times, in order to preserve the ancient look, the British prohibited the use of any building material except the stone in the Old City.

The Christian Quarter is dotted with churches, convents, religious schools, and religious libraries. The patriarchs of the Ethiopian, Orthodox, Coptic, and Latin sects are also within this quarter.

Mosque of Omar

We'll stop next at the *Mosque of Omar,* a twelfth-century building marked by two minarets. After his armies conquered Jerusalem in 638, Caliph Omar prayed in this courtyard near the Church of the Holy Sepulchre. The tomb inside the church is not recognized by devout Moslems as the tomb of Jesus. Although the mosque on Temple Mount is often called the Mosque of Omar, it would appear that this is not accurate.

Nearby you'll see *Khankah Salahiyya*, a mosque that is off-limits to non-Moslems. It was built by Saladin as a convent for Sufi mystics in A.D. 1188. This mosque stands on the site once occupied by the Crusader Patriarch's home. By the way, Caliph Omar was one of the more benevolent Moslem rulers. He cleaned up the Temple Mount area, which had become something of a town dump, and later the Dome of the Rock and El-Aqsa Mosque were built there.

Church of the Holy Sepulchre

From the Mosque of Omar you descend the small flight of steps that leads down into the courtyard of the Church of the Holy Sepulchre. This church, which was built on the site of Golgotha (the place where, according to the New Testament, Christ was crucified and buried), occupies a supreme place in the Christian world. During Christ's time, this area was not part of the city and was in fact a burial site. It was Helena, mother of Emperor Constantine, who identified this place (which at the time was beneath Hadrian's temple to Venus) as the spot where the True Cross lay. In 326 the foundations for the basilica were laid and a magnificent church, with an octagonal central building, was constructed.

The Persians destroyed the church in 614 but it was rebuilt and stood till 1009, when the Fatimid Caliph Hakim obliterated it. In the eleventh century, the Byzantines rebuilt the church but were unable to raise enough money to build as grand a structure as Constantine had. Only the magnificent rotunda was duplicated. When the Crusaders arrived, they added a Romanesque church to the rotunda and, in spite of a major fire and severe earthquake, the building you see today is similar to that of the Crusaders. A major renovation took place in the 1950s but we've never been inside the church when at least one chapel or mosaic wasn't being renovated.

What is most striking is that the church, unlike those in Rome, is hemmed in on all sides by houses and shops and, because of its renovations, does not have a beautiful architectural line. Confusion exists inside too, for the church has been divided into sections like a pie. Every part of the church has been assigned to one of six different communities and this has resulted in lines being drawn in the center of a pillar or down the floor. For example, the Greek Orthodox sect (which controls most of the church) administers the north side of the Golgotha; the Latins (Roman Catholics) administer the south side. The other communities involved are the Armenians, Syrian Orthodox, Copts, and Abyssinians. Only the Stone of Unction and Tomb of Christ are administered jointly. Every ritual has an exact time and place, according to a strict timetable worked out in 1852. Fortunately, the keys to the front door are held by two Moslem families (a tradition since Saladin's time) who act as guards and arbiters. Obviously, with each sect responsible for its area, there is no unifying design. Nevertheless, the important sites within the church are moving.

The stairs that are on the right, inside near the entrance, lead up to Calvary. From the Chapel of Adam you can see the actual rock of the summit where the Crucifixion took place. *The Stone of Unction* actually dates from 1810, although it was part of the church from the twelfth century. *The Tomb Monument*, built in the nineteenth century to mark the spot of Christ's rock tomb, seems much too elaborate, and a far simpler and more dignified marker might have been more fitting. Five of the Stations of the Cross are within the church. In the Roman Catholic chapel, where Christ was stripped of his garments, is Station X. Station XI is where he was nailed to the cross. Station XII is within the Greek Orthodox chapel. This is the spot where Christ died on the cross. Station XIII, where Christ's body was taken down by Joseph of Arimathea, is between the Catholic and Greek chapels, and the tomb itself is Station XIV.

Make sure to buy an English guide to the church. They are sold very inexpensively at the Christian Information Center and in the church shop.

If you enjoy ecclesiastical pageantry, don't miss the annual appearance of the Holy Fire. It happens on Greek Orthodox Easter (a different day every year, usually two to four weeks after Roman Catholic Easter). The pilgrims crowd into the church (the diehards stake out a spot the night before), the air is thick with excitement, and everyone holds an unlit candle. The Patriarch enters the tomb and a miraculous and spontaneous flame — the "Holy Fire" — ignites his candle. He exits the tomb and in a matter of minutes, the church is ablaze with the warm glow of candlelight. The flame, like an Olympic torch, is relayed to Greece for Easter Day celebrations there. It's quite an occasion and a spectacle worth seeing. The church is open from 4 A.M. to 7 P.M.

The Muristan

On the opposite side of the stairway that brought you down to the church, there is an open square called the *Muristan* (from the Persian word *bimaristan*, meaning "hospital" or "hospice"). This square is especially interesting because of the far-flung associations it has with the Knights of St. John of the Hospital, who went on to greater fame and fortune in Malta and Rhodes. The hospice that existed in the ninth century was erected by the Emperor Charlemagne on land that was a gift from the Caliph Hauen El-Rashid. The Egyptians destroyed the hospice, library, and Church of St. Mary in 1099, but the merchants of Amalfi restored the structures. The Church of St. John the Baptist (discussed earlier) was intended as a hospice for the poor, while the Church of St. Mary (a women's hospice) no longer exists.

Church of the Redeemer

The Lutheran Church of the Redeemer occupies the location where St. Mary Latina (a hospice for men) once stood. Several of the knights who came to Jerusalem with the Crusades in 1099 were wounded in a skirmish and were cared for at St. John's hospice. A few of these men decided to stay and help the sick. They became the Knights of St. John of the Hospital, or the Hospitallers. These men later lost sight of their original purpose and went on to acquire great wealth in Rhodes and Malta. Nevertheless, the good work of the Muristan carried on into the fifteenth century, until the Ottoman Empire. The best spot from which to view the city and specifically the entire Christian Quarter is from the top of this church tower, which is 150 feet high. (No elevator — 177 steps.) The church is open from 9 A.M. to 1 P.M. and 2 to 5 P.M., Friday 9 A.M. to 1 P.M. The Bell Tower, incidentally, was planned by Kaiser Wilhelm II in 1898.

Retrace your steps to Christian Quarter Road and follow it to Greek Orthodox Patriarchate Road. This road is where the Greek Orthodox Patriarch lives and where the charming little *Museum of the Greek Orthodox Patriarchate* is located. The museum is generally open Monday through Saturday from 10 A.M. to 4 P.M., and a kindly old priest is usually there to explain the especially notable acquisitions in the museum's possession. Among the artifacts are the sarcophagi of Herod and members of his family, pottery from the Byzantine periods, and a splendid wood and ivory door salvaged from the Church of the Holy Sepulchre when a fire in 1808 ravaged it almost completely. Other items of interest are the Egyptian scarabs and Antinoos' Cross (Antinoos was a favorite companion of Emperor Hadrian of Rome). One of the most peaceful places in the Old City is surely the blooming garden behind the museum, a medley of roses and dahlias to soothe the eye and spirit.

From the museum, walk to the end of the road, where you will see a shop with the name Rittas written on a yellowed old placard above the door. Enter this disheveled little emporium of new and used bric-a-brac, and you are entering the Jerusalem of yesterday. The family who runs the shop today are direct descendants of old Mr. Rittas, a Greek originally from Constantinople, who set up shop here over 150 years ago. Mr. Rittas catered to the Greek and Eastern Orthodox pilgrims who came to the Holy Land with little more than faith to tide them over. His great-grandsom, Vassilis, will tell you stories of how the old chap would give them food and lodging—and if he didn't receive monetary compensation, he did achieve a measure of immortality. The dusty corners of the shop contain curiosities worthy of the most serious scavenger: authentic photographs of Allenby entering the city, a painting of the first Patriarch and a reverent photograph of the present one, a vast collection of icons, religious calendars, beads, and crosses — and a bust of Homer.

Wandering through the quarter is fun and if you like you can leave through New Gate, which leads into a newer Christian neighborhood. If you want to follow the Via Dolorosa you should start from Lions' Gate or Herod's Gate. Many of the Christian sites, such as the Church of St. Anne and the Pools of Bethesda, are in the Moslem Quarter.

Take bus #1, #3, #13, #19, #20, #23, or #38 to the Christian Quarter.

The Via Dolorosa

The Street of Sorrows

The route followed by Christ from the Roman hall of judgment (*praetorium*) to the site of his Crucifixion on Calvary is called the Way of the Cross. Along the way there are fourteen stations (biblical references allude to incidents along the route) that pilgrims have observed throughout the years.

The last five Stations of the Cross occurred in what is now the Church of the Holy Sepulchre; the nine that precede them took place in what is today the Moslem Quarter. One can follow the Stations by observing the signposts along the way — but it is confusing and you are better off tagging along with a group of pilgrims who meet regularly on Fridays at 3 P.M. at the Antonia Fortress (in the Monastery of the Flagellation). Before you start your walk, you should explore the *Antonia Fortress*.

The *Antonia Fortress*, which has only recently been open to the public, covered a five-acre area when it was built by Herod the Great in the years 37–35 B.C. He named it Antonia after Marc Antony, and it served as a palace, a fortress, and later on, as a residence for Roman governors. The excavations here have unearthed fabulous things. The *Lithostrotos* is the paved courtyard where the trial and judgment of Jesus took place. Most of the flagstones, which were quarried from local limestones (*lithostrotos* in Greek literally means "stone-paved"), are in good condition. The cuts that you see on the surface are water channels that drained off the rain through holes leading to the water reservoir below.

The *Cistern* (actually a double cistern), part of which lies under Lithostrotos, was built by Herod the Great and is fifty-three yards long and fifteen yard wide. The winter rain poured through the porous stones in the roof, passing under the arches to fill the reservoir underneath the Lithostrotos. The water is fresh and clean, and the reservoir is still in use.

On the flagstones of the Lithostrotos you can still see where the Roman soldiers carved out games for their own amusement. One game, called the Game of the King, shows a spiked crown near the initial *B* (which stands for Basilinda), and a line of life cut by a sword. This game, known in Babylon and India, denotes a puppet king who would be mocked at a carnival and then sacrificed to pagan gods.

To help you refresh your memory, here are the fourteen stations. By the way, if a chapel or door is locked, try knocking. A nun or priest will sometimes let you in.

I.   Station I is located in the courtyard of the Al Omariye College. This is the point where Jesus was condemned to death (at the ruins of the Antonia Fortress, near Temple Mount).

II.   Station II is where Jesus received the cross, and the site is marked at the entrance to the Flagellation Convent.

Ecce Homo   Between Stations II and III you will see Ecce Homo Arch. Part of a triple arch built by Hadrian in A.D. 135, it was at the entrance to his city, Aelia Capitolina. The arch that spans the Via Dolorosa is nineteen feet high. It is said that under this arch Pontius Pilate said "Ecce homo" (behold the man), when he showed Christ, dressed in a king's robe and a crown of thorns, to the crowd.

III.   Station III is where Jesus fell for the first time under the weight of the cross (near El-Wad Road at the Polish Archeological Museum).

IV.   The entrance to the *Church of Our Lady of the Spasm* marks the place where Jesus met his mother.

V.   At the point where the Via Dolorosa (Street of Sorrows) ascends to Golgotha, the cross was taken over by Simon of Cyrene.

VI.   St. Veronica's Church marks the spot where the saint of that name wiped the sweat from Jesus' face.

VII.   Jesus fell for the second time near the Ethiopian Patriarchate at the bazaar crossroads.

VIII.   The Greek monastery of St. Charalampos marks the place where Jesus consoled the women of Jerusalem (look for a Latin cross on the wall).

IX.   Jesus fell for the third time near the Coptic Monastery.

The last five stations are within the Church of the Holy Sepulchre (previously mentioned).

To visit the Via Dolorosa, take bus #23 or #27 to Damascus Gate.

West Jerusalem Sights

West Jerusalem is the "today" part of town. A modern Israeli city with wide streets, lovely parks, and new urban areas, it is cosmopolitan yet not overly sophisticated. Its sights, scattered throughout, are contemporary ones. The core of the city is commercial and residential, with the industrial areas on the fringes of town. Since most hotels, restaurants, and nightlife activities are centered here, it is the part of Jerusalem you'll get to know best. We've planned our walk to touch on some of the distinctive neighborhoods and sights, and you'll find many more on your own.

A Walk Through West Jerusalem

Zion Square is the heart of this area. The streets radiating from it are filled with good shops, restaurants, and small businesses. Walk along *Harav Kook* (from the square), where you'll pass several handicraft stores and, across from them, *Ticho House*. This small house, part of the Israel Museum, has an exhibit of artist Anna Ticho's works and articles used by her doctor-husband, one of Palestine's first eye specialists. There is a lovely coffee shop as well. Museum hours: Sunday through Thursday 10 A.M. to 5 P.M., Friday till 1:30 P.M.

The next cross-street is *Rehov Haneviim* (Prophets' Street). Named for the Jewish prophets, it now houses many of Jerusalem's Christian institutions. Notice the buildings here. This is one of the city's oldest areas. On *Ethiopia Street* (Rehev Hahabashim), look for the Abyssinian Church (Ethiopian) which has a Lion of Judah carved on its gate. This lion was the symbol of Emperor Haile Selassie, who traced his lineage back to a meeting between the Ethiopian Queen of Sheba and King Solomon.

Turn right on *Rehov Rabbi Shmuel Salant*. This is *Mea She'arim*. If you feel as if you've just stepped back four hundred years, it's understandable, for the ultrareligious, mystical sect, the Hassidim, live here today much as they did in the shtetls of sixteenth-century Poland and Russia. The community, established in 1875, was one of the first outside the city walls. It still has winding, narrow streets with ornate wrought-iron balconies lining the buildings. Its name derives from Genesis. "Then Isaac sowed in the land and received in the same year a *hundred-fold*" (in Hebrew, *Mea She'arim*).

Walking beside you will be men with full, bushy beards, many reddish-gold in color, or thin, pale-faced youths, heads virtually shaved but for long sidecurls called *peyot*. All will be wearing long black silken coats, tall black hats, some rimmed with fur (*shtreimels*), white tieless shirts, and black shoes. In very hot weather, they may discard the coat and roll up their shirt sleeves. You'll notice a fringed shawl beneath the shirt. The men will studiously ignore you while conversing in Yiddish, for Hebrew is reserved for prayer.

You'll see Hassidic women less frequently, but you'll recognize them immediately, for they wear ankle-length dresses, no makeup, and a kerchief tightly bound over their heads (or a wig to cover their shorn heads). You will see many children in the area, for Hassidim do not believe in birth control.

While there is no specific route, you'll notice many *yeshivas* (schools), synagogues, and shops selling religious articles. There are many bakeries and glatt kosher butchers. Make it a point to find the market on *Rehov Mea She'arim*. Here you will see women shopping, whereas in the city market you'll only see Hassidic men. There is no mingling of the sexes—at school or even in this casual shopping situation.

While a walk through this neighborhood offers a glimpse of a unique group of people, you cannot help but feel uncomfortable, for the Hassidim do not pretend to welcome you. Signs everywhere warn women to wear modest dress (elbows, shoulders, and knees covered); no displays of affection are permitted (including holding hands); and no photographs are allowed. Hassidim have been known to spit and curse at offenders and to stone cars that wander too close on the Sabbath.

Leaving Mea She'arim, turn left on *Natan Straus* back to *Jaffa Road*, where you head uphill (right) to *Mahane Yehuda*, the lively city market whose streets are named after fruits.

Running from *Jaffa Road* to *Agrippas Street* there is a covered lane as well as a parallel open street. Although it is primarily a produce market, you'll also see pickles, olives, smoked and raw fish, meat, and baked goods. Arabs as well as Israelis from every walk of life shop here. An offshoot of Mahane Yehuda, the *Iraqi*

Market, which fills an alley off Mahane Yehuda's open street, has items of poorer quality and a less affluent clientele. If all this foods makes you hungry, head to Agrippas Street, where you'll find several excellent Middle Eastern eating spots. Two popular ones are *Simma* at number 82 and *Ima* number 189. Both stay open till the wee hours. Both are kosher.

Retrace your steps to Jaffa Road and return to Zion Square. If you haven't already walked along *Ben Yehuda Mall* (and the streets joining it), you should do so now. Ben Yehuda, Jerusalem's answer to Tel Aviv's Dizengoff Street, is very pretty but not as "hip." We have already mentioned some of the cafés here (see Restaurants), and the promenade also has some good shops. Try *Iran Bazaar* for Yemenite jewelry, *E. Ben David* for hammered copper and brass, *Steimatsky Books* if you've run out of reading material, and *Alexandra*, which stocks wonderful Hassidic figures sculpted in dough and gaily painted.

Turn left onto *King George V*, a wide, tree-lined boulevard with the IGTO, several hotels, parks, and public buildings.

The complex of tan stone buildings around a fenced courtyard is the *Jewish Agency*. Now housing such organizations as the Jewish National Fund and United Jewish Appeal, it functioned as the unofficial government of the Jewish people during the Mandate period. Incredibly, security, which still looks tight, was breached in 1948 when an Arab chauffeur drove a booby-trapped U.S. Embassy car into one of the buildings.

Just beyond the Jewish Agency, you'll see two imposing modern buildings: the *Great Synagogue* and the *Seat of the Rabbinate Building (Hechal Shlomo)*.

Solomon's Mansion, the religious center of Israel, is a tall, domed building designed to resemble the Temple. It houses both the Ashkenazi and Sephardic Rabbinates, a museum, and a lovely Italian synagogue. Visit the *Wolfson Museum* (the building is named for philanthropist Isaac Wolfson's father and not the king) on the fourth floor. Small, it concentrates on religious art and articles. The Persian rugs are beautiful and the display of marriage contracts is very interesting. Stop to see the 3-D miniature display of key times in Jewish history, and don't miss the view from the balcony. Museum hours are Sunday through Thursday 9 A.M. to 1 P.M., Friday 9 A.M. to noon. You can attend Friday night or Saturday morning (8 A.M.) services at the Great

Synagogue, but I suggest those in the more intimate synagogue that once stood in Padua, Italy. Check on times here.

The neighborhood just to the west (right) is *Rehavia*, Jerusalem's most exclusive residential area and home to the Prime Minister and other Israeli politicians. You might like to walk through the area and see the attractive one-story homes with lovely gardens.

King George V heads downhill here and its name changes to *Keren Hayesod*. At the base you'll see *Yemen Moshe* to your left and *Liberty Bell Park* (lots of children's playgrounds) to your right. Many fine hotels are nearby.

In 1860, Sir Moses Montefiore visited Jerusalem and was shocked to find the Jewish quarter overcrowded and unsanitary. He decided to build a new neighborhood outside the walls and chose a site across the Hinnon Valley (south of Jaffa Gate). He called it *Mishkenat Sha'ananim*. The original building, long and low, now houses a French restaurant of the same name (see Restaurants) and a guest house for visiting artists. Around this building sprang up Yemin Moshe, a middle-class area. Caught in the crossfire in 1948 and 1967, and within sniping range during the years of Jordanian control, the area languished. But after 1967, it was reconstructed and now it is lovely. Stone houses on many levels house artists' workshops, studios, and galleries. The community center here often has concerts and art shows. Do walk through here, and don't miss the windmill at the point. Montefiore built it to provide the community with an energy source, but there wasn't enough wind. It now houses a tiny museum about Montefiore, and his ornate carriage stands nearby.

At this point, you can head along King David Street to the YMCA and a fabulous view of the Old City and surrounding areas from its tower (there's a fee). Or you may head downhill on King David Street to St. Andrew's Church and Jerusalem's Cinematheque. You will be across the Hinnon Valley from Mount Zion at this point.

The Israel Museum/Knesset/Valley of the Cross

A contemporary urban area in West Jerusalem houses the Israel Museum and the Knesset (Parliament). Other government buildings are in the area, *Kiryat Ben Gurion*, too. Nearby, the community of *Givat Ram* is home to the new campus of Hebrew University. As happens so frequently in Israel, adjoining these new areas is an ancient monastery in the *Valley of the Cross*.

The Israel Museum

Opened in 1965, the museum, built on the Hill of Tranquility, incorporates five entities: *The Bezalel National Museum of Fine Arts, Judaica, and Ethnography; The Samuel Bronfman Biblical and Archeological Museum; The Billy Rose Art Garden; The Ruth Young Wing;* and *The Shrine of the Book*. Consisting of a complex of modular cubes, the museum from a distance looks like a small village hugging the hillside.

Just beyond the entrance, you will see the white dome of the Shrine of the Book, the building that houses the Dead Sea Scrolls and the Bar Kochba finds. The white dome (which resembles the lids of the jars in which the scrolls were found) and the black basalt walls of the circular building are symbolic of the struggle between the Sons of Light and the Sons of Darkness, which is a recurrent theme in the scrolls. The subterranean atmosphere is reminiscent of the caves in which the scrolls were found in 1947 near Qumran on the Dead Sea. Written on parchment, mostly in Hebrew with a few in Aramaic, the scrolls belonged to the Essenes, a sect who lived two thousand years ago and were decimated in the Jewish war against Rome when the Temple was destroyed.

The second group of manuscripts dates from the Bar Kochba revolt, when a group of Jews from En Gedi, near the Dead Sea, sought refuge in caves near the Judean Desert. Discovered and eventually killed by the Romans, they left many documents in the caves. These papers were hidden in a waterproof pouch made of the entire hide of a sheep.

The Dead Sea Scrolls are enclosed in a glass case that you can illuminate. They contain the Essenes' code of rules, a military manual which outlines the battle between the Sons of Light and Darkness, psalms, and commentaries on the Books of the Bible. A facsimile of the largest scroll, the Isaiah, is displayed in the central platform. It is the oldest one found, a thousand years older than the others, and contains all sixty-six chapters of the biblical

Book. The exhibits downstairs contain objects from the Bar Kochba period, including palm fiber baskets, skulls and bones, keys, and glassware. The letters of Babata, a wealthy divorcee, are located in the long entrance hall. They provide unique glimpse into life in Judea 1,800 years ago. Hours for the Shrine of the Book are Sunday, Monday, Wednesday, and Thursday, 10 A.M. to 5 P.M.; Friday, Saturday, and holidays, 10 A.M. to 2 P.M.; Tuesday 10 A.M. to 10 P.M. For Saturday entry, buy a ticket in advance or from the van at the entrance on Saturday morning.

Continue along the garden path until you reach. *The Billy Rose Art Garden*, set in a rock garden designed by the Japanese-American sculptor Isamu Noguchi. Noguchi has managed to integrate the works with the natural rise and fall of the land so successfully that you are hardly aware of it. While everyone will have a favorite or two, the Henry Moore pieces do stand out. The *Vertabrae* bronze on its own platform is special, but my favorite, *Homage to a Garment Section* (parts of a sewing machine embedded in concrete), reminded me of my father, a garment worker.

Inside the museum, head downstairs to the archeology section. Always a first-rate collection, which was formed around pieces collected by the Israel Department of Antiquities, this department has recently acquired the Moshe Dayan collection. With this acquisition, the museum has definitely earned itself the right to claim one of the finest archeological collections in the world.

Dayan was controversial in life, and his collection has created further controversy. You will find many Israelis who believe Dayan was an out-and-out pilferer who dug up these treasures illegally and hoarded them in his basement to reap a huge profit from them, since they were legally the property of the government. Others consider the country fortunate that he bothered to collect these pieces and care for them or they might never have remained in Israel. One million dollars was paid to Dayan's wife for this superb group, which has been called "A Man and His Land." It was a steal. Dayan's interest in necrology is much in evidence, for many of the pieces are funerary objects. Among the most breathtaking are the life-size anthropoid coffins from the Late Bronze Age, sculpted ceramic animals used as charms to alleviate the harsh forces of nature, and gravestones with portraits of the deceased engraved on them. Incredibly, the collection is not displayed in glass cases but is on open platforms, where the items can be touched. A group of pieces from the museum was brought to the United States for exhibit in late 1986.

Rooms nearby display Jewish ceremonial art. Handwrought and painted, woven and carved, intricate and very simple are the objects used by Jews, sometimes secretly, to pray. Menorahs, Torah cases, Sabbath lamps, wine bottles, kiddush cups, and candlesticks donated by families from India, the United States, Germany, France, and Spain are on display. They will remind some of you of things you saw in the home of your grandparents or parents or that have been handed down to you. An entire synagogue from Vittorio Veneto, Italy, is on exhibit as is a painted wooden *sukkah*.

The ethnography section is only two large rooms, but it reconstructs Jewish life in various Diaspora nations. You will be astonished when you see how the outer trappings vary but the religious practices hold firm. Six ethnic groups are highlighted, and the exhibits focus on daily life in each community.

Other exhbits include Islamic and Israeli art, ethnic art, and ancient art of neighboring cultures. Depending on your interests, the Israel Museum could occupy an entire day of your visit. Set aside a minimum of a half day. Hours are Sunday, Monday, Wednesday and Thursday, 10 A.M. to 5 P.M.; Tuesday, 4 P.M. to 10 P.M. and Friday, Saturday and holidays, 10 A.M. to 2 P.M.. Buy tickets for Saturday in advance. The museum closes on Rosh Hashana. There are gift shops and a cafeteria on the grounds.

The Knesset

It's a short walk from the museum to the *Knesset*, and the spectacular flowers in the Wohl Rose Garden lead the way. Look for the building with a sixteen-foot menorah at its entrance; that is the Knesset (Israel's Parliament). The seven-branched bronze candlestick, which is the symbol of Israel, was a gift of the British Parliament. The columned building, behind a heavy iron gate, has beautiful tapestries and wall and floor mosaics by Marc Chagall. There are guided tours (in English) on Sunday and Thursday from 8:30 A.M. to 2 P.M., when the Knesset is not in session. During a session, you can buy a ticket for the visitors' gallery. Sessions are conducted in Hebrew. Passports are required for entry. Take bus #9 or #24.

The Bible Lands Museum

New to our list of "musts" in Jerusalem, the *Bible Lands Museum* is home to one of the world's most important collections of ancient art and artifacts from biblical times. Exhibits depict the civilizations of the ancient lands of the Bible bordered by Afghanistan, the Western Mediterranean, the Caucasus Mountains, and Nubia. This museum is located in the Museum Compound Givat Ram, between the Knesset and the Shrine of the Book, at 25 Granot Street. Hours are Sunday, Monday, Tuesday, and Thursday from 9:30 A.M. to 5:30 P.M.; Wednesday from 9:30 A.M. to 9:30 P.M.; Friday and holidays from 9:30 A.M. to 2 P.M.; and Saturday from 11 A.M. to 3 P.M. Tickets for Saturday must be bought in advance, as the box office is closed that day. Take bus #9, #17, #24, or #99.

Monastery of the Cross

Providing a total contrast to the modern museum and Knesset buildings, the Monastery of the Cross, in the nearby Valley of the Cross, is an eleventh-century building built on the foundations of older churches. The stark, windowless wall around the monastery gives it a foreboding look. Inside, the domed church has mosaics from the Byzantine period. Legend has it that Lot settled here and planted seeds of cedar, cypress, and pine. They grew together as one and formed the tree that supplied the wood for Christ's cross, hence the monastery's name. Hours are Monday through Thursday from 9 A.M. to 5 P.M.; Friday from 9 A.M to 1:30 P.M.; and Saturday from 9 A.M. to 5 P.M. Bus #19 is the most direct. Buses #9, #17, and #24 also pass by.

Mount Herzl/Yad Vashem/En Kerem

On the outer fringes of West Jerusalem, you'll find two memorial sites, Mount Herzl and Yad Vashem. Plan to visit them in sequence, but note that Yad Vashem is the more interesting of the two. If time permits, continue to En Kerem, a picturesque town nearby with historic churches, art galleries, and restaurants.

Mount Herzl, a beautiful hilltop park on the city's western edge, is the final resting place of Theodor Herzl, the founder of the modern Zionist movement. In 1896, Herzl, an Austrian newspaperman, published his book, *The Jewish State*, which called for the creation of an independent Jewish state, and his words gave impetus to the growing movement. Buried in Europe, his remains and those of his wife and parents were reinterred here in 1949. Nearby are the tombs of Ze'ev Jabotinsky, the brilliant revisionist leader and founder of the Irgun, and Golda Meir. A small museum near the entrance has documents, photos, and books about Herzl's life and work; his study was brought here intact.

Also on Mount Herzl is a military cemetery holding the remains of thousands of young people and some not so young, who died in defense of Israel and who were buried en masse. The tombstones are dated chronologically.

Part of the cemetery is a memorial to those who died at sea, and in a pool of water you'll see tablets with a psalm, "I will bring my people from the depths of the sea." Sadly, Mount Herzl is used as a training camp for young recruits, and behind many a towering cypress tree or verdant pine is a coil of barbed wire and a beardless young man with a rifle slung over his shoulder.

Museum hours are 9 A.M. to 4:45 P.M. (till 1 P.M. on Friday); the museum is closed on Saturday. Take bus #17, #20, #23, #24, #39 or #99.

Yad Vashem

Just beyond Mount Herzl stands *Har Hazikaron* (Hill of Remembrance) and the Yad Vashem Memorial. The name, literally "a monument and a name," refers to a passage in Isaiah (Chapter 56, Verse 5): "I will give in my house and within my walls a place and a name that will not be cut off." Yad Vashem is troubling and terrifying, for it is a poignant memorial to the six million Jews killed by the Nazis. It is also a monument to those who tried to help. The long entrance, the Avenue of the Righteous, is lined with trees, each tree a tribute to a non-Jew who saved Jewish lives. A small rowboat commemorates the actions of Danish citizens who, at the risks of their own lives, rowed Jews out to

Swedish ships offshore—and to safety. But six million Jews did not escape, and the *Historical Museum* tells the frightening story of the Holocaust, which unfolds in authentic photographs, newspapers of the period, and captured documents. Hitler's rise to power and Germany's policy of expansion are explored. Slides show life in the shtetls and the increasing persecution by the Third Reich. Photos taken after the start of the war show Jews being herded into ghettos, stripped of all they own except their dignity. Soon that too was lost as they were herded into transports to die in gas chambers. The bewildered faces of wide-eyed young children with yellow stars pinned to their tattered coats will stay with you for a long time, as will the photos of those liberated at the war's end. Symbolic headstones record the number of dead in each country.

Nearby the *Hall of Remembrance*, a rectangular building whose foundation is a mass of irregular boulders, is so simple and stark that in the hush all you hear is the sharp intake of breath all around you. As your eyes adjust to the dim lighting, you'll realize that the words on the floor are *Auschwitz, Treblinka, Dachau*, and the names of nineteenth other infamous death camps. The eternal flame, lit at 11 A.M. each day, is beside a vault holding ashes brought from these camps. You are alone with yout thoughts, for there are no speeches or ceremonies.

Other exhibits include a memorial garden to children who died in the camps, an art museum exhibiting works done under the most trying conditions, and an archive which has information about all who perished. Other memorials are under construction.

Works of art are located throughout the complex and each is moving, but none more so than *In Memory of the Victims of the Concentration and Death Camps*. It depicts human forms in all positions of agony and is horrifying.

Yad Vashem, born of unspeakable horror, will stay in your mind's eye for a long time. Hours are 9 A.M. to 5 P.M., Friday till 2 P.M. Closed on the Sabbath. Take bus #17, #18, #20, #21, #23, #27, or #99.

En Karem

On a wooded hillside just five minutes from Yad Vashem is the lovely town of *En Karem*. The drive is beautiful, for the town is

surrounded by olive groves and towering cypress trees. It was
here that St. John the Baptist was born, and there are two
churches here associated with his life. Until 1948, En Karem was
a picturesque Moslem town, but since then it has become an
artists' colony of sorts with several galleries and restaurants. You
might consider spending an evening here.

As the road descends into town, look for the towering spire of
the *Church of St. John the Baptist*. It will be to your right. A
Franciscan church built in 1674, it is over the grotto where John
the Baptist was born. From the church you can descend to the
grotto. While some renovation work was being done in 1885, an
earlier chapel was found, perhaps fifth century, which contained
two rock tombs, and still another with a beautiful mosaic floor.
Look for the painting of *St. John in the Wilderness* over the sac-
risty door. It is a copy of a Murillo. Hours are 8 A.M. to noon, 2:30
to 5 P.M.

Cross the narrow road and you'll see a mosque (no longer in
use). Directly in front of it is the *Virgin Spring*. It's in a cave and it
is said that the Virgin Mary drew water from the well when she
visited John's mother, Elizabeth. It is fenced in now, however.
The *Franciscan Church of the Visitation*, on the hill nearby, is
the site of the cottage where Zacharias and Elizabeth, the parents
of St. John, lived. Elizabeth was related to the Virgin Mary, who
came to visit her here, and there is a lovely mosaic which depicts
that visit. The church has two levels; the lower was built in the
late nineteenth century and the upper in 1955. A lovely garden
surrounds the church.

Today's En Karem

The nicest art gallery in town is *Bet Mayan*, which adjoins the
Virgin Spring. Local artists work in a variety of media and there
are some unusual pieces. Definitely worth a look. As you wander
through town you'll see some smaller galleries.

Two restaurants share the building next to the gallery. *The
Barn* is a rustic, comfortable dining spot with white-washed
walls, plain wooden tables, and lots of greenery. In keeping with
the decor, the food consists of ribs (beef), barbecued chicken,
burgers, soups, and good steaks. Beer and soft drinks are served
as well. The Barn is open for lunch and dinner and is very popu-

lar at night. *Michael's*, the more formal eating spot, is open only for dinner. Small, with only a half dozen tables, it has an interesting menu that includes seared sirloin with homemade mustard sauce (rather like blackened steak) and filled chicken breast with yakitori sauce. Quiet and more elegant dining here. Both are kosher and accept American Express.

At the entrance to town stands *The Goulash Inn*, which is designed to look like a Swiss chalet. It is so totally overdecorated that it is impossible to describe; suffice to say that there is something hanging everywhere. The nonkosher food is Hungarian and is very good. Goulash and paprikash are the specialties here, and you should try the cherry soup. There is polka music at night. Open noon to 3 P.M. and 6:30 P.M. to 12 midnight seven days a week.

There are several Middle Eastern restaurants, as well as pubs and bars, in town. The *Targ Music Center* often has concerts. Check at the IGTO or in the *Jerusalem Post*. Take bus #17.

Exploring East Jerusalem

While East Jerusalem does not have many specific sights to visit, you should definitely reserve some time to walk through it, for this area, the home of Jerusalem's Arab residents, adds a special flavor to the city. It is slower paced, with small shops and very courteous merchants, and you will feel the different rhythm immediately. The "downtown" area is a small one and within easy walking distance of Damascus and Herod's Gates. You might combine a walk through East Jerusalem with Old City sightseeing. To get a feel for East Jerusalem, walk north on Nablus Road (from Damascus Gate) to St. George Cathedral, then head south on Salah-ed-Din to Herod's Gate. En route you will pass many of the sights listed below and you can stop in if you like.

Rockefeller Museum

The museum, built in 1927 to 1929 (during the British Mandate period) looks like a Crusader castle, with a rotunda and Moorish and Ottoman influences. It is built around an inner courtyard, surrounded by colonnaded rectangular and octagonal galleries.

The museum boasts a collection of artifacts from all periods of Palestine's history—from the Stone Age to the eighteenth century. The simplicity of the layout and the chronological order of the finds makes it easy to explore this fine collection. Particularly interesting is the complete reconstruction of rooms from Hisham's Palace in Jericho and an extensive collection of Paleolithic bones. The South Gallery has the remains of the Carmel Man who lived 100,000 years ago, and nearby is skeleton from a crouched burial who still looks uncomfortable after ten thousand years. An inexpensive pamphlet will guide you through this fine collection. Endowed by John D. Rockefeller, Jr., with two million dollars, the Rockefeller Museum is East Jerusalem's most interesting stop. It is located on Sultan Suleiman Street (near Jericho Road). Hours are Sunday through Thursday 10 A.M. to 5 P.M. Friday and Saturday 10 A.M. to 2 P.M. Free (English) guided tours Friday at 11 A.M. Phone 282251.

Other Sites in East Jerusalem

Tourjeman Post
A once-lovely Arab house became the Israeli military post overlooking the Mandelbaum Gate, which from 1948 to 1967 was the only crossing point from Israel to Jordan. When the city was reunified, a museum was created to describe the history of the city in those years. It contains some humorous photos, audiovisual displays, and documents. Hours are Sunday through Thursday, 9 A.M. to 4 P.M. and Friday, 9 A.M. to 1 P.M. (Closed Saturday) The museum is located at 1 Chail Hahancasa St. Phone 28178. Take bus #1, #11, #27, or #99.

Garden Tomb
Maintained by the Anglican Church, this lovely garden and tranquil spot was developed around a tomb that some believed was Christ's actual burial spot (since disproved). Services Sunday at 9 A.M., otherwise locked. The Garden Tomb is located on Nablus Road.

Tombeau des Rois (Tomb of Kings) (Saladin Street)

Maintained by the French government, to whom it was left by a French Jewess, this site was believed to house the tombs of the kings of Judah, but in reality contains the tomb of Queen Helena of Adiabene (who was a Jewish convert) and her family. Helena's Jewish name, Queen Sarah, written in Aramaic, was found on the sarcophagus, which was taken to the Louvre.

Zedekiah's Cave (Solomon Quarry)

In the Old City wall, near Damascus Gate, is Solomon's Quarry, where the stones that built the Temple were quarried. It is also called Zedekiah's Cave, for here the last Jewish king hid while attempting to escape from the Babylonians. He didn't make it and was taken to exile with his people. Moslem and Jewish legends say that the tunnels leading from these quarries went as far as Jericho and the Sinai. Hours are 8:30 A.M. to 4:30 P.M. daily (Friday till 2:30 P.M.). A lighted path takes you into the caves and under part of the Old City.

The American Colony

Located northeast of the city, the American Colony was founded by American Christians in the nineteenth century. Today it is home to the U.S. Consulate, St. George's Cathedral, the East Jerusalem YMCA, and the legendary American Colony Hotel.

The Artists' House

The Jerusalem Artists Association runs this lovely gallery which doubles as a center for many of Israel's aspiring artists. International artists are invited to display their works here as well, and poetry readings, lectures, and music recitals are often held here. The building, one of the most picturesque in Jerusalem, dates back to the Turkish occupation and was remodeled in 1965 to make the most of its natural lighting. Located at 12 Shmuel Hanagid Street, it is open Sunday through Thursday 10 A.M. to 1 P.M. and 4 P.M. to 7 P.M.; Friday morning only; and Saturday from 11 A.M. to 2 P.M. Take bus #4, #7, #14, #19, #21, #31, #32, or #48.

The Gabriel Sherover Promenade

Extending from Naomi Road in Abu Tor to Talpiot, the Gabriel Sherover Promenade offers an unsurpassed view of the Old City, the Judean Hills, and the desert. A lovely escape from the crowded streets of Jerusalem, its paths are lined with native trees, flowering plants, and herbs. It also features a playground for the kids and a gazebo serving snacks and beverages. Take bus #8 or #48.

Shopping

THE PALESTINIAN NEEDLEWORK SHOP

79 Nablus Road   8 A.M. to 7 P.M.
                                                     (closed Sunday)
                                                   No Credit Cards

Cotton cloth is hand-embroidered in intricate patterns by Palestinian women living in West Bank towns and in refugee camps. The placemats, tablecloths, guest towels, and altar cloths are beautiful to own, and they make unusual gifts. This folk art tradition began during the Turkish era, and patterns reflect the traditional patterns worn by women in different parts of the country. The shop is across the street from the Ambassador Hotel.

Mounts and Valleys

Many of the mountains that are integral parts of Jerusalem's skyline have figured prominently in the city's history. They also offer excellent vantage points for taking photos of the Old City. You can drive to these mountains or take a bus. You can walk as well.

Mount of Olives

The Mount of Olives stands east of the Old City and is separated from it by the Kidron Valley, a description of which appears later in this section. Named for the olive trees that grew here in ancient times (and still do), the mountain was mentioned in the Old Testament.

The small white headstones visible on the Mount's southern slope mark the oldest Jewish cemetery in the world. Many a wealthy Jew was buried here within sight of Judaism's most sacred site, the Western (Wailing) Wall. Many headstones were removed during the period of Jordanian control and used to build local roads and retaining walls. For years after they recaptured the Mount, Israelis retrieved family headstones by digging them out of walls or roads.

It is still a favored burial site (you will see new headstones as well as ancient ones), and it is believed that on the day the Messiah comes, all the dead will be resurrected and will follow him from the Mount into Jerusalem through the Golden Gate. To prevent this, the Moslems sealed this gate and built Moslem cemeteries in the intervening Kidron Valley, reasoning that an Orthodox Jew would never walk over such unholy ground. Nearby is the *Tomb of the Prophets*. Haggai, Zechariah, and Malachi are believed to have been buried here with their disciples. Thirty-six recesses mark those sites inside the cool, candlelit cave. There is a small entrance fee. Open Sunday through Friday, 9 A.M. to 3:30 P.M.

The Mount of Olives is studded with churches, monasteries, and crypts that are closely associated with the life of Jesus and the events surrounding his capture and Crucifixion. During Jesus' life, the Mount of Olives was a place of quiet introspection, where the Nazarene would spend hours talking to his disciples and contemplating the lack of faith he encountered. He would often walk to the Mount from the nearby town of Bethany, where his friend Lazarus lived. From here Jesus embarked on his triumphant march into Jerusalem and from it he ascended to heaven.

While the sites are not in a straight line but are scattered on the mountainside, we have detailed them approximately from the summit down. It's easier if you are walking it. Bus #75 from Damascus Gate will leave you nearby.

The Place of the Ascension (Chapel/Mosque)
At the mountain's highest point, near the small Arab village of Et-Tur, this chapel (actually a mosque) is where, according to

Luke, Jesus ascended to Heaven on Easter Sunday. The structure visible today was built by the Crusaders over a Byzantine site which has been in Arab hands since Saladin's times in 1198; hence it is, in reality, a mosque. Inside a small vestibule, a stone in the floor bears the mark of Jesus' right foot. The stone with his left-foot imprint was taken to El-Aqsa Mosque in the Middle Ages. Ask the guard to allow you onto the gallery above the mosque — the view of the Old City and the Jordan Valley is unsurpassed. The Feast of the Ascension is celebrated here forty days after Easter.

Nearby stands the *Russian Monastery*, which was built in 1880 and has been home to an order of White Russian nuns since 1909. A hole in the mosaic floor marks the spot where John the Baptist's beheaded body was buried. There is a small museum and a 200-foot bell tower, which for followers of the Russian Orthodox faith marks the site where Christ ascended to Heaven. The nuns sing vespers at 4:30 P.M. each day. It's an awkward time to be here, but the service is very lovely to hear.

Pater Noster Church (Our Father)

Emperor Constantine, who built both the Church of the Nativity (Bethlehem) and Church of the Holy Sepulchre (Old City), also built a church here to mark the spot where Jesus prophesied the final judgment day to his disciples. The church, the Eleona Basilica, was destroyed by the Persians. The Crusaders built a new church here, which they called Pater Noster, for they believed that it was here that Jesus taught the Lord's Prayer, which begins with the phrase, "Our Father ...." The present church, built through the fund-raising efforts of a French princess, is almost a century old. A delightful touch is the Lord's Prayer in sixty-two languages, painted on tiles near the entrance. Hours are 8:30 A.M. to 12:30 P.M. and 3 to 4:30 P.M.

Dominus Flevit Chapel

Dominus Flevit means "the Lord wept," and the dome of this beautiful Franciscan church resembles a tear. Tradition marks this as the place where Jesus stopped before he entered Jerusalem and cried as he prophesied the city's destruction. The Crusader church built on this site was replaced by a mosque. The modern church you see today, built over an earlier Byzantine chapel, was erected in 1953. During the excavations, workers uncovered the former chapel and a first-century Jewish cemetery. Artifacts are on display nearby, and the mosaic floor of the early chapel is visible. A Greek inscription tells us that the former chapel was built by Simeon, a friend of Jesus. Hours are 7 A.M. to noon and 3 to 6 P.M. (5 P.M. in winter).

Garden of Gethsemane and the Church of All Nations

At the foot of the Mount, the Garden of Gethsemane is tranquil and flower-filled, and it retains the ancient olive trees that gave this garden its name—olive press. It was here that Judas betrayed Jesus with a kiss and also where, after the Last Supper, Jesus withdrew from his disciples and prayed on the night before he was arrested. To commemorate his agony, the Church of All Nations (also called the Basilica of the Agony) was built here in 1924, over a Crusader building. Built with funds contributed by several nations, the church is stunning outside. It has twelve mosaic domes. Inside, it is rather dark, but the rock on which Jesus prayed is near the altar. Hours are 8:30 A.M. to noon and 3 to 7 P.M. (garden open till 5 P.M.). Take bus #36 from Damascus Gate.

Russian Church of Mary Magdalene

Quite near the Church of All Nations is another striking building, this one in typical Russian style, with golden onion-shaped domes. Built by Czar Alexander in 1888, it is a sixteenth-century-style edifice. You can see the domes from the Old City. A crypt inside holds the remains of a grand duchess killed during the Russian revolution. The garden adjoining the church is very old. Hours are Thursday and Saturday 9 A.M. to noon and 2 to 5 P.M.; Sunday 10 A.M. to noon.

Tomb of the Virgin and Grotto of Gethsemane

On the other side of the Church of All Nations is a steep staircase that leads down into an underground shrine. Halfway down are the tombs of Mary's parents and her husband, Joseph. You can see the Virgin's tomb behind a Greek Orthodox altar. Armenians

and Abyssinians also have altars nearby. It is quite dark here.
Hours are Monday through Satuday 6 to 11:30 A.M. and 2 to 5 P.M.

Near this tomb is the cave where Jesus' disciples slept while
Jesus prayed in the garden. The cave is cared for by Franciscans.
Hours are 8:30 A.M. to noon and 3 to 7 P.M.

Bethany and Bethphage

There are two other sites you might consider exploring if you
have a car. They are Bethphage and Bethany. *Bethphage*, which is
now a Franciscan complex, marks the place where the ancient
town of Bethphage stood. Jesus sent two disciples here to bring
him a donkey that had never been ridden and which would be
tied at the town's entrance. This is the donkey that Jesus rode
into Jerusalem. Bethphage is the traditional start of the Palm
Sunday procession, which follows Jesus' path to St. Anne's
Church in the Old City.

Bethany was a small village that Jesus visited often, for his
friend, Lazarus, and Lazarus' sisters Martha and Mary lived here,
as did Simon the Leper. Here Jesus raised his friend from the
dead. The Crusader church on this site was razed, and a mosque
was built in its place. A modern Franciscan church was built here
in 1953. Bethany is on the Jerusalem—Jericho road. Take bus
#36 from Damascus Gate.

Kidron Valley/Mount Ophel (The City of David)

Also called the Valley of Jehosaphat, this valley lies between the
Temple Mount and the Mount of Olives. King David built his city
on the ridge of Mount Ophel, which overlooks the valley. This
area, which lies to the south of the Temple Mount and outside
the present walls, was in 1000 B.C. the administrative seat of
David's kingdom. It is one of the oldest parts of Jerusalem.

In the valley to the east of the Arab town *Silwan* is a vast
necropolis dating back to the first century A.D. There are several
tombs here; the most impressive is called *Absalom's Tomb*—but
it isn't. Absalom, King David's rebellious and disobedient son,
was killed by his father's soldiers and buried under a pile of
stones in a forest. The tomb here, carved out of the rock with
sturdy columns and a zany conical dome, has been the object of
Jews' scorn for centuries; some even stone it.

The Tomb of Zachariah has a pyramidal roof and is a monolith that served as a tomb and as a funereal monument for the multichambered catacombs in the cliff behind it. There are other tombs, and a cliff nearby exhibits square rock-cut openings that lead to burial chambers of the eighth and ninth centuries B.C.

The *Gibon Spring* was, in ancient times, more like a geyser, spitting forth an abundant supply of water, then lying still for an indeterminate period. This spring supplied the City of David with water. Solomon, realizing its importance, had a channel dug from the spring to the city. When the city was under attack by Assyrians, King Hezekiah became fearful that his enemies would block his water supply, and he had a closed tunnel built to bring the precious water to the city. The tunnel, 1,600 feet long, ended in the *Pool of Siloam*. The pool, which was actually a spring, according to the historian Josephus Flavius, had curative powers and was known to people in the area. Silwan, the town in the valley, has over the years diverted the water from this spring, and it is in a sorry state today.

The City of David, on Ophel Ridge, is the site of a major archeological dig, started in 1978. The first section of what will one day be an archeological garden can be visited. You can go on your own; the entrance is south of Dung Gate and to your left through a bus station. But you will learn a lot more and have a lot more fun if you join a group. We did and loved it. The Archeological Seminars Tour is excellent. Check the schedule at their office at 34 Habad Street. The tour lasts about two hours and is preceded by a slide presentation and discussion. After the tour, you can walk through Hezekiah's tunnel to the Pool of Siloam. This is optional and will take about forty-five minutes. There is often water in the tunnel, so dress appropriately.

Mount Zion

The hill with a cluster of buildings atop it just southwest of the Old City is Mount Zion. The buildings are the *Dormition Abbey* and *King David's Tomb*, with the *Cenacle* (site of Jesus' Last Supper) above it. A new addition, the *Chamber of the Holocaust*, is in an adjoining building.

In 100 B.C. this southern extension was part of the city and within its walls. These walls and the Hinnon Valley below acted as a natural defense against the Roman invaders. Emperor Hadrian excluded Mount Zion from his Latinate city, Aelia Capitolina, but the Byzantines included it within their city walls. Suleiman's architects neglected to include it within the present walls, drawing his wrath. The architects are buried beside Jaffa Gate.

The *Church of the Dormition* ("sleep") was built by German Catholics in the early 1900s. It stands on an area where a Byzantine church stood. According to tradition, this is the place where Mary, mother of Jesus, "went to sleep" (died). The church is very beautiful and is filled with mosaics.

It features a mosaic of Mary and Jesus in the apse; a mosaic on the floor of the rotunda, which represents the Word of the Tri-une God spreading through time and space; and a mosaic in the crypt, down below, where the house of Mary stood. The hexagon in the center marks the place where she slept, or passed away. The icon above the table of the western altar (its column support is a relic from one of the earlier churches) shows Mary on her deathbed, surrounded by her family and the apostles. Notice the three flames that unite into one. They represent the Holy Trinity.

Note the interesting chapels (donated by various countries) that encircle a statue of Mary.

The Tomb of David is a rock-walled room where Jews come to light candles and rekindle the memory of their greatest king, David. Above the tomb is the Cenacle, the site of the Last Supper, where Jesus broke bread with his disciples for the last time.

I'm sure you aren't surprised to hear that these attributions are open to question. Many places in the Bible are attributed to the wrong spot. In all likelihood, David was buried on nearby Ophel and not on Mount Zion, and it is also likely that the Last Supper was not actually held here.

The Museum of King David

In a medieval building nearby, a new museum has opened which contains exhibits about Jewish life in the time of King David. The Psalm Room contains an exhibit of handwritten psalm books in Hebrew, and another room has a display of musical instruments. Ceremonial objects are also on display. Hours arc Sunday through Thursday 8 A.M. to 6 P.M., Friday till 2 P.M.

The Chamber of the Holocaust

Rather eerie, this Holocaust memorial is a small room illuminated by flickering candles. Part of the exhibit contains articles of those who died in the camps. Worth a look, but it isn't nearly as poignant as Yad Vashem. A small yeshiva is next door.

On the eastern slope of Mount Zion is *St. Peter in Gallicantu*, or St. Peter at Cockcrow. The church is a modern, blue-domed structure built in remembrance of the prophecy of Jesus, that Peter would deny him for the third time at the second crowing of the cock. Some Christians believe that High Priest Caiaphas' house once stood here. Jesus was imprisoned here overnight and taken to Pontius Pilate the next day for judgment. This has been negated by more recent finds in the Armenian Quarter; nevertheless, a monastic church of the sixth century A.D. definitely stood on this spot.

Mount Zion is an easy walk from the Armenian Quarter or from King Street, at the bottom of Jaffa Road.

Between Mount Zion and the Yemin Moshe section is the *Hinnon Valley*, also called Gehenna. Gehenna is associated with Hades or Hell and it is said that children were sacrificed here in the seventh century B.C. to a god called Moloch.

Mount Scopus (Har Hatsofim)

Named Observation Mount for its sensational views, Mount Scopus is the least interesting of the peaks surrounding the Old City in terms of ancient history. It does, however, have the most intriguing modern history of the three, for Mount Scopus remained in Israeli hands during the nineteen years of Jordanian rule. Because it was cut off from West Jerusalem and other Israeli-held areas, a special agreement was required between Israel and Jordan. The area was required between Israel and Jordan. The area was demilitarized, although it would seem that arms were smuggled in, for the police on the Mount held their own during the 1967 war. Every two weeks, for nineteen years, a convoy of policemen and maintenance people rolled through the Mandelbaum Gate and East Jerusalem, escorted by the U. N. police. Atop the mountain, *Hebrew University* and *Hadassah Hospital* were also cut off and closed down. A new campus was built in Givat Ram, and the new Hadassah Medical Center was built on the western fringe of the city. In 1967, when the city was reunited, the two became operational again. You can visit them, as well as a *British World War I Cemetery*. The best reasons to visit Mount Scopus are the views, which include the Old City, West Jerusalem, the russet-brown Judean Hills, and as far away as the Dead Sea.

Scattered Sights

Model of Ancient Jerusalem

On the grounds of the Holyland Hotel, southwest of the city, stands a meticulously detailed model of ancient Jerusalem in A.D. 66 at the beginning of the revolt against Rome. Constructed of marble, stone, wood, copper, and iron (all materials in use at that time), the plan follows the Mishnah, the Talmud, and the New Testament. You'll see the walls, towers, theaters, and market—all in scale. The city had fabulous palaces—Herod's, Hasmon's, and Caiaphas'. Hours are Sunday through Thursday 8 A.M. to 5 P.M., Friday 8 A.M. to 3 P.M. Buy a ticket in advance for Saturday or holidays. There is a modest fee. Take bus #21, #21A, or #99.

Ne' Ot Kedumin Biblical Landscape Reserve

The landscape of Biblical and Talmudic Israel has been recreated on this 625-acre reserve. Fascinating. They have gathered many of the plants, nearly one hundred animals, and many birds that lived here in biblical times. You'll see camels, gazelles, lions, and crocodiles. Cages are often marked with a biblical phrase mentioning that animal. It's a fun way to spend an hour or two. Open Sunday, Monday, Wednesday, and Thursday from 8:30 A.M. to 4 P.M.; Tuesday till 6 P.M.; and Friday and holidays till 1 P.M. No tickets sold here on Saturday, but you can buy them in advance. Take bus #471.

Sanhedrin Tombs and Park

In a beautiful garden in the northernmost region of the city are the rock caves and tombs that are the burial places of the judges of the Sanhedrin, ancient Israel's highest court. It had seventy-one members and met near the Temple. The cave has three stories with alcoves where the coffins were placed. It's dark inside.

Hadassah Medical Center

The largest medical center in the Middle East, it was built to replace the hospital on Mount Scopus which couldn't be used from 1948 to 1967. To the west of the city, it is famous for the Chagall stained-glass windows in its synagogue. The twelve colorful windows depict the twelve tribes of Israel. You can visit the synagogue from 8 A.M. to 1:30 P.M. and from 2 P.M. to 4 P.M. Sunday through Thursday. There is a modest fee. Take bus #19 or #27 from Jaffa Gate.

Shopping

Antique buffs, those with an interest in Judaica (either contemporary or old and rare), and lovers of handicrafts will have a great time shopping in Jerusalem. Good buys here include 18-carat gold jewelry set with ancient coins and glass, olivewood carvings, religious articles, and both Arab and Israeli crafts. The *souk* in the Old City is the best in the country, and you'll love shopping there. There are shops in the Old City too. There are two interesting arts-and-crafts centers and a tiny street that specializes in Judaica.

Shopping Hours

Hours vary but the most common are 9:30 A.M. to 1 P.M. and 4 P.M. to 7 P.M. Sunday through Thursday, and 9:30 A.M. to 2 P.M. on Friday. No shopping hours on Saturday. These hours apply to West Jerusalem and the Jewish Quarter. In East Jerusalem and the Arab Market, stalls open at 9 A.M. and close at 6 P.M. Many stalls are closed all day on Friday.

Credit Cards

Shops here accept major credit cards and also dollars and pounds. You save the VAT if you pay in non-shekel currency (that includes traveler's checks) but if you pay VAT on any purchase over $50, make sure to ask for a redemption certificate. No credit cards are accepted in the market.

Jewelry

Jewelry design and stone cutting and polishing were traditional means of earning a living for Ashkenazi Jews in the shtetls and cities of Europe. Here in Israel, these old-timers still work their magic while passing on these demanding skills to young North African Jews. You'll be delighted when you see the jewelry here. Fabulous multicolored gemstones, diamonds, and ancient coins and glass are placed in 18-carat gold settings. Styles range from classic and traditional to the contemporary and avant-garde. Some pieces are collectibles; the price range is enormous. Casual jewelry and antique jewelry are also popular.

H. STERN JEWELERS

Jaffa Gate   Open 9 A.M.–6 P.M. (till 2 P.M. Friday)
Major Credit Cards

H. Stern, a Brazil-based jeweler, is Israel's most prestigious jewelry concern. The bilevel Jaffa Gate shop is Jerusalem's main branch. There are smaller shops at many of the city's deluxe hotels (including the Seven Arches). The Stern shops offer a wide variety of fine jewelry as well as a broad price range. Brazil's fabulous gemstones, in every color of the rainbow, are set in 18-carat gold settings. The Jerusalem shops feature the designs of famous Israeli artists, including American-born David Levine, whose designs are classic and traditional. Many pieces incorporate antique glass and antique coins (with certificates of authenticity). They are unique and simply stunning. Shops also stock gold and silver religious items and charms. Each item comes with a year's guarantee and can be exchanged during that time as well. Stern has shops in thirteen countries.

RUTH MATAR GALLERY

23 Pele Yoez Street, Yemin Moshe   Phone 245886
Sunday–Thursday 8:30 A.M.–6 P.M.,
Friday till 2 P.M.

First-quality jewelry crafted around ancient coins is a specialty in this lovely shop, which also has a wonderful collection of Judaica. The pieces are handmade and are frequently one of a kind; some incorporate diamonds and other precious stones. The Judaica collection has sterling silver spice boxes, kiddush cups, and candlesticks.

SARAH EINSTEIN

22 Rivlin Street   10 A.M. to 7 P.M.
Antique jewelry originally created by master craftsmen from the Middle East and North Africa is recrafted by the very talented Sarah Einstein. Each piece is unique and a terrific remembrance of your stay in Jerusalem.

THE RING

17 Jaffa Road   Phone 231032
Jewelry made to order is the lure here. Owner Bob Faber will make your "dream" in 14-carat gold. Wedding bands for both men and women, with or without stones, are the most asked-for items. Bob also specializes in modernizing family heirlooms. Originally from Southern California, Bob has lived in Israel for more than ten years.

THE BEDOUIN MUSEUM

37 David Street (Market)

Jamal, Munir, and Ziad have quite a collection of Bedouin jewelry. The jewelry has coins, chunky glass, and colored stones, and it's fun to wear. Inexpensive if you bargain hard. They also have a lovely selection of hand-embroidered dresses and blouses, as well as copperware and rugs. "The Arches," across the street, also theirs offers jewelry and souvenirs.

Crafts

HUTZOT HAYOTZER ARTS AND CRAFTS LANE

(Just south of Jaffa Gate)   Sunday–Thursday 10 A.M. to 5 P.M.
Friday till 2 P.M.

A dozen shops, galleries, and workshops line this restored street that was formerly a stable and market. The shops are small, and each has a unique product. There are artists working in oils, in silver, and in copper and brass; others sculpt or weave tapestries and rugs. There are ceremonial art objects and contemporary leathers. This is an interesting place to browse, and the complex has several restaurants too. The shops we liked include Or Hayotzer for leather goods, the Engel Gallery, Roup Rock Shop, Stella Soper Weaving, Studio Alsberg–Ancient Jewelry, and Morris Studio. Take bus #1, #2, #3, #13, #19, #20, #30, or #38 to Jaffa Gate, or take bus #5, #6, #18, or #21 to King David Street.

JERUSALEM HOUSE OF QUALITY

12 Hebron Road   **Phone 717430**
Sunday–Thursday 10 A.M. to 6 P.M.
Friday till 1 P.M.

You can watch the artisans and craftsmen at work on the second floor of this art center and buy their works in the gallery below. This gallery is alongside Jerusalem Cinematheque, and buses #4, #5, #6, #7, #8, #10, #14, #18, and #21 will get you there. Opened in 1968 in a building that was formerly an ophthalmic hospital, its crafts are all award winners, having been passed by a board of experts. You'll see enamel, pottery, wood, glass, metal, and copper sculptures and jewelry. Batiks and embroidered paintings on display when we visited were not seen elsewhere.

WIZO SHOP

34 Jaffa Road   Phone 256155
Sunday–Thursday 8:30 A.M. to 7 P.M.
Friday till 2 P.M.

To get an overview of Israeli arts and crafts, head to WIZO, run by an organization that uses profits to aid schools, and children. WIZO stocks handwoven dresses, caftans, batiks, silver and brass religious articles, glassware, and exquisite paintings of Jerusalem handpainted on silk. Hand-embroidered tablecloth sets and children's clothing are best buys. No bargaining. Items are priced in line with those elsewhere and it's nice to know that your money is helping those who need it. WIZO also operates shops in Tel Aviv, Haifa, and other parts of Israel.

MUNIR BARAKAT

3 locations: 9 A.M. to Midnight
The American Colony Hotel, Nablus Road
The Hyatt Regency
David Street

Antiques, fine Persian and Oriental carpets and wall hangings, copperware, Armenian jewelry, 16th– to 18th–century glass, Bedouin embroidery and other fine *objets d'art* are displayed at all three shops. Collectors and less serious shoppers alike should stop in at any of the three shops.

STUDIO SAKALOVSKY CERAMICS LTD.

4 Gal-Ed Street (Jewish Quarter)   Phone 894298
9 A.M. to 8 P.M. in Winter,
9 A.M. to 11 P.M. in Summer,
Fridays till 2 P.M.
(closed for Sabbath)

Shortly after moving to Israel from South Africa in 1976, ceramic artist Lorna Sakalovsky developed the unique figurines which have earned her an international reputation. As individual as human beings, her figurines are hand-fashioned using the finest stoneware and porcelain clays and Ms. Sakalovsky's own special process. Highlighting her work are chess sets and Shabbat candlesets, as well as individual figurines. You can even order portraits of yourself or loved ones. Just supply the necessary information or a photograph. Don't pass up a visit to her studio.

MASKIT

6 Eliash Street (Rejwan Square)   Sunday–Thursday
8:30 A.M. to 6:45 P.M.
Friday till 1:45 P.M.

This is the largest shop in this well-known chain. Here too you'll get an overview of Israeli crafts; the second floor is filled with textiles in dresses, tablecloths, and children's clothing. Maskit has Shalom of Safed posters and beautiful small rugs to hang.

ARIEH KLEIN

34 Bar Ilan Street   Phone 732666

Olive trees have been part of the landscape here for hundreds of years. Carved and polished olivewood items make lovely gifts. Many souvenir olivewood carvings are sold in the city, but the best assortment is found in this shop. Biblical figures, ashtrays, bookends, key rings, and candlesticks are all precisely carved. All prices.

GABRIELI

2 Ben Yehuda Street

Gabrieli boasts the most beautiful hand-woven items in Israel. Are they right? You'll have to decide for yourself.

In the Old City

The Souk (Market)

You'll want to shop in the *souk* for Arab handicrafts. These include ceramic plates and jugs, clocks, and bells. The color blue predominates. Armenian pottery is the top of the line. Many stalls have chunky jewelry that features colored stones, old coins, and beads. These should be inexpensive. Bedouin dresses, which have beautifully embroidered bodices, are popular for use as beach robes, but they cost more than you think—if they are authentic. Olivewood carvings, copper and brass, woven carpets, baskets, and glassware are all sold here. How good a buy you get will depend on your bargaining technique.

Armenian Art Center, on Armenian Patriarch Road, is a very nice shop selling local handicrafts. Look at the tiles with homilies and messages; they make nice gifts. (Armenian Quarter)

Jerusalem Pottery, Via Dolorosa (Sixth Station) has a vast selection of Armenian pottery and others too. (Christian Quarter)

Shoshana, near Tiferith Yisrael Street, is for the needlework fan who'd like a kit with Israeli motifs. Directions given. (Jewish Quarter)

Old City Art Gallery, 33 Hayehudin Street, has lovely paintings and old maps. (Jewish Quarter)

Courtyard Gallery, near Hurva Synagogue. Owned by Gloria Kramer, a transplanted Chicagoan, this new gallery specializes in fiber arts. Woven pieces, batiks, and crocheted, embroidered, and knitted items by some of Israel's best-known artists are on sale here. Motifs are from the Bible and Jewish tradition. (Jewish Quarter)

Judaica

Yochanan Migush Halav Street

This small street near the Old City is the place to head if you have an interest in Judaica. Judaica can be new, but most shops here specialize in fine antiques. This includes kiddush cups, spice boxes, Hanukkah menorahs, Sabbath lamps, Torah ornaments, and paintings and prints with Jewish themes. Shops include *Eitan Amiel*, at number 15, which specializes in ritual art in silver and enamel. Phone 243742. *Catriel*, at number 17, specializes in Judaica carved out of woods such as jacaranda, atimoya, cocobolo, and ebony. *Oded Davidson*, number 19 (phone 246416), features silver and brass objects, and shares space with *Korman's* which has ceremonial objects such as *betubot*, *megillot*, and *mizrahim*.

Leathers/Sportswear/Furs

Israeli leathers are supple, come in a variety of colors, and are high-styled or classic in style. There are more choices in Tel Aviv, but some well-known manufacturers have shops here too.

Beged Or has a shop on Ben Yehuda Mall. It sells leather jackets, skirts, pants, and coats for both men and women.

Ateret, 19 King David Street, carries Israeli designer clothes from casual sportswear to elegant evening fashions. Good workmanship and fair prices.

Other Shops to Explore

FRANK MEISLER GALLERY

28 King David Street   Phone 228781

Delightful sculptures with movable parts are fashioned in pewter with gold or silver overlays. Biblical and Israeli themes. There is another branch in Jaffa.

ESTHER DORAN

9 Shlomzion Hamalka Street   Phone 227528

Antiques and modern pieces for your home—all one of a kind—as well as unusual furnishings are featured here. Check what's in stock when you walk by.

KUZARI

10 Rehov HaBukharim   Sunday–Thursday
(Bukharan Quarter)   8:30 A.M. to 1 P.M.

Another interesting ethnic group in the city, from Bukhara (now Russia), has a terrific embroidery shop. Decorative pieces, Persian cosmetic bags, Yemenite shirts—all hand-embroidered—are sold here.

For Book Lovers   Gur Arieh, located at space #8 in the Nachalat Shiva pedestrian mall, has a fine selection of new and used books. Steimatsky Books on Ben Yehuda Mall is also worth browsing.

Sports

Tennis   Israel Tennis Center, 5 Elmaliach Street, Katamon Quarter, has eleven all-weather courts. Hours are 8 A.M.–2 P.M. Inexpensive. Phone 791866.

Men's Softball   Givat Ram Stadium at Hebrew University. Fridays at 2:30 P.M.

Bicycling   Join the Jerusalem Biking Club on two rides each week. Different routes. For rental and information, phone 344452.

Fun Run   Sundays at 4. Liberty Bell Park, phone 248313.

Swimming   Jerusalem Public Pool, 43 Enek Refaim Street, 8 A.M.–5 P.M. YMCA Aelia Capitolina Hotel on Nablus Road allows guests for a small fee. The Kibbutz guest houses near Jerusalem also allow guests at their pools. (See Hotels.)

Sundown to Sunup

While Jerusalem can never be called a "night town", it does have a good range of evening activities. Most are low-key and are tame by New York, London, or Tel Aviv standards. Check the *Jerusalem Post*, particularly Friday's edition, which has a special pullout, "In Jerusalem." Pick up the "Events in Jerusalem" listing at the IGTO. On Friday nights, West Jerusalem pulls in the carpet at sundown and many Israelis head to Talpiot, where restaurants and clubs are quite crowded.

Sound and Light Show

The history of Jerusalem is fascinating, and the Sound and Light show reenacts key events by illuminating different parts of the Citadel. It lasts forty-five minutes and you'll really get into it. At this writing the English show is at 8:30 every night except Friday. You can get tickets at the Citadel.

Good Music for Listening

Jerusalem Sherover Theater, 20 David Marcus Street. Classical music concerts by the Jerusalem Symphony Orchestra and Israel Chamber Music Ensemble. Phone 617167.

Henry Crown and Rebecca Crown Concert Halls   These smaller auditoriums are part of the Jerusalem Theater Complex. They have concerts, dance programs, and plays.

Pargod Theater, 94 Bezaled Street, phone 228819. Jazz sessions every Friday afternoon at 1:30—free. Shows include Israeli rock singers, jazz, guitar music, Jewish songs and stories (sometimes in English), and Irish bands. Bezalel Street is the continuation of Ben Yehuda Street after crossing King George V.

Concerts are frequently scheduled in some of Jerusalem's most interesting historical sites. Watch for them at the *Israel Museum*, *David's Tower*, *Dormition Abbey*, the *Targ Music Center* in En Karem, *West Jerusalem YMCA*, the Artists House, and the Ticho House. Be sure to check concert listings in the "In Jerusalem" pull out.

Good Music and Light Food

Ticho House, Harav Kook (near Zion Square), phone 245068. Classical music and dairy food, open late. Nice terrace overlooking a garden.

Zion Confederation House, Emil Botta Street, Yemin Moshe, phone 245206. Classical and popular music and dairy food draws an "arty" crowd.

Cellar Bar, American Colony Hotel, East Jerusalem, phone 282421. Jazz, piano, and light food.

Pubs

31 Jaffa Road   The courtyard at 31 Jaffa Road is lined with pubs. Each has indoor dining spots and outdoor tables. The food varies but the beer and drinks are plentiful. Unusual, for most stay open seven nights. Look in on The Yard, Morris, and The Finger Pub. This is a good spot to meet Israelis.

Champ's Pub, located at space #5 on the Nachalat Shiva pedestrian mall, is similar to a U. S. sports bar. NFL flyers adorn the walls and draft beer is the favorite drink. Light fare, music, and dim lighting complete the picture. Open until 2 A.M. daily. For a different ambience, try the *Jazz Town Pub & Restaurant* nearby.

Herod's Inn   King David Street. One of the city's nicest pubs. The food is good here too.

Cinema

Cinematheque, Hebron Road (between Mount Zion and Yemin Moshe). The Israel Film Archives is located here, and the theater shows foreign-language films (not dubbed) and classics. Check for schedules or call 724131. *La Moon* restaurant in the complex serves dairy specialties. Movie theaters are located throughout the city and first-run U.S. films are shown in English with subtitles. Check the newspaper for information. Here are some of the more convenient ones: *Eden*, 5 Agrippas Street, near King George V; *Orion and Habira*, on Shamai Street, near Ben Yehuda Mall; *Kfir*, 97 Jaffa Road; *Or Gil* and *Orna* on Hillel Street (near Ben Yehuda Mall).

Israeli Nightclubs

The Khan, David Remez Square, phone 718281. Built in the nineteenth century, when it was a roadside stop for travelers, the Khan is Jerusalem's most popular night stop. It houses a theater, a café and restaurant, a bar where you can drink and dance, and the Khan nightclub, with shows that feature folk singing and dancing. It's lively and you can join in. There is a cover charge. Make reservations on Saturdays.

Similar in style and substance is *Marrakesh*, 4 King David Street, which has dinner and a show that features a belly dancer. You can come just to drink and watch the show. Phone 221208.

Sefer Ve Sefel (Book and Mug)   An unusual stop, this is a cluttered bookstore with books in several languages, and it is also an ice cream parlor. It's open Sunday through Wednesday, 9 A.M. to 8 P.M., Thursday till 11 P.M. Look for the sign at 4 Yavetz Street (off Jaffa Road near Zion Square). Chess and backgammon next door.

Talpiot, formerly an industrial center, is now home to many of Jerusalem's most popular restaurants and nightclubs. Yad Haruzim Street is virtually lined with nightclubs. A few to try are Blue Moon at #3, Expose at #13, and Pitagoras at #11. The concierge at your hotel should be able to recommend others. Many reserve certain nights for particular age groups, so be sure to phone ahead before venturing out.

Ben Yehuda Mall   The cafés here are open late and you can sit outside, sip a cappuccino, and watch the action—what little there is of it.

Hotel Stops   The city's deluxe hotels have bars and lounges that stay open late. Try the Hilton in Givat Ram, the Seven Arches on the Mount of Olives, and the Hyatt Hotel's Castel Lounge.

Jerusalem Potpourri

Jerusalem Sightseeing Ticket   Offered by the Ministry of Tourism, the sightseeing ticket covers admission to David's Tower, the Museum of the History of Jerusalem, the Israel Museum, and three other sites of your choice. You also get discounts at many theaters, stores, and cafés. A ticket can be purchased at various sites throughout the city, as well as at most hotels.

IGTO The most accessible office is at Jaffa Gate. The main office is 24 King George Street (near Ben Yehuda Mall). Hours are 8 A.M. to 5 P.M. Sunday through Thursday, till 1 P.M. on Friday. Phone 754910 or 754888.

Jerusalem Municipality Tourist Office, 34 Jaffa Road, same hours as above.

Rent a Bicycle, 14 Shlomzion Hamalka Street (near Jaffa Gate), phone 249530, daily 8:30 A.M. to 4:30 P.M.

Second-Hand Books   Popular English books are very expensive in Israel. Try the *Book Stop* at 6 Yosef Du Nawas Street (off Jaffa Road near Zion Square) or *Book Shuk* on Hahavatzelet Street nearby for large selections, fairly priced.

Ticket Offices Cahana-On, 1 Dorot Rishonim Street (near Ben Yehuda), phone 222831; *Klaim Agency*, 8 Shamai Street (near Zion Square), phone 2409896; *Ben Naim*, 38 Jaffa Road, phone 224008.

Tradition   It is tradition for Orthodox Jews to ritually cleanse their hands before eating. You'll notice a ceramic pitcher and basin at the entrance to many restaurants.

Excursions from Jerusalem

Bethlehem

While the town of Bethlehem has changed dramatically since Jesus was born there, the surrounding area seems unchanged by the passage of years. Only eight miles from Jerusalem, the road (route 60) curves through gently rolling hills covered with flowering almond trees, olive and fig trees, and lazy vines. Neat farms worked by white-garbed Arab men and their families are visible on either side of the road. Arabic *Beit Lahm* means "house of meat"; Hebrew *Bet Lehm* means "house of bread"; both refer to this area's fertility. You'll pass grinning boys prodding their heavily laden donkeys and shepherds sitting quietly on huge rocks while their sheep and goats graze nearby.

Firmly identified with the birth of Jesus, Bethlehem was also intricately involved in the lives of the Patriarchs. Abraham, Jacob, Rachel, and Ruth the Moabite, whose progeny include Obed, the grandfather of David, all lived here when the town was called Ephrat. Traditionally a Christian Arab town, half of Bethlehem's residents are now Arab Moslems, displaced by the wars. Bethlehem is in the West Bank/Judea-Samaria.

Orientation

Getting There

Arab bus #22 (from Damascus Gate) or Egged buses #34 and #44 (West Jerusalem Bus Terminals) will drop you in Manger Square, as will sheruts from Damascus Gate. If you drive, follow Hebron Road (route 60) south out of town through the Talpiot industrial area.

En route you will pass the *Mar Elias Monastery* (on your left) and *Rachel's Tomb*. You might like to visit the tomb, which seems very Moslem. Rachel was Jacob's wife and she died in childbirth on her way to Ephrat (Bethlehem). The small rectangular domed building is often crowded with praying, weeping women. (You need a head covering.) When you leave the tomb, bear left. You are only one and a half miles from Bethlehem.

Major Streets

Manger Square is the center of town. The local IGTO is located here between the Andalus Hotel and the Mosque of Omar. Phone (02) 741581.

What to See

The Church of the Nativity is most important, and you might also like to visit the Milk Grotto and the Shepherds' Fields. Don't forget the local market and shops, where religious articles abound. These are in Manger Square and near the Milk Grotto.

The Church (Basilica) of the Nativity

When Jesus was born, Bethlehem was no longer an important city, for David, who had been crowned king there, made Jerusalem the capital of his kingdom. Jesus was born in a manger (now below the church), for there was no room at the local khan. In Roman times, Hadrian sacked Jerusalem and in a heathen rage forbade Jews to enter both that city and Bethlehem. Jesus' parents took their infant to exile in Egypt and on their return made their way back to Nazareth, in the Galilee, where Jesus grew up.

The first church here was built by Constantine (under the guidance of his mother, Empress Helena) in the fourth century. The Samaritans destroyed it, but a new church was built in the sixth century. The energetic Crusaders arrived on the scene centuries later and surrounded Justimar's building with massive stone walls and added a convent. They spruced up the church, adding marble siding, mosaic walls and floors, and a lead roof. This is basically the church you see today, although it has been repaired several times. The Crusaders crowned their first king, Baldwin I, in this chapel on Christmas Day. When the Crusader's kingdom fell, the church lapsed into disrepair, but it was not destroyed by invading armies nor in more recent battles.

Your first glimpse of the church will be disappointing, for it looks like a citadel. Only the wide expanse of courtyard to its left gives the structure dignity. You enter through a low doorway—so low that you have to bend over—called "the door of humility." Some say it was built to prevent infidels from riding horses into the church, while others say that you must bend low as a sign of respect.

The Corinthian pillars within are peach-colored and bear pictures of the apostles. The ceiling and floors are almost rustic in appearance, with wooden beams and stone and wood floors. You can see the Crusaders' mosaic floor through small openings. Plenty of gold and silver shimmers from the heavy chandeliers and ornate lamps.

The church and the grotto below it are under the supervision of the Greek Orthodox Church, but Armenians and Roman Catholics have areas that they administer according to a strict timetable worked out by the British during the Mandate period. This was necessary because there were fights for control of parts of this sacred site.

Go down the stone staircases that descend from either side of the altar to the manger where Jesus was born. If you can nudge your way through the wall-to-wall pilgrims and tourists, you'll see the silver star that marks the place of his birth. This star was placed here by an Ottoman sultan in 1852 to replace an earlier one placed by the Franciscans in 1717. Thousands of lips have kissed this star, and you'll notice quite a few people weeping aloud and hundreds of flashes from cameras. There are two altars here, for the Altar of the Nativity (where the star is) is off-limits to

Roman Catholic priests, who instead conduct services at the Altar of the Manger nearby.

Adjoining the basilica is the Roman Catholic *Church of St. Catherine* (a door leads from within the basilica), where Roman Catholic services are traditionally held. If you walk down a small staircase in the church, you'll see parts of the original manger and a series of catacombs and rock-filled rooms. Not fixed up, it looks far more authentic than the grotto under the Church of the Nativity.

It's interesting to note the clergy of the various Christian sects, for each is dressed distinctively. The Franciscans wear brown robes, tied with a rope around the waist, and open sandals; the Greek Orthodox priests wear more formalized black robes and have bushy breads; the Armenians wear purple-and-tan robes with pointed headdresses. By the way, St. Catherine's is one of the few places where you will be directly asked for a contribution by all involved.

Manger Square

The town's main square is filled with cars, tourist buses, and scurrying people. Hotels, restaurants, and shops are located here, and all around the square and the streets leading to it are churches of various Christian denominations in different styles and sizes. We saw Greek Orthodox convents, Coptic Orthodox, Syrian Orthodox, and Greek Catholic churches, and one lonely mosque which was built during Jordanian control.

Christmas Eve in Bethlehem

If you've ever seen this ceremony on TV (it is broadcast by satellite), you know that it is magnificent. Choirs from Christian countries all over the world gather in Manger Square and sing hymns and carols. Inside the Church of St. Catherine (Roman Catholic), Midnight Mass is celebrated. The service is dignified, and the ritual is repeated in churches around the world. The service is led by the Roman Catholic Patriarch of Jerusalem, who arrives in a colorful procession. Your chances of getting into the chapel are minimal (in fact, you need a special pass to enter Bethlehem on December 24 or 25, obtainable at the IGTO in

Jerusalem), but the service is broadcast on a huge television monitor in the square.

Note: Prices go up here for Christmas week. It can get very cold and even snow, so bring warm clothing, especially boots. Restaurants stay open well into the night, so you can warm up with hot coffee.

Milk Grotto Church

Southeast of Manger Square is Milk Grotto Street, and this Franciscan church was built over the cave where Mary spilled a few drops of her milk while nursing Jesus. These drops, it is said, turned the entire area of black stones chalky white. The stone is powdered and sold as a souvenir.

Shepherds' Fields

Four kilometers from Bethlehem is the Arab Christian village, Beit Sahur, where the shepherds who were tending their flocks saw the shining star announcing the birth of Jesus. Incredibly, there are two fields just east of the town; the Roman Catholic field is to the left of the Greek Orthodox one. Bus #66 will take you here from Bethlehem, but it isn't too far to walk.

Other points of interest in town are David's Wells on King David Street and Ruth's Field near the Milk Grotto, where Ruth the Moabite was picking barley when she met her husband-to-be, Boaz.

Want to Stay Over?

Hotels are basic but immaculate, and the owners are friendly and hospitable.

AL ANDALUS GUEST HOUSE

| Box 410, | Phone (02) 741348 |
| Bethlehem | *No Credit Cards* |

In Manger Square, the Andalus is well maintained and the view from your room—the Jordanian hills, olive groves, church spires, and minarets—is almost poetic. Breakfast included, showers only. *Inexpensive*.

PALACE HOTEL

Manger Square   Phone (02) 742798
No Credit Cards

Twenty-five rooms and a location right next to the basilica are what the Palace Hotel offers you. Some rooms have balconies and all have private bathrooms. *Inexpensive*.

Dining Options

These restaurants serve Middle Eastern food, do not accept credit cards, and are inexpensive.

St. George Restaurant, in the Municipality Building (next to the IGTO), has umbrella-covered tables, fresh flowers, and music. Good kubbeh, stuffed pigeon, and vegetables.

Al Andalus Restaurant, in Manger Square, has nicely grilled meats with a delicious dipping sauce. Unfortunately, tour groups at lunch here make for mass confusion and noise.

Shopping

Paul VI Street has a Bedouin shop and several "factories" where you can buy items made of olivewood and mother-of-pearl. The New Tourist Shopping Center is not a bad shopping stop either.

Herodion and Mar Saba Monastery

Two detours from the road to Hebron are quite interesting.

Herodion, nine kilometers from Bethlehem on route 356 (Beit Sahur Road), is where Herod the Great built another mountaintop fortress, similar to the one at Massada. It's an impressive sight, for the king had the mountain shaped into a cone by piling debris on it. At the flattened summit he built his palace and the two hundred white marble steps leading to it. Stone benches from a synagogue and a *mikveh* have been uncovered. Herod was buried here, and the view of the Judean desert, the Dead Sea, and Bethlehem is stunning. Part of the National Park System. Hours 8 A.M. to 4 P.M. daily. There is a modest fee.

Mar Saba Monastery is fourteen kilometers east of Bethlehem. Most of the trip is on Route 398. Mar Saba is the most interesting monastery in the Holy Land, they say. We cannot relate any first-hand experiences here, for women (even female animals) are not permitted to enter. We stood on a tower overlooking the monastery. Built on a canyon wall, Mar Saba was founded in the fifth century but was totally destroyed by invaders. Rebuilt by the Czar in 1840, a special room houses the skulls of monks killed in those attacks. The reclusive monks, some of whom live in nearby cave and don't communicate with one another, belong to the Greek Orthodox sect. Although the monastery may have housed five thousand monks at its zenith, we did not see many, and friends who went inside said there were only a few elderly monks there.

En Route to Hebron

From Bethlehem, Route 60 South leads to Hebron, a Moslem Arab town which is twenty-six kilometers away. The countryside is pastoral and the road bypasses Arab villages and farms. On your left you'll see a sign to *Solomon's Pools*. The three giant, rectangularly shaped cisterns, surrounded by towering trees, were an important water source for Jerusalem. Though more likely Herodian than from Solomon's day, they were in use through the British Mandate period. If you feel like having a snack, there is a small restaurant here.

On your right at about thirteen kilometers from Bethlehem, you'll see a right to *Kfar Etzion*. The original settlement of ultrareligious Zionists was established in the early 1900s, only to be overrun by Arab forces in 1948. All the defenders were killed, and the settlement was reduced to rubble. This new settlement, actually a group of small settlements under the umbrella name Etzion Block, was established after the 1967 war. Symbolically, many of the settlers are descendants of the people who died here. These people and many other Israelis believe that the Jews historically had influence in this area and should have a vital presence there now. The Arabs of Hebron oppose these settlements vehemently. This is not a peaceful environment, as you will note when you see the rolled barbed-wire enclosures.

This uneasiness is part and parcel of a visit to Hebron, and before you decide on a visit here you should be aware of the difficulties. Check with the IGTO and read the *Jerusalem Post* to see if there is a flareup of tensions. Stick to the major tourist routes. It's not a bad idea to take a bus from Bethlehem, leaving your car there for pickup on return.

Hebron

Called the City of the Patriarchs, many of whom are buried here, Hebron is a Moslem Arab town nestled in the Judean Hills at three thousand feet above sea level.

Biblical Hebron (the tel is nearby) was a fruitful agricultural area and Abraham lived a nomadic life here, settling in this area for many years. His family tomb, the *Cave of Machpelah*, is what gave hebron its designation as one of ancient Judaism's four holy cities.

In the center of town, you will see a commercial district. There is a glass factory (the industry brought here by Jews in the sixteenth century), a pottery factory, and a woodcarving factory, as well as many other shops. You should walk through this area for a bit. You might notice an Israeli or two in the shopping area. These, part of the in-town settlement, Qiryat Arba, are always accompanied by Israeli soldiers.

When you tire of shopping, continue past this area and bear left to Abraham's Tomb, which is marked by a road sign. A red sign points to the Jewish Cemetery, which is 3,700 years old but has been virtually destroyed, and a bit farther along (past the homes of Arab craftsmen), you'll see the Moslem cemetery. Here the road widens and you'll see Abraham's Tomb.

The Cave of Machpelah

Abraham bought this land as a burial site for his wife, Sarah, and later he was buried here, as were the patriarchs Isaac and Jacob and their wives Rebecca and Leah. The spectacular tomb over the cave was built by Herod, and the resemblance to the stones of the Western Wall is striking. The Crusaders added a church, which was converted into a mosque in the twelfth century. At that point, the Moslems decreed that non-Moslems were forbidden to enter the tomb and so it remained till 1967. For all those centuries, the closest that Jews could get to the tomb of their Patriarchs was the seventh step. Today, open to all, the ornate Moslem-style building has beautiful 700-year-old stained-glass windows and green-and-gold cloths over the tombs. It is open to the public from 7:30 to 11:30 A.M. and 1:30 to 5 P.M. The building remains in Moslem control, and so from 11:30 A.M. to 1:30 P.M., it is used for Moslem services and it is closed on Friday, the Moslem Sabbath.

Hebron is where the uneasy truce between the Arabs of the West Bank, who consider themselves Palestinians, and the Israelis becomes most apparent. Since the solution does not appear to be imminent, you will have to use good common sense when visiting there.

The Dead Sea Region

Jericho, Qumran, En Gedi, and En Boqeq

he Dead Sea has fascinated travelers, both ancient and present-day, with its strange reputation for curative powers and its unique and forbidding associations with immorality and vice. The area of land that lies on Israel's side of the Dead Sea coast possesses not only a stunning natural diversity but a dramatic inspirational past. The entire Dead Sea region represents, perhaps more than anywhere else in Israel besides Jerusalem, that burning faith which, through centuries of oppression and annihilation, could not be extinguished and led finally to the creation of the modern state of Israel.

At this point you have several options—all delightful—dependent on your time frame and your future itinerary. Jericho, which is only twenty-four miles from Jerusalem, normally can be visited on a half-day excursion with a return to your Jerusalem hotel for the evening. A full day's excursion will allow you to take a peek at Jericho, visit the Massada, and float on the Dead Sea, with a return to Jerusalem in time for a hot bath and dinner. However, Jericho will now be administered by the new Palestinian authorities. Provisions to be made for tourists are unclear as this is written, so check with the IGTO when you arrive. If that is all that time permits, then you should certainly go for it, but if you have two days or if you are driving to Elat, the best way to experience this region's wild loveliness and moving history is to drive along Route 1 from Jerusalem to Jericho, making stops en route, then head south to Qumran, site of the Dead Sea Scrolls' discovery, the En Gedi Nature Reserve, and Massada with a late-afternoon arrival at the En Boqeq hotel area. Here you can float on the Dead Sea and relax for the evening at one of the seaside hotels. The next day, after a refreshing mud pack or massage, you can continue along this coastal road to Elat or head inland to Beersheba and its exciting Bedouin market.

In this best of all possible worlds, we will assume that you have the time to explore this region at a slower pace. You'll notice that the most interesting places to see are in fairly close proximity to one another and there is a momentum created when you visit these history-rich places in sequence. Every stop along the route is like a living chapter in history.

Jericho

The twenty-four-mile ride from Jerusalem to Jericho takes Israelis just forty-five minutes, but there are several points of interest en route, so it will take you somewhat longer. Leaving Jerusalem is nearly as beautiful as entering it—the silver-green olive groves and glistening domes dissolve behind you and the encroaching dry scrubland of the Judean Desert stretches far into the distance. This expanse of arid land grows less and less populated as you venture on, the Arab villages grow fewer and farther between, and, with the exception of Bedouin tents that spring up haphazardly along the roadside, you are alone. The stratified rock is everywhere. Hewn out of this Mesolithic fantasy are valleys, gorges, and gently rolling sunbaked hills, often crowned with small communities at their summits. The houses on the parched hilltops are surprisingly lavish in contrast to the bleak landscape, and they appear to be newly constructed. Life does go on here, and the Judean Desert is home to a special breed of people. Some are nomads who have crossed the desert as a matter of habit and have chosen to join the rest of the world to some extent by settling down. Others are displaced persons who, disenfranchised after the War of Independence, were placed in these settlements. Many road signs in this West Bank region are only in English and Arabic. This might be your first chance to glimpse the Bedouins and their nomadic lifestyle. Being strict Moslems and extremely clannish, Bedouins cling to their traditional ways and resist change. It is a long-term process to erase thousands of years of tradition and habit, and maybe it is a mistake to try. The typical Bedouin is eternal—the women wear heavy ankle-length robes of black cotton with brightly embroidered bodices, and the men still prize their camels above all else. Bedouin ways are as old as time and deserve respect.

Even the Bedouin settlements thin out eventually, and the silent earth formations and withered, wild brushland recall an ancient time. Very little has changed along this road for thousands of years, except for a rare Coca-Cola sign (in Hebrew) and the vehicles that ply the dusty route.

The Inn of the Good Samaritan is on your right a bit more than halfway to Jericho. Once a *Khan*, an ancient inn whose Arabic name was *Khan el Ahmar* (Red Inn) for the red clay used to build it, the inner courtyard was filled with horses, camels, donkeys, and Bedouins all together. What you see today is mostly a Turkish construction several centuries old; the well in the central courtyard is so deep that you cannot see the bottom. Most importantly, it marks the spot where, according to the parable, the good woman of Samaria dipped into the well and drew water to quench Jesus' thirst.

Back on Route 1, watch for the old Jericho road turnoff on your left. The sign reads *St. George's Monastery* (Khoziba) and the monastery, five miles away, is near the spring of Wadi Qelt. This spring, whose waters irrigate part of Jericho today, once ran through the aqueducts of Herod's time. The Greek Orthodox monastery, built during the Byzantine period, seems to cling perilously to the side of the cliff. Nearby, the cliff face is marked by cells where the monks retreat during the week, returning to the monastery for prayers on Saturday night and Sunday.

When you return to the main highway, you'll start a steep descent (our ears popped), for Jericho is below sea level. If you choose, you can make one more interesting detour before the Jericho turn. It lies off the road to the right; the sign reads *En Nebi Mousa* (tomb of Moses). At first glance it looks like an abandoned army barracks (it was), but the ancient mosque here marks the site where, according to Moslem tradition, Moses was buried. In Jewish tradition, Moses never returned to the Holy Land but died during the forty years of wandering in the desert. Some believe that Moses' tomb is actually at Mount Nebo (Jordan), from which he is believed to have viewed the Holy Land before he died. Nonetheless, annual pilgrimages are made to the shrine here and it is a desired final resting place for devout Moslems.

As you turn left onto the Jericho highway, you'll see adobe shacks lining both sides of the road. These semi-deserted refugee camps for Palestinians displaced by the wars and those on the other side of town are stark reminders that you are in the West Bank. Where the people in the camps will live now that Jericho is under Palestinian administration remains to be seen. When visiting the West Bank, stick to the main roads and stay abreast of the current political situation.

Jericho today, a fair-sized sprawling town that is home to eight thousand Arab inhabitants, does not have much to offer the visitor, and its past glory is its present attraction. As you enter Jericho (on Route 90) the bustle of small-town traffic envelops you.

Soon you're in the downtown district and the scents, the sights, and the colors assault your senses. Fruit and vegetable stalls display artistically arranged eggplants, cauliflower, cabbages, and tomatoes. Enormous mangoes and oranges are stacked in pyramid formation; dates and bananas hang in profusion from the fruitsellers' stands.

This is a traditional Arab town, and the veiled women who scurry by may cast curious glances at you. This bountiful street is called Jaffa, and you are in the Baladiya (Main Square) when you reach the busy intersection. There are some enticing things to buy in Jericho—the hand-woven baskets and small rugs beckon from makeshift stalls and more solid retail establishments. Walk around the town for a time and don't forget to buy some fruit. You'll appreciate having it later in the day. *Tel Jericho*, the mound marking the biblical city, the *Mount of Temptation*, and the other archeological sites you have come to visit are just north of the modern town. English signs point the way.

Lunch Choices

The *Mount of Temptation Restaurant* near Tel Jericho is a good stop for lunch or a soft drink. Other bright, cheerful places marked by striped awnings and hanging plants are in the strip between Jericho and Tel Jericho. The *Seven Trees, Youni's* and *The Green Valley Cafeteria* all serve Middle Eastern cuisine, and because these are Arab kitchens the spicing is a tad different.

Jericho Sights

Archeologists have never ceased to be intrigued by the lore and history of the place where "Joshua fit the battle." Jericho's history is impressive. It was an important Canaanite town in 3000 B.C., when Joshua and the Israelites destroyed it. In later years, it became the property of the Ptolemies and, in fact, Mark Antony presented the town to Cleopatra as a gift. She subsequently sold it to King Herod the Great, who built his winter palace here and died in it in 4 B.C.

Christ's presence was felt here, and in the Christian Era Jericho served as the seat of the Episcopalian See. It was stormed by the Crusaders, who abandoned it, and the unceasing years of Arab habitation began.

Tel Jericho

Biblical Jericho lies near the ***Jebel Qarantal***, called the Mount of Temptation, and here Jesus sequestered himself for forty days and withstood the devil's temptation to break his fast and weaken his faith. The mountain, which rises 1,130 feet above Jericho, has at its top Hasmonean and Frankish ruins, in addition to a Greek chapel, silently attesting to the diverse people who were drawn to this spot. Nearby, you will see Elisha's Fountain. It was here that the prophet Elisha, when told of the water's acrid taste, caused it to become sweet. The waters of Jericho have been sweet ever since. Note: Do not attempt to reach the Greek Orthodox monastery from the road here. This is a hiking trail. Instead return to Tel Jericho and follow road signs to ***Ramallah***, where you'll see the proper turnoff.

The excavations carried on in Tel Jericho (which is an enormous mound) over the last eighty years have revealed remnants of a Canaanite city and its walls, bronzes, primitive flint tools, and little else. In a country where stunning archeological sites are commonplace, Tel Jericho is a disappointment. Jericho's most interesting site, a fabulous ruined palace, is a mile northeast of Tel Jericho and is of Arab origin.

Hisham's Palace

Tel El Mafja, or *Hisham's Palace*, was the winter residence of
the Caliph Hisham in the eighth century. Much of the palace has
been carted off to the Rockefeller Museum in East Jerusalem and,
in fact, you can appreciate what the palace looked like by viewing
the totally reconstructed room on permanent display at the museum. However, much that is notable remains at the original site;
pay particular attention to the mosaics found on the floors of
various rooms that have survived surprisingly well over the
centuries (due to the dry desert air). They depict pastoral scenes
and stunning geometric patterns that are reminiscent of fabrics
used by today's best decorators. Pillars and columns of various
styles represent the interrelationship of different cultures and reveal the fact that Jericho was probably a very cosmopolitan city
where artistic innovations from other parts of the world were
adopted and used. You will see traces of Byzantine, Hellenistic,
Arabic, and Roman architectural styles. The grand walls decorated with stucco arabesques and the six-pointed star (it looks
a bit like the Star of David) give a Moorish feeling to the palace
and foreshadow the palaces of Alhambra and Granada to a de-
gree. Part of the National Park System, Hisham's Palace is open
10 A.M. to 5 P.M. daily, 10 A.M. to 2 P.M. Fridays.

Ancient Synagogues

Jericho's synagogues form an important link with the past. Several important ancient synagogues are located in the area between Elisha's Fountain and Hisham's Palace (a narrow road
swerves to the right coming from Tel Jericho). You will see an
Arab house that was built atop a synagogue. Below, on the lower
level, an intricate menorah and the words *Shalom Ak Israel*, or
"Peace upon Israel," can be seen. There is another example of
mosaic work on the floor of the *Noara Synagogue*, but the
main part of the floor, *Daniel in the Lion's Den*, is on display at
the Rockefeller Museum.

Retrace your route through Jericho until you reach Route 90.
Turning south, you continue to descend to the shores of the
Dead Sea, which is a strange, artificial-looking aquamarine blue.

It won't be long (twenty kilometers) before you reach Qumran and the caves that held the Dead Sea Scrolls.

Qumran

Qumran is the beginning of an intensely personal experience for most travelers. This area was first settled in the eighth century B.C. and then remained deserted for a long time after. This desolate area stands as a paean to idealism, scholarship, and single-minded devotion. The abandoned settlement, once the site of an ancient religious community, overlooks the northwestern shore of the Dead Sea, and from here—in the haze of the desert—one can still see for miles in all directions. The thoroughly excavated building complex at Qumran is called the monastery; this main building is thought to have been built some time around the first century B.C. by an all-male monastic order of ascetics called the Essenes. These men were fundamentalist Jews who were opposed to the direction Judaism was taking in the religious centers of what was then Judea. It is speculated that John the Baptist and Jesus himself ascribed to the philosophy of the Essenes, who occupied their time with manual labor and the study of the Torah. Marriage was prohibited to them, and accepted practices of the time, like animal sacrifices and slavery, were strictly taboo. Coins found in the area have been immeasurably helpful to archeologists in charting Qumran's history. Activity is this area seems to have taken place from 140 B.C. to A.D. 67.

Some of the other important structures at Qumran include a scriptorium (writer's room), the remains of small shelters, potters' workshops, ritual baths or *mikveh*, and a large cemetery. There are numbered plaques on each of these structures which bear full explanations of what you are seeing. The monks of Qumran survived due to a remarkable water-supply system that collected floodwater from the little rain that fell each year.

The small community here was vanquished by the Roman troops in the years A.D. 60–67. Fortunately, some of the members of the sect hid the Sacred Scrolls (found in 1947) in large clay jars in the nearby caves—and today, as a result of their foresight, civilization can better understand itself. The two Bedouins who inadvertently happened upon the scrolls while searching for wayward goats knew they had something when they spotted the cylindrical jars (forty to sixty of them) in the caves. The jars contained scrolls made of parchment and sewn together with linen thread. Among these priceless documents (many of them are wonderfully displayed in Jerusalem's Shrine of the Book) are a twenty-three-foot-long and twenty-five-inch-high complete manuscript of Isaiah and the Book of Discipline. Most of the scrolls are dated from the beginning of the Christian Era and the destruction of the Temple by the Romans in A.D. 70. Qumran and its caves have yielded some of the most tangible historic evidence of the Jewish faith in practice.

Qumran, part of the National Park System, is open from 8 A.M. to 4 P.M., with a 3 P.M. closing on Friday and holiday evenings. There is a moderate entrance fee.

On to En Gedi

Continue south along Route 90, which parallels the Dead Sea for much of the time. There is little to interrupt the hush around you until you reach the oasis *En Feshkha (Einot Zukim)*, which has become a popular weekend beach destination for landlocked Jerusalemites. You do not swim in the Dead Sea, but rather in two pools of springwater right near the shore. Changing rooms and a snack bar are available at a modest fee.

Just beyond the beach you'll see the sign to *Mitzpe Shalem Kibbutz*. The paved road to the kibbutz (six kilometers) climbs all the way; along its circuitous path are numerous observation points and photo opportunities. The road is too narrow to permit U-turns, so you'll have to go all the way up to the kibbutz, which is very special. You'll learn more about Mitzpe Shalem and its Metzoke Dragot Climbing School later in the chapter.

Perhaps because of the heat and the fact that you've spent much of the day exploring dusty ruins surrounded by brown craggy mountains and eerie unpotable water, the forty-five kilometers from Qumran to En Gedi seem to take forever. By the time the Sodom green apple trees and date palms of this oasis come into view, you'll have an unquenchable thirst and great empathy for those who wandered through this desert with Moses for forty years.

En Gedi Oasis

En Gedi is as old as time. Its history dates back to about 3000 B.C. —the Chalcolithic Age. The biblical references to this lush and fertile spot are numerous. King Solomon rhapsodized over the fragrant flowers, spices, and flowing streams of En Gedi in his Song of Songs. King David sought refuge here from Saul, and successive civilizations (including the Byzantines) and various nomadic cultures inhabited En Gedi as far back as six thousand years ago. Evidence of these inhabitants has been found in and around the canyons and caves of En Gedi. Coins, tools, and a fourth-century synagogue with a fine mosaic floor have been discovered here. En Gedi is long-famous for the abundant fruit that grows here year-round: dates, melons, tomatoes, cucumbers, and grapes. It was also a center for the production of balsam, a highly prized aromatic substance used for cosmetic and medicinal purposes.

The development of the En Gedi Oasis area is due to the work of the kibbutz nearby. There is the kibbutz guest house, a beach area, a gas station, and a spa. It all began in 1949, when the kibbutz was established as a *nahal* (defense) outpost near Israel's pre-1967 border with Jordan. Needless to say, rooms were easily obtainable then, but since 1967 the guest house has been enlarged to accommodate the ever-increasing demands for space.

EN GEDI KIBBUTZ 3★

Mobile Post, Dead Sea 86980   Phone (057) 584757

This 120-room kibbutz guest house offers accommodations in rustic one-story cottages (two families per unit) surrounded by lawns, flowers, and plants. The double rooms here are fully air-conditioned and heated and have showers and hot plates. Meals are served family-style and guests are expected to maintain their own rooms. (Supplies upon request.) Your rate includes three meals and daily transport to the nearby spa, if you choose. There is a swimming pool, and on-site activities include miniature golf, tennis, basketball, and organized field trips into the desert and to Massada. Reserve here will in advance. *Expensive.*

At this point you'll want a change of pace, a break in this day of travel and history-rich sightseeing, and nature has provided it for you at the ***En Gedi Nature Reserve***. Look for the sign that reads *David's Spring* just before the gas station. Here you can relax, kick off your shoes, and take a refreshing shower in the spring, where the water drops from three hundred feet, sparkling clear and delightfully cold. Of course, you'll have to hike to reach it, but the path is lined with pine and palm trees, hanging vines, and multicolored wildflowers.

Tip: Bring a bathing suit and change at the snack shop.

As you climb the marked path which crosses the stream at several points, you'll encounter some sharp and steep twists and turns. Certain places are covered with palm fronds, causing the walkway to become slimy and sometimes slippery, so be careful. You'll be rewarded with glimpses of wildlife—spectacular birds, goats, even an ibex if you're lucky. The sign at the entrance warns you to beware of leopards, but the chances of even spotting one are pretty slim. It will take you about a half hour to reach the cascading falls and the cool sweetwater pool at its base. The green vegetation here seemingly clings to the rock face, and this hollowed-out niche is a water sprite's playground. The large flattopped stones in the pool are often obscured by smart hikers who wear bathing suits under their clothes and strip down for a dip—it's an enchanting place to cool off.

Serious hikers can follow other marked trails, some short and some extended, through the reserve to other waterfalls, hidden caves, and ancient Chalcolithic ruins. The En Gedi field school has information about these trails. Part of the National Park System, En Gedi Reserve is open from 9 A.M. to 5 P.M. daily. There is even a hostel and a camping site nearby if you want to be one with the environment.

En Gedi Hot Springs

The spa at En Gedi offers a variety of programs with an emphasis on the therapeutic qualities of the Dead Sea and the Hot Springs, which are helpful in the treatment of respiratory, muscular, and joint ailments, as well as problems with psoriasis and blood circulation. There is a pool and a restaurant as well. These Hot Springs are located two miles south of the En Gedi Beach area.

Massada

Leaving the green world of En Gedi, you will reenter the scorched Judean Desert and approach the tragic and dramatic phenomenon that is Massada.

If you find yourself tiring at this point, continue on to En Boqeq and visit Massada in the morning before continuing your journey.

Massada is only eight miles to the south of En Gedi, but as soon as you have identified this red-hued cliff with the flat top as the one and only Massada, or *metzuda* (fortress), the last stronghold of the Jews against the Roman invaders, history and legend sweep you up and you are eerily compelled to reconstruct the past.

The story of Massada is thrilling and awesome. It is inspirational yet disturbing, but it lives and breathes and few Israelis or thoughtful travelers can help but feel the power of this place. The early history of this stony citadel has been traced back to Judah and Jonathan, two of the Maccabees who rebelled against the Greeks. Years later, it was Herod's hiding place, the place where he installed his family and entourage to protect them from his enemies. When the mighty Herod became king, he began to build the structures, the remains of which can still be seen today. Herod died, but the Roman threat did not, and a group of Jewish religionists, called Zealots, took hold of the city of Jerusalem. When that city fell, the Zealots knew their time was running out and they fled to Massada in order to protect themselves and to repel the advancing Roman hordes. The Roman soldiers did not lack persistence; for a year they attempted to seize Massada. Finally, on the night of the Jewish Passover in A.D. 73, the 967 men, women, and children under the leadership of Eleazar Ben Ya'ir realized the fate that awaited them. The Romans had set their formerly impenetrable walls on fire, and the flames were spreading uncontrollably inward.

The Zealots could not see themselves under the yoke of the Romans, living in slavery, forced to abandon their self-respect and their sustaining belief in one God. The decision was taken. When the Romans entered the smoldering settlement, not a soul was left alive, save for two women and five children who lived to tell the tale. According to the Jewish historian Josephus Flavius, each man was to slay his own family, thereupon ten men were chosen to kill the other men, and of these final ten, one was chosen to slay the nine who remained and then to put the sword through his own heart. It was a gruesome scene that confronted the eyes of the Roman soldiers. By the second century A.D., the awful events at Massada were shrouded and forgotten. The fortress was abandoned and remained so until the fifth century, when some Christian monks rediscovered the cliff fortress and built a monastery at the summit, as well as a Byzantine church with a mosaic floor that exists today. The events that colored Massada entered the realm of folklore. No one really knew where this place was or if the story was fiction to begin with. Providentially, the spot where the horrible drama was played out was identified in 1838 by a Christian missionary. In the course of time, other explorers and travelers verified Massada's existence, and finally, through the efforts of Professor Yigael Yadin and Shemaria Gutman, with the help of thousands of volunteers and the Israeli army, a two-year excavation (1963–1965) proved successful. Massada came to life as the remnants of a poignant reality were pieced together.

The palace, the Zealots' houses, sacred scrolls, and many other treasures were uncovered. Today, a trip to Israel without having seen the Massada is truly a loss—because it is here that country's raison d'être is most painfully apparent.

Sites at Massada

One can spend an hour at Massada and manage to see everything, but to really feel Massada, a careful and thorough visit to the site is recommended. Two hours are usually sufficient for most people to experience the place, but others spend far more time. Proceeding clockwise from the western gate, there are certain structures that are very affecting; the synagogue and the Byzantine church, the northern palace and the store rooms, and the ritual baths *(mikvehs)* are of particular interest. Make sure you descend to all three levels of Herod's cliff-hanging palace. The lower section is a thrill to behold, as you stand on the wind-swept precipice of sheer rock, with the vast desert and the treacherous ravines looming in front and behind you and the grandiose ruins of a power-hungry king all around you. The synagogue at Massada is the oldest one in existence so far. There are well-preserved frescoes and mosaics at the site. Large cisterns and storage rooms contained the precious water and food staples that kept the community alive, and the tiny dwellings and ritual baths of the Zealots tell their own story of sacrifice and humility.

Getting to the Peak

At soon as you reach the base of the cliff, you'll see a phalanx of tourist buses, the cable-car station, and several snack and gift shops. These gift shops sell a lot of Massada-related souvenirs, including the best-selling "I Climbed Massada" T-shirts. The colorful cars, which hold about forty people, zip you to the top in under five minutes, but you'll wish it took a bit longer, for the views of the surrounding area are simply breathtaking. The cable-car schedule calls for one every half hour, but the cars actually run when there is a group waiting and can thus run every few minutes. The first car up leaves at 8 A.M. and the final car makes the ascent at 4 P.M. (2 P.M. on Fridays). It is advisable to go early in the day or in late afternoon, to wear sunglasses or a hat and very comfortable shoes (not sandals), and to drink as much water as possible before your visit.

You can also walk to the peak, and lots of purists (young, hardy types) insist it is the only way to go. There are two paths. The more popular one, which leads from this cable-car station (the other is near the town of Arad), is known as the Snake Path, more for the way it snakes up the mountain than for the reptiles on it. This path opens at 7:30 A.M. and closes at 3:30 P.M. Your fitness will determine the length of time required, but a general consensus was that one and a half hours was the minimum time for the uphill climb. Bring a canteen. The Arad Path, or the Battery (for the Roman battery that was built there), is easier to climb. By the way, there is a fee for using either path, and there is an entrance fee as well. However you arrive at the summit (the cable car puts you at the eastern gate), buy Yigael Yadin's booklet, which will serve as your tour guide around the ruins. There is also an exhibit of things found during the excavations at the Metzada Museum on the Snake Path (Dead Sea side) but it is open only by request of a tour guide. Massada phone (057) 584207.

Now that you have explored the most important sights in the Dead Sea region, you will undoubtedly be ready for the En Boqeq hotel area, where you can look forward to a peaceful respite and, if you are so inclined, first-rate spa facilities.

Before discussing the En Boqeq spa hotels, some background on the Dead Sea itself is in order.

Dead Sea/En Boqeq

The Dead Sea has figured briefly in everyone's fifth-grade geography class. It was that notorious body of water (a lake, in fact) that festered at 398 meters below sea level. It's still down there, and it is so salty that life cannot be sustained in its briny water. The Dead Sea story sounds pretty grim, but there is new life on the shores of this sea in the form of fine spa-hotel resorts that are filled with tourists who come for a "cure" or just a little rest and relaxation.

Geographically, the Dead Sea is seventy-six kilometers long and 14 kilometers at its widest point. To the west of the Dead Sea are the Judean Hills, and to the east the Moab mountain range slices the horizon. The southern section of the Dead Sea (it is divided by the Lashon peninsula—*lashon* means "tongue") is quite shallow now, due to the excessive drainage caused by the numerous chemical plants that operate on the shore. The northern part is much deeper. The Dead Sea has fired people's imaginations for obvious reasons throughout the centuries. It is the lowest point in the world, it is 30 percent salt and contains the highest mineral content anywhere, its water is a shocking shade of blue, and it sits in the middle of the most desolate place on the planet. The sea has had many names in its time. Israelis call it *Yam*

Ha-Melah, or Salt Sea. It has been called the Sea of Sodom, the Arava Sea, Sea of Zo'Ar, and Bahr Lut, or the Sea of Lot, by the Arabs. The Dead Sea's exploitation began in the 1930s with the first desalinization plants and chemical works mining the rich assortment of minerals from the water. It was around this time that its future as a resort area, specializing in the treatment of skin and respiratory ailments, became a reality. Today, En Boqeq is a major tourist center, not for its waters alone, but also for the historical sights that are only a short distance away.

Hotels

The special programs offered at the Dead Sea's finer hotels take full advantage of the mineral-rich water, acknowledged by doctors and laymen to help cure a multitude of medical problems. You need not suffer from psoriasis, rheumatism, or arthritis to benefit from the restorative qualities associated with the Dead Sea. (These diseases have, however, been treated at a marvelous rate of success.) The bromide-rich water contains 10 to 15 percent more oxygen, and this, say the medical experts, is calming to the nerves and a natural tension-reliever.

Legends have a way of becoming big business, and the Dead Sea cosmetics and cleansers, marketed under several brand names, love to remind you of the fact that immortal beauties like Cleopatra cleansed their lovely limbs and smoothed their furrowed brows with this oily seawater and the gooey black mud from the seabed.

The Dead Sea climate is ideal. It is virtually rainless and although the temperature can vary from a low of 51°F in January to as high as 102°F in August, it is always dry—so the heat is never disturbing. The high air pressure limits the influence of the sun's ultraviolet rays, which means you will get a great tan without sunburn. The Dead Sea has a pervading mystery about it that a profusion of hotels and tourists cannot strip away. Everything and everyone accommodates itself around the sea—and that includes the activities in the region. It's unique, really; there is nowhere to go outside of the hotels for shopping, nightlife, etc. So, let's take a look at the hotels.

Hotel Generalities

High season at the Dead Sea usually refers to the periods between April 1 and May 31 and October 1 and November 30. Rates are higher at those times, but check with the individual hotel, for these dates do vary a bit. Hotels here do not have restaurants per se, although they may have lounge areas where light food is served. Instead they have dining rooms where three meals a day are served, family-style, with fixed menus that are posted in the lobby. Most guests take half or full board. Until recently you had no other option, for there were no restaurants anywhere in the area. There is one now, however, and we do suggest that you eat breakfast at your hotel and any other meals at the delightful *Kapulsky*.

En Boqeq Hotels

THE MORIAH DEAD SEA SPA HOTEL 5★

Sedom 86910   Phone (057) 584221/24
Fax (057) 584238
Major Credit Cards

This was first five-star hotel-spa at the Dead Sea, and it carries on a tradition of excellence. The hotel is right on the beach, permitting the facilities of an on-site luxury spa to do its good work directly on the water. The resort, home to the Moriah Dead Sea Spa Health and Beauty Center, has mineral pools, mud packs, dry and underwater massage, vapor inhalation, cosmeticians, and a physiotherapist. Personal supervision makes this the ultimate place to pamper yourself. This attractive hotel sits imposingly on its own private beach, and all rooms have private balconies. A promenade and running path link the Moriah to the En Boqeq area. *Deluxe*

NIRVANA RESORT & SPA 5★

Mobile Post, Dead Sea   Phone (057) 584626
Fax (057) 584345
Major Credit Cards

The name says it all. The Nirvana provides world-class five-star luxury, taking full advantage of the unique spa treatments afforded by its Dead Sea location. Spa treatments include mineral-rich mud packs, hydrotherapy, thalassotherapy, and aromatic and therapeutic baths featuring Dead Sea water or water from a nearby sulphur spring. Medical check-ups and diet and nutrition consultations are also available. The Nirvana boasts a private beach, sweetwater pool, fitness centers, fine dining, plenty of evening entertainment, and children's activities. *Expensive*.

THE MORIAH GARDENS HOTEL 4★

Mobile Post, Dead Sea 86939 Israel   Phone (057) 584351
Fax (057) 584238
Major Credit Cards

The Moriah Hotel is also on the Dead Sea shore—but it's closer to the other hotels in the En Boqeq area. It deserves its four stars. The well-kept grounds, bright lobby, and lounge area are comfortable; there's a coffee shop, a dining room, and a discotheque in the hotel; all rooms have bath and shower, radio, TV, video, direct-dial telephones, and air conditioning. There are special facilities and guest rooms for the disabled. An outdoor sweetwater pool, solarium, and psoriasis treatment center and an indoor health club featuring heated Dead Sea water, Jacuzzi, and massage make this hotel an excellent choice. Special events include barbecue evenings at poolside, and a pianist entertains daily from 6 A.M. to 12 P.M. in the lobby. The bar is open from 10 A.M. to midnight. *Expensive*.

THE GALEI ZOHAR 4★

Dead Sea   Phone (057) 584311
Fax (057) 584503
Credit Cards

This four-star hotel has an extensive array of facilities for guests' benefit. The hotel will arrange sightseeing tours for you and will even pick you up from Ben Gurion Airport. There are two medical clinics on the premises, specializing in dermatological and rheumatic/arthritic treatment (with professional medical supervision at all times). The Zohar and En Gedi thermomineral springs are fully utilized for treatment. Facilities at the hotel include a fully equipped health spa, a Dead Sea water pool, a rooftop solarium, massages, mud packs, a cosmetic treatment center, a disco and piano bar, a game room, a coffee shop, and a shopping mall with mini-market, beauty salon, barbershop, and coin-operated laundry. *Expensive*.

THE HOD HOTEL 4*

En Boqeq

Phone (057) 84664
Fax (057) 84606
Major Credit Cards

The region's newest four-star hotel, the Hod has a private beach, a sweetwater swimming pool, a health spa featuring a large indoor pool (filled with water from the Dead Sea), a fine restaurant, a nightclub, and activities for the kids. Its 204 rooms and 14 suites are tastefully furnished. All have color TV, radio, and private bath, and are, of course, air-conditioned. *Expensive*.

EN BOQEQ HOTEL 4*

Mobile Post,
Dead Sea 86930

Phone (057) 584331-4
Fax (057) 584162
No Credit Cards

The En Boqeq is a modest four-star hotel. Its ninety-seven rooms are all air-conditioned and have baths and showers. The pool and garden are visible from the large, light-filled lobby; a comfortable and roomy video room often shows first-rate movies. *Moderate*.

THE LOT HOTEL—DEAD SEA 4*

En Boqeq 86930

Phone (057) 584321-4
Fax (057) 584623
Major Credit Cards

The Lot Hotel is on the beach and has a large pool, gift shop, TV, video room, bar and restaurant, discotheque, and plenty of comfort at reasonable cost. All two hundred rooms are air-conditioned and nicely furnished. *Moderate*.

TSELL HARIM HOTEL 3*

En Boqeq, Sedom

Phone (057) 584121
Fax (057) 584666
Major Credit Cards

This fairly new hotel has a pool, and all 184 rooms have private balconies. The hotel has a large dining area and lobby lounge, and many evening activities are planned for guests, including movies and dancing. *Moderate*.

Dining

Don't expect to discover any cute out-of-the way restaurants in this part of the world. En Boqeq has two small informal eateries —both overlooking the beach. To avoid the family-style meal service in your hotel dining room, head to Kapulsky's, near the Galei Zahar Hotel. Part of the nationwide chain of dairy restaurants, Kapulsky's serves sumptuous salads, terrific sandwiches, hot soups, and rich pastries. A short walk will bring you to Hordus Beach, which has a self-service restaurant (dairy) and a vast salad bar.

Shops and Nightlife

The En Boqeq Center, a one-level shopping arcade, has half a dozen shops selling beachware, foods for take-out, and jewelry. The local IGTO is here too. Hours are 11 A.M. to 1 P.M. and 4 P.M. to 6 P.M. daily; 11 A.M. to 1 P.M. only on Friday and Sunday. (Closed Saturday.)

My Pub is a local evening hangout. Most of the clientele work at nearby hotels. It features drinks, finger foods, and piped music.

Spas at En Boqeq

The *Hamei Zohar Thermal Baths* are situated beyond the Moriah Hotel. The admission charge allows you to use the beach and to swim in the open-air sulphur pool. You can purchase the medicinal mud and rent bathing suits and reclining chairs. There are rest rooms, showers, and a snack bar on the premises.

Nearby is the *Kupat Holim Hamei Zohar*. This is a spa with medical bathing facilities, sulphur pools, rest rooms, and showers. There is an admission fee. The telephone number is (057) 84161. Another treatment center has opened nearby at Hordus Beach.

Swimming in the Dead Sea

Actually, *floating* is the more correct term, for the water is so dense it actually feels thick and it is hardly refreshing. You have to wade out quite a distance to get to waist-high water level, and the catch is that the bottom has lots of sharp stones. The water leaves an oily residue on your skin, which aficionados leave on till they shower for dinner but I shower off immediately. It is very good for your skin, but it can sting your eyes and tastes bitter, so keep your mouth closed. The facial mask using Dead Sea mud did leave my skin, which had gotten dry from all the sun I was in, feeling very soft and smooth. If at this point you are wondering why you should venture into this rocky, oily, bitter lake, it's because it is fun. You simply cannot sink! You'll have a ball bobbing up and down on the water like an apple on Halloween, and it's an experience that you cannot have anywhere else. Bring your camera.

Metzoke Dragot Desert Tour Village

Just south of the En Gedi Oasis a sign reads "Mitzpe Shalem Kibbutz Desert Tours." We couldn't pass that up and assumed that the village would be just off the road. Six kilometers later, all of them uphill, we spotted a few scraggly trees and a miniature village. This desert settlement was started by young Israelis who had explored the Sinai Desert when it was in Israeli hands. When it was returned to Egypt, they transferred their ambition to an exploration of the Judean and Negev Deserts, and established the kibbutz so they could share their expertise with people who had similar interests.

Their most popular tour, A Desert Safari, lasts for a week and is offered once a month. It includes visits to Bedouin camps, hidden monasteries (including Mar Saba, which women may not enter), and isolated caves. The high point of the safari is rappeling down a Negev cliff. You will be given an intensive course in rappeling as part of the safari, and the hosts assured me it was not as hard or dangerous as it looks. Rappeling practice includes trial trips down mini-cliffs until you feel comfortable, but if you don't care for this part of the safari you can watch the others. Rappeling is the technique of going *down* a sheer cliff, using a rope, rather than scaling it. Metzoke Dragot rumbles through the

desert in specially constructed open-sided trucks, and if you are
game you can have the adventure of your life. Two- and three-day
tours are also offered by Metzoke Dragot and by the En Gedi
Kibbutz Field School and the Israeli Nature Protection Society.
For more details write: *Metzoke Dragot*, Kibbutz Mitzpe Shalem,
Mobile Post Dead Sea; *Israel Society for the Protection of
Nature*, 3 Hashfela Street, Tel Aviv, Israel; *En Gedi Field School*,
Mobile Post Dead Sea, Israel 84757.

Just five miles from En Boqeq, the town of *Newe Zohar* has a
gas station and the *Bet Hayotzer Museum*, which explains various
Dead Sea industries. Hours are 9 A.M. to 12:30 P.M. and 1:30 P.M. to
5 P.M. daily. Admission is free.

As you continue south on Route 90 to Elat, you will pass
Sodom. Sodom's reputation is far more sordid than its present
reality. In fact, it has no present—its days of wantonness and sin
are entombed in legend, albeit a legend that is eternally fascinating. Strange and fantastic formations of salt surround you—but
in Lot's day, legend has it, this area was green and fertile.

Sodom is a derivation of the word *Sidim*, which means
"devils"—an apt name for a town where wickedness was commonplace. If you've forgotten the story—Abraham's nephew Lot
and his family were given a chance to save themselves from im-
pending destruction. God ordered them to leave Sodom and not
to look back at the shameless city. Lot's wife's curiosity overcame
her—she looked back and immediately became petrified into a
pillar of salt. Look for her at the peak of Mount Sodom, where
her anthropomorphic form can be discerned. There are old salt
quarries in the canyons of Sodom that are worth investigating.

Public Transportation to the Dead Sea

You can reach En Gedi and En Boqeq by bus from Jerusalem,
Beersheba, and Tel Aviv. Check at Egged for schedules. Getting
from one spot in the area to another is the big problem; there are
no buses or taxis.

Decisions! Decisions!

From the Dead Sea region, you can continue along the coastal
road (Route 90) to Elat, at Israel's southern tip (two and a half

hours). Or, you can turn inland at Newe Zohar and head to Beersheba, passing through the town of Arad. The primary reason for visiting Beersheba is a stop at the Bedouin market, which is in full swing by 6 A.M. every Thursday and is dying out by noon. You should consider this when planning your trip. We prefer to follow Route 90 to Elat, for it is an easy drive, but we always return to Beersheba along the older, inland Route 40. If you decide to drive to Elat and to fly back to Tel Aviv or Jerusalem, by all means take Route 40 now and spend some time at Avdat, En Avdat, Sde Boqer, and Mitzpe Ramon. We will detail that exciting trip after the Elat chapter.

For Those Headed to Beersheba

Arad

The road from Newe Zohar passes the planned city **Arad**, which is very clean and attractive. It does not have much to interest you, however, except for the tel nearby. If you are passing here, by all means stop for a while and walk through the town, If you are not on this road, there is no reason to detour to Arad. It's a seventeen-mile drive from the Dead Sea to Arad on the Sodom-Arad road, which continuously ascends from its point below sea level and winds its way through the rocky Judean wilderness, and finally reaches a plateau where some signs of life become apparent. In a matter of minutes, you will be in Arad. This pleasant and well-planned city is surprisingly modern—it looks as though it belongs in the American Southwest. Arad is known for its pure air and, as a result, is a popular vacation spot for asthma sufferers. Founded in 1961, it now houses ten thousand people, most of whom work at the Dead Sea chemical plants.

Tel Arad is ten kilometers west. Biblical Arad was a Canaanite kingdom, later conquered by Joshua and settled by the Kenites. Captured by Egypt, rebuilt by the Persians, it was then rediscovered by the Romans. Archeologists date Arad's beginning during the Chalcolithic Age (about five thousand years ago). The excavation site is open from October through March from 8 A.M.

to 4 P.M.; the rest of the year, it remains open until 5 P.M. There is an entrance fee.

It's only a forty-five minute ride from Arad to Beersheba. Watch closely here; you will notice the landscape changing from arid and parched to wide open spaces with fields of rippling yellow grasses. For a moment, you'll think you're in Kansas.

The Bedouins start appearing slowly at first, their tents giving way to corrugated tin houses. Then you'll see shepherds with herds of sheep and goats; the lone Bedouin woman and child on a donkey; loping camels that form noble outlines on the sky—you are approaching Beersheba, the heart of the Negev.

Eilat/ Elat

s you drive mile after mile through the Negev, with hills that look like cones of vanilla fudge ice cream looming up on all sides and an awesome stillness in the air, the realization strikes you that Elat is far removed geographically from the rest of Israel. After you've been in the city for a short while, you'll realize that Elat is far removed from the rest of Israel in lifestyle as well. It seems that the geographical barrier of dune and desert that isolates Elat from the rest of Israel physically does so too in terms of tradition. Elat's lifestyle is extremely casual and easygoing (the average age of an Elati is 26), and the city's secular, international flavor appeals to Israelis and Europeans who come with carefree fun on their minds.

Elat offers a vast number of activities that involve the sea, but if your idea of a vacation is lots of suntan oil, an engrossing mystery, and a tall, cool drink, you can relax and enjoy. Blessed with a perfect climate, a sea rich in marine life, and fantastic coral reefs unsurpassed anywhere in the world, Elat will be a liquid Paradise to the person who takes water sports seriously.

Elat will also make a perfect base for desert explorations (of both Arava and Sinai) on horseback, by camel, or by jeep. King Solomon's mines, unusual biblical animals, and a rare bird sanctuary are all within easy reach of the city.

Elat is like a precocious youngster. When a dispute arose regarding the switch to daylight savings time and its start was postponed for several weeks, Elat went right ahead and declared its own daylight savings time. For one month it functioned one hour ahead of the rest of Israel. You can't help but admire Elat's brash spirit of independence.

As you travel through Israel, a neutrality of color envelops you. The silver-green of olive trees, glints of dull gold from the dome of a mosque, and the pale pink of Jerusalem limestone remain in the mind's eye. Red is the color of Elat. The absolutely gorgeous sunsets really seem to turn the waters red and red is the color of the hills on which Elat is perched. Astride these hills, which look like an infinite number of pennies crushed into mounds by a master hand billions of years ago, sits a city that is relaxed, vivacious, and "red-hot."

Orientation

When Route 90 nears the city limits, it becomes Derech Ha'Arava (Arava Road). This main street, which runs directly to the Red Sea before skirting it on its way to Coral Beach and Egypt, acts as a demarcation point for you. To your right as you enter is the town itself, built on gently rolling hills which retreat from the sea. At the core of this downtown area are three commercial centers in which scores of restaurants, shops, and city services operate. These centers, on the town's main streets, are the beachfront multilevel **New Tourist Center** on Derekh Yotam and the **Rechter** and **Shalom Centers** on Hatmarim Boulevard. The Egged Bus Station and the local IGTO are here as well. To the left of Arava Road, you'll see the local airport and beyond it **North Beach**, Elat's major hotel and beach area.

A stunning horseshoe-shaped lagoon has been constructed in this area, doubling the space for hotels, which was actually quite limited. The lagoon functions as a marina, and a delightful arched footpath leads from one shore to the other. The dazzling city you see in the distance is Aqaba, Jordan.

Arava Road wends its way out of town, bypasses the city's modern port facilities, and brings you to Elat's other beach strip, **Coral Beach**, a border of thick white sand that forms the western shore of the gulf.

Coral Beach, a resort unto itself, draws a younger, somewhat less affluent crowd. Club Med has a village here, and there are a few hotels, very good restaurants, and the famed coral reef. Part of the beach strip here is for topless bathers. At the far end of

Coral Beach you'll see the border control kiosk for those crossing into Egypt, and just beyond it the tiny disputed sand strip, **Taba**. The stunning Elat Princess Hotel is on Taba just before the border.

Some General Information

In years past many Israeli families spent winter vacations in Tiberias. Now their children head to Elat for long weekends or extended midwinter vacations. Europeans, particularly Germans and Scandinavians, have also discovered Elat as a winter hideaway. Hotel space is very tight from November through April and prices rise about 20 percent. Weekend space is tight year round, for many Israelis arrive on Thursday evening and leave on Sunday. Elat can get very hot in the summer, with temperatures exceeding 110F. But the sea remains refreshingly cool, all hotels and restaurants are air-conditioned, and it gets far cooler in the evening. If you are planning a midwinter trip to Elat, reserve far in advance.

Elat has a large number of hotels and restaurants solely because it is a resort area. It is actually a very small city and the downtown area consists of only a dozen square blocks.

And now to bed down.

Hotels

Elat has a great many hotels for a town its size, and since occupancy rates here are high year round, many more are under construction. Most are resort-style establishments with swimming pools, shopping arcades, and planned activities. Your best bet is to stay at one of the hotels on North Beach and around the lagoon. A stop here puts you near the action-oriented public beach, the town center, and the local airport. North Beach is the center of activity in Elat. Because the hotels are so close to one another, it's easy to check out the goings-on at a neighboring hotel. It's a matter of a few minutes walk.

As we've noted previously, many Israelis and European visitors eat in hotel dining rooms. Again, we urge you to eat only breakfast in your hotel (if it is included in your rate). There are lots of eateries nearby. The King Solomon and Elat Princess Hotels have terrific restaurants on the premises that operate independently of the dining room. Coral Beach, a smaller beach area about five miles away, has a few choice hotels, fine swimming, and water activities and excellent restaurants. Several new hotels have opened on the beach between Coral Beach and the Taba border crossing. They are a ten-minute ride from the center of town. Those are your option—all delightful ones.

Note: All hotels in Elat accept major credit cards.

North Beach

KING SOLOMON'S PALACE HOTEL 5★

North Beach, Elat 88106   Phone (07) 334111
                                             Fax (07) 379589

Shining like a bauble on the beach, the 419-room King Solomon, built in 1984, dominates and sets the tone for the North Beach area. Its King's Wharf promenade is the center of attention at night, housing several good restaurants, a lively pub, and good shops. During the day, the Red Sea Sports Club attracts water-sports activists to its wharf headquarters. The hotel has three pools (one heated), a huge sun deck, a health club with sauna, two tennis courts shaded by towering trees, and a children's playground. This hotel is where the action is. *Expensive*.

MORIAH PLAZA EILAT HOTEL 5★

North Beach   Phone (07) 332111
                                              Telex 7775
                                            Fax (07) 334158
                                        U.S. 1-800-221-0203

Another five-star choice, the recently renovated Moriah Eilat features Elat's largest convention center and a great location on the public beach. The hotel's two hundred rooms are large and comfortably furnished and some have balconies overlooking the beach. The good-sized pool has a large sunning area around it, and there is a tennis court, floodlit for night play, as well. The hotel has a piano bar, an especially comfortable lounge area decorated in soothing grays and taupes, and several world-class restaurants, including La Promenade, The Continental, La Trattoria di Moriah and the Capricio Gourmet Restaurant. *Deluxe*.

Neptune Hotel 5★

North Beach	Phone (07) 334333
Box 259, Elat	Fax (07) 379889

The Neptune, another five-star hotel, is one of the quieter "veteran" hotels on the scene. Prized for its attentive service and subdued atmosphere, it enjoys the highest occupancy rate of any hotel in Israel. A wealth of facilities and services includes two swimming pools (one heated), Eddie's Bar at poolside (open from 11 A.M. to midnight), and the Neptune Nightclub (jumps every night except Sunday). All 165 rooms feature balconies with a sea view. The west wing, currently under renovation, will add one hundred more rooms to the hotel. There is a fine shopping arcade where you will find an H. Stern and a Steimatzky. The Rondo coffee shop had some wicked-looking pastries. A permanent orchestra and terrace entertainment add to the pleasure of this hotel. Ask about the Theme Evenings—if you are lucky enough to be there on Ali Baba Night, you will see a modern-day Salome or Scheherazade explain the mysteries of the East undulatingly. There is a private synagogue. Full access for the disabled is available throughout the hotel. *Expensive*.

The Lagoona Hotel 4★

North Beach,	Phone (07) 333666
Box 1111	Telex 7765
Elat 88000	Fax (07) 333744

This hotel takes its nautical name to heart—the painted murals on the lobby walls depict scenes of a watery world. The Red Lagoon restaurant, the Lost Lagoon bar, the Golden Lagoon coffee shop, the Lagoon Island Bar, the Lagoon pool snack bar, and the Blue Lagoon cinema are at your service. The La Boite disco stays open into the A.M. If you think this hotel sounds all wet, take a look at the blue and brass decor in the bar—it's a positive sedative as you sip and watch the bodies turn brown at poolside.

There is a gift shop in the hotel and a long list of activities to participate in, including pool games, backgammon, gymnastics, sports competitions, bridge, and table tennis. *Moderate.*

EILAT SPORT HOTEL 4★

North Beach   Phone (07) 333333
Fax (07) 332765

Sports enthusiasts should find plenty to keep them active at the Sport Hotel. Its centerpiece, the Country Club, is an ultramodern sports club featuring floodlit tennis courts, air-conditioned squash courts, courts for racquetball, basketball, and volleyball, as well as badminton, jogging, aerobics, a fully equipped gym, and, of course, sauna, jacuzzi, and massage. The 327-room hotel is set around two large swimming pools and offers both informal and formal dining and plenty of evening entertainment, including theme parties and live entertainment every night. *Expensive.*

PARADISE HOTEL 4★

North Beach   Phone (07) 335050
Fax (07) 372327

Minutes from the beach, the modern Paradise Hotel wraps around tropical gardens and swimming pools. Its children's club with separate play area and kiddy pool make it an attractive option for parents traveling with small children. Facilities include a health club, a creative arts room, hotel shop, beauty parlor, two dining rooms, and an informal poolside restaurant. *Expensive.*

LA COQUILLE 4★

North Beach   Phone (07) 370031
Fax (07) 370032

If you're planning an extended stay in Elat, or simply prefer the added value of a suite hotel, then consider La Coquille in North Beach. Classic European style highlights the decor of La

Coquille's fifteen suites. Each has its own fully-equipped kitchen-ette, color television and a sun porch. Some even have a Jacuzzi. As a special treat, breakfast (at no extra charge) is served in your room, or even on the sun porch. La Coquille also has its own mini mart and pub as well as a gourmet French restaurant presided over by Chef (and hotel manager) Robert Sonego. *Moderate*.

THE SHULAMIT GARDENS HOTEL 4★

North Beach   Phone (07) 333999
                                               Telex 7738

The Shulamit Gardens Hotel is located on the lagoon and within minutes of the town center. The Shulamit's lounge area is es-pecially tasteful, with plenty of deep-cushioned seating and pan-oramic views of the lagoon from the wall-high windows. The Aquarium Lounge serves a dairy menu and is decorated in dark red and green velvet, with an abundance of healthy plants; the dining alcoves along the walls are intimate; the Lagoon Bar adjoins the lounge. The Shulamit has a wide range of facilities: a gift shop, a hairdresser, a lobby bar, a TV and video room, two dining rooms, a pool, and an à la carte restaurant. Young people tell us that the Shulamit's Disco is number one in Elat, with shows from 10 P.M. on. The Pub is open from 7 to 10 P.M. nightly. *Expensive*.

THE CAESAR HOTEL 4★

Box 888,   Phone (07) 333111
Elat 88107   Telex 7732
                                               Fax (07) 332624

The Caesar has been one of Elat's better hotels right from the start.Recently renovated, it consistently maintains a high standard of comfort and service. The hotel overlooks both lagoon and sea, and provides the usual resort-hotel amenities: an outdoor pool, movies and video in the film club, tennis courts, and the Mythos discotheque—one of the nicer hotel dance clubs. The Lotus

Chinese restaurant is run by the Caesar and serves good Oriental food (see Restaurants). There is a snack bar and a coffee shop as well. This traditional hotel also has a synagogue and plenty of parking space. All 240 rooms have radio and direct-dial telephones. *Expensive*.

THE QUEEN OF SHEBA 3★

Box 196	Phone (07) 334121
North Beach, Elat	Telex 7776
	Fax (07) 334126

This hotel is a real down-to-earth choice for your vacation. This homey establishment is well suited to families with children, and it does get a bit noisy by the pool, but it's all in the name of good, clean, Israeli-style fun. The location on North Beach is excellent, with all rooms facing the sea. There are eleven garden cottages for families and a lot of special activities like camel tours, miniature golf, video games, tennis, billiards, Ping-Pong, and water sports. The Queen of Sheba's lounge has a cool subterranean feeling about it; like a stalactite cave, it's dimly lit, with stone planters and desert vegetation blooming in the darkness. There is a minimarket adjacent to the hotel, a card room, a snack bar, a souvenir shop, a piano bar, a restaurant, and a discotheque. Chez Pierre is the outdoor café and it is very pretty with its white wrought-iron lawn furniture and flowering vines. The hotel also features frequent pool-side barbecues in a somewhat questionably "authentic" Bedouin tent. Moderate.

RED ROCK HOTEL 4★

Box 306 North Beach	Phone (07) 373171
Elat 88102	Fax (07) 371530

You'll have to look for the Red Rock. It's off Arava Road as it heads past the New Tourist Center toward Coral Beach. The Red Rock, although not a fancy place, is extremely bright and well kept. Rooms are large with spacious sitting areas and wall-to-wall carpeting. It's a short walk to the public beach, or you can swim in the hotel pool. A poolside snack bar, organized games, exercise sessions, and water sports are part of the day's "work," and

you can "work" on a cocktail in the Red Rock nightclub or
Rondo Bar at night. *Moderate.*

GALEI EILAT 3★

North Beach	Phone (07) 334222
	Telex 7718
	Fax (07) 334184

The Galei Eilat adjoins and is managed by the Neptune. The feeling of this place is relaxed and informal; the freshly whitewashed look of the hotel and its semiprivate beach make it a
sound choice. The Galei has an attractive lounge area (sandwiches, ice cream, and drinks served here), a pool, a gift shop,
and a hair salon. The Seaview restaurant specializes in Moroccan
cuisine as well as barbecued meat and fish. The Gishron Bar is
open till midnight; room service is available till midnight, too.
Inexpensive.

THE AMERICANA EILAT 3★

Box 27 North Beach	Phone (07) 333777
Elat	Telex 7749
	Fax (07) 334174

This long, low hotel is situated near the lagoon on the north
shore of the Red Sea. Its 106 rooms are fully air-conditioned, and
have direct-dial phones and radio. The hotel offers a gift shop, a
cafeteria, a lobby bar, a TV-video and games room, a lively disco
and pub, and a restaurant. Plenty of recreational activities include
organized water sports and aerobic dancing. *Inexpensive.*

In-Town Stop

SONESTA SUITES HOTEL 4★

Derech Ha' Arava	Phone (07) 376222
Elat	Fax (07) 372125

Just beyond the New Tourist Center on Arava Road, the Sonesta
Suites Hotel opened in January 1993. Its three hundred accom-

modations are either studios or multibedroom suites with sitting areas. They are colorfully and attractively decorated and make you feel right at home. The hotel has a huge pool and sundeck area and you can easily walk to nearby Sonesta Beach. It has several restaurants, a kids' club, and a fitness center. Nice choice. *Expensive.*

Coral Beach Hotels

Coral Beach is the quieter beach strip, with a few hotels, very good restaurants, and the best water-sports action in Elat.

THE "CLUB IN" ELAT

Coral Beach, Elat   Phone (07) 334555
                                                Telex 7730 RESOR
                                                Fax 334519

Managed by Hilton International, the unique "Club In" doesn't call itself a hotel—what it *is* is a "villa-resort" and a rather well-planned one, at that. The 168 villas, set on beautiful grounds, are completely self-contained and air-conditioned; each accommodates six people, with two bedrooms, a fully equipped kitchenette, and a lounge with a private terrace. Amenities at the "Club In" include a heated freshwater pool, an outdoor Jacuzzi, "multisports play area," the restaurants, a takeaway snack bar, and a poolside barbecue. It's so complete, you need never leave the compound, with its own minimarket, lounge bar, and cabaret. There's even a special "Kids' Mini Club" to keep the little ones busy. The "Club In's" nightclub is one of the best in Elat. "Club In" is the perfect stop for families. *Expensive.*

CARLTON CORAL SEA 4★

Coral Beach   Phone (07) 333555
                                                Telex 7790
                                                Fax (07) 334088

This smaller hotel, with only 145 rooms, has a terrific location just minutes from the beach and Coral World. It has its own pool, a dining room, and coffee shops. Kosher meals are served in the dining room. The Hut, an Israeli nightclub, is a popular nighttime haunt. All rooms face the sea, a great feature, especially at dusk. *Moderate*.

CARAVAN SUN CLUB HOTEL 2★

Coral Beach   Phone (07) 373145
                                                    Telex 7753
                                                Fax (07) 374083

The Caravan Sun Club only merits a two-star rating but seems nicer to us. Perhaps it's because only forty rooms have tubs. The other sixty-odd have showers only. They are all air-conditioned and there is a good-sized pool and kiddie playground. The Caravan is Coral Beach headquarters for the Red Sea Sports Center, so there's lots of activity here. A fun place. *Inexpensive*.

Taba Beach

EILAT PRINCESS HOTEL 5★

Taba Beach (Israel)   Phone (07) 373030
                                                Fax (07) 373333

Situated in a breathtaking and secluded setting ten minutes south of Elat, the Eilat Princess is a haven of luxury and tranquility. Inaugurated in late 1992, the hotel features luxuriously appointed guest rooms, all with spacious balconies overlooking the sea and mountains. Guests are pampered (or put to the test) at the spa and fitness center with its indoor Jacuzzi, finnish and Turkish saunas, aerobics, state-of-the-art gymnasium, private massage and treatment rooms, underwater massage bath, and hydro-reflexotherapy bath. The Princess also boasts a beautifully landscaped pool, tennis courts, private beach, and, of course, plenty of water sports. Dining choices range from informal pool and beachfront dining to à la carte gourmet restaurants. *Expensive*.

HILTON TABA 5★

Taba Beach (Egypt)   Phone (07) 376191

Located in what is now Egyptian territory, Hilton Taba (formerly the Aviya-Sonesta Hotel) is a great choice for families. This first-rate resort is set on carefully tended, lush grounds that exhibit the full blooming glory of desert cactus and swaying palms. Its 326 rooms face either the desert or the sea. Public areas are classy and low-key—perfect foils for the starkly modern chandeliers and Israeli sculptures. The resort's unique lotus-flower pool with a bar in its center is just steps away from the private beach. In addition to scuba expeditions, snorkeling, windsurfing, sailing, and other water sports, guests can enjoy unlimited tennis on five floodlit courts, fitness classes, archery, and other activities. A qualified counselor heads up the Kids Mini Club, and for even younger tots there's a baby listening service.

The Hilton Taba features several restaurants. Marhaba specializes in Arabic cuisine and international fare is served in elegant surroundings at Casa Taba. Lighter meals are served at the Bedouin Tent, frequent site of beachfront cocktail parties. In the evenings, entertainment is on tap at the hotel's "end of the world" night club.

To reach the hotel you must cross the border passing from Israeli checkpoints to Egyptian ones. You need a passport and a visa (which you'll get at the initial checkpoint). The process does not take a long time normally, but may take longer on the weekends when Israelis and others cross into the Sinai to scuba dive. You cannot drive a rental car across the border. *Expensive.*

Restaurants

Elat's restaurants are a heterogeneous bunch. There are several superior dining choices on the beach strips and hidden away in town that consistently serve well-prepared dishes in handsome surroundings, and you'll be delighted at some of our gourmet finds as well. Following up on a totally unscientific survey conducted on the beach and poolside, we found many of the city's most highly advertised spots to be overpriced and pretentious. *Caveat emptor!*

Because days in Elat are invariably hot, sunny (approximately 360 sunny days each year), and activity-filled, the city's classiest eating houses open only for dinner. In Elat's vast majority of restaurants you will encounter the same sort of fare you've tasted throughout the country—perfectly grilled and skewered meat or crisply fried fish. Elat's restaurants offer not gracious dining but rather good eating, utilizing indigenous foods like fish and dairy products that do not have to be imported from the north.

Many restaurants have been built with open terraces facing west, so you can marvel at the brilliant red color as the sun sets over the harbor. Restaurants open for dinner at 6 P.M., but are most crowded from 7:30 to 10 P.M. Since most restaurants are rather small, reservations are a must in peak periods or on weekends. All is not lost if you neglect to reserve, if you don't mind dining late in the evening. Israelis seem not to linger over dinner.

Casual dress is *de rigueur* in Elat, but men will feel more comfortable in a sports jacket than in shirt sleeves at our gourmet dining spots. Ties are out—everywhere.

Restaurant prices are a bit higher here than in other parts of the country, even though Elat is a duty-free zone, because so many items must be flown in. Shipping costs get passed down to you. Please note that many restaurants here do not accept credit cards.

By using our suggestions, you can choose a different type of restaurant each night of your stay and enjoy each thoroughly.

Note: Few restaurants in Elat close for the Sabbath.

Gourmet Dining

CASA ITALIANA

Adjacent to Pipson's on Coral Beach   Phone (07) 371995
Open 6 P.M. to midnight
Visa, MasterCard

Murals of Italian cities and countryside add local color to the whitewashed walls of this fine Italian restaurant on Coral Beach. Homemade pastas served with sixteen different sauces dominate the menu along with a number of different pizzas. The osso buco and veal schnitzel in picant sauce are recommended. The seafood or avocado salad appetizers are great ways to start your meal. *Moderate*.

AU BISTROT

Rue Eilot, Elat   (07) 74333
Major Credit Cards

Michel is the owner of Au Bistrot, and his good taste is reflected in the sedate dark-blue and white decor—and the serious French cooking that goes on in the kitchen. Au Bistrot has the reputation of being one of Elat's premiere restaurants, and Michel will help you select what is seasonal and fresh. The avocado mousse, the filet of beef in green pepper sauce, and the shrimp provençale are always excellent. Fabulous desserts. The five-course prix fixe menu is worthwhile. *Expensive.*

PAPA MICHEL GOURMET RESTAURANT

Hatemarim Blvd.   Phone (07) 374131
next to the Etzion Hotel   Noon to 3 P.M., 6 P.M. to 11 P.M.
                                                       Kosher

The varied menu features fresh fish, both oven-baked and charcoal-grilled, fine steaks and many different dishes including lamb prepared with couscous. Recommended by the Ministry of Tourism and our friends in Elat. The original Papa Michel restaurant is in Beersheba. *Moderate.*

EDDIE'S HIDE-A-WAY

63 Eilot Street   (07) 371137
                                              6 P.M. to midnight
                                          Visa, Diner's Club

The pleasant atmosphere, an off-beat and interesting menu, and the ebullient personality of Eddie himself are enough to recommend this place, which isn't easy to find (ask a taxi driver or look for the lighted tree). In a town where eating might prove to be the least adventurous pursuit, Eddie conjures up some magical mélanges like Chicken Spartacus—half a bird slowly roasted with date syrup and brandy and stuffed with ground barley and pine nuts. The beef en brochette has been marinated in onion juice, ginger, garlic, and cumin, and then broiled in a peanut-butter sauce. The Nairobi shrimp and the Shanghai fish are two more intriguing choices. Ceiling fans cool the three small dining rooms, which are whitewashed and wood-beamed. Not a fancy place, but there is clever, interesting cooking going on. Eddie's mixes a mean drink—try the Goombay Smash. Say hello to Eddie for us. He's there every night. *Expensive.*

LA COQUILLE

North Beach   Phone (07) 370031
                                                   7 P.M. to midnight
                                                   Major credit cards

Located in the hotel of the same name, La Coquille is consistently rated one of Elat's finest restaurants. Exquisite French cuisine is served in lovely European surroundings. Specialties of the house, according to Chef Robert Songo, include the stuffed trout in pastry, Veal Cordon Bleu, and a dish that I "discovered"—Squid Bedouin-style (not as rubbery as squid often is). *Expensive.*

Superior Dining Choices

TANDOORI

Lagoona Hotel   Phone (07) 333879
King's Wharf   12:30 P.M. to 3:30 P.M., 7 P.M. to 1 A.M.
                                              Reservations Required

The shimmering batiks along the walls, flowers on your table, soothing Indian music (live) accompanied by typical dancing, and subdued atmosphere combine to make Tandoori Elat's most elegant restaurant. The chefs and staff are all from India, making your dining experience nothing less than authentic. The mulligatawny soup is among the best we've ever had and the lamb dishes are superb. *Expensive.*

MANDY'S ON THE BEACH

On Coral Beach, near AquaSport   Phone (07) 372238
                          Noon to 3 P.M., 6:30 P.M. to midnight
                                                        Visa

The first Chinese restaurant in Elat is still going strong. Both of its dining rooms overlook Coral Beach. The larger one is more appealing, with its green chairs and white accents. A beachy-looking thatched roof and bamboo accessories provide the swept-away look and the food is good—traditional Chinese. Shark fin of wanton soup for openers, beef and shrimp in hot garlic sauce, and lemon chicken are a few delicious choices, and the prices will not make you wince. *Inexpensive.*

THE LAST REFUGE

Opposite Club Med and
Coral Sea Hotel

Phone (07) 372437
1 P.M. to midnight
Major Credit Cards

This Israeli seafood restaurant looks like a ship, complete with anchor and old lanterns. You can dine indoors on shrimp, grilled fish, and salads, but the dining terrace in the rear is better with its thatched roof and fishing nets and windows that open out onto the sea. The shark fin and turtle soups are sure to please you. *Moderate.*

NEVIOT VILLAGE '82

On the shore at North Beach

Phone (07) 372030
Open 24hrs.
No Credit Cards

La dolce vita was very much in evidence at this casual spot, where all types of appetites might be aroused. This beachside restaurant and watering hole is popular! The grilled meats and the fried Red Sea fish are especially fine here. There is a wide selection of salads and omelets. (Serves breakfast.) *Moderate.*

MES AMIS

Red Sea Hotel
Rechter Center Hatmarim
at Boulevard

6 P.M. to midnight
Major Credit Cards

This is our choice for the most attractive restaurant in the Rechter Center. The dining room's bright white tablecloths are set off with blue accents and glow with candlelight. Intimate. First-class food is accompanied by soft music. Shrimp au poivre, duck à l'orange, juicy grilled lamb chops, and lobster à la crème are our favorites from an extensive menu. *Moderate.*

LE FRANÇAIS / CHEZ HENRI

Rechter Center, opposite Post Office   Phone (059) 75008
Major Credit Cards

You can eat well and reasonably inexpensively in this small white and wood-beamed restaurant. A four-course meal and aperitif are offered for twenty-seven shekels. The marmitte dieppoise and the lobster au gratin are top choices on this menu; the trout meunière was exceedingly fresh. *Moderate*.

THE BLUE FISH

Coral Beach   Phone (07) 372529
5 P.M. to 12:30 A.M.
Diner's Club, Visa

When you imagine a seafood restaurant, don't be surprised if visions of The Blue Fish come to mind. Fishing nets, turtle shells and other like articles decorate the interior of this quaint restaurant overlooking the Bay of Akaba and the Coral Reserve. Grilled fish served with a variety of sauces is the specialty, along with French-style seafood dishes and grilled meats. Its twenty-five-year reputation for fine seafood is well deserved. *Moderate*.

MOULIN ROUGE

Rechter Center   Phone (07) 373887
Sunday through Thursday, noon to 3 P.M.,
5 P.M. to midnight;
Friday, noon to 3 P.M.
No Credit Cards

Climb up the spiral staircase to the second floor and enter the dining room—all chandeliers and whitewashed walls (white walls are the rage in this town). All this brightness does indeed reflect on the selective menu here. Choose the poisson aux noisettes, sole à la marinière, entrecôte à l'oriental. There is a fifteen shekel menu which cannot be beat and gives you salad, a choice of fish or meat, dessert, and a half-bottle of wine. *Moderate*.

We usually advise against eating in hotel restaurants; however, two restaurants of note are to be found in the King's Wharf at King Solomon's Palace Hotel:

THE CAFÉ ROYAL

King Solomon's Palace Hotel   12:30 P.M. to 4:30 P.M.,
5:30 P.M. to midnight
(closed Saturday)
Major Credit Cards

This delightful place resembles a gazebo—you're even serenaded here by the feathered brigade in the huge gilded cage in the center of the floor. The feeling is bright; the food is light and dairy. Sit under the big umbrellas and treat yourself to some healthy food. Try the Ha'Emek French onion pie, the omelets, and the salads—great for the times when you're not feeling carnivorous. *Inexpensive*.

THE BRASSERIE

King Solomon's Palace Hotel   Phone (07) 334111
7 P.M. to 11 P.M. (closed Friday)
Major Credit Cards

The Brasserie has class—more formal than the Café Royal, handsome, and tasteful, with a substantial menu that features smoked goose breast (a wonderful appetizer), chicken diablo, and trout Ali Baba (baked in tehina and tomato sauce). The mallard with onion and raisin sauce was exceptionally tender and the desserts can be good, if run of the mill. *Moderate*.

Good Food, Less Ambience

TEDDY'S PUB-RESTAURANT

Opposite Shulamit and Caesar Hotels   Phone (07) 372731
North Beach, Elat   Noon to 2 A.M.
No Credit Cards

This "western" style restaurant is set in a quiet parklike spot, near the miniature golf course, and within view of the Arkia airport. There are picnic tables in front of this rustic place, which provides a lot of draught beer, country music, and a warm atmosphere. The stars on the menu are the thick grilled steaks and the chile con carne. The shrimp and calamari platter is a super companion to all the beer you may be drinking. *Inexpensive*.

EL GAUCHO

At Ha'Arava Road, entrance to Elat   Phone (07) 331549
Noon to 1 A.M. daily
No Credit Cards

This Argentine grill restaurant is off the beaten track in the industrial area. The whitewashed walls and Argentinian gunpowder horns are pretty hohum, but the "gauchos" serving you are really dressed for the part. The empanadas and chorizo sausage make a lovely appetizer and the large portions of beef, veal, and chicken are reasonably priced. South American music several nights a week. *Moderate*.

HALLELUYAH

Eilat Tourist Center   Phone (07) 375752
Edomit Hotel   11 A.M. to midnight
(closed Friday)
No Credit Cards

The food at Hallelujah is made the way your mother might prepare it—if she was Moroccan, kept a kosher kitchen, and was a whiz at the grill. The Middle-Eastern food here is the best you'll find in Elat—freshly made, cooked to order, and authentic. Typical dishes like shishlik and kebabs, and more involved ones, like Tunisian couscous and beef tongue Madeira, are fine. The Halleluyah bean soup is a satisfying potage that is as filling as a meal. Rachel is the hostess and is always ready to answer questions about Elat, Israel, and food. The staff is eager and just as friendly. *Inexpensive*.

THE GOLDEN FISH RESTAURANT

Bldg. #3, Elat Tourist Center   Phone (07) 375306
(on the 2nd level, tucked in corner)   Noon to 3 P.M.,
6 P.M. to midnight daily
No Credit Cards

Probably the best eatery in the New Tourist Center, The Golden Fish serves dishes like sole aux champignons, pepper steak, and stroganoff in a comfortable wood-and-stucco dining room. Prices are low—typical of places in the Tourist Center—but this one is a cut above the others and Elatis say the fish here is good and fresh. *Inexpensive*.

OASIS

Between the Moriah and
Caesar Hotels near Marina

Phone (07) 372414 or 376628
1 P.M. to midnight
No Credit Cards

The decor (like a *taverna*) is uninspired, but somehow it works in the context of Elat. The embalmed fish tangled up in the nets that hang from above and the opaque window panes do not detract from this busy place, which serves a wide variety of Red Sea fish and grilled chicken and lamb specialties. Prices are very modest and portions are enormous here. *Inexpensive*.

THE LOTUS EILAT

Adjacent to Caesar Hotel and
Israel Palace Museum

Phone (07) 376389
Noon to 3 P.M.,
6:30 P.M. to midnight daily
Major Credit Cards

The Lotus is small and personal with unusually attentive service. The take-away service is nifty (think about an Oriental picnic on the beach) and the place serves business lunches. (Who does business in Elat?) The attraction here is the food: chicken in garlic sauce, sweet and sour pork, crispy duck—follow the "one from Column A, one from Column B" approach and you'll taste Chinese food as good as Elat has to offer. Prices are extremely reasonable. *Inexpensive*.

OFF THE WHARF

King Solomon's Palace Hotel

Phone (07) 334111
7:30 A.M. to 11 P.M.
(closed Friday)

A large charcoal grill is the centerpiece of this outdoor restaurant poolside at King Solomon's Palace. The simple menu features grilled fish (of course) as well as slightly more exotic dishes such as the gravet lox and the smoked fish terrine. The atmosphere is casual, as is seating: wooden tables and benches. *Expensive*.

THE ORIGINAL PANCAKE HOUSE

In the Shalom Center   No telephone
8 A.M. to midnight
Major Credit Cards

Informal and friendly, the Pancake House serves main courses (grilled chicken, steaks, and burgers) but their raison d'être are pancakes, sixteen kinds of them—thick American-style pancakes served with butter and maple syrup, or cherry, raisin, pineapple, walnut, and applesauce versions served with whipped cream, or savory pancakes topped with omelets, salami, and frankfurters. Haviv is the hospitable manager and the entire staff is earnest and helpful. It's a nice place for breakfast and you can have your eggs cooked any way you like. Chili, sandwiches, and blintzes are all good and the portions are massive. *Inexpensive*.

ROVALIT

Red Sea Tower Hotel, North Beach   No telephone
5 P.M. to midnight
No Credit Cards

Ivan Jarbec and his son were busy installing brand-new appliances and refurbishing this rooftop dairy bar where the view is the all-in-all—the lagoon, the sea, and the stars. You can enjoy a pastry or ice cream, or maybe sip a drink and watch the boats drift by. It is very pretty at night, with music most of the time. *Inexpensive*.

EL MOROCCO RESTAURANT

Tourist Center   Phone (07) 371296
Noon to midnight
Major Credit Cards

This is Moroccan kosher cooking at its most basic, and here, "basic" means well-prepared grilled and charbroiled meats, stuffed vegetables, spicy "cigars," and the exotically fragrant tehina. Real North African delights like pastilla, mouchoui, and couscous are made every day. *Inexpensive*.

NARGILA

Park Ofira Opposite the Neptune	Phone (07) 371355
and Caesar Hotels	Open twenty-four hours a day
North Beach	

This lovely window-lined restaurant is part of a national chain specializing in Yemenite food. Favorite dishes include melawach (a phyllo dough pastry stuffed with a wide range of fillings, including puréed tomatoes, cheese, and mushrooms) and Ziva, (a long tortilla-like pastry stuffed with cheese, mushrooms and onions). Additional offerings include eggplant, tahina, hummus, meatballs, kebabs, and other traditional fare. *Inexpensive.*

Also on King's Wharf

If you just want a quick bite, or need a taste of home, you'll be pleased to know that Ben & Jerry's and Pizza Hut have both set up shop on King's Wharf.

Pninat Elat, North Beach

Clustered in this small food court on North Beach are a number of fast-food and café-type eateries with both indoor and outdoor seating, including a MacDavid's, a Mr. Lak's Ice Cream, and a branch of the famed Kapulsky Café best known for its delicious cakes and pastries.

Sunup to Sundown

Although a town named Eloth was mentioned in the Bible, the modern city of Elat, just over forty years old, shows no trace of its glory days nor its inglorious ones. There are no ancient tels to be unearthed, no impressive ruins to explore, no historical paths to follow, and no museums exhibiting artifacts proving human abilities and accomplishments. Surprisingly, for Elat seems content to be exactly what it is, the city has paid its respects to "culture" and built a museum. The Israel Palace Museum, a combination of Madame Tussaud's Wax Works and Marvel Comics, sits next to the Caesar Hotel on North Beach. The museum presents Israel's history, heroes, and legends in diorama style, using over one thousand wax models. Save your visit for a snowy afternoon!

Your daylight hours in Elat will revolve around the sun, which shines 360 days each year, and the sea. The Red Sea waters and those of the Gulf of Elat (Aqaba) are perfect for swimming, snorkeling, fishing, sailing, and windsurfing. You can snorkel over a portion of the world's finest coral reef or, if your are certified, you can dive down and discover it from close up.

Don't let the brilliant sunlight and sparkling waters blur the fact that Elat is enveloped by two great deserts—the Israeli Arava (southern part of the Negev) and the Egyptian Sinai. Exploring these deserts, whether on camel, on horseback, or by jeep, is an experience not to be missed. The Arava, one of the world's driest deserts, supports an amazing animal life and it has flora as well— you just have to ferret out the hidden gorges and wadis. Nature has crafted beautiful cliffs and thrown in red-hued sunsets. Visiting the Sinai is easy to do and requires a minimum of effort.

Excursions from Elat include an ancient copper mine (King Solomon's), a biblical animal reserve, and, for bird-watchers, a rare opportunity to see unusual species up close.

A Capsule History

Although Elat is a very young city, it has a long, well-documented past in which Jews played a key role.

The Bible tells us that wise King Solomon built a port at Ezion-Geber near the town of Eloth on the Red Sea. This port would give him access to Arabia and Africa. It also gave the Queen of Sheba access to the king. She, according to legend, landed at the port on her way to Jerusalem. Solomon's ships sailed to Ophir (Sharm-El-Sheik) from Elat and returned with exotic cargo fit for a great monarch.

In the years that followed, conquests and occupations were the city's fate. It attracted the Ptolomies, Nabateans, Romans, and Byzantines. Each renamed the city, which accounts for the variety of names associated with this area. Saladin built a fortress here and in the sixteenth century it was defended by the Mamelukes, who repulsed the Portuguese, who wanted to make this a trading station for their ships returning from the east. Amazingly, Jews maintained a high profile in the area throughout all these conquests and often were dominant in its affairs. The rise of Islam in the tenth century and the fervor of its adherents affected Elat as well. It became a rest point for North African pilgrims on their way to Mecca.

Elat's history grows dim and on March 11, 1949, when a small contingent of Israeli paratroopers took the city from the Egyptians holding it, it was nothing more than a dusty and forgotten place. It hardly seemed worth the effort, but as elsewhere in Israel, plucky pioneers arrived to establish an Israeli presence. In 1950, Arkia Airlines, the country's domestic carrier, started freight service to Elat, where the settlers had to rely on airlifts for their most basic needs. This was the lifeline that Elat needed to be more than just a political statement.

In 1952, a road was carved out of the desert (Route 40), which facilitated overland traffic and firmly established Elat's links to the north.

With the completion of the Arava Coastal Road (Route 90) in 1971, Elat's future became brighter, although problems of water supply and labor remained. The Six Day War in 1967 opened the Gulf of Aqaba for Israeli ships, making Elat an important port and allowing Israeli access to the stunning beaches that stretched into the Sinai. Even the return of the Sinai and its beaches to Egypt in 1982 has not dimmed Elat's light. Tourism is now the city's major industry, and an international airport, capable of handling jumbo jets, at Ouvda, forty miles away, has made the area easily accessible to Europeans. In fact, many European vacationers come to Elat and never visit the rest of the country.

Sightseeing

The Coral World Underwater Observatory

If Morris Kahn, an Israeli businessman, had not punctured an eardrum while scuba diving, Coral World would never have been built. That would have been a real loss for people like me, who would never get to see Elat's famed coral reef and the curious marine animals and plants that inhabit the Red Sea.

Unable to dive again, Kahn realized that most people never have an opportunity to see the rich ocean life, and he set out to change that. He worked with a marine biologist to come up with the novel idea of an underwater observation tower, which would not destroy but enhance the natural environment and would allow people a glimpse of the underwater world. The tower opened in 1975 and a replica of the Red Sea reef and three saltwater pools were added in 1982. All the water utilized at the complex is fresh, untreated ocean water, which accounts for the amazing variety of indigenous and rare species of sea life that flourish in this environment. The complex includes the Underwater Observatory, which is connected to the shore by a one-hundred-meter-long bridge; the marine aquarium, which displays species of sea life that are not easily seen from the observatory; and the Red Sea reef, which contains three hundred thousand liters of seawater and some very rare fish, including a favorite, the Picasso fish, which looks more like a Jackson Pollock with all those splattered blue dots.

The observatory is below water level and surrounded by open area. No nets keep the creatures here, so the picture from each of the huge windows is constantly in flux. The coral reef is as beautiful and as varied as any flower garden.

You can take a look at the stingrays (often called devilfish, for obvious reasons) who live amicably with the sand sharks and the turtles in the turtle pool. It's not only great fun to watch the different species of marine life, but very soothing as well. This attraction is also an educational and research tool for marine biologists and students of all ages. Viewing the exotic denizens of the deep from the safety of an all-steel, air-conditioned underwater cabin, eighteen feet below sea level, it's hard not to get enthusiastic about conserving our environment.

With the recent addition of Jaqueline, the observatory's own "Yellow Submarine," you can tour the Coral Reserve at a depth of twenty-five to sixty meters below the surface. It's an exhilarating experience, to say the least. Incidentally, the reserve's new observatory, which towers twenty-four meters above the city, offers an unparalled view of four of the nations surrounding the Red Sea—Saudi Arabia, Jordan, Israel, and Egypt.

The complex includes a gift shop, a jewelry store where the blue Elat stone from the surrounding hills is crafted into some attractive pieces, a buffet, and the Pearl Bar, where you can purchase an oyster (but not a cocktail) and be sure that there will be a genuine pearl inside. Coral World, on Coral Beach, is open daily from 8:30 A.M. to 4 P.M. A bus departs from the Moriah Eilat Hotel every half hour for the five-minute trip.

Texas Ranch

At high noon on a day that you've reserved for seeing the sights, mosey down to Texas Ranch. This is, by far, one of the oddest structures in Elat. The story goes that some Hollywood moguls commissioned this "ghost town" for a western starring Gregory Peck. The film has long since been forgotten, but the town (which is only a façade) brings back those buckaroo days when Elatis were fighting Indians and keeping varmints out of town. The Texas Ranch has a mock prison, a marshal's office, a Wells Fargo, and a saloon on a dirt street—you get the idea. It's good for little bronco-busters, and there is horseback riding on this seven-and-a-half-acre area, as well as a restaurant and shops. Entrance fee is modest.

Water Sports

Scuba

AQUASPORT / INTERNATIONAL RED SEA DIVING CENTER

Coral Beach,   Phone (07) 334404
Box 300
Generally acknowledged as the leading scuba center in Elat, Aquasport offers a two-star diving course.

The course begins every Monday at 9:30 A.M. and ends at noon on Saturday. There is a hostel which offers bed and breakfast, but it is a better idea to take bus #5 or #15 from the center of town or from the hotel area (they leave every half hour). Aquasport also offers special seven-day packages and programs of unlimited diving and windsurfing and six-day diving and camping safaris.

RED SEA SPORTS CLUB KING'S WHARF

Two locations:	Phone (07) 379685 (North Beach);
North Beach	(07) 376569 (Coral Beach)
Coral Beach	

Moving up fast, the Red Sea Sports Club has the distinction of being Israel's largest water-sports and adventure center.

The divers' boat sails twice daily; ten compulsory dives complete the requirements for two-star qualification. The diving safaris in the Sinai stop at points like Devil's Head, Sharm-El-Sheik (ancient Ophir), and Ras Hamasid. You can even attend a seminar in underwater photography.

Note: A chest X-ray and a diving medical exam must be presented before undertaking any program. You can call 379685 for more details.

Both Aquasport and Red Sea Sports Club rent equipment to certified divers. You must present your diving certification, logbook, and diving medical exam results.

Snorkeling

CORAL BEACH NATURE RESERVE

At Coral Beach	Phone (07) 376829, 372722
	9 A.M. to 5 P.M. daily
	Admission fee

The special feature of the Coral Beach Nature Reserve is that it has three wonderful marked paths (signposted with explanations) that have been traced for the swimmer in this underwater wonderland. The Gulf of Elat's coral reef, composed of stony and soft coral in a blend of color, shape, and texture, appears landscaped. The gulf's water temperature is high (28°C) and the water is clear enough for the sun's rays to penetrate deeply. This factor, plus an absence of storms that might stir up sediment and impede the growth of coral, has helped create a highly accessible reef. A haven for invertebrates and shelter for thousands of fish (clown, butterfly, and parrot among them), the reef plays host to an occasional sea turtle, barracuda, and shark. The Japanese Gardens Trail adjoins Coral World Observatory and is similar to it; the larger Winding Trail and intricate Moses Rock Trail vary a bit. You do not have to be a great swimmer to follow these trails, but you cannot walk them. The visitors' center will provide you with specifics and good safety advice, and will even rent you equipment for an additional fee.

RAFFI PIPSON'S

Coral Beach   Phone (07) 372909

In this offbeat place with a bohemian look, Raffi rents equipment for surfers, snorkelers, and certified divers—also floats for sunbathers who want to dangle and beach chairs for those who don't. You can snorkel off Raffi's beach, which adjoins the Nature Reserve. Shower facilities and snack shop. The open-air roof is used for disco dancing at night.

DOLPHIN REEF ELAT

Southern Beach   Phone (07) 371846
                                               9 A.M. to 5 P.M. daily

If you've ever dreamt of swimming alongside a dolphin, don't pass up a visit to the Dolphin Reef. You'll observe dolphins and sea lions in their natural environment and watch their hourly training sessions from specially built piers and observation points. Nature films featuring marine mammals are shown continuously in the air-conditioned auditorium. Additional facilities include a complete diving center, photo center (with underwater photography), restaurant, souvenir shop, and a beach front pub which stays open till the wee hours. Bus #15 from your hotel or the center of town will get you here.

Day Cruising

There are sailboats that ply the waters of Elat. These pleasure cruisers follow a usual route from the marina to Coral Island (which is in Egyptian hands) and last about seven hours. There is swimming, snorkeling, wind-surfing, and diving at Coral Island (but you won't actually set foot on the island). Most of these cruisers offer lunch with wine and night cruises if there is enough interest generated. Information and registration can usually be arranged at your hotel reception, at a local travel agent, or best of all, directly at the marina where the sailboats are docked.

Some highly regarded cruisers: The *Jadran* (former Adriatic yacht of Marshal Tito of Yugoslavia) docks at the marina; The *Cormoran* (holds 18 people) Phone: 331717, 375998; *L'Amie* (features diving safaris) Phone: 376465, 376070; *The Pirate* (kosher food) Phone: 372436, 373024; *Andromeda* (a maxi 84 sailboat, Red Sea Sports Club) Phone: 379685

Windsurfing / Waterskiing / Parasailing

Windsurfing looks easy, but if you're a beginner, stick to the lagoon. The northern coast is for more advanced surfers and Coral Beach is for pros. Equipment is available; you can get your international V.D.W.S. qualification from a professional instructor.

Instructions in waterskiing and surfing, as well as in using equipment like advanced underwater cameras, are offered at reasonable rates.

Check at the Caravan Sun Club desk for windsurfing, waterskiing, and parasailing on Coral Beach; phone (07) 371345; at Red Sea Sports Club, King's Wharf, for windsurfing only in the lagoon. On the beachfront adjacent to the Neviot Restaurant, you'll find the Beach Boys. They rent kayaks, motorboats, and other gear, and give lessons in waterskiing, parasailing, and all the water sports you an possibly think of, at reasonable rates. They are open from sunup to sundown. Friendly, young staff.

Sport Fishing

Walking along the dock behind the Caesar Hotel, I saw a posterboard nailed to the mooring. Tacked to it were a dozen snapshots of smiling people, each with an unhappy-looking fish hanging upside down behind them. Sure enough, late that afternoon, another happy group came ashore with fish in hands. If you'd like to smile at a tuna, dorado, or barracuda, call Robert of *The Pequod* at 378558. Red Sea Sports also organizes fishing trips.

Glass-bottomed Boats

Yet another way to survey the watery depths in dry comfort is on the glass-bottomed boats that set sail daily from the Elat Marina and proceed down the coast to the port and the Coral Reserves. Sailing time is about one and a half hours. Israel Yam departs from the marina at 10 A.M., noon and 2 P.M. Tour Yam has hourly departures from the glass-bottomed-boat pier opposite the Club Med, Coral Beach. There are two half-day cruises to Taba every day, leaving at 9:30 A.M. and at 2:30 P.M. from the northern marina (the boat stops at the glass-bottomed-boat pier at 10 A.M. and 3 P.M. to pick up additional passengers). There is a bar on board and a night cruise can be arranged. To confirm schedules and make reservations, phone (07) 374428 or 332325.

Also at the marina is the Jules Verne Explorer, a state-of-the-art "mobile underwater observatory." Below deck transparent walls surround you, forming a seemingly thin barrier between you and the marine life gliding past. The vessel's modern design allows it to travel through remote dive sites once accessible only to experienced divers. A bar, restaurant, plenty of sunbathing, and even entertainment are above deck. Day and night tours are available. For reservations, call (07) 334668. Cost is approximately $17.

Equipment Rentals

Venezia, located on the boardwalk at North Beach, is another outfit that will be happy to rent you all kinds of water-sports equipment, including small boats. They also operate a small snack bar that's open twenty-four hours a day. The phone number is (059) 73817. You might also try Red Sea Sports Club, King's Wharf— (07) 334111, ext. 1353. The club rents pedal boats, twin-seater canoes, mini-speedboats (for four people in a six-horsepower boat), and a speedboat with a driver/water-ski instructor, stereo music, ski equipment, and a parachute.

Water Slides

WHITE RHAPSODY

On the North Shore

Phone (07) 332123
8 A.M. till after midnight
Slides open 10 A.M. to 7 P.M.
Evening sliding on Sat.
No Credit Cards

By day, it's a water-amusement center; by night, it's a pub and coffeehouse with music and dancing. Rumors have White Rhapsody in the red, however, and since it was closed at the time this was written, it may be gone by the time you arrive.

Touring the Desert

Back on terra firma, you can explore the nearby Arava Desert (the southern Negev), and with a minimum of fuss you can visit the Sinai as well. You can do your exploring on horseback, on camel, or in that four-wheel-drive animal, the Jeep. Here's how:

Camel Riders of Elat and Neot Hakikar have put together the Sunset Caravan. You can ride a camel for two hours or ride that noble beast into the desert sunset and return to Elat in the evening. The two-day Desert Caravan features vegetarian meals prepared as in biblical times. The local office is in the Etzion Hotel on Hatmarim Street.

The people of Kibbutz Ketura have organized kibbutz desert and riding tours on horseback. Excursions are for a full or half day. Lunch and transportation to and from your hotel are included in the price. Contact them at (07) 373169 or Egged Tours at (07) 373148-9 or 375161.

Geographical Tours Ltd. is located in the Moriah Hotel. This outfit offers exciting tours of the Sinai and Jeep-treks into the mountains around Elat. Danny Tzam and Fabienne are on hand to answer questions and book tours in their extremely friendly way. Call them at (07) 372151-2.

Ne' Ot Ha Kikar Desert Tours/Jabaliya Trekking has a terrific reputation for operating excellent tours of the Sinai, the Negev, and the Judean deserts. These tours are really desert safaris and emphasize camping and experience-oriented ways of seeing the desert. Meals are cooked over campfires and participants are expected to pitch in, as in pitching a tent, drawing water, cleaning up.... All necessities (including sleeping bags) are provided, however.

These people pride themselves on hiring highly skilled outdoor experts who know the land from the bottom up. You can sleep under the stars or in a nomad's tent, but don't expect bathing facilities like the ones you've grown accustomed to. A deep plunge into a swimming hole with a bar of soap will do the job nicely. In the Footsteps of Moses is a five-day safari and departs from Jerusalem, later picking up more passengers in Elat. The Grand Sinai Safari from Elat to Cairo also takes five days.

Mountain treks in the Sinai with Bedouin guides and self-satisfied camels to carry all the paraphernalia will last a week. Ne' Ot Ha Kikar also has two- and five-day Diving Safaris for licensed divers only. Since there are many itineraries, you should call Ne' Ot Ha Kikar in Jerusalem, (02) 699385 or 636494, or in Tel Aviv, (03) 463111-3, for specifics. Egged Tours at the Elat Central Bus Station has information on these excursions, (07) 71329, or you can visit the Ne' Ot Ha Kikar office in the Etzion Hotel (off Hatmarim Blvd.) at (07) 376908. The hours there are 8:30 to 1 and 4 to 7.

The ubiquitous *Red Sea Sports Club* operates on land too, organizing small groups to ride horses, camels, or in Suzuki jeeps. Horseback-riding lessons take place at the Texas Ranch. The camel safaris can last a half day or a week (it's up to you) under the stars of the Arava sky, sailing on the ship of the desert. This is your chance to be like Lawrence of Arabia. On the Suzuki jeep safari (self-drive, four people to a vehicle), there is a guide who drives ahead in a lead vehicle and provides detailed explanations of desert terrain and wildlife.

Yaalat Tourist Services, Shalom Center
Yaalat organizes small groups for visits to some interesting spots near Elat, such as half-day trips to En Netafin Red Canyon, near the Egyptian border, Har Tze-fakhot Mountain, near Coral Beach, and Solomon's Pillars in Timna Valley. Phone (07) 72166.

To the Sinai on Your Own

Since you cannot drive your rented car from Israel into Egypt, the only way to go on your own is by public bus #15. Leave procedural time to pay your Sinai travel tax at the Taba border (don't forget your passport) and complete other formalities—all told, about two hours. Make sure you are through the border by 2 P.M., when the only Egyptian bus of the day arrives. It will take you to Sharm-El-Sheikh at the Sinai's southern tip. The snorkeling/scuba diving is unparalleled. Bus returns each morning to Taba. Bring sleeping bags, camping equipment, and food. For experienced campers/divers only.

"Over the Sinai"—Arkia Airlines

Arkia, Israel's domestic carrier with offices in the Tourist Center, operates a super tour into the Sinai. Fly over the desert (it's gorgeous), landing near St. Katerina Monastery. After passing customs (perfunctory), you bus over to the monastery and Mount Sinai. Cost includes lunch and Egyptian fees. Expensive but very special.

To the Sinai—with a Group

JOHNNY'S DESERT TOURS

Shalom Center	Phone (07) 376777
Box 261, Elat 88102	

Johnny's, with an office in the Shalom Center, is the largest tour operator from Elat into Egypt. Johnny's organizes several one-day Sinai tours, as well as a two-day and a five-day tour. The one-day tours visit wadis, oases, and unique ancient ruins and offer a Bedouin-style lunch and a swim in the Red Sea. Johnny's most popular tour, the two-day safari, visits St. Katerina monastery and climbs Mount Sinai. Johnny's also organizes five-day trips into Cairo and Luxor. If you are interested, write for information in advance. To visit the Sinai, take your passport to the Taba border station and pay the fee for the special Sinai travel tax. This takes the place of a visa, but it is good only for the Sinai for up to fourteen days. For Cairo visits, you need a standard Egyptian visa, which you should get before you leave home. You can get it here, but why waste vacation time?

Excursions from Elat

Timna Valley (Timna Park/Solomon's Pillars/ Timna Copper Mines)

One of the most popular excursions from Elat is the Timna Valley. Located about thirty kilometers north of Elat and covering an area of about fifteen thousand acres, Timna is the site of the biblical copper mines.

Timna is a geological document of antiquity. Rocks from the Precambrian, Paleozoic, and Mesozoic eras point to the millions of years of evolution represented in this area. The landscape looks like a moonscape of natural arches and caves and eerie rock formations caused by erosion. On the slopes that surround the valley can be seen circular patches; these are silted-up mining shafts. Most of these abandoned shafts were used by the Egyptians in the fourteenth through twelfth centuries B.C. They were also responsible for the rock-drawings (look for them near the carpark, on a high vertical rockface above the wadi) depicting herds of ibexes and ostriches, hunters, and wheeled chariots and battle-axe-wielding Egyptian soldiers. At about 1150 B.C. the Egyptians abandoned the mines and the subsequent waves of conquerors saw the value of these copper-rich mines.

The area called the Mushroom Camp is the site of the ancient copper-smelting furnaces (only one is preserved), and at the southern end of the camps stands what may have been a Semitic shrine of the Kenites and Midianites who also worked the mines. The Slave Hill opposite Solomon's Pillars, located on top of a mountain, is one of the most impressive smelting sites. The Mining Temple, built by Pharaoh Seti I and dedicated to the cow-eared goddess Hathor, is located at the foot of Solomon's Pillars. Take a look at the rock-drawing at the top of a flight of steps, depicting the Pharaoh worshiping the goddess Hathor.

There are marked walking paths at Timna. Most walks take from four to eight hours to complete; if you're game, you can obtain more information at the entrance to Timna Park. Part of the National Park System. Open 8 A.M. to nightfall. Moderate fee. For further information, call (07) 375126 or (07) 356215.

Hai-Bar Biblical Wildlife Reserve and the Yotvata Visitor's Center

The Visitors' Center at Yotvata is only minutes away from the Hai-Bar Biblical Wildlife Reserve; both are only about twenty-seven kilometers from Elat. The center (run by Yotvata Kibbutz) is a modern building filled with various informative exhibits (in English) that will acquaint you with the true nature and evolution of the Arava Plain and the surrounding desert. When you leave Yotvata, you'll have a better understanding of the area's history, topography, unusual features, plant and animal life, and agriculture.

There is a brief film shown in the auditorium, highlighting Elat's special attractions. The Yotvata Visitors' Center is open from 7:30 A.M. until nightfall Sunday through Thursday, 9 A.M. to 2 P.M. on Fridays, and 10 A.M. to 2 P.M. on Saturdays. The Dairy Bar, located just off the highway at Yotvata, is excellent. Treat yourself to a creamy custard cone, made from the sweetest milk in Israel.

Kibbutz Gerofit is a working holiday village nearby; if the desert heat threatens your sanity, there is a pool you can swim in for a nominal fee.

Hai-Bar

The Nature Reserve Authority of Israel has performed the Herculean task of preserving, restoring, and bringing to bloom the ancient landscape of Israel—planting roses in granite, so to speak. The Hai-Bar Arava Biblical Wildlife Reserve is the answer to a twentieth-century Noah's Ark. *Hai-Bar* means "wildlife." The idea to restore the animal species mentioned in the Bible (today, many of these are near extinction) to the land in a protected environment was realized in 1977 after seventeen years of planning. This wildlife reserve (one of three of its kind in Israel) provides a sanctuary and breeding grounds for animals that once roamed free and now face an uncertain future. The long-term goal is to bring the numbers of these animals up high and then to release them into their natural environment. Hai-Bar, with its natural grazing pasture, is an actual savannah, where acacia trees grow in abundance. Animals at Hai-Bar include Saharan oryxes; Somali wild asses; that largest of all living birds, the ostrich;

addaxes; the wild goats called ibexes; and the animal that symbolizes beauty and love and Israel itself—the gazelle.

Certain predatory animals are mainly active at night and, therefore, seldom seen. Among these carnivores are the wolf, the fox, the hyena, and the caracal (a rare feline). The Hai-Bar Reserve is situated off the Elat highway near Kibbutz Yotvata. Visiting in the morning or afternoon is recommended. You are not permitted to leave your vehicle for any reason (except near the observation tower). Open from 6:30 A.M. till late afternoon. (Hours are irregular.) Part of the National Park System. Moderate fee. For further information, call (07) 376018.

Excursions Nearer the City

The *Amram River Valley* and the *Pillars of Amram* are located thirteen kilometers north of Elat. To get there by car, turn off the Arava Road after nine kilometers (there is a sign). Travel westward along the riverbed and you will arrive at a fork in the road. The blue arrows pointing to the right lead to the Amram Valley; park your car in the lot here. A ten-minute walk and you will reach the Pillars of Amram.

The *Red Canyon* Shani Valley is located thirty kilometers north of Elat. The canyon is the uppermost part of the Shani riverbed and was cut out of the mountain by flood waters, exposing vivid red sandstone and large limestone boulders. The trails start at the parking lot at the side of the road. After you park your car, proceed on foot down the valley. The path is marked by green arrows. The return path is marked in brown and leads you along the bank of the riverbed to the exit at the end of the ravine. A new, direct road is planned from the main highway.

The *Netafim Spring* is ten kilometers west of Elat near the Egyptian border. You take the road past the hospital to the west —Derech Yotam—and make a right turn onto an unpaved road after ten kilometers. After another eight hundred meters, you will see the carpark. From that point, continue on foot, walking along the narrow path that leads to the spring. The way back is marked by arrows, on a path starting 100 kilometers north of the spring. You should look for the highly colored Nubian limestone faultine and the drops of water falling through openings in the steep walls of the ravine.

Tsfachot Summit is located seven kilometers southwest of Elat. The trip is well worth the walk because of what is waiting for you at the top—a gorgeous view of the Gulf to Elat with Aqaba in the distance. To get there, turn right about six kilometers south of Elat (not far from Coral World). The sign says Wadi Shlomo. Continue up the valley until you reach the junction of two dry riverbeds—the Shlomo and Tsfachot riverbeds. From here follow the trail marked by green arrows to the summit.

All the interesting sights we've discussed are easy drives from Elat and are easily negotiable by car. If you aren't renting a car, the proliferation of tour buses and operators makes getting there comfortable and economical. Check with Egged at the Elat Central Bus Station or Dan United Tours in the Shalom Center. Public transportation is not a feasible alternative.

Bird-watching Expeditions

Elat is a bird-watcher's delight, for a large number of migratory birds and interesting regional species can be seen at the salt ponds and date groves nearby. The annual migration from Europe to Africa is from September to November and the return is between March and May. The best bird-watching months are February, March, and April, and the *Elat International Bird-watching Center* organizes groups during that time. But you can certainly go on your own. The organization's office on King's Wharf opens at 5 P.M. each day, phone (07) 374276, or you can ask for information at the Coral Beach Nature Preserve, phone (07) 376829. Egged also offers bird-watching tours.

Sundown to Sunup

Elat carries on at night as it does in the daytime, offering plenty of the good life for people with the taste for it. Pubs and discos scattered through the city come into their own when the sun dips behind the red hills. But it is the hotels that are the centers of Elat's nightlife and they offer varied programs catering to different whims. Discos and piano bars, bingo and bridge, belly-dancers and folksingers are integral parts of the hotels' evening schedules. Pick up a copy of the monthly listing of special events at the local tourist office in Rechter Center to find out what's happening.

The Philip Murray Cultural Center at Ha-Tivat Ha-Negev is a museum that houses primarily contemporary art and moonlights as a cinema. The Cinematheque Club shows American movies and opens at 5 P.M. on Sunday, Tuesday, Wednesday, and Thursday. Check any of the free tourism pamphlets (like *This Week in Elat*) for film schedules. They are distributed to the reception desks of most hotels. Many of the hotels show first-rate films in their lobby TV/video rooms. Cinema Elat in the Rechter Center provides a more authentic space for moviegoing.

Israeli Folklore Evening in the Kibbutz

An evening of Israeli folklore featuring the Elat Dance Company and the Ye'elim Ethnic Dance Band is held every Saturday evening from 7 to 10 P.M. at the Kibbutz Elot. An Israeli buffet dinner, drinks, and transportation to and from the Kibbutz are included in the $14 admission fee. For reservations and to arrange for transportation, call (07) 375468.

The Khan Amiel Center, near the Shulamit Garden Hotel is a circular one level shopping area. Cafe Mozart, which is open seven days from 10 A.M. to 10 P.M. has both outdoor and indoor tables. Freshly made salads, sandwiches, soft drinks and beer are popular and at night the German-style pastries and capuccino top the list.

Clubs and Discos

A popular and pulsating discotheque at the North Beach Marina is *Yatush Barosh* (translated, it means "a flea in your ear"). The name may sound uncomfortable, but Elatis and tourists alike fill this place to capacity at night. There are lots of cozy booths downstairs and good music—Israeli and pop/rock.

King Solomon's Palace Hotel's disco, with flashy lighting, glitzy decor, cocktail waitresses in "Sultan's Favorite" costumes, and tall mixed drinks in every color, seems to top the hotel disco list. It attracts lots of singles and presents the best opportunity for meeting the opposite sex if you are in Elat solo.

Young Elatis told us that the clubs at the *Shulamit Gardens* and the *Americana Hotel* were very hot. Each has closed-circuit video screens and electronic ceilings. The *Spiral Club* at the Red Sea Tower is another hot club with the younger set.

The *Tropicana* nightclub at the "Club In" Hotel and the open-air disco at *Raffi Pipson's* are late-night meccas on Coral Beach, while the *End of the World* disco at the Hilton Taba packs them in and allows outside guests. Most clubs and all hotel discotheques have an entrance fee that includes a first drink.

The Hut, an Israeli nightclub at the Coral Sea Hotel (Coral Beach), has folksinging and dancing nightly with well-known entertainers on Friday night, as does the *Amanim Kashim Pub* next to La Coquille restaurant.

Yacht Pub on King's Wharf has live music and outdoor seating on Friday and Saturday nights.

Open-air concerts (usually on Sunday and Tuesday) are held under the stars on North Beach near the Moriah Hotel.

Coral Beach is a good place for a late-night drink with the *Jonathan* and *Hitchkok* pubs along the strip an the Tent at the *Dolphin Reef*. Piano bars at the Moriah, Lagoona, and Caesar Hotels are free, pay by the drink spots as is the *Red Lion Pub* in the New Tourist Center.

Shopping

There are bargains to be had in this free-trade zone and, although shopping is not one of the main attractions in Elat, the New Tourist Complex, the Shalom Center, and the Rechter Center will all help to lighten your purse very nicely. Check out the shopping arcades at the Princess, Neptune, and King Solomon hotels as well. One of the best buys in Elat is the jewelry made from the brilliant blue Elat stone.

Cadurite Manufacturers have a mouth-watering collection of jewels and set stones at reasonable prices. They are the biggest producers of Elat stone jewelry and pottery. The pottery used contains a high percentage of iron and copper and, after the glazing process, resembles malachite. Hours are 8:30 A.M. to 6 P.M. daily and 9 A.M. to 1:30 P.M. on Friday and Saturday. Located at the Elat Art Center on the Ha'Arava road.

The Elat Diamond Center Ltd. and the *Israel Jewelry Exchange* (in the Shalom Center) provide you with the chance to purchase beautiful diamond jewelry at prices that would be hard to beat. The Exchange is state-owned and reliable. Open 9 A.M. to 1 P.M. and 4 to 8 P.M. daily.

H. Stern shops are located in the larger hotels, and feature jewelry using the local Elat stone as well as the fabulous Brazilian gemstones they are noted for. Prices are slightly lower here due to the city's duty-free status.

The Carnival Shop on the King's Wharf contains the cream of Israel's crop under its roof—Gottex and Gideon Oberson swimwear, Beged-Or leather fashions, WIZO Israeli Art and Handicrafts, unique handpainted silks, and natural cosmetics, as well as a small branch of H. Stern. You'll find variety and quality in the merchandise at this shop.

Yolande Antal is a textile artist who lives and works in Elat. Her exclusive handpainted pieces are wearable art and you can visit her studio at 184 Edom Street. Phone (07) 376629 for an appointment.

The New Tourist Center, built in 1974, is situated just a stone's throw from the North Beach hotel area. Be warned—it does not represent architecture at its zenith but is rather a hodgepodge of shops and restaurants perched on several levels like a rookery. It does supply resident and visitor with more shwarma, shishlik, and stuffed squid than they can consume in a lifetime. *Nimrod* is an Israeli sandal and a rightfully popular one. It's also a shop in the center that sells the 100 percent genuine leather article and other fashionable footwear. Open 9 A.M. to 1 P.M. and 4 to 8 P.M., Fridays 9 A.M. to 3 P.M. (07) 375351. There are scores of souvenir shops, but the *Negev Bazaar* seems to provide for a wide range of tastes. You can buy just about anything here, but the Nazareth glass pieces, including a beautifully crafted menorah, looked especially nice. A store nearby displayed a sign with this message, "Buy here—we need your money." (Ah, subtlety—not yet a lost art!) By the way, if hunger pangs strike you while you are shopping, try the *Grand Marrakesh* upstairs or the *Lido* for decent Italian fare. *Bank Leumi* has a branch here.

The Central Bus Station area is not only a place to catch the Egged buses to everywhere; there is a *Steimatzky's* here that has the fine print—all the newspapers, paperbacks, and maps you'll require during your stay. And don't forget that emporium of plenty: the *Hamashbir Lazarchan, the* department store of Israel. This HL branch offers everything from pantyhose to thirsty beach towels—all under one roof.

Finally, the *Shalom Center*, that new spherical shopping mall opposite the Arkia Terminal, has a few boutiques that carry some offbeat fun items. Check on Ellast Patio—it's a good place to find sporty, casual clothes and slightly outré accessories. Colorful beachwear and summer footwear too.

New shops open and close with frequency; summer resort areas are notoriously transient when it comes to businesses catering to the tourist trade, so don't be surprised if one or more of these places has gone the way of the sand dunes. The fun is finding the new spots before everyone else does.

Elat Potpourri

Bicycle Rental   A fun way to get around town is to rent a bicycle. Red Sea Sports Center, King's Wharf. Phone 379685 or 371926 evenings.

Camping   Campgrounds on Coral Beach with tents or mobile homes; electricity and showers are available. Across from the Nature Preserve. Phone 372133, ext. 350.

Car Rentals   Hertz, Shalom Center, phone 376682; Eldan, Shalom Center, phone 374027; Inter Rent, New Tourist Center, phone 374893; Budget Hotel Etzion, phone 376139; Europcur, Taba Hilton, phone (02) 763544.

Going to Egypt   You can cross the Taba border by getting a special Sinai stamp on your passport. It acts as a visa for a stay of fourteen days—Sinai only.

Health Club   The King Solomon's Health Club admits non-guests for a fee. You can pump iron, work out on the machines under expert supervision, and get a massage.

Driving North on Route 40

The road from **Qumran** to Elat that hugs the shore of the Dead Sea is an autobahn compared to the snaking old route that passes through the hills and open expanses of the Negev to Beersheba and on to the north. You can, of course, return to the north the way you left it, on Route 90—but that would be a shame. The old road winds past **Shivta and Avdat**, sites of vanished civilizations; a kibbubz, **Sde Boqer**, admired by Ben-Gurion and his final resting place; **Mitzpe Ramon**, a lunar landscape where a small town, a brilliant geological museum, and a desert observatory perch on the rim of an extinct volcanic crater; and some fascinating quirks of nature like **En Avdat**, a spring whose waters cascade down the cliffs through natural rock pool formations, ending up in a large spring at the bottom of a gorge—all sights that are rare and worthwhile.

Before leaving, check your gas and water. Fifty kilometers from Elat (on Route 90), you will see the left turn to Route 40, which will take you through the heart of the Negev to the north. The Negev has great variety in color and contrast. Here, the geological story of the planet is more evident; the giant rifts that were created in prehistory—long before the advent of humans—have left their mark on this scarred terrain. The ridges and cliffs form a jagged horizon line in this red-tinted, alien-looking landscape. There appears, however, every now and then, a spot of green, and you start imagining oases that won't appear. The route is well marked and you will notice places like **Ouvda** and **Shizzifon Junction**, which are either tiny settlements or military outposts.

The road is a curvy one that runs past wide stretches of parched, open land and desert dunes, with virtually not a house or a soul in sight. Keep in mind that it's also a narrow road, and should an occasional truck or bus pull up behind you to pass, it's best to yield. It can become swelteringly hot and there isn't a service station or a rest stop until you reach Mitzpe Ramon.

Mitzpe Ramon Geological Park and Reserve

When David Ben-Gurion talked about conquering the desert lest it conquer Israel, he was dreaming of a place like Mitzpe Ramon.

This kibbutz, founded in 1956, today has a population of four thousand. The people here like to feel that Mitzpe Ramon is a reflection of Israel—hardship and beauty in one.

The Visitors' Center

Exhibition Hall is a modern structure perched on the edge of a cliff overlooking the park. From this vantage point, the fabulous view of the red valley with the huge crater and the surrounding hills will leave you breathless. The kibbutz is involved in several key industries and is planning to construct a scientific center and a geological garden. What is here already is of significant importance: a highly educational and interesting geological museum.

The museum features informative displays of the minerals, flora, and fauna of the area (the Nubian ibex and the hyrax are two of these desert dwellers). The displays are housed in a striking building that is a bit like the Guggenheim Museum in New York, circular and stairless.

The anthropological exhibits are well done, explaining the settlement patterns in the Negev from the Middle Bronze Age (Canaanite) to the bright period of the Nabatean Kingdom (300 B.C. to A.D. 30) and through the Byzantine and Early Arab periods (fourth through eighth centuries A.D.).

There is an audiovisual program every half hour (in English). Mitzpe Ramon is for anyone who is interested in learning about the geological history of the Negev—its rocks, caves,and valleys, the animal life of yesterday and today—and about the nature of our planet. Don't miss the exhibit on the Makhtesh; the valley, surrounded by steep walls, was drained by a single wadi (a dry riverbed). There is a huge blowup of a NASA photo that shows the craterlike Makhtesh in great detail—it looks just like the surface of the moon.

The *Mitzpe Ramon Geological Observatory* is open Saturday through Thursday from 9 A.M. to 4:30 P.M. Fridays and holidays from 9 A.M. to 2 P.M. There is an entrance fee. There is a hostel and a rest house here, as well as a snack bar and restaurant (for light food) on Mitzpe Ramon's main street.

The Inn at Mitzpe Ramon

Isrotel, one of Israel's leading hotel chains, has built an inn at Mitzpe Ramon. It was not complete when we visited and we were unable to get any details. If you want to explore the Negev region, this is an excellent base. Call Istrotel's U.S. sales office at (201) 816-0830 for the most up-to-date information and for reservations.

Avdat

Just a few miles north of Mitzpe Ramon is one of the most impressive sights in Israel. The grandeur of the *Nabatean Kingdom* can still be felt in the ruins that sit high above the empty desert, a limestone Arabian acropolis on a cliff-top plateau. Who were these ancient desert people who were responsible for building Petra in Jordan and this lofty city? The Nabateans were nomads who built Avdat as a caravan stop between the Saudi Arabian trading posts and their capital at Petra, in the first century B.C. These once-great people fought with the Maccabees against the Greeks and controlled a great portion of the Negev, Transjordan, and Gaza. They traded in gold, precious stones, and spices, amassing great wealth along the way. Avdat was the grandest of their caravan stations, but resources in the wilderness were non-existent. Houses had to be built of intricately fitted stone. Rainwater had to be collected via a complex system of irrigation ditches and cisterns. Agricultural experts today still marvel at the genius of yesterday's farmers–the desert dwellers provided methods for growing food in the barren land that were light-years ahead of their time.

Avdat's decline was heralded by the Roman invasions, around A.D. 106. It fell to ruin until the fourth century, when it was utilized as a fortress by the Romans, who were also on their way out. Byzantine monks resettled the city in the sixth century A.D. and transformed the temple into a Byzantine church. They added several churches and structures to what existed there at the time, but they too faded into oblivion. The Arabs seized Avdat in the middle of the seventh century A.D., and it sat dormant until 1871, when it was rediscovered. It wasn't until 1935 that excavation was started and now, thanks to the Israeli Historical Sites Authority, Avdat can reveal its former splendors.

To reach Avdat, proceed cautiously. The road to the summit is a bit tricky; keep your vehicle in low gear. At the foot of the hill, there is a booth where you can pick up booklets on Avdat and En Avdat (described below). There is also a cold-drink stand opposite the booth. You will come to a point where you must park your car and ascend the rest of the distance on foot. This is the highest point in the desert and was a perfect natural fortress for those old Nabateans, who would be able to see the enemy hordes invading from far away.

The hike up is really not so exhausting; whenever you get short of breath, just stop and survey the windswept vista of the Negev that stretches out for miles. The ruins here are worth the climb: a small museum housed in a Byzantine bathhouse (exhibiting beautiful examples of Nabatean pottery), the workshop of a Nabatean potter, and a large military encampment are highlights. Note the winepress and the juice-collection vat; they are superb examples of ways of utilizing the natural decline of the hill. Part of the National Park System. Open 8 A.M. to 4 P.M. (Fridays till 2 P.M.)

En Avdat

This icy-cold pool of water, fed by flood waters that flow through channels in the rocks, lies at the foot of a canyon below Avdat. This fountain, which cascades into the deep rocky canyon, is one of the most intensely beautiful sights in the dry and barren wilderness of the desert. It can be confusing to find it, however, for just as you pass Avdat, you'll see a sign to En Avdat off to the right. If you follow this dirt road you will be atop the canyon, where the Parks Authority has installed an observation post. You can see the water below and if you speak loudly or shout, the sounds will bounce around the canyon, scaring off any ibex drinking there.

To reach the pools themselves, continue on Route 40 to Institute Sde Boqer. Turning right, you will see the road that leads down into the canyon. If you are lucky, you will spot a gazelle or an ibex drinking the clear, cool water. You'll walk along the dry riverbed, which runs between the massive canyon walls, then climb up sixty stone steps (I always count steps) to the first water-fall and pool and even further to the second pool, which is sur-rounded by bamboo shoots. No swimming, but if no one is look-ing you might dip your toes for a bit.

Sde Boqer Institute and Kibbutz

When you return to the highway, make an immediate right into the Sde Boqer Institute, which includes a school for foreign students, a center for study of the Negev, and a teachers' college. As you follow the magnificently landscaped path, with flora from deserts all over the world, you realize that Ben-Gurion's dream, of populating and greening the Negev is still possible. On a grassy slope overlooking En Avdat ravine are the simple graves of Ben-Gurion and his wife, Paula.

The kibbutz, a few miles north, is a green world in a vast brown wilderness. Orchards, neatly tilled fields with crops cov-ered with plastic, and flowering trees and bushes are everywhere. About three hundred people live here in neat one-family homes, with laundry hanging out to dry and young children riding bicycles and playing basketball. Notice that each home has a wall on its eastern side that acts as a buffer against the sand-storms that move in this direction.

You will find the Paula and David Ben-Gurion hut of consider-able interest. They lived here after his retirement, from 1963 to 1973. This plain, humble dwelling tells more about the man than any book or history lesson; the focal point of this tiny house is the library, where you can see perhaps a thousand books on many subjects lining the bookshelves. This scholarly man's tastes ran to religious, scientific, and biographical works. His sensitivity shines forth in the numerous mementos he saved throughout his busy life—a photograph of Gandhi, small plaques and flags given to him by youth groups from all over the world, honorary medals, and personal and family photographs.

Shivta

The last stop along Route 40 before you reach Beersheba is **Shivta**. Shivta is thirty miles southeast of the Negev capital, another slightly less dramatic example of Nabatean ingenuity. Shivta's name may be derived from the Nabatean word *Shevet*, which means "tribe." Shivta was not a main stopping point for caravans and was not destroyed by the Romans, as was Avdat. It seems that Byzantines liked to repopulate abandoned cities, and during the fifth and sixth centuries A.D., Shivta experienced a revival. The remains of several Byzantine churches, public squares, two- and three-story buildings, and water cisterns were excavated and reveal that Shivta must have been a fairly large town. The Moslems followed and added a mosque to the site. This city remains much as it did in the fifth century. You can walk through the streets and terraces of town. Shivta represents the best-preserved Byzantine ruin in the Negev.

Shivta, the only site not directly on Route 40, is reached by making a left turn onto Nizzana Road. It is only a short detour (about five miles), but the paved road gives way to mostly dirt about halfway there. At this point, you are fifty kilometers from Beersheba, the capital of the Negev.

Beersheva/ Beersheba

eersheba, the town of the Patriarchs, has always been a point of demarcation in the desert. Israel's fourth largest city and the only major city in the southern half of this land, it lies on an imaginary boundary line that separates the more fertile northern regions from the barren terrain of the south. What makes Beersheba interesting is not that it is a modern city of nearly 113,000 people who have literally built the wide tree-lined streets, lush parks, and housing developments in this wilderness since 1948—admirable but not terribly exciting. What gives Beersheba rhythm and a special beat is that it has always been and continues to be a prime center of Bedouin life. Bedouins have come to this place for millennia—to water their flocks at the wells, to do business, and to socialize.

Excavations at Tel Beersheba have revealed signs of ancient nomadic peoples dating back six thousand years. Many of these tribal wanderers live as they did then, moving silently across the desert, settling for a time near grazing lands for their sheep and goats, and then moving on to a new oasis. As you approach Beersheba, particularly from the east (Arad), you'll see hundreds of tiny encampments. Here too, Tel Sheba, the first permanent Bedouin settlement, can be found just outside the city. Many residents keep tents pitched nearby just in case claustrophobia sets in. During Wednesday night, the caravans (camels and pickup trucks) start for town, arriving at dawn for the start of the famous Bedouin market, which starts at 6 A.M. This market ain't what it used to be, but it is still a special experience. Beersheba is the Bedouins' capital city, and that is what makes a two-day stay here a lot of fun. If you are not going to Elat, you can use Beersheba as your base for desert exploration as well.

Orientation

Getting There

We have already detailed Route 40 from Elat and the Arad road (see *Dead Sea*). Excellent roads link Beersheba with the north. *Sheruts* from Tel Aviv and Jerusalem are available, but if you have the time, you can take the train from either city.

Getting Around Town

You will spend most of your Beersheba hours, both daylight and evening, in the downtown old town, which was laid out by the Turks. During the day, it is best to park in one of the free lots nearby and walk. Many of the streets here are one way or dead end, so keep your eyes peeled for the red circular sign with a white slash—it indicates No Entry.

City buses link all parts of the city, but the sights outside the city limits (like Tel Arad) are not serviced. To reach them, you will have to take an intercity bus (to Arad) and get off as close as possible and hike. Not the best!

Major Streets

David Tuviyahu Boulevard is the major street in the new part of town. It becomes *Elat Road* just south of the old town, and this is where the Bedouin market is located. *Hanessim Boulevard* is the other main street in the new city. When it crosses David Tuviyahu Boulevard into old town, it becomes *Herzl Street*. *Herzl Street, Ha'atzmaut* Street, and *K.K. Le Israel* are downtown's three busiest streets. *Smilansky Street* is the center of evening activity in Beersheba.

Hotels

The standard of luxury at most of Beersheba's hotels is more in the realm of "standard" than "luxury" and Beersheba, not yet organized for tourists, has very few hotels. Listed below are the pick of the lot, offering comfortable, clean accommodations and that must—air conditioning.

THE DESERT INN—BEERSHEBA 4*

Box 247	Phone (057) 424922
Beersheba 84102	Telex 5266
	Fax (057) 412772
	Major Credit Cards

The class act in town, the Desert Inn is a resort hotel and a five-minute drive from the old city along David Tuviyahu Boulevard. All one hundred rooms have phones, radios, and full baths. There are several types of rooms, however, and some are minuscule. But the hotel's swimming pool will revitalize you after a day of sightseeing in the heat, and in the early evening you may feel up to a set of tennis on one of the hotel's courts. There are two dinning rooms and the second-floor *Grill Room* functions as a restaurant, serving good grilled meats and fish. The grounds are parklike—lush and tropical—and there is plenty of parking out front. At night a keyboard player entertains in the comfortable bar. *Moderate.*

THE ARAVA HOTEL 2*

37 Ha' Histadrut Street	Phone (057) 78792
	Major Credit Cards

This 27-room hotel, tucked away on the second floor of a nondescript building, has its central location as a real advantage. Right in the heart of the old town and near the shops and restaurants, it offers air-conditioned rooms with tiny bathrooms (showers only). The reception desk is on the second floor. *Inexpensive.*

HA NEGEV HOTEL 2*

26 Ha-Atzmaut Street	Phone (057) 77026
at Trumpeldor Street	*Major Credit Cards*

This hotel is in a 200-year-old building and maintains strict kosher standards. The old section of the hotel has nine rooms, while the new wing has twenty-one—most of them with air conditioning and bathrooms (shower only). The location is central and you won't find a quainter atmosphere anywhere in Beersheba—the old building used to house the Sultan's harem. No television in rooms; there is a set in the lounge. *Inexpensive.*

HOTEL AVIV 2*

40 Mordei Ha-Getaot   Phone (057) 78059
                                       No Credit Cards

The small (twenty-two rooms) Aviv is also in the old part of town. All rooms have private bath (but most have showers only) and are clean if small. Breakfast is included in the rate. *Inexpensive.*

If all the previously listed hotels are booked, try *The Rol*, 29 Ha-Palmach Street (across from the Aviv). Its twenty-eight rooms are air-conditioned, but have no private bathrooms.

BIET YATZIV YOUTH HOSTEL

79 Ha'Atzma'ut Street   Phone (057) 277444

The Biet Yatziv offers both youth hostel and hotel-style accommodations. The young-in-spirit and low-in-funds should opt to stay in the hostel itself, which offers a bed (eight beds to a room) and bath at $13 for Youth Hostel members, and just a few dollars more for non-members. There are also family rooms with four beds. Hotel accommodations are in the adjacent guest house, which has moderately priced air-conditioned singles and doubles. There is a large outdoor swimming pool on the grounds. Breakfast is included. *Inexpensive.*

Restaurants

The traveling gourmets among you will be fighting a losing battle here, for Beersheba is a culinary wilderness. The city has a surprisingly large number of moderately priced restaurants, but their menus are virtually identical. It would appear that the definitive desert taste is olives, humus, and tehina, followed by shiskliks or kebabs—all well-prepared, however. We did manage to find several non-Middle Eastern eateries, and these too serve tasty food in comfortable but not elegant surroundings. Listed below are our finds with an eye to variety of fare.

PAPA MICHEL

95 Histadrut Street

Monday—Thursday,
noon to midnight,
Friday till 7 P.M.
(closed for Sabbath)
Visa

The food in this simply decorated restaurant will not astound you but it will please you; it's plain and, due to the freshness of the ingredients, better than what you'd find at most of the other restaurants in town. Middle Eastern specialties include baked lamb, couscous, mixed grill, and twelve variations on salad. You can dine in the garden or indoors, where it's cozy and candlelit. Plaques on the walls from the Ministry of Tourism announce Papa Michel's status as a winner in the restaurant sweepstakes. It's a family operation here, and the waiters take good care of you. *Moderate.*

THE JADE PALACE RESTAURANT

79 Histadrut Street

Noon to 3:30 P.M. and
7 P.M. to midnight
Not Kosher
Major Credit Cards

This will be a favorite place of yours when you're in Beersheba—simply because it's unique. Its cinnamon exterior with oriental touches is reminiscent of a pagoda—not original, but in Beersheba, quite amusing! The chef really is Chinese, so the food is authentic. Indoors, the Chinese lanterns, the large aquarium, and the predominantly pink, red, and purple color scheme complement the dishes like sweet and sour pork and shrimp with garlic, and beef in mushroom sauce.

PALACHINTA

98 Histadrut Street
Corner of Yair

No Credit Cards

Should the craving for blintzes prove too much for you to bear, head toward Palachinta straightaway. Not only are the crêpes and blintzes (all reasonably priced) stuffed with a wide variety of goodies from fruit to nuts to caviar and sour cream, but you'll be sitting in one of the oldest buildings in Beersheba, built by the Turks and nearly crumbling at its limestone foundations. (How's that for ambience?) The restaurant is across the street from the Jade Palace.

ILLIE'S STEAK HOUSE

21 Herzl Street
Phone 278685
Sunday—Thursday,
noon to midnight,
(open after Sabbath)
No Credit Cards

Unless you simply adore poster-sized camels, you will not be bowled over by Illie's decor, which is rather basic. But the cuts of meat and fish, straight from Beersheba's market, look fresh—and they are. Charcoal-grilled and served with a variety of salads, these are your best bets here.

BET LIMON

18 Ha' Histradrut Street
Phone 271095
Sunday—Thursday,
10 A.M. to Midnight
Kosher
No Credit Cards

A bright yellow-and-white stop, Bet Limon serves Middle Eastern specialities such as couscous and lamb kebobs. Named for the lemon tree that grows in the dining room and that gives the restaurant its distinctive aroma, Bet Limon faces Gan Ha-Nassi Park.

THE BULGARIAN RESTAURANT

112 K.K. Le Israel Street
Sunday—Thursday,
8 A.M. to 10 P.M.
closed Friday,
open Saturday
Visa

It looks primitive, with its plain wooden tables that get so crowded with businesspeople and shoppers at lunchtime that you may have to share table space. The atmosphere here is homey, the staff is eager to please you, and the food is so plentiful (at minimal prices, too) that lunch or dinner at the Bulgarian is a good idea. The usual salads are all fresh and well prepared, and the roasted and grilled meats are cooked to order. The soups are stellar—a chorba sheep soup (a staple for Bulgarian sheepherders) translates into a hearty and filling lunch. There is a bar on the premises.

MINA KONDITOREI

on Histadrut Street, near Hadassah Street
Mina has what we consider to be the best selection of pastries, cookies, and cakes in the Negev. The coffee (which often falls short of the mark in Israel) is excellent.

HUNGARIAN RESTAURANT

Histadrut Street 51–1   Phone 27740
As you would imagine, goulash and paprika dishes rank high on the menu, along with a number of very filling soups. Also on the menu are five types of blintzes—cheese, meat, mushroom, vanilla and marmalade— and salads. Located not far from the new aqueduct.

For a Quick Bite: Canion Center

For a light snack or quick meal, you'll find plenty of options at the Food Court on the lower level of the Canion Center Shopping Mall. Old standbys include Pizza Hut, Burger Ranch, fried chicken and a salad bar at Quicki, and a Chinese take-out. Cafe George is perfect for coffee and pastries; or, go more typical with shwarma and veggies.

K.K. Le Israel Promenade

Finding a place to eat in Beersheba is much less of a problem since the expansion of the mall on K.K. Le Israel Street at Histadrut Street. The falafel places are literally climbing on top of each other, and ice creameries, or dairy bars, try to attract the most attention with their colored plastic streamers and balloons and the rainbow-hued umbrellas that provide welcome shade. There is something of a carnival atmosphere at this place; it's young and noisy and what modern Beersheba is all about. Try the Café Panorama on the second level of the mall at the corner —it's the one with the prettiest awnings that tilt charmingly over the windows looking out onto the street. Sit here for lunch and watch the shoppers file by in search of a bargain, or go late at night and watch the singles action.

Dining in a Bedouin Tent

What may be the most unusual place to have dinner is actually a bit out of town at Tel Beersheba. The eatery, part of a shop/restaurant/peacock farm/archeological dig mélange is open for dinner only. Inside the large tent, the tables are so low you feel as if you are on the floor on pillows. Middle Eastern food is served by costumed waiters. Prices are higher because of the ambience and yes, it is all a setup and not authentic, but what the hell, you aren't coming back tomorrow. For reservations, phone 460103 *Moderate*.

Sunup to Sundown

Unless you are using Beersheba as a base for desert exploration, two days is a fair amount of time here. Try to arrive on a Wednesday so you can walk around the city, rising early on Thursday morning for the Bedouin Market. The market is in full swing by 6 A.M. and runs out of steam by noon (although it is officially open till 2 P.M.). Beersheba was an important city in biblical times, when Abraham lived here, but for centuries it was little more than a dusty desert outpost and has few must sights. It does have a lovely museum that you will enjoy and a puzzling war monument outside of town that you will like.

A Capsule History

The name *Beersheba* literally means "well of the oath" and probably dates back to the days of Abraham. The Patriarch watered his flock at a well here that was owned by King Abimelekh. As a peace offering, Abraham offered the king seven ewes, and the two swore an oath of friendship. In the Bible, the land of ancient Israel stretched from "Dan (in the northern Galilee) to Beersheba." Tribes of Jews returned from captivity in Egypt and Babylonia to settle here. The Romans and Byzantines followed, but until 1900 Beersheba was merely a place for Bedouins to water their flocks. When the Turks came, they built a small town whose purpose was to serve as the administrative center for the scattered nomads of the Negev. The old town is still there (in part) today; the fine museum is in a Turkish building. It was in Beersheba that Lawrence of Arabia was captured and imprisoned by the Turks. He had entered the town disguised as a Bedouin in an attempt to learn about its fortifications, but was captured and supposedly tortured by the Turks. (For the full story, rent the movie!) Beersheba was the first town in Palestine taken by General Allenby and the British. In 1948, three thousand people lived here. The Egyptian army controlled it as the Mandate came to an end, but in fierce fighting, in an operation called Ten Plagues, the Israelis took the area in October 1948.

A Walk Through the Old City

The old city as it exists in its present form isn't so old. The Turks built this area in 1907. A few of the best examples of Turkish architecture are still around today—the Great Mosque is now the town museum, and the old city hall in a Turkish bath is now an administrative building surrounded by a restful garden called Allenby Park.

Start your walk where David Tuviyahu Boulevard meets Herzl Street (there is a parking lot here). As you walk along Herzl Street, a busy commercial area lined by low old buildings, you will notice that the Israelis of Beersheba are more often than not new immigrants, for this city is rather comparable to a city in the American west during the gold rush days—a new frontier. You'll see dark-skinned, lithe Ethiopians, some in tie-dyed saris and others in western garb, and you'll overhear conversations in Russian at many outdoor cafés. When you reach Ha'atzmaut Street, turn right and walk past Allenby Park to the mosque, which is the *Negev Museum*, a compact jewel. It's in the loveliest old building in Beersheba (fine Moslem architectural details, for it was originally the Great Mosque) and contains an impressive collection of ancient artifacts from different historical periods.

Most of the items exhibited here were found in the central Negev, south of Beersheba. Fine examples of pottery from the Persian period (late sixth through fourth centuries B.C.) and the Upper, Middle, and Early Fortress periods (seventh through sixth centuries B.C.) constitute a major part of the collection.

The Byzantine relics, however, are the most important finds here. Wonderful mosaic floors, Corinthian columns, slabs of marble engraved with ancient Greek inscriptions—imperial edicts and dedications—are in fine condition. The most important example of Byzantine art is the Kissufim Mosaic from a church floor (dated sixth century A.D.), which was found in the town of Kissufim in the western Negev. It is almost perfectly intact, depicts two benefactresses of the church, and has Greek inscriptions.

The Negev Museum is open from 8 A.M. to 5 P.M. Sunday through Thursday, from 8 A.M. to 1 P.M. on Friday, and from 10 A.M. to 1 P.M. on Saturday. There is free admission on Saturday. The phone number is (057) 34338.

Leaving the museum, continue along Ha'atzmaut Street, where en route you will pass a cemetery. These graves mark the final resting place for British soldiers who died wresting this city from the Turks. It is well cared for.

Return to Herzl Street and turn right into K.K. Le Israel Mall with its cafés and shops. This may be the time for a soft drink (we consumed vats of liquids here—it gets very hot) and a newspaper break. The *Jerusalem Post* and *International Herald Tribune* are sold at Steimatzsky's nearby. When you're ready to continue your walking tour, make a right onto Hehalutz Street, which is lined with flowering trees, and follow it to Smilansky Street. This street has several pubs and art galleries, and you will want to return here at night. Turning left onto Smilansky, follow it to the dead end, which is Trumpeldor Street. This corner (Smilansky at Trumpeldor) houses several discotheques and pubs.

Follow Trumpeldor Street back to K.K. Le Israel and turn right; you'll soon find yourself at the riverbed (Hebron Street). The Tourist Office literature says Abraham's Well is located here, but much to our surprise, there is no longer a well but a wall plaque marking the spot where the Well of the Oath stood four thousand years ago. At any rate, the city market is nearby and that is interesting to see.

To see the more modern parts of town, return along Elat Road to Hanessim Boulevard. Turn right and you'll notice wider streets; taller, newer buildings in white stone; large parks; and government buildings. This is where the 110,000 residents of Beersheba work and play. Nearby stand the modern City Hall and *Yad Labanim*, the Soldiers' Memorial House of Beersheba. This monument also houses a library, the city archives, an educational center, and a museum. The first floor is strikingly simple. The names of fallen soldiers are engraved into the black basalt pillars that support the ceiling. A display shows different stages of the Liberation War, and artifacts from Tel Beersheba and the Negev are here as well. No English explanations yet. Hours are Sunday through Thursday 9 A.M. to noon and 5 to 8:30 P.M.; Friday 9 A.M. to noon; and Saturday 10 A.M. to 1 P.M. Admission is free.

The Bedouin Market at Beersheba

Every Thursday, starting at 6 A.M., a most curious assemblage of what is old and what is new takes place in a special area near the municipal marketplace, at the south-eastern edge of town. *The Bedouin Market* has been a fixture and a weekly event in Beersheba for as long as anyone can remember. More than a bazaar or a flea market, it's a chance for the Bedouins to pause from their nomadic ways, set up their stalls, sell their wares, trade and barter for livestock, and get as good a look at us as we're getting at them. The variety of salable merchandise is endless: gaudy costume jewelry, colorful embroidered vests, purses, gowns, belts, and caps (usually less than top quality and overpriced), brass and aluminum kitchenware, hand-dyed skeins of wool that shock the eye with their brightness, and a medley of Bedouin handicrafts that make nice gifts and souvenirs.

It will hit you rather quickly—"What is wrong with this picture?" you say, as you look at tables, piled sky-high with stone-washed denims, plastic shoes, and battery-operated toy cars. You'll see some Bedouins selling cuckoo clocks and polyester curtains; the market has obviously become a retail outlet and everybody's got a stake in it. It doesn't seem right; it takes away from the authenticity of the scene—but you cannot hold back the tide of commerce. The trick is to ignore this element of the market and focus instead on what remains of the old ways: the dark, swaddled women with nose rings and tattoo arabesques under their eyes, sitting amid burlap bags of spices—cumin, turmeric, and *hel* (used for flavoring Turkish coffee). Wander to the outskirts of the market area to see the ruddy, wind-burnt men in white desert habits haggling over the price of sheep and camels, while puffing on water-pipes in crouched huddles, and the women pinching the thighs of live chickens and turkeys in anticipation of the evening meal. Let one of the *kaffiyeh* vendors tell you how great you'll look in that black-and-white checkered cloth with the black satin cord—as he practically forces you to put one on.

There is plenty of free parking at the market. Keep your eyes open for the better buys, like the gleaming brass and copper Turkish coffee cups with trays, carved wood, rugs, baskets, and Arabian saddles, and don't be shy—bargain hard. It's expected of you.

Andarta Monument and Tel Beersheba

Two of Beersheba's most interesting sights lie just outside the city limits on the road toward Arad.

The first, the Monument to the Negev Fighters, also known as the Andarta Monument, is an unusual memorial built on Hill 369. This is the most imaginative, paradoxically whimsical yet effective war monument you may ever see. At first it looks like a futuristic playground, but as you approach the hill you realize it isn't a park. Built in 1969 on the hill that affords the most sweeping view of the area, the memorial is for the brigade that captured the Negev during the 1948 war. The eighteen sections of the monument are made of concrete, cast into a jungle-gym style of shapes that symbolize army bunkers, trenches, and a pipeline. The entire Ten Plagues campaign is part of this memorial—watch and water towers and the dome with the inevitable listing of the fallen and the dates they died. You become a living extension of the symbols by walking, climbing, and crawling up, through, and around these abstract forms. Hopefully you will feel some of the pleasure the soldiers who survived must have felt as they surveyed the vast desert they'd won, and just a tinge of pain for those who perished. In a country full of striking memorials, this is one of the most moving.

No car? Bus #388 Beersheba–Arad passes the monument (it's still a hike to the top). Admission is free.

Just beyond the Andarta Monument is the Tel Beersheba complex, which we mentioned in the Restaurant section. An ancient Israelite city has been unearthed; its walls and gates, an unusual circular street lined with buildings, and a deep well are already visible at this huge mound. Many of the artifacts are in the Negev Museum. Adjoining the Tel is a shopping/restaurant complex. The shop is run by a lovely English-speaking woman who had terrific gift items that we hadn't seen elsewhere. (The secret was out when we saw her bargaining hard at the Bedouin Market.) But do stop in because she has a good eye for the unusual and her prices were in line with elsewhere.

Adjoining the Tel Beersheba complex is the Man in the Desert Museum, which focuses on man's adaptation to a desert environment and has a terrific exhibit about Bedouin life. Hours are 10 A.M. to 1 P.M. and 4 to 6 P.M.; the museum is closed Friday and Saturday.

Nearby is Tel Sheba, a village with recently constructed homes for Bedouins willing to give up their nomadic lifestyle and settle down. The Bedouins themselves had a hand in designing this village; but we saw several tents set up nearby—just in case. Interesting to see, and the children are delighted to see you.

Visit a Bedouin Village

We were informed about this tour by a woman at the Beersheba tourist office, and although we were unable to take the tour ourselves, we are passing along the information. Travel agents in town organize group visits to a nearby Bedouin camp. Here, with Bedouin music as a backdrop, you can have coffee with the local sheikh and ride on a camel. Dinner tours include a typical meal eaten while sitting on rugs inside the large black tent, as well as the camel rides. Setup for the tourists? You bet, but on the other hand, how many sheikhs will invite you for dinner? Worth a look! Contact A. Zakai at 75 Rehov Hehaluz (phone 77477) or Teper Tours, Passage Srul (phone 34625).

Sports

Swimming Pools

A refreshing afternoon swim will feel very good about 3 P.M., when the hot sun has been baking on your head for hours. Try one of the following. Desert Inn Hotel Pool, April through October, closed Saturday, phone 74931 (fee); Municipal Pool, Shikun Gimmel, May through September (small fee); Country Club, April through October, phone 33444 (fee); University Sports Center, April through October, phone 37983.

Tennis

Reserve courts for early in the morning or late in the afternoon. The Desert Inn Hotel, Country Club, and University Sports Center all have courts. To reserve, see numbers previously listed.

Horseback Riding

For horseback riding, try the Neve Noy Horse Ranch, Nizzana Road (about forty kilometres away).

Desert Trips

Metzoke Dragot (see Dead Sea) and Neot Hakikar Desert Tours (see Elat) also operate from Beersheba. The Society for the Protection of Nature in Israel has an office in Beersheba. Their phone number is 232156. Also check at the IGTO near Egged Bus Station.

Sundown to Sunup

While most Beershebians are early-to-bed people, there is some action for night people. Here are some late-night possibilities.

Clubs

Mandy's Discotheque, 57 Hadassah Street, phone 35609. Beersheba's most popular watering-hole, Mandy's is open for drinking and dancing into the morning. It's wedged between shops and restaurants in the old town. The music is sometimes live and when it is, there is a cover charge which includes a drink. Open 9 P.M. to 3 A.M.

Beit Ha'Ajekef, 52 Smilansky Street, phone 78746. Look for the lit Budget Rent-a-Car sign and you've found this delightful pub/club. Hardly any English is spoken here and menus are in Hebrew only, but another patron will always help out. Head for the garden in the rear, which has rattan armchairs and encircling wall made of beer barrels piled atop one another. Live or taped music. Fish, steak, salads, and plenty of beer—at least that's what we got. Opens at noon. No credit cards.

Barnash, 15 Trumpeldor Street (9 A.M. to 3 A.M.), Simta, 16 Trumpeldor Street (in an alleyway), and Chaplin's, 18 Rehov Ha'avot (at Trumpeldor) are three neighborhood pubs that stay open late and draw only locals.

Shva Tea House, 29 Smilansky Street, phone 71454. An intimate place where young artists rub elbows, Shva is frustrating to find because there is no sign. Just watch where people are walking or where lots of cars are parked and you'll have found it. An eclectic assortmemt of art adorns the walls, and light fare is served. It's best to come here for pastries and coffee. The young people here are rather different from their hearty pioneering parents who built this city. No credit cards.

Bet Ha'am Community Center (Sderot Shazar). The center is open from 8 A.M. till 11 P.M. every day, and lots of activity goes on all day and into the night. Chess, bridge, and an occasional game of gin rummy can be found. There are concerts, lectures, and exhibitions (some in English), and dance troupes are often on hand.

The Rubin Conservatory and Academy of Music on Hameshahremim Street is Beersheba's own municipal conservatory, and the natives are justifiably proud of the fact. The Chamber Orchestra (founded in 1973) performs frequently at schools, youth centers, and clubs. For information, call (057) 31616 or 76019. Beersheba is also home to a Municipal Theater, the Dance Institute *Bat-Dor*, a youth Art Center, and a Center for Visual Art. Ask at your hotel's reception desk for details—or better yet, call Dafna Mora at the IGTO on Nordau Street (057) 36001.

Cinemas

There are many cinemas in Beersheba, and American films are always popular, so the language won't be a barrier. Here are several of them: the Be'et Ha'am, the Chen (at Einstein and Bialik Streets), the Gilat, the Eshel, and the Keren (near City Hall), the Merkaz (on Hapalmach), the Orten, the Orot on Hama'apilim. They often show first-rate films.

Art Galleries

Art galleries on and around Smilansky Street are open well into the night, but make sure to pinpoint them in daylight. Nights on Smilansky Street are black voids.

The Liarz Art Gallery, 25 Smilansky Street (76747), is in a quaint old Turkish building surrounded by a high garden wall. Open 9 A.M. to 1 P.M. and 5 P.M. to midnight, seven days a week.

Beersheba Potpourri

Egged Bus   Rehov Hebron. Phone 74342.

IGTO   Rehov Nordau (near the Bus Station). Hours 8 A.M. to 5 P.M. Sunday through Thursday, 8 A.M. to 1 P.M. Friday. Phone 2360013.

Phone Code for Beersheba   (057).

Post Office   Located on Hanessim Boulevard near David Tuviyahu Boulevard.

Train Station   The new railroad station is near the bus station on Rehov Hebron. It will be in operation when you get here. Check before you leave your embarkation point.

Tel Aviv/ Jaffa (Yafo)

Jerusalem, a fabulous combination of the modern and the ancient, breathes history and legend. Tel Aviv, Israel's largest city, has both feet firmly planted in the twentieth century. In fact, Tel Aviv, the first all-Jewish city in modern times, did not even exist until 1909, when a group of sixty disgruntled families decided to leave the narrow confines of their homes in Arab Jaffa and move slightly northward. Aided by the Jewish National Fund, they purchased several tracts of land, virtually all sand dunes. For a time the settlers were badly outnumbered by snakes and lizards.

Symbolically, they named their new settlement Hill of Spring. As the population increased, they continued to buy land in irregular parcels, which may explain the circuitous—often downright strange—paths taken by some downtown streets.

Tel Aviv, more than any other city in Israel, reflects the character both of the country and of its native-born *sabras*. To savor the sweet fruit of the sabra, a prickly pear, one has to patiently peel off the irritating outer layers. Tel Aviv is rather like that. At first glance, it is an unattractive city with undistinguished architecture, crowded streets, and brusque people. But as you spend time here, you'll find that brash, cosmopolitan Tel Aviv is where the action is in Israel.

Hundreds of sidewalk cafés serve as meeting places for Yiddish-speaking old-timers by day and for Reebok-shod youngsters well into the night. The city has fine museums, lovely parks and beaches, concert halls and theaters, elegant restaurants, and chic shops. You'll soon find that your taxi driver and waitress and the people eating at the next table have relatives in London or Los Angeles, have visited them several times, and before you know it, they'll have filled you in on their family history and Israel's political problems and asked you a hundred questions about yourself.

Most of all, Tel Aviv is a delightful city for strolling and browsing. The beachfront promenade is open year-round, Dizengoff Street's chic boutiques and funky shops stand side by side, and Ben Yehuda Street has musty old antique shops. The Carmel Market in the Yemenite quarter and Jaffa's Flea Market are bargainers' delights, while the art galleries and craft centers on Gordon Street are outlets for Israel's most creative talents. We think you'll enjoy Tel Aviv's special charm.

Orientation

Getting into Town

Taxis make the trip from Ben Gurion Airport to North Tel Aviv in just twenty-five minutes. If you pick up your rental car at the airport, follow the English signs to Tel Aviv and, once you reach the city, look for those that read Beach Hotels. You might opt for the shuttle bus, which runs on the hour, and makes stops along Hayarkon Street near the major hotels. There is no sherut service to Tel Aviv, but if you get together four people, you can share a cab. The sixty-two kilometer run from Jerusalem to Tel Aviv, along a modern four-lane highway, takes just under one hour.

A Capsule History

During the First World War, the Turks occupied Tel Aviv, forcing the Jewish residents to flee. After the war, spurred by the 1917 Balfour Declaration, which promised the Jews a homeland in Palestine, a wave of immigrants from Eastern Europe poured into the town. In 1921, Tel Aviv, home to fifteen thousand people, elected Meyer Dizengoff its first mayor and became independent from Jaffa. During Israel's War for Independence in 1948, the Haganah launched an attack against the Arabs in Jaffa, who fled, turning an ancient Arab city into a ravaged Jewish one. In 1950,

Tel Aviv and Jaffa, (Yafo in Hebrew) were again united as one municipality. The city expanded rapidly after independence, spreading northward and eastward. Ramat Gan, Ramat Aviv, the ultraorthodox Bnei Brak, and Petah Tikvah form a large urban area with almost one and a half million people. Since these communities are of little interest to you as a visitor to Tel Aviv, you'll spend much of your time exploring the older downtown sections where you'll find the restaurants, theaters, shops and sights—all within easy access from the seafront hotel strip. This downtown section is bounded on the north by the Yarkon River and on the south by Jaffa. The Mediterranean Sea forms the city's western border. House numbers generally run from the sea eastward and from south to north. Note: The Hebrew word for *street* is "rehov" as in Rehov Hayarkon (Hayarkon Street).

Major Streets and Landmarks

Herbert Samuel Promenade   The lovely mosaic-tiled beach beach-front—front promenade stretches from the Hilton Hotel in the north to Jaffa. Several beach areas, a large marina, swimming pool, sidewalk cafés, and clubs are on the strip.

Hayarkon Street   A major thoroughfare that is home to Tel Aviv's finest hotels, with the most elegant on the western seaside. Look for Atarim Square (Kikar Namir), an elevated platform filled with outdoor cafés and shops. Open every night till the wee hours, Atarim Square is on the corner of Ben Gurion Boulevard.

Ben Yehuda Street   A commercial center best known for its antique shops and the city's fur district.

Dizengoff Street   Tel Aviv's answer to the Champs-Élysée, Dizengoff is the liveliest street in town, crowded with boutiques, sidewalk cafés, and shopping centers. Dizengoff Square, actually an elevated pedestrian platform, is a local hangout and meeting place, especially at night.

Allenby Street   A commercial street in the older downtown part of the city that is a middle-class shopping area.

Kikar Ha-Medina   A vast circular plaza that houses the city's designer boutiques and fine houseware shops. A twenty-minute stroll from the beach, Ha-Medina is encircled by some of Tel Aviv's most posh real estate.

Old Tel Aviv   At the northern tip of town where Hayarkon, Ben Yehuda, and Dizengoff Streets merge is a Greenwich Village-type area where much of the city's nightlife is located. Elegant restaurants, outdoor cafés, pubs, and rock clubs keep the streets alive every night of the week. Yirmiyahu Street is at the heart of this area.

Tizmoret Square   The city's cultural center, at the southern tip of Dizengoff Street, houses the Mann Auditorium (Israel Philharmonic), the Habima National Theater, and the Helena Rubenstein Art Pavilion, which offers special exhibits and is part of the Tel Aviv Museum.

Kerem Ha-Temanim   The city's Yemenite quarter has narrow streets and old buildings that house several fine restaurants. The raucous outdoor Carmel Market (Shuk Ha-Carmel) is here as well. Check out the small design studios, art galleries, and cafés on Shenkim Street near the market.

Jaffa (Yafo)   A four-thousand-year-old city just south of Tel Aviv, with a lively flea market, excellent restaurants, nightclubs, and a restored center filled with art galleries, outdoor cafés, and shops. This is a must stop and you'll want to spend both daylight and evening hours here.

Ramat Aviv   A ten-minute cab or bus ride from your hotel, Ramat Aviv is home to the notable Beth Hatefutsot Diaspora Museum on the campus of impressive Tel Aviv University and the nearby Ha-Aretz Museum Complex. This expanding museum has several buildings, each devoted to a unique aspect of Israel's past. Tennis players flock to the nearby National Tennis Center.

And now that you have your bearings, it's time to bed down.

Hotels

Tel Aviv's finest hotels dot Hayarkon Street, the seafront thoroughfare. A stay here puts you on the beach and within easy walking distance of fine shops, restaurants, and nightlife. Public transportation is easily accessible as well. Five-star hotels are on the seaside with four- and three-star choices across the wide street. As we previously noted, hotels with the same rating do not necessarily have identical amenities. Within each rating we have listed the hotels subjectively in the order that they appealed to us. Hotels accept major credit cards except where individually noted.

Tel Aviv Hilton 5★

Independence Park   Phone (03) 520222
Tel Aviv 63405   Fax (03) 5272711

The seventeen-story, six hundred-room Hilton has the best location in town. Set back from bustling Hayarkon Street on a private hillside in a lovely city park, the Hilton has all the amenities of a resort hotel plus all the big-city facilities too. You'll enjoy the large saltwater pool and sundeck, the first-rate health club, and floodlit tennis courts. Attractively decorated, unusually large rooms have comfortable sitting areas, minibars, in-house TV channels and twenty-four hour room service. The Hilton shopping arcade includes an H. Stern shop (fine leather and sportswear), boutiques, El Al, car rental agencies, and banks. Several restaurants, including the elegant King Solomon Grill, are on the premises, and a seafood eatery, Seaspoon, is on the beach. The Executive Business Center is manned by well-trained personnel from 8 A.M. to 10 P.M. Sunday through Thursday, with a 1 P.M. closing on Friday. Reserve through Hilton International stateside. *Deluxe*.

Tel Aviv Sheraton 5★

115 Hayarkon Street   Phone (03) 5286222
                                              Fax (03) 5280805

It may seem strange to describe a twenty-two-story, four-hundred room hotel as intimate, but the Sheraton has created a special, warm ambience with several small seating and eating areas in the large lobby. There is a multilevel shopping arcade as well as two outdoor pools and a sundeck on the mezzanine. Excellent restaurants include the Twelve Tribes, posh and romantic, and the sedate Danceotheque, which sways to the sounds of the 1950s and 60s. The Sheraton is a top-of-the-line choice. Reservations through Sheraton stateside service. *Deluxe*.

DAN HOTEL 5*

99 Hayarkon Street   Phone (03) 5241111
Tel Aviv 63903   Fax (03) 5249755

The Dan Tel Aviv, flagship of a fine Israeli-owned hotel chain, was Tel Aviv's first deluxe hotel. By constantly upgrading and adding to its facilities, the elegant, modern Dan remains at the center of the city's social whirl. The thickly carpeted, crystal-chandelier-lit, multilevel lobby is a prime meeting point for Israeli political leaders and businessmen, as is the lower-level Dan Grill. The 290 guest rooms are good-size with thick brown carpets, minibars, and TVs. The open-air pool is enclosed for winter use and there is a Jacuzzi. The Dan's health club has a sauna and a steambath as well as exercise machines. The Tent Bar is popular for late-afternoon cocktails, as is the lobby piano bar. *Deluxe.*

CARLTON TEL AVIV HOTEL 5*

10 Eliezer Peri   Phone (03) 5201818
Off Hayarkon Street   Fax (03) 5271043
Tel Aviv 61064

Another excellent choice, the fourteen-floor Carlton is right at the heart of things. Adjoining Atarim Square and fronting the city's marina and pool, the Carlton's 280 rooms are small but tastefully furnished, with sitting areas, minibars, and in-house TV. Another nice touch is the hair dryer in each bathroom. A rooftop pool and sundeck, several restaurants, and lounge areas round out the hotel's pluses. One drawback is the ''For Men Only'' sauna. The Carlton's business center offers access to international stock exchanges and secretarial and translator services. *Expensive.*

RAMADA CONTINENTAL 5*

121 Hayarkon Street   Phone (03) 5272626
Tel Aviv 63573   Fax (03) 5272576

Bright, comfortable, and luxurious are words to describe the Continental, where all 330 rooms have balconies that face the sea. Color coordinated with twin or double beds, rooms have direct-dial phones, individually controlled air-conditioner/heaters, and color TVs. The heated indoor pool and well-equipped health club are rarely crowded, and there is a direct walkway to the beach. Restaurants include the Asia Grill Room, where Chinese specialities are served. Reservations can be made through Ramada's stateside reservation service. *Expensive*.

MORIAH PLAZA TEL AVIV 5★

155 Hayarkon Street	Phone (03) 5271515
Tel Aviv 63405	Fax (03) 5271065

Watch the sun set behind the Mediterranean from the balcony of your room. All 350 rooms at the seventeen-story Plaza have ocean views. Rooms are carpeted and have writing desks, easy chairs, minibars, and TVs. The saltwater pool and sundeck are on a terrace off the lower lobby. The Plaza has a coffee shop but all meals are served in the main dining room, where an à la carte menu is available for dinner. The Plaza is not as luxurious as the other hotels with a five-star rating. *Expensive*.

YAMIT TOWERS 5★

79 Hayarkon Street	Phone (03) 5171111
Tel Aviv 63903	Fax (03) 5174719

A new stop on Tel Aviv's hotel strip, the Yamit is an all-suite hotel. While there is no minimum stay, most guests book for an extended period. Two-room suites with a large bedroom, a living area, and a fully equipped kitchenette were designed for double occupancy; three-room suites (two bedrooms) can accommo—date four. Suites are deluxe but highly functional. This is a great stop for families with young children. The Yamit has an outdoor pool and Jacuzzi off the smallish lobby and a highly regarded French restaurant, which also serves breakfast. *Expensive*.

BASEL HOTEL 4★

156 Hayarkon Street	Phone (03) 5244161
Tel Aviv 63451	Fax (03) 5440005

It's no wonder that guests return to the top-value Basel year after year. The 138 guest rooms are compact but comfortable and immaculate. The staff is very friendly and helpful, going that one extra step to make you feel really welcome. Most guests eat all their meals in the lower-level dining room, where breakfast is also served. A block from Atarim Square and the beach, the Basel has a small outdoor pool and sundeck. Free parking. Good choice. *Moderate*.

CONCORDE HOTEL 4*

1 Trumpeldor Street   Phone (03) 5659241
Tel Aviv 63902

Tucked on a small street between the promenade and Hayarkon Street, the Concorde is a far nicer choice than a quick glance at its location and crowded lobby would indicate. The ninety-two rooms, many of which have terraces overlooking the promenade, are well laid out to maximize your comfort. The hotel has a dining room for breakfast and a terrific sidewalk café. *Moderate*.

GRAND BEACH HOTEL 4*

250 Hayarkon Street   Phone (03) 5466555
Tel Aviv   Fax (03) 5466589

Guests at the 208-room Grand Beach return each year for the excellent location—only a short walk from the Hilton Beach and the Little Tel Aviv nightclub/restaurant area. The ample rooms have modern furnishings with minibars and in-house TVs, and a copy of the *Jerusalem Post* appears at your door each morning. The pool is large and there is a sauna. Business travelers can use the hotel's cable and telex system. *Moderate*.

TAL HOTEL 4*

287 Hayarkon Street   Phone (03) 5442281
Tel Aviv 63504   Fax (03) 5467687

The Tal's outer façade, a peculiar shade of green, is the only unattractive feature of this popular 126-room hostelry. The small lobby and dining room are often filled with young guests attracted by the Tal's location only a few blocks from the city's nightlife center and the Hilton beach. A good value choice. *Moderate*.

THE SINAI 4*

11 Trumpeldor Street	Phone (03) 652621
Box 26505	Fax (03) 660297
Tel Aviv 63803	

With 250 rooms spread over sixteen floors, the brown-stone Sinai rises above the buildings nearby, giving upper-floor rooms an unobstructed view of the beach and the promenade. The largest four-star hotel in the city, the Sinai has several five-star amenities, including a large outdoor swimming pool and sundeck on the mezzanine and room service. The dairy coffee shop and lobby cocktail lounge are usually crowded with guests. By the way, a nice sitting area is one flight up from the lobby. Staff is very helpful here. *Moderate*.

PARK HOTEL 4*

75 Hayarkon Street	Phone (03) 651551
Tel Aviv	

Another of Tel Aviv's tower hotels, the smaller 99-room Park has the most southerly location on the strip. Easy walk to Jaffa and the Yemenite Quarter from here. A few rooms have only showers but all are comfortably furnished and well cared for. Ask for a room with a balcony facing the Mediterranean. *Moderate*.

ASTOR HOTEL 4*

105 Hayarkon Street	Phone (03) 223141
Tel Aviv	Fax (03) 5237247

Back rooms have ocean views and less street noise at this recently renovated 68-room hotel. Rooms facing Hayarkon Street can be very noisy. Located near the deluxe Dan Hotel, the Astor's biggest pluses are the Panorama (nouvelle cuisine) and the Second Floor dairy restaurant in the lower lobby. *Moderate*.

RAMAT AVIV 4*

151 Derech Namir	Phone (03) 6990777
Ramat Aviv, Israel	Fax (03) 6990997

Museum lovers with cars or children might consider the attractive 114-room Ramat Aviv, a five-minute walk from the Ha'Aretz

Museum. Surrounded by lavish gardens, the hotel looks rather like the house in *Great Expectations*. There is a pool. *Moderate*.

Three-Star Hotels

If you arrive in Tel Aviv sans reservations and find the five- and four-star hotels booked solid, here are some three-star options—all are on or near the beach strip, well maintained and with air conditioning.

SHALOM HOTEL 3★

216 Hayarkon Street   Phone (03) 5243277
                                    Fax (03) 5235895

Forty-two rooms (only thirty doubles) in a modern, five-story hotel. Only doubles have tubs. The hotel faces Independence Park. *Inexpensive*.

FLORIDA HOTEL 3★

164 Hayarkon Street   Phone (03) 5242184
                                    Fax (03) 5242184

Fifty-two rooms, all carpeted with full baths. Some rooms face Atarim Square, so if you are a light sleeper ask for a back room. *Inexpensive*.

CITY HOTEL 3★

9 Mapu Street   Phone (03) 5246253
                                    Fax (03) 5246250

Near the four-star Basel, the ninety-six room City is also near the beach. All rooms have tubs. *Inexpensive*.

Restaurants

Tel Aviv's cosmopolitan nature is accurately mirrored in the enormous number and variety of restaurants that thrive here. It is the rare block that does not have several eating spots—ranging from fast-food eateries, to European-style konditoreis, sidewalk cafés, and elegant restaurants. Weather permitting, as it does much of the year, tables are set out on the sidewalk. Whether you want to sample Eastern European specialties, kosher or nonkosher Chinese dishes, or French, Italian, or Middle Eastern cuisine, you'll find a host of restaurants to satisfy you. While fine restaurants are scattered throughout the city, we've sought out those that are within walking distance of your hotel, in areas near theaters and concert halls, and those easily accessible by public transportation.

Kosher restaurants close for the Sabbath after lunch on Friday and reopen for Saturday-night dinner. Restaurants here open at 11:30 A.M. and usually stay open till midnight or thereabouts. Restaurants are most crowded between noon and 2 P.M. for lunch and 7 and 9 P.M. for dinner. Most are informal and quite small. Since Israelis eat out frequently, it is advisable to make reservations for dinner, especially on Saturday night. Major credit cards are accepted except where noted.

French Restaurants

As elsewhere in the world, the French restaurant in Tel Aviv epitomizes elegant dining, fine food, and good wine.

CASBA

32 Yirmiyahu Street	Phone 602617
Little Tel Aviv	Lunch and Dinner
	(closed for Sabbath)

Considered among the city's finest restaurants, French or otherwise, the Casba's garish outer façade masks one of the most elegant dining spots in Israel. The bilevel restaurant has whitewashed walls, and graceful arched doorways lead from one small dining area to another. Every table is adorned with a bouquet of fresh flowers and fine china and stemware. Soft piano music in the background and the well-trained waiters' attention to detail make your dining experience here special. Artichoke hearts vinaigrette or delicate smoked salmon are delicious starters, and owner Emil Gatlin is proud of the tournedos chasseur au poivre and the canard (duck) flambé for entrées. Leave room for the sweet liquor-filled crêpes. *Expensive*.

HIPPOPOTAME

12 Yirmiyahu Street	Phone 448729
Little Tel Aviv	Lunch and Dinner
	Diner's Club, Visa

Hippopotame is Tel Aviv's French brasserie. Its two indoor dining rooms and sidewalk café attract a younger, hip crowd looking for delicious French dishes in a less formal, less expensive atmosphere. The lure here is the prix fixe dinner (three courses), consisting of salad, soup, a choice of main course, and either wine or beer. Less hungry? Scallops St. Jacques and a variety of pâtés are on the à la carte menu. Pastry, ice cream, and mousse are offered for dessert. Open late. *Moderate.*

Fine Hotel Dining

We rarely recommend hotel restaurants, which tend to serve uninteresting food at inflated prices. However, Tel Aviv, with many restaurants but few elegant ones, has three exceptional restaurants in its deluxe hotels. These serve French and Continental specialties in posh surroundings, and are definite possibilities for a business dinner or big night out. All are strictly kosher and serve limited menus on Friday night if they open at all.

KING SOLOMON GRILL

Hilton Hotel	Phone 5464444
	Lunch and Dinner
	Major Credit Cards

Located in the Hilton's lower lobby, the heavy carved wooden doors open onto an elegant dining room with plush high-backed chairs and widely spaced tables. Live piano music in the background accompanies the smoked goose breast on melon (smoked game tastes like prosciutto) or the deep-fried stuffed mushroom caps. Prime ribs are carved to your taste, as is the roast veal loin. Service is slow and attentive. Indulge yourself in the light souffle for dessert. Open Friday evening with a limited menu, but closed for lunch on Saturday. *Expensive.*

THE TWELVE TRIBES

Tel Aviv Sheraton Hotel   Phone 5286222 ext. 3824
Dinner only, 7 P.M.
Major Credit Cards

The Twelve Tribes offers superb French food in a romantic candlelit dining room. Attentive waiters seem to anticipate your every need as they serve the thinly sliced goose liver with apples and smoked salmon with capers and onions. Tournedos Rossini and tender filet mignon are house specialties. Parfaits, mousse, and crêpes are the finishing touches to a delightful dining experience. Good wine list. *Expensive*.

DAN GRILL

Dan Hotel   Phone 5241111
Lunch and Dinner
Major Credit Cards

Because it is located in the heart of Tel Aviv's commercial district, the Dan Grill is most popular for lunch, when it offers a prix fixe menu as well as an à la carte one. Serve yourself from the hors d'oeuvres cart and the salad bar, which features raw vegetables and prepared mixed salads. Soup arrives, followed by a choice of meat, which will be carved at your table. A dessert cart follows.

You can eat well here in a short time or you can linger over lunch if you prefer. Evening fare leans toward superbly prepared French dishes, including duck and seafood. Closed for Sabbath. *Expensive*.

Eastern European Cuisine

CAFÉ DAN

147 Ben Yehuda Street   Phone 220988
Major Credit Cards

Friends who live in Tel Aviv and consider themselves mavens of Eastern European Jewish food insist that Café Dan has the best in town. After eating my fill of the kishke and the tongue with a tangy sweet-and-sour sauce with tiny raisins, boiled beef, and schnitzel, I have to agree. The dishes taste exactly the same as my grandmother's did (Polish-based) and the portions were just as large. All ingredients are kosher, but because Café Dan does not close for Sabbath observance, it cannot be certified. Little ambience. *Moderate.*

BATIA

197 Dizengoff Street at Arlosoroff	Phone 221335
	Visa, MasterCard

Vying with the Café Dan for top honors is Batia, a block away on Dizengoff Street. Similar in style with small indoor dining rooms and a covered street terrace, Batia's menu is slightly more diverse. Here we tried the delicious stuffed cabbage, which was served as an appetizer but was actually enough for an entire meal. I passed on the jellied calf's feet (*petchka*), but my friends liked it. On Friday and Saturday, Batia serves the traditional cholent, a meat, potatoes, and barley stew with kishke. Fruit compote with peaches and plums was tangy and the perfect end to a filling meal. Again here, only kosher ingredients are used, but because it is open on the Sabbath, Batia is not kosher-certified. *Moderate.*

TULIPAN

7 Pasteur Street	Phone 817979
(at the entrance to old Jaffa)	Open noon to 3 P.M.,
	7 P.M. to midnight
	(closed for Sabbath)
	Major Credit Cards

The only kosher Hungarian restaurant in Tel Aviv, Hungarian specialties are served in a colorful Hungarian setting dominated by tulips and waiters in national costume. We especially enjoyed the Hartobagy, pancakes stuffed with spicy ground meat and topped with a creamy tomato sauce and the goose liver appetizer. Paprika is used quite liberally in many dishes. *Moderate.*

BABUSHKA'S

20 Yirmiyahir Street	Lunch and Dinner
Little Tel Aviv	*Major Credit Cards*

An informal dining spot for lunch and dinner or a late evening nosh, Babushka's serves Eastern European specialties prepared in the Russian mode. Cold yogurt or borscht (beet) soup, kreplach, and blintzes. The house specialty is crêpes filled with chopped vegetables or ice cream. *Inexpensive*.

Seafood

THE CORNER

317 Hayarkon Street	Phone 5443864
Little Tel Aviv	Dinner only
	Major Credit Cards

Very small, with two indoor dining rooms and a covered sidewalk terrace, the Corner serves excellent seafood. We enjoyed the smoked trout appetizer, served with a tangy horseradish sauce, and the fish soup, which had large chunks of fish and seafood in a spicy broth. The grouper with capers and mushroom sauce is in demand, as is the steamed trout in almond sauce. Fried bananas and pineapple are light desserts. Reserve. *Moderate*.

SHALDAG

| 256 Ben Yehuda Street | Phone 5465030 |
| Little Tel Aviv | *Major Credit Cards* |

You don't need Sherlock Holmes to tell you that Shaldag is a seafood restaurant. The outer façade, whitewashed stucco embedded with stained glass fish, is the first clue, and the clincher is the fishnet hanging from the ceiling, complete with seahorses and crabs. Case closed. Now for the good part—the food. Shaldag's chefs prepare a scrumptious shrimp platter with very large shrimp in a provençale sauce or with a garlic-tomato sauce. Sole meunière with sliced almonds and lobster, shelled or broiled in the shell, are expensive but certainly delicious. Shaldag has been awarded the Tourist Ministry's award for fine food several times. Desserts are commonplace. *Moderate*.

Yemenite Restaurants

Make sure to eat at least once in Kerem Ha-Temanin, Tel Aviv's Yemenite Quarter, where a cluster of small, informal restaurants serve the city's tastiest Middle Eastern food. You'll also enjoy walking through the area, which is one of the city's oldest districts. An unusual feature in each of these restaurants is an "exclusive" dining area (room or annex). The exclusive section frequently has exotic furnishings, tablecloths, air conditioning, a few extra dishes, and slightly higher prices. Yemenite restaurants are kosher, so they are closed on the Sabbath. How to choose between them? Stroll around till you find the one that suits your mood.

ZION EXCLUSIVE

28 Peduyim Street   Phone 658714
Lunch and Dinner
Major Credit Cards

Walk past the outdoor tables and indoor dining rooms to the "exclusive," a small room decorated to look like the movie set for *Dinner in Bagdad*. Damask walls, silver table tops, intimate booths covered by flimsy scarves, and dim lighting make for a romantic, exotic setting. Service is unhurried. A delicious soup with beef chunks and beans or vine leaves stuffed with ground lamb and rice are delicious. Lamb, which is the house specialty, is served as chops, on a skewer, or sliced. Ouzi, a Bedouin lamb stew, has lots of meat, rice, and vegetables in a rich brown gravy. Desserts, which are very sweet, include honey-dipped cakes and caramel custard. *Moderate*.

SHAUL'S INN

11 Elyashiv Street   Phone 653303
Lunch and Dinner
Major Credit Cards

There is nothing special about Shaul's exclusive dining room downstairs, unless you cannot eat without a tablecloth, so we suggest you head for the ground-floor main dining room. It has stone floors, dark-brown wooden tables, and a huge photograph of a Yemenite wedding filling one wall. Shaul's attracts a noisy, fun-loving crowd on Saturday nights, and it often spills out into the street. Share a mezze (assorted vegetable salads), which you can dip up with pita bread, or some stuffed vine leaves. Osso bucco (stuffed leg of lamb) is the specialty of the house, but you'll enjoy the shashliks and shish kebabs too. *Moderate*.

PNINAT HAKEREM GAMLIEL

47 Hakovshim Street   Phone 661537
Major Credit Cards

The Gamliel at number 47 and its less-fashionable sister at number 38 have several dining rooms and lots of hanging greenery. Number 47 has stained-glass windows and red tablecloths. Both offer identical menus, which include delicious hot vegetable soups and small salads, including falafel. The stuffed vegetables are superb, with delicately seasoned ground meat and rice filling the cavity of an eggplant or green pepper. Entrées include skewered meats and grilled steaks. *Moderate.*

Italian (and Quasi-Italian)

VITTORIO

106 Hayarkon Street   Phone 5246837
Lunch and Dinner
Major Credit Cards

This attractive restaurant is open for lunch but we prefer it for dinner, when there is more time to savor the food and unwind in the comfortable ambience. Despite the chianti bottles hanging overhead and the Neapolitan songs on the tape, Vittorio's menu roams the globe. Minestrone soup and herring filets, spaghetti with meat sauce and beef stroganoff, seabass Hawaiian—I'm sure you get the idea! Small, with only a dozen tables, so it's best to reserve. *Moderate.*

ME & ME

293 Dizengoff Street   Phone 5443427
Little Tel Aviv   No Reservations
Lunch and Dinner
No Credit Cards

Small and dimly lit, Me & Me rarely has tables at peak dinner hours, since the food is good and the prices quite low. A white picket fence at the very end of Dizengoff Street tells you that you've arrived, as does the delightful garlicky aroma of freshly baked pizza, lasagna, and cannelloni. Veal and chicken dishes are very good too. The atmosphere is informal, with checkered cloths on the tables, and the service is slow but steady. *Inexpensive.*

OSTERIA DA FIORELLA

44 Ben Yehuda Street
(corner of Bograshov)

Phone (03) 5288717
Open Sunday through Thursday,
noon to midnight, Friday,
noon to 3:30 P.M.,
Saturday, 6:30 P.M. to midnight

This small corner eatery is authentic Italian from the red-and-white checkered tablecloths to the Chianti bottle with a candle on every table. Owner and chef Fiorella hails originally from Rome and the proof is in her cooking. Homemade gnocchi is served on Sundays and Thursdays with a variety of different sauces including Bolognese and quattro formaggi (four cheeses) while pasta, chicken and veal dishes are offered every day. Any of Fiorella's soups make a delicious starter or a light meal. Charming. *Moderate*.

BOCCACCIO

106 Hayarkon Street

Phone (03) 5246837
Lunch and Dinner
Monday through Saturday

Fine Italian cuisine is served in a lovely setting, complete with chandeliers. Pastas are homemade and the ravioli is especially good. The menu features a number of beef and fish dishes, including scallopine. *Moderate*.

CACTUS

66 Hayarkon Street

Phone 5105969
Noon to midnight every day
Visa

Tex-Mex cuisine is served in a lovely Southwestern-style setting featuring light woods, beamed ceilings, terra cotta tiles and scenes reminiscent of Arizona. Popular entrées include *Drunken Chicken* (chicken in Tequila Sauce), taco salads, frittatas, and the *Santa Fe Sandwich* (smoked beef with barbecue sauce). *Moderate*.

CHICAGO PIZZA PIE FACTORY

63 Hayarkon Street

Phone (03) 657505
Lunch and Dinner Daily
Major Credit Cards

As you can tell from the name, deep dish pizza, Chicago Style, is the specialty here. "Everything But the Pan" is our favorite, generously topped with pepperoni, sausage, mushrooms, green peppers, onions, olives, and lot of cheese and tomato sauce. Sports posters for Chicago teams hang throughout the fire-engine-red dining room. Look for the door with the sign that reads "To the Johns"; pass through and you'll have a choice of "Elton John" or "Olivia Newton John." Definitely a lot of fun. The Tel Aviv restaurant joins others in London, Paris, and Barcelona. *Moderate.*

Romanian Restaurants

MON JARDIN

186 Ben Yehuda Street

Phone 5231792
Noon to midnight
Major Credit Cards

Head for Mon Jardin if you are very hungry. Portions are huge, particularly the trademark grilled or pan-sautéed entrecôte steak, smothered with onions. Start with such Eastern European favorites as chopped liver, gefilte fish, or stuffed peppers. A popular business lunch eatery, the Mon Jardin is less crowded at night. *Moderate.*

MAMAIA

192 Ben Yehuda Street

Phone 5237784
Noon to midnight
Major Credit Cards

Mamaia, a long, narrow restaurant a few steps away from Mon Jardin, is also popular with those who enjoy Romanian cooking.

Romanian kebobs are served here, as well as charcoal-grilled meats and fish and a whole range of appetizers and mixed salads. *Moderate*.

South American Choices

BAIUCA RESTAURANT

103 Yehuda Hayamit (Jaffa Port)	Phone 827289

7 P.M. to 11 P.M.
(Closed Sunday)
American Express

Tucked in its own building near the Jaffa Customs House (lots of parking here), the twelve-table Baiuca is Israel's only Brazilian restaurant. It is always crowded; reservations are a must. Diners are drawn by the spicy crabmeat appetizers (*siri*) and the perfectly grilled meats (beef, pork, lamb) served on skewers, family-style. Share a platter of *feijoada*, Brazil's national dish, which is a tasty mix of pork, sausage, and black beans served over white rice. Wash your meal down with a cool Brazilian beer or *caipirinha*, a gimlet-like cocktail. The menu is in Portuguese and Hebrew , but the amiable staff speaks English and will gladly explain the dishes for you. *Expensive*.

EL GAUCHO GRILL

4 Shaul Hamelech Boulevard	Phone 6950079

Lunch and Dinner
American Express, Visa

Very informal, this Argentine grill (part of a chain) has both an outdoor terrace overlooking the beach and an indoor dining area. The meats (beef, veal, lamb, and chicken), grilled over an open hearth, are brought to your table on a small hibachi, which keeps them warm. Waiters in full gaucho regalia serve sliced tomato and onion salad, fried potatoes, and *chorizo* (a very spicy sausage eaten as an appetizer). If you have room for dessert, try a traditional *flan* (caramel custard) to cool your taste buds down. *Moderate*.

Eclectic Dining Spots

LITTLE OLD TEL AVIV

300 Hayarkon Street   Phone 455539
Little Tel Aviv   *No Credit Cards*

One of the city's "in" dining spots, funky Little Old Tel Aviv is the place to meet and greet. Its crowd is young, lively, and modishly dressed. The decor features old movie posters, ceiling fans, Salvation Army furniture, and an ancient piano which adds to the cacophony every evening. The menu is also eclectic, with omelets, spaghetti dishes, burgers with various toppings, spare ribs, chili, and pizza. Apple pie and cheesecake are excellent. You can spend the evening at the popular bar, which features daiquiris and pina coladas. Fun spot! *Moderate.*

APROPO

Jacob's Garden   9 A.M. to 2 A.M.
Mann Auditorium   *American Express*
Tizmoret Square

Surrounded by trees and hanging planters and often the sounds of practicing musicians, Apropo is one of my favorite spots in Tel Aviv. After a morning of sightseeing, I gratefully sink into a wicker chair and relax until the cold cucumber yogurt soup arrives, followed by a salad or an omelet. This is a dairy restaurant and fish is featured in the most filling dishes. All have musical names, such as maestro sandwich and Peter, Paul, and Locus fish. After a concert, the pastries are warm and so are the crêpes. Outdoor covered terrace plus indoor dining rooms. *Moderate.*

TABOON

Old Jaffa Port   Phone 811176
                                          Major Credit Cards

There are a half dozen restaurants on the fishermen's wharf of biblical Jaffa—but Taboon stands out. Painted white with turquoise accents, it looks as if it would be at home in Greece. The name comes from the unique Middle Eastern oven that lightly smokes food as it is baking it. Seafood is the specialty here. Shrimp tempura in a corn flour and beer batter is excellent, as is the St. Peter's fish in a wine sauce. *Moderate.*

MIMOUL

---

118 Hayarkon Street   Phone 5236105
                                                       11 A.M. to 2 A.M.

Friendly staff and comfortable tables in a small dining room with a few tables on the terrace make Mimoul an especially lovely choice. The menu roams the globe with a smattering of French, Italian, and Israeli dishes. The house specialty is stuffed vegetables. Try an artichoke stuffed with chopped meat and marinated in wine or lemon juice, or plums stuffed with meats, almonds, and raisins. Italian specialties include cannelloni, osso bucco, and pizza. *Moderate*.

HENN'S CORNER

---

108 Hayarkon Street   Phone 236859
                                                       Lunch and Dinner
                                                       No Credit Cards

A quick stop for lunch when you've been out shopping or sightseeing, Henn's Corner has only eight wooden tables in a tiny serving area. The waiters keep things moving here and the kitchen is fast as well. Assorted cheese and vegetable plates, vegetable omelets, and St. Peter's fish grilled in a light butter sauce are popular at lunch. Goulash is the house specialty—it's a stew thick with chunks of meat and vegetables in a tomato-based sauce. Delicious! Home-baked pastries and pies for dessert. *Inexpensive*.

CAFE TNUVA

---

34 Ben Gurion Boulevard   Phone 5272972
                                                       8 A.M. to 1 A.M.
                                                       Major Credit Cards

This lively café is always crowded at mealtimes. You can dine indoors or outside at one of the colorful wicker tables on the verandah. The menu features bistro-type fare including quiche, lots of salads, blintzes, sandwiches, and pasta dishes, as well as homemade cakes and pastries. A terrific spot for a late afternoon break. *Moderate*.

Delicatessen

ME & ME

49 Bograshov Street	Phone 5287382
(Downtown)	Lunch and Dinner
	Visa, Diner's Club

If you are in a hurry, you can eat at the bar or at one of the small counters set up for that purpose. Greek salad, shrimp kebabs, fried fish and chips are good for quick stand-up eating. But if you want to dine at a slower pace, wait for a table in the attractive wood-beamed dining room, which is crowded with business-people at lunchtime. Barbecued meats, prepared to your taste, are the most-ordered entrées, with pork steak, filet mignon, and lamb kebabs also on the limited menu. Side dishes include salads, onion rings, and French fries. Try a sticky sweet baklava for dessert. *Moderate*.

American-Style Food

BONANZA

17 Trumpeldor	Phone 5285803
	Lunch and Dinner
	Major Credit Cards

A popular pub and singles' stamping ground, Bonanza's tables are crowded for lunch and its bar area is wall-to-wall from 5 to 7 P.M. weekdays. Very rustic, its wooden walls decorated with scenes of the British countryside and Beefeater guards, Bonanza specializes in powerful drinks, spare ribs, burgers, and pasta. *Inexpensive*.

STAGECOACH

216 Hayarkon Street	Phone 5241703
	Lunch and Dinner
	Major Credit Cards

A western-style saloon, Stagecoach has a long wooden bar, high stools, and steers and stirrups on the walls over wooden booths. Live country/western music every night but Friday and a lively crowd of cowhands often sings along. Chicken in the basket or

Druze style (spicy with onions and potatoes), T-bone or sirloin steaks, and burgers with assorted toppings are the usual fare, but there are several daily specials too. Desserts include ice cream sodas and sundaes (Stagecoach isn't kosher). *Inexpensive.*

STEAKHOUSE WHITEHALL

6 Mendele Street   Phone (03) 5249282
                                          Noon to midnight daily
                                          Major Credit Cards

Whatever your appetite, there's a steak to match it at Steak house Whitehall. Steaks come in a variety of cuts and sizes, but what makes them extra delicious is that every cut is tenderized for two to three weeks before it reaches your plate. The menu also features an extensive selection of appetizers including mushroom-filled pastry, seafood cocktail and grilled pâté de foie gras, and tempting desserts such as chestnut mousse. A prixe fixe lunch menu, including steak, salad bar, garlic bread, potato, and beverage, is offered from noon until 6 P.M. *Expensive.*

Oriental Dining

THE RED CHINESE RESTAURANT

326 Dizengoff Street   Phone 448405
Little Tel Aviv   Lunch and Dinner
                                              American Express

The *red* in the restaurant's name has less to do with the owner's ideology than with the vivid tint used on the walls, tablecloths, and napkins in this always-crowded choice. The Red Chinese, with several small dining rooms and a covered sidewalk café, is known for its extensive menu. Dishes are seasoned to your taste, so if you like your food hot and spicy ask for the Thai dishes. Try the duck with pineapple, Thai-style, or chicken with lemon sauce. Steamed fish was moist and flaky. Sample several dishes. Great take-out for picnics. *Moderate.*

SUKI YAKI

302 Dizengoff Street   Phone 5443687
Little Tel Aviv   Lunch and Dinner
American Express, Diner's Club

Serving Chinese, Thai, and Japanese dishes, the multilevel Suki Yaki is rather overly decorated with gilt mirrors, paintings, and Chinese lanterns. Savor exotic Singapore Slings, or Mai Tais with the fried wontons or mixed appetizer plates. Then share a Fujiyama chicken, the house specialty. A whole chicken with spicy skin, it tastes rather like Peking duck. Hot shrimp Szechuan and steamed fish with soy sauce are delightful too. Service is impeccable and the live guitar music makes Suki Yaki a nice spot. *Moderate.*

Dining in Old Jaffa

Jaffa's restored area has some exceptional restaurants and some informal dining choices, all in Kikar Kedumin, the main square. Here are two elegant eateries and a delightfully informal choice.

Toutonne, at 1 Mazal Dagion Street, phone (03) 820693, has a delightful setting in a private garden adjoining the square. As at its sister eatery, the Toutonne Elat, the fare is French and non-kosher. Specialties include tiny shrimp stuffed in avocado and escargot à aïl (with garlic) as openers and steak au roquefort or St. Pierre fish with mustard sauce as entrées. Share a profiterole with chocolate sauce for dessert. Toutonne, open for dinner seven nights a week, does not accept credit cards. *Expensive.*

Yamit, at 16 Kikar Kedumin, is an open-air dining choice whose terrace overlooks Andromeda's Rock and the twinkling lights of Tel Aviv. Casual dining at its loveliest. Specialties include poached bass and sole meumière. Beware—we ordered bowls of fish soup as appetizers and could barely eat the main course. Open for lunch and dinner seven days. No credit cards accepted. *Moderate.*

Via Maris, at 6 Kikar Kedumin, phone (03)828451, is where my friend, spending her sabbatical year studying in Israel, took me to dinner. A multilevel dining room in a restored fortress, its many tables face the sea and are cooled by the breeze. Via Maris serves both meat and fish dishes prepared in French style. The salad had a thick roquefort dressing, and the sole, delicately poached in white wine, was flaky and moist. Veal cordon bleu was tender enough to slice with a fork. Here too, desserts are delicious but fattening, so if buttoning your skirt or trousers has become difficult, stick to fresh strawberries or raspberries sans whipped cream. Not kosher. Open seven nights and week for dinner. Via Maris accepts major credit cards. *Expensive.*

Blintzerias

Blintzes, cylindrical dough pouches bursting with soft, sweet cheese, fresh fruit, or chopped vegetables, lightly sautéed or baked and served with sour cream or apple-sauce, are commonplace in American Jewish homes and in Tel Aviv's sidewalk cafés. Head to place that specializes in them and not a place that serves them in addition to other things. Being a blintz maven, I found some delicious choices. Of course, none were as good as those my grandmother made—but they were close.

Shoshana and Uris, 35 Yirmiyahu Street, Little Tel Aviv, is a "formal" blintzeria, for it has tablecloths and only serves dinner from 6 P.M. to 1 A.M. (except Friday). The blintzes are Hungarian-style and in twenty-seven varieties. Order a hearty bowl of soup first. *Moderate.*

Plintzi, 23 Yirmiyahu Street, is an all-pink blintzeria, from its tablecloths to its striped awnings. Try the spinach-apple blintzes with sour cream. They were stuffed and very good. Open Sunday through Friday for lunch and dinner (except Friday night). *Moderate.*

Hungarian Blintzes at Dizengoff Square serves blintzes filled with melted chocolate (heresy!) that were too sweet for me. I enjoyed the eggplant-cheese variety better. Open for lunch and dinner, seven days a week. *Moderate.*

Afresmon Blintzes, Dizengoff Street at Jabotinsky, had an unusual poppyseed-and-date blintz that my friends loved. I'm a traditionalist, however, and stuck to cheese. *Inexpensive.*

Vegetarian Restaurants

The food served in Tel Aviv's vegetarian restaurants invariably looks fresh—as if they'd just plucked the zucchini or pepper as you ordered it. Vegetarian restaurants, which serve much the same food as many of the city's dairy spots, throwing in a tofu burger or carrot cocktail, are most popular at lunch. We found two we think you'd enjoy: *The Naturalist*, 60 Ben Yehuda Street (downtown) and *Banana*, 334 Dizengoff Street (Little Tel Aviv). Vegetable platters, vegetable quiches, mushroom and cheese omelets, blintzes, and sandwiches are all attractively served and delicious. Greek, Waldorf, and Niçoise salads are always fresh. Specials include cheese *moussaka*, cigars, and soya goulash. *Inexpensive.*

Sidewalk Cafés

Sidewalk cafés are in fashion in Tel Aviv, where restaurants augment their small space with glass-enclosed or roof-topped terraces. *Ben Yehuda Street, Herbert Samuel Promenade*, and *Yirmiyahu Street* are the areas with the nicest cafés. Dizengoff Street's cafés are rather like fast-food stops. Cafés serve a variety of light foods, with croissant sandwiches vying with filled crêpes and pastries as late-afternoon favorites.

London Konditorei, 186 Ben Yehuda Street and 15 Yirmiyahu Street, is like a European coffeehouse with small sandwiches, freshly baked pastries, and several teas and coffees. Pleasant ambience. *Inexpensive.*

Le Croissant, 155 Ben Yehuda Street (and other branches), is a newcomer on the Tel Aviv noshing scene. Sandwiches on croissants, filled sweet croissants, and flaky croissants with butter and jelly are the best choices. There are non-croissant choices too. *Inexpensive.*

Cherry, 166 Dizengoff Street and 145 Ben Yehuda Street, serves flavored frozen yogurt, pizza and pastries. There is another location: Cherry on the Promenade at 90 Herbert Samuel Promenade. *Inexpensive.*

Next door to Cherry on Dizengoff Street, at 168, is a branch of the very popular *Kapulsky Cafe* which first opened in Haifa and now has branches springing up in cities across Israel.

Promenade Café, 82 Herbert Samuel Promenade, serves late-afternoon cocktails and hors d'oeuvres-type appetizers that you nibble as the sun sinks below the sea. *Inexpensive.*

Atarim Square Restaurants

Outdoor tables, shaded from the sun by wide thatch or rain-bow-colored umbrellas, spread across this square from a half dozen kitchens. It's hard to tell where one restaurant begins and the other ends. They are all open late into the evening, when they serve as meeting places for Tel Aviv's young set. *Safari*, marked by a gorilla over its main door, is the most popular eatery here, serving charcoal-broiled hamburgers, steaks, and ribs along with daily specials. There is a well-stocked serve-yourself salad bar. Adjoining it is *The Rondo*, which serves burger-type food but adds several varieties of pizza, lasagna, and ravioli. Restaurants nearby serve ice cream and drinks.

Fast Food

Israel's answer to McDonalds is *MacDavids*, a hamburger eatery with a nonkosher branch (you can get a cheeseburger) at Frishman Street near Dizengoff. The Burger King of Israel is *Burger Ranch*, also on Dizengoff Street. Pizza by the mini-pie or the slice is sold at several spots along Dizengoff Street. The most popular fast foods here, however, are *falafel* (fried, ground-chickpea balls) and *shwarma* (sliced beef or lamb served in a pita and garnished with raw vegetables and tehina sauce). These items, sold like hot dogs by street vendors who prepare them for you, are also sold at stands where you garnish them yourself. Best falafels are sold in Jaffa. For a quick slice of pizza, try Ray's Pizza at 71 Ben Yehuda Street. It's sold by the slice or by the pie.

Sunup to Sundown

You will find yourself juggling your daytime hours here because there is so much to see and do. Interesting walks, fabulous museums, Old Jaffa, two markets, and of course, you'll want to shop. We'll try to give you an idea of what the "don't miss" spots are and then it's up to you to juggle.

To savor the beat of a city, we suggest that you walk through it. Tel Aviv is a particularly good city for strollers, since it is essentially flat, and, while there are many interesting places to see, none is crucial to your enjoyment and understanding of the city. Most stops are within easy walking distance of your hotel, so if you tire you can easily return another day.

Three vital stops, Jaffa and two Ramat Aviv Museums, are not within easy walking distance, so set aside time to visit them. Although you can walk to Jaffa, we suggest you save your energies for exploring the city itself, which is quite hilly. The museums in Ramat Aviv are a ten-minute bus or cab ride from your hotel.

And now, on your feet! (Make sure to pick up a free city map at the local IGTO at 7 Mendele Street, near the Dan Hotel.)

A Walk Through Tel Aviv

Start your walk at *Kikar Namir* (Atarim Square) overlooking the seashore where Hayarkon Street meets Ben Gurion Boulevard. The square, part of a hotel/shopping complex, has several open-air cafés serving light fare, ice cream, and cocktails. These, open from early morning to early morning, seven days a week, are local late-night meeting spots. Nearby, you'll see the city's marina and outdoor swimming pool.

Walk down the steps along tree-lined *Ben Gurion Boulevard*. On your left at number 17, marked only by a tall hedge and a kiosk, stands the unimposing house in which Paula and David Ben-Gurion lived. All their personal effects have been kept just as they were when the Ben-Gurions lived here before moving to Sede Boqer Kibbutz in the Negev. Ben-Gurion's library, with over twenty thousand books in several languages, is the most impressive room in the simple dwelling. The photos are what I enjoyed most, for they are a history of Israel's independence movement and the people who led it. Open Sunday, Tuesday, Wednesday, and Thursday 8 A.M. to 3 P.M.; Monday, 8 A.M. to 5 P.M.; and Friday, 8 A.M. to noon. The museum is open from 11 A.M. to 2 P.M. on the first Saturday of each month.

When you leave the Ben-Gurion house, continue along the boulevard for two blocks to *Dizengoff Street*. You'll know that you've arrived because the sounds of traffic and people will rise several decibels. Turn right onto Dizengoff, Tel Aviv's—and perhaps Israel's—most sophisticated, liveliest promenade, where fashionable shops stand next to mod ones, and scores of sidewalk cafés are jammed day and night. The amalgam of people is fascinating. You'll see young soldiers on leave with rifles slung casually over their shoulders; attractive matrons, neatly and fashionably dressed, carrying bulging shopping bags; purple- and orange-haired teens in cut-off jeans, T-shirts, and Nikes; and black-robed Hassidim gently tugging the hands of tiny boys with peyots, who would like to dawdle.

Hebrew, of course, is the primary tongue, but you'll hear English, Yiddish, French, and Spanish too. This is a cosmopolitan street in a cosmopolitan city. If you can't resist the shops, they are open from 9 A.M. to 1 P.M. and 4 to 7 P.M. Sunday through Thursday and 9 A.M. to 1 P.M. on Friday (see Shopping).

As you wend your way along the street, you'll suddenly see a raised pedestrian platform. This is *Dizengoff Square*, the heart of the city, especially interesting at night when it is crowded with revelers. If you need a short rest, you can sit on one of the benches on the platform, shaded by towering royal palm trees, or cool off near the multicolored fountain in the center.

Continue to walk south along Dizengoff until you see *Dizengoff Center*, the towering five-story shopping/office center with a few good shops and lots of promotions. Stores here do not close during the afternoon. When you leave the center, cross King George Street into a quiet residential area. Slightly uphill, only a few blocks ahead you will reach *Sderot Tarsat* and, on your right, a trio of modern white edifices. These form Tel Aviv's cultural center. The first, the *Helena Rubenstein Art Pavilion*, is a special exhibit hall, part of the Tel Aviv Museum (several blocks away). The day I visited, the Pavilion was between exhibits and was being used for finger-painting and giggling sessions by a very dirty group of five-year-olds. Normally, exhibit hours are 10 A.M to 8 P.M. Sunday through Thursday; Friday, 10 A.M. to 2 P.M; and 10 A.M. to 3 P.M. on Saturday.

Behind the Pavilion is a delightful oasis, *Jacobs's Garden* (Gan Yaakov), with benches, tall trees, and spraying fountains. Beyond it stands the *Mann Auditorium*, home of the famed Israel Phil-harmonic and where visiting orchestras from all parts of the world play. It can seat three thousand people and is almost always sold out. Founded in 1936, even before Israel was a state, it offered a creative outlet to musicians who had fled for their lives from Eastern Europe. Apropo, a delightful café, is located beneath the building's terrace.

Across the square is the recently renovated *Habimah National Theater*, which houses a repertory company that stages Hebrew performances of works by Shakespeare, George Bernard Shaw, and Eugene O'Neill. Founded in Russia by Stanislavsky, it opened to raves in Palestine in 1927 and has been performing here ever since. Some performances are simultaneously translated into English through earphones. The building also supports exper-imental companies of dance and theater.

From the theater, follow Ben Ziyyon (Zion) Boulevard down-hill for two blocks. Turn left onto King George Street and on the next corner (Shera Hashikmin) you'll see a brown building at number 38 which houses the *Jabotinsky Institute* (Metzudat Zeev). The institute is involved in historical research into the acti-vist groups within the Jewish Resistance Movement. These in-clude the infamous Irgun and Stern Gang units, which operated against the British during the Mandate Period. Jabotinsky, a writer, a journalist, and a fiery orator, was the founder of the Jewish Legion, whose members fought with the British against the Turks in the First World War. Jabotinsky was the spiritual and political mentor of the former prime minister Menachem Begin. The first-floor museum, dedicated to his life, depicts the resist-ance movement in a different light from the one you've been used to. All signs are in Hebrew, but for a very small fee you can buy an English pamphlet. Not many non-Israelis come here; the staff were very surprised to see me.

When you leave, continue walking south (left as you leave) along King George. This area, a commercial shopping district for Tel Aviv's middle class, has only a few shops that will interest you and these sell freshly baked pastries that you can munch on as you continue.

At Kikar Magen David, where King George joins Allenby Street (the area's major thoroughfare), you will hear a babble of shout-ing voices. This alerts you to the fact that you have reached *Shuk*

Ha-Carmel (the Carmel Market), the city's largest and rowdiest outdoor market.

Running for a dozen blocks, its stalls are filled with colorful fruits and vegetables, assorted homemade cheeses, and fresh breads and cakes. Burlap bags of spices send unusual aromas into the breeze, as do the smoked fish, olives, and pickles. Inexpensive clothing, pots and pans, and small appliances are also sold. The noise level is incredibly high due to the singing, hawking, cajoling, and shouting patter of salespeople pushing their wares and their customers haggling over the prices. It's great fun and you can gather a feast for a delicious seaside picnic.

At this point, you have several options. If you are tiring, leave the market, turn right to Hakoveshim Street, which passes through the *Yemenite Quarter* on the way back to Allenby Street and the beach. You'll enjoy *Kerem Ha-Temanim* (the Yemenite Quarter), which is one of the city's oldest areas. It has winding, narrow streets, small pink-and-white apartment buildings, and several excellent restaurants (see Restaurants). At Allenby Street, turn left to the sea. You'll see the new Dan Hotel/shopping complex here. By the way, the square at the foot of Allenby is called *Kikar Ha-Knesset*, for it was here that the Knesset met until the capital was moved to Jerusalem.

If you are not tired and want to continue to explore this downtown area, retrace your steps through the market to Allenby Street and turn right (east) to follow this wide street until you pass Montefiore. Just ahead, at 314 Dizengoff Street, you'll see the *Great Synagogue*, the largest in Tel Aviv, which was built in 1926 and renovated in the 1970s. Its white stone dome with stained-glass windows is lovely, but I found the interior disappointing. The Ashkenazi Chief Rabbi is installed here.

At the next corner (Ahad Hiam) turn right and glance up. Ahead of you is *Migdal Shalom* (Shalom Tower), a thirty-six-story commercial/shopping center, and Israel's tallest building. On this site previously stood Gymnasia Herzliya, the first secular high school, where all subjects were taught in Hebrew. Built in 1957, the tower housed the country's first department store and has added a wax museum, electronic game center, skating rink, and scores of small shops. Do take the glass elevator to the Observation Tower for a splendid view of the city and areas nearby.

Still game? Follow Herzl Street downhill for one block to tree-lined *Sederot Rothschild*. At number 16 stands *Independence Hall*, formerly the home of Meyer Dizengoff, founder and first mayor of Tel Aviv. It was here that David Ben-Gurion proclaimed a Jewish state on May 14, 1948. The house is filled with photos and newspaper headlines of those times and of the war that followed. Open Sunday through Thursday 9 A.M. to 1 P.M.. Closed Friday and Saturday.

The fountain you see in the middle of the next cross street is *Founder's Monument*, a three-tiered bas-relief which depicts the phases of Tel Aviv's growth.

At number 23, the *Israel Defense Forces Museum* (Bet Eliahu), which is popularly known as the *Haganah Museum*, will prove of great interest to history buffs. Located in the second-floor apartment of Eliahu Golomb, the founder of the Haganah, the building has been enlarged (keeping the original two secreted rooms intact) and its four floors hold exhibits tracing the birth of the Hashomer (the kibbutz defense forces) through the War of Independence, the Six-Day War (1967), and the Yom Kippur War (1973). The old photos, showing the ingenious ways weapons were hidden from the British, are fascinating. Most captions are in Hebrew; however, for a few argorot you can buy an English walking guide. Hours are 8:30 A.M. to 3 P.M. Sunday through Thursday, 8:30 A.M. to noon Friday. The museum is closed Saturday. Modest admission fee.

This walk has taken you through the older parts of the city, where most of the historical sites are located. Although it is written as one walk, there is no reason for you to do it in one day. Feel free to break off at any point and continue at another time. Bypassing those places that do not interest you is another good technique.

Other Interesting Parts of Town

Kikar Malkhei Israel — King of Israel Square

Ten minutes from Hayarkon Street (follow Sderot Ben Gurion) is a favorite holiday gathering spot for Tel Avivians. During Purim, costumed children from the surrounding neighborhoods party here, and on Independence Day, school bands play, fireworks light up the sky, and speeches are drowned out by laughter and dancing. The twelve-story building in the plaza is City Hall. Good view from the top.

Kikar Ha-Medina

A vast circular plaza a twenty-minute stroll from Hayarkon Street (follow Jabotinsky Street), Ha-Medina Square is the city's most chic shopping and residential area. Boutiques for men, women, and children are stocked with imported and Israeli designer clothes, European-style leathers, shoes, and housewares. Some shops definitely worth a peek are Leopard and Machos (for men); Pat and Nicole, Ouiset, and Rodier of Paris (for women); and Boom for the yuppie in your life.

First Cemetery

Opened in 1903 as a cemetery for Jaffa's Jews, it now holds the remains of Tel Aviv's founding fathers and several well-known writers and poets. A common grave holds the victims of an Arab massacre in 1920, while a black tomb symbolically notes the victims of Auschwitz. A lonely old caretaker will show you around (every single headstone if you let him), but since he speaks only Hebrew and French, I'm not sure if I've got my facts straight.

Safari Park (Ramat Gan)

Tel Aviv's zoo, located in the suburb of Ramat Gan, is actually a drive-around park where you follow five miles of trail through a two-hundred acre plain and observe animals in their natural habitat. You can stop as long as you please for the admission price. Young children may be frustrated by the fact that they cannot touch any of the animals, but if you don't have children with you, there is no great reason to make this trip. Hours: are 9 A.M. to 6 P.M. summer, to 5 P.M. rest of the year; 9 A.M. to 2 P.M. on Friday.

Tel Aviv's Two "Must See" Museums

Tel Aviv's two finest museums, located within a mile of one another in the near suburb of Ramat Aviv, are only ten minutes by cab or bus (#13, #24, #25, or #45) from your hotel.

Beth Hatefutsoth

Beth Hatefutsoth, the Nahum Goldmann Museum of the Jewish Diaspora, located on the campus of Tel Aviv University, is a unique institution. It houses an incredible amount of information about the basic tenets of Jewish life, how those tenets were maintained, and how a people who were scattered all over the world for 2,500 years survived. And what makes the museum such a fascinating place to visit is not the information alone, but the variety of media mustered to present the information.

The museum is arranged by topic, rather than chronologically. As you move through the three exhibit floors, you will find various aspects of each topic, such as "The Family" or "Holidays" using realia, slides, films, reconstructed buildings, models, photographs, and dioramas (with everything explained in a variety of languages). Stop at a mini-cinema for a ten-minute film contrasting Jewish life in Eastern Europe's shtetls with those in Morocco and Salonika, Greece, and don't miss the model of a thirteenth-century community peopled with realistically attired tiny figures and an ornately painted ceiling from a seventeenth-century Polish synagogue. There are individual study centers with films on a variety of topics, a Chronosphere where an audience of fifty can view an audiovisual presentation about the migrations of the Jewish people, and a vast computer center. This section is full of bittersweet memories for Ashkenazi Jewish visitors whose families lived in Central Europe. The computer is programmed with information about more than three thousand Jewish communities worldwide, and by punching in the name of the town or a family name, a printout appears with information about the community. Unfortunately, the bottom line for virtually all the communities of Eastern Europe is that they no longer exist. A sad but illuminating experience.

Each time I visit Beth Hatefutsoth (and I do each time I visit Israel), I overstay the time I've allotted myself. Be forewarned and leave enough time (three hours at least) so you can enjoy it at your own pace. Dairy cafeteria, book and gift shop. Hours: Sunday, Monday, Tuesday, Thursday 10 A.M. to 5 P.M.; Wednesday 10 A.M. to 7 P.M.; Friday 9 A.M. to 2 P.M.; closed Saturday. Entrance fee; additional fees for computer printouts and study halls.

Ha-Aretz Museums

A large museum complex with nine individual buildings (and others under construction), each focused on a different aspect of Israel's past. The entire complex, in a garden setting, is grouped around the Tel Qasile excavation site where since 1948 archeologists have unearthed a Philistine city. Built in the eleventh century B.C. and then destroyed, it was rebuilt in the tenth century B.C. during the reigns of kings David and Solomon. Streets, houses, a bronze workshop, and public buildings have been identified. The artifacts found here are exhibited in a nearby pavilion and at appropriate buildings on site.

The other buildings include: *Man and His Work*, which illustrates how tools and methods of working the land have evolved through the ages; *Kadman Numismatic Museum*, where exhibits include primitive moneys and coins in copper, gold, and silver, and comparative costs and pay scales in various societies are shown; *Ceramics Museum*, in a beautiful building that exhibits pottery dated back to the Neolithic period and illustrates several uncommon uses for pottery; *Glass Museum*, with ancient glassware from the sixteen century B.C. and many unique finds, including toilet vessels from a first-century steambath; *Nehushtan Pavilion*, in an architecturally interesting building resembling a limestone cave, which illustrates copper mining and smelting from the Stone Age to the present; *Ethnography and Folklore*, which has a fine collection of Judaica with ceremonial objects and clothing most visible; *Lasky Planetarium*, in a small domed building at the far end of the complex, with English shows on Monday and Wednesday at 8 and 9 A.M; *Museum of Science and Technology*, which is devoted to aviation and other methods of tranoportatioii aiid eiieigy; *Alphabet Museum*, where the history and development of writing and alphabets are explored.

Ha-Aretz has a well-stocked gift and book shop, but no eating facility at this writing. Hours: Sunday, Monday, Wednesday, Thursday, Friday 9 A.M. to 2 P.M.; Tuesday 9 A.M. to 5 P.M.; Saturday 10 A.M. to 2 P.M.. Free on Saturday. Buses #24, #25, #45 will whisk you here from Tel Aviv. Note: Check schedules here. They seem to change frequently and you'll want to coordinate with the Diaspora Museum hours. Phone 6415244.

Tel Aviv's Other Museums

Tel Aviv Museum of Art, 27 Shaul Hamelech Boulevard. (Downtown) Permanent and rotating exhibits of paintings, sculptures, prints, and photographs by Israeli and foreign artists. Films, concerts, and lectures are held here as well. Check Friday's *Jerusalem Post* for listings. Museum hours: Sunday through Thursday 10 A.M. to 9 P.M., Friday 10 A.M to 2 P.M.; and 10 A.M. to 2 P.M. and 7 P.M to 10 P.M. Saturday. Phone 261297. Bus #18 and #70.

Bialik Street, downtown, is home to three small museums that you might enjoy:

Bet Bialik Museum, number 22—This was the home of Israel's national poet and author of nearly one hundred books (translated into several languages), Haim Nahman Bialik. His letters, paintings, photos, and archives have been maintained in this small museum. Hours: Sunday through Thursday 9 A.M. to 7 P.M.; Friday 9 A.M. to 1 P.M.; closed Saturday.

Museum of the History of Tel Aviv, number 27—Photos, a model, an English-language film, and documents of the period trace the history of the city's founding and its early days. Hours:Sunday through Thursday 9 A.M. to 3 P.M.; Friday 9 A.M to 1 P.M.; closed Saturday.

Rubin Museum, number 14—Ruevin Rubin used Palestine, Jerusalem, and Zefat as his themes and his beautiful oils, watercolors, and sketches of pre-statehood days are exhibited here. Hours: Sunday, Monday, Wednesday and Thursday 10 A.M. to 2 P.M.; Tuesday 10 A.M. to 1 P.M. and 4 P.M. to 8 P.M.; Saturday 10 A.M. to 3 P.M.; closed Friday.

Jaffa (Yafo)

Jaffa, *Yafo* in Hebrew, an ancient city with a long and colorful past, has a colorful, exciting present. While Jaffa is part of the Tel Aviv/Jaffa municipality, it is distinct from it and you'll sense the difference in rhythm and beat immediately. The flavor is definitely Middle Eastern, with an Arab market and streets so narrow and hilly that they resemble alleyways. Lining them are peeling, centuries-old buildings, an occasional minaret, and the best falafel and Middle Eastern pizza stands in this part of the country. The restored area, **Old Jaffa**, on a promenade overlooking the old port, has a nifty mall with art galleries, craft workshops, and *The Israel Experience*, an audiovisual show. Nearby are fine restaurants, Israeli nightclubs with a belly dancer or two, and some interesting historical sights. You'll want to visit Jaffa both during the day and at night.

Orientation

Getting There

Jaffa is to the south of Tel Aviv. Buses link the two, and if you are fit you can walk to Jaffa along the shore.

Major Streets

Jerusalem Avenue The wide thoroughfare that links with the streets from Tel Aviv at Tarshish Boulevard.

Yefet (Japhat) Street Home to Jaffa's major landmark, the Ottoman Clock Tower, the street then heads uphill to Old Jaffa.

Haganah Square Just beyond the Clock Tower. Make a right on Mifratz Shlomo Street here and walk uphill into Old Jaffa.

Oley Tsiyon (Zion) Two blocks uphill on Yefet Street, make a left onto Tsiyon for the Arab Market and its funky curbside adjunct, which I've dubbed the "Junk Market"

Pasteur Street Main street of restored Old Jaffa with terrific shops, clubs, and a great view of the sea and Tel Aviv.

Kikar Kedumin The main square of Old Jaffa. Small cobble-stoned streets leading from it are named after the signs of the Zodiac.

Getting Around Jaffa

The part of the city that is of interest to you is in a very small, heavily trafficked area. You can drive to Jaffa, but then park your car and walk.

Free Walking Tours of Old Jaffa, led by knowledgeable and friendly English-speaking members of the Association for Tourism, leave from the Clock Tower at 9:30 A.M. every Wednesday. Take their advice and wear comfortable shoes.

Andromeda Walks: a local tour operator runs these walks on Mondays and Thursdays at 10 A.M. Fee.

Using this guide, you can easily walk through this area on your own.

A Capsule History

Jaffa, an important seaport in ancient times, became the gateway to Jerusalem under the rule of King Solomon. It was here that the towering Lebanon cedars that were used to build the Temple were delivered from Hiram, King of Tyre. The unusual name, legend states, came from Noah's son Japheth, who established the city after the great flood. Many legends are associated with Jaffa's harbor. During the reign of the Maccabees, Jaffa's Jews were forced to take shelter on boats by their hostile Greek neighbors, who promptly sank the ships, killing off a considerable part of the Jewish population. One hundred years later, history repeated itself as the Jews took refuge on ships to elude murderous Roman legions, and storms sank the ships in the harbor. With a happier ending we find the Greek legend of Andromeda, a lovely lass who was sacrificially chained to a huge rock in the harbor by Poseidon, god of the seas. He hoped she would assuage the local sea monsters. Instead she was rescued by Perseus, who married her. You can still see the rock today.

Jaffa, the port of entry for thousands of pilgrims over the centuries, later served as the gateway for thousands of Zionists who came to Palestine to start a new life. In 1921, Arab riots forced most of the Jews to flee to nearby Tel Aviv, and Jaffa stagnated until 1948, when it was captured by the Haganah amid vast destruction. In 1950, Jaffa and Tel Aviv were reunited and the Israeli government undertook a vast restoration project. The result, Old Jaffa, will restore your faith in slum clearance.

A Walk Through Old Jaffa and Jaffa's Flea Market

We'll start our walk at the city's most photographed landmark, the *Ottoman Clock Tower* at Haganah Square, just as you enter the city. The tower, built in 1906 by the Turkish Sultan Abdul Hamid II, marked the thirtieth anniversary of his ascension to the throne. Others stand in Jerusalem and Akko. Its newer stained-glass windows, the work of a local kibbutznik, depict events in Jaffa's history. Haganah Square and the city's two main thorough-fares, Jerusalem Avenue and Yefet Street, are filled with local shops, falafel stands, and traffic.

At this point, you can head uphill on Mifratz Shlomo Street (right) directly to Old Jaffa or you can visit the flea market. We'll take the latter option, anticipating the biggest bargains early in the day.

Continue along Yefet Street for one block and turn left at Oley Tsiyon Street, which leads to Jaffa's frenetic market. As you ap-proach the market, two blocks away, passing stores that reek of fish and slabs of meat hung from hooks, you'll notice peddlers with their wares dumped on blankets and spread on the side-walk. This is not the Arab market, which is tucked into two nar-row streets on your left. This, the Jaffa Junk Market (my name), is rather like a garage sale with second-hand clothes, battered pots, and "jewels." If you are a junk maven you might find something to make your day, but if you want something more upscale and want to put your bargaining skills to good use, plunge into Shuk Hapishpeshim.

Two covered alleyways, lined on both sides with stalls, the market features hammered copper and brass plates, mirrors, and samovars, Oriental jewelry, Persian carpets, interesting old maps of the Middle East, and lots of clothing. There are also stores in the market area. Make no mistake about it, the sell is hard here, but shrewd bargaining will get you a fair discount. Most merchants speak some English and all of them understand "too much money." When you tire of shopping, return to Yefet Street and turn left, uphill, for three blocks to *Pasteur Street*. On your right at number 4 you'll see the *Old Jaffa Mall*.

Here you can see the hour-long audiovisual presentation called "The Israel Experience" or eat at the rooftop Emerald Restaurant. Stop at the *Shalom of Safed* shop, especially if you aren't going to Zefat. Although you will see Shalom's posters in WIZO and Maskit handicraft shops throughout the country, this is the only shop that carries all his work. Shalom Moskovitch, a Hassidic watchmaker with a small shop near Zefat's bus station, painted when business was slow, which it often was. An Israeli artist noticed his work, and at age 65, Shalom became an overnight sensation and a collectible artist. By the time he died at age eighty, his work, using biblical themes and scenes of life in Israel, had been hung in museums in Paris and New York. This shop sells signed lithographs, posters, batiks, and tiles. Also in the mall area, you can watch glassblowers and potters at work. (At this writing Old Jaffa Mall is in the red and many shops have closed. An influx of new money should perk things up again.)

The better shops, however, are not in the mall but all around it, where cobblestoned streets and narrow alleys with names taken from signs of the Zodiac lead into art galleries and potters' studios, jewelers' workshops, antique shops, and boutiques. Individual shops we liked are listed in the shopping section (see Jaffa Shopping).

When you tire of browsing through the shops, take a break by walking over the small wooden bridge behind the mall to the grassy knoll overlooking the sea, where you'll see the unusual sculpture *Jacob's Dream*. This is a favorite photo spot for newlyweds and it's not unusual to see white-gowned brides and their tuxedo-clad grooms posing here. Time to head to *Kikar Kedumin*, the central square of Old Jaffa, which is filled with outdoor eateries, elegant restaurants, nightclubs, and some historical sights.

Before you reach the steps leading to the plaza, walk down the stone stairs to the left on *Shimon Habursk Street*. The heavy wooden door facing you will be locked, but you can gain entrance by ringing the bell. Christian tradition marks this site, home of Simon the Tanner, as the place St. Peter stayed after restoring Tabitha to life. The courtyard has a well that was in use during the time of Christ and an ancient carved stone coffin which the Moslems used as a washstand to purify themselves for prayer.

Remember the Greek legend of Andromeda? A marked path through the outdoor restaurant, Yamit, leads to the best vantage point to see and photograph the rock in the nearby harbor. In the plaza, you'll notice a fenced-off area. While reconstruction was taking place here, workers came upon the ruins of a third-century B.C. village and catacomb. The antiquities were moved to a nearby museum and the area was left as it was.

Beyond the plaza, the gold-orange brick building on your left is *St. Peter's Monastery*, built on a medieval citadel. Administered by Franciscan fathers, the church can be visited from 8 to 11:45 A.M. and 3 to 5 P.M. daily, with a Sunday morning service. As you continue downhill on Mifratz Shlomo Street, you'll see several nightclubs and the small *Museum of Antiquities*, which exhibits the pieces found in the plaza and other archeological sites nearby. Hours here are 9 A.M. to 2 P.M., Sunday through Thursday; also 4 to 7 P.M. on Tuesday. Also on the street is the *Mahmoudiya Mosque* and its lovely cloister. If you haven't wandered through the narrow streets off Kikar Kedumin, do so before you leave the area.

Mifratz Shlomo Street has kiosks selling sweet pastries and Middle Eastern minipizzas (chewy with salty cheese, eggs, and spinach) for a light lunch, but if you want something more substantial or you are here for dinner, you'll want to head to one of the eateries in the plaza or in the nearby old port area (see Restaurants).

Buses #10 and #46 will take you back to Tel Aviv in just a few minutes.

Shopping

While shopping at home is a necessary task, it is something I always look forward to when I travel. Over the years, I've gathered quite a few objects that I treasure, for each reminds me of a great vacation. Shopping in Tel Aviv is a lot of fun. The articles that are good buys range from fine jewels and furs to sleekly styled bathing suits; the shops are often as not raucous flea markets and, since they are in several parts of town, you are sightseeing at the same time. A strictly personal pet peeve is that the sales personnel in boutiques here hover over you, commenting on each item you finger. It takes several "I'd like to look first" comments for them to move away. Of course, many shoppers enjoy being "helped" and if you do, you'll enjoy this aspect of Tel Aviv shopping

Major Shopping Areas and Their Specialties

Dizengoff Street for sportswear, swimwear, shoes, leathers; *Ben Yehuda Street* for antiques (particularly Judaica), and furs; *Gordon Street* for art galleries,crafts; *Jaffa* for copper/brass, ceramics, inexpensive jewelry (The Market), arts, sportswear, and antiquities (Old Jaffa); *Shalom Tower/Dizengoff Center* for shopping centers with scores of shops of mixed quality.

Shopping Hours

Shopping hours vary tremendously. Most common are 9:30 A.M. to 1 P.M., 4 to 7 P.M. Sunday through Thursday, 9:30 A.M. to 2 P.M. Friday; closed Saturday. Shopping centers have no afternoon closing.

Credit Cards

Except for small antique shops, most stores take major credit cards. If you pay in nonshekel currency and are charged VAT (purchase over $50), save the receipt and ask for a redemption certificate.

Jewelry

The demanding skills required to produce an exceptional piece of jewelry have been passed down from father to son in Jewish families for generations. In Eastern European shtetls, in the cities of North Africa, in South Africa, and in the U.S., Jewish designers, stone cutters, setters, and goldsmiths have long been identified with the creation of fine jewelry. With so many master jewelers immigrating to Israel, it was only a matter of time before Israel's jewelry industry boomed. Fabulous colored gemstones, diamonds, ancient coins and glass, and the blue Elati stones are meticulously incorporated into 18-carat gold or silver designs with many one-of-a-kind pieces. Classic and Oriental styles as well as avantgarde styles are available and the distinctive traditions of various cultures are also evident. Immediately identifiable is the delicate filigree style of the Yemenites. Arab and Druze craftsmen are also highly skilled, although their creations rarely use gold or fine stones. Fine jewelry is tax-free in Israel and free of customs duty in the U.S. and European Economic Community countries.

H. STERN JEWELERS

Hilton Hotel Arcade   8 A.M. to 11 P.M.
Dan Hotel   (Early Sabbath closing)
Daniel Tower-Herzlia
Sheraton

H. Stern, a highly respected international jeweler with headquarters in Brazil and over 150 shops worldwide, is Israel's most prestigious jeweler. All purchases at Stern shops from the least expensive charm to the most costly diamond come with a worldwide guarantee (as to quality) and an exchange or repair can be made within one year of purchase.

The Stern trademark, the fabulous multicolored gemstones of Brazil, are featured here as well. Aquamarine, tourmaline, topaz, and lapis have been joined by Israeli-cut diamonds and Elat stones. Each stone sparkles in an 18-carat gold setting which was designed to fit the individual stone. The Tel Aviv shops feature the original designs of Amitar Kav, a sabra who creates just a handful of pieces each year. When you see them, you'll realize why. Each piece is a hand-sculpted work of modern art. Pieces include brooches, earrings, necklaces, and bracelets that are absolutely stunning. Stern also carries more traditional pieces and typical religious symbols. Shops also in Jerusalem, Elat, and Ben Gurion Airport. Major credit cards.

Padani Jewellers

185 Hayarkon Street   9 A.M. to 7 P.M. (except Saturday)

The Padani shop on the beach strip features designs from their own workshops, using 18-carat gold and silver. Pieces are set with diamonds, emeralds, sapphires, and pearls. Pedani sells watches too, but prices seem in line with most in the U.S. Designs are not unique or as contemporary as those at Stern, but the quality is there. Credit cards.

Yaniv Jewelry

113 Ben Yehuda Street   9 A.M. to 1 P.M., 4 to 7 P.M.
                                        Early Sabbath Closing

Yaniv has less-expensive jewelry in 14-carat gold and silver settings. Most pieces are set with pearls or small diamond chips, and there are inexpensive chains as well. A more casual outlook here. Major credit cards.

Menora

40 Allenby Road   9 A.M. to 1 P.M., 4 to 7 P.M.
                                    Early Sabbath Closing

If you like antique jewelry you should head to Menora, a delightful shop for browsing and buying. Ornate brooches, dangling earrings, and unusual rings are the special items here. Modern jewelry in silver is also sold, as are antiques for the home. Major credit cards.

Leathers

Articles of clothing made of leather and suede are particularly good buys here. The leather is supple, comes in a variety of colors, and styles vary from classic to modish. Leathers are less expensive than in the U.S. and U.K., but are not cheap. Handbags and shoes may have excellent leather but the styling is not up to snuff.

REEM LEATHERS

101 Ben Yehuda Street	9 A.M. to 6 P.M., Friday till 2 P.M.
	Open Saturday evening

Reem was highly recommended by friends in Tel Aviv. The selection in the storefront shop is small because most items are made to order in Reem's second-floor factory. That way you get a perfect fit (if you are leaving, they'll mail it) and you can choose both the style and color you like. Helpful, English speaking staff. Major credit cards.

BEGED OR

Dizengoff Center	10 A.M. to 1 P.M.; 4 to 7 P.M.
104 Ben Yehuda Street	

Beged Or, a name that was synonymous with Israeli leathers, seems to be slipping just a bit. Styles were as imaginative as ever and the leather felt soft and buttery, but all three shops were very low on inventory. If I found a jacket I liked, they had neither my size nor a color I wanted. I may just have caught them midseason. Beged Or is definitely worth a stop before you buy elsewhere.

GINGETTE

307 Hayarkon Street	Old Jaffa
	9 A.M. to 1 P.M., 4 to 7 P.M.

Gingette had the most trendy, modish leathers I saw in Tel Aviv. Stunning bright colors—reds, rusts, blues—and sexy styling make Gingette popular with the sleek set. They do alterations and offer tourists a 25 percent discount.

TADMOR

99 King George Street	9 A.M. to 1 P.M., 4 to 7 P.M.

A downtown location, this small store had terrific suedes in tans and rusts. Good selection for men when I visited. Women's styles were conservative.

SAFARI HANDBAGS

147 Dizengoff Street

Safari's bags—for both daytime and evening use—are highly styled but not sleek or elegant.

BAG

154 Dizengoff Street

An Israeli outlet store with shoes, sandals, belts, and bags. Their shop at number 187 has very modish accessories.

Furs

Israel has a thriving fur industry. Furs are tax-free and customs-exempt in both the U.S. and E.E.C. countries. Most furriers will deliver the garments to the airport when you leave, saving you the chore of redeeming the VAT. The city's fur district is at the southern end of Ben Yehuda Street. Shops are small because most garments are made to order and rarely brought off the rack. Two fittings are required and garments are often shipped to you after departure. Mink, Persian lamb, and fox seem most popular. Here again, fine workmanship is the key. Israelis don't wear furs too frequently here but do when they travel abroad. All accept major credit cards.

ANNA GRENFOR

80 Ben Yehuda Street   Phone 5246333

Ms. Grenfor has a lovely flair for design and styling. Ask her to suggest something or bring a photo of your fantasy.

Handicrafts

Israeli handicrafts are both religious and secular. Brass, copper, enamels, silver, glassware, ceramics, and woven rugs and wall hangings are just the tip of the very deep iceberg. Typical items are always nice gifts and also are reminders of the trip.

JAFFA MARKET

Zion Street   9 A.M. to 5 P.M.

You'll love wandering through the two long alleyways that comprise this fun shopping area. Lined by small stalls on either side (and similar shops nearby too), the market is the place to shop for brass, copper, ceramics, clothing, and *chachkus* (small gift items). Bargaining a must.

WIZO

94 Ben Yehuda Street   87 Allenby Road

A potpourri of handicrafts, Judaica, gifts, and clothing. A great stop to get an overview of what's available. Items are all of the highest quality. Salespeople are all volunteers and members of the Women's International Zionist Organization, a worldwide group that helps women and children. Fixed prices.

MASKIT

13 Frishman Street

Similar to WIZO, Maskit shops are known for the wide selection of items and the high quality of their merchandise. Many unusual craft items here.

CACTUS

30 Shenkin Street   Phone 283502
Yemenite Quarter

A very different type of craft is sold at this small design center owned by several young talents. They design textiles (silk scarves, ties, and bedspreads), hammer jewelry, and sculpt ceramics. You'll like this store, and the enthusiasm of these young entrepreneurs is contagious. You'll feel happy as you explore the other studios, antique shops, and galleries on this "Soho" block. Small cafés too.

Bathing Suits

GOTTEX

148 Dizengoff Street   9 A.M. to 7 P.M., till 1 P.M. Friday
Closed Saturday

Sold abroad, Gottex swimsuits are high-quality garments, and you'll see even more styles and colors here. Styles are one-piece and bikinis. Gottex suits are sold in many boutiques and at their shop above. Discontinued styles and seconds at their outlet, in Ramat Gan. Ask at number 148 for directions.

GIDEON OBERSON

4 Yirmiyahu Street

Oberson suits are not well known abroad but are best-sellers here. Same high quality and even nicer fabrics and sexier styling than Gottex. The shop carries their beachwear too. Oberson's factory outlet in Ramat Gan is open 10 A.M. to 6 P.M. (till 2 P.M. on Friday). Call 751863 for directions.

Art Galleries

We almost put this information in the sightseeing section, for Tel Aviv's art galleries and craft centers, which are arrayed along Gordon Street (from Hayarkon to beyond Dizengoff) and the tiny streets intersecting it, are charming to browse in even if you aren't interested in buying. There are least two dozen galleries here and exhibits (which change frequently) range from the avant-garde to the antique and highly traditional. Art galleries unfortunately are often marginal businesses, so if the gallery we mention is gone, you can be sure another is occupying that space. We are only mentioning the few that caught our eye, but keep in mind there are many others. Galleries open 10 A.M. to 1 P.M.; 5 P.M. till all hours. Closed Saturday. Most take major credit cards.

Dvir Gallery, number 26, features paintings by Israeli artists and international masters including Picasso and Chagall. *Givon,* number 35, features works from the 1920s and 1930s by Israeli artists, and lithographs. Other interesting galleries to browse through are the *Engel Gallery*, number 26, the *Ephrat Gallery*, number 21, *Gallery Gordon*, number 30, and *Shulamit*, number 29.

Galleries in Old Jaffa

FRANK MEISLER GALLERY

Behind Jaffa Mall

This is the main store of this famous Israeli artist and it has the largest selection of his unique pewter sculptures, which are then plated with gold and silver. His works have movable parts; his famous camel, made to honor Anwar Sadat, has a movable head. His Hassidic figures at prayer are fabulous.

CERAMIC HOUSE

Behind Jaffa Mall

Need an unusual gift and don't want to spend lots of money on it? Head to Ceramic House, where you'll find clay plant holders with imprints of natural plants baked in. Far better pieces too. (No credit cards here.)

HANDELMAN STUDIO

Behind Jaffa Mall

Original silk-screens of Hassidic life; children playing, men praying—no women. The delicate technique includes painting on the glass that covers the screen.

Antiques

Antiques in Israel fall into three categories. First is Judaica, which consists of family heirlooms brought to Israel by immigrants. Then we find archeological antiques, such as artifacts and coins found at digs. These must be certified to be removed from the country. And third, we find the brass/copper "antiques" sold in the Arab Markets, most of which are made in small workshops in the West Bank. Make sure you know what you are buying if you are paying for an antique in the market.

Judaica Antiques

Clustered on Ben Yehuda Street are tiny, musty old shops that sell Judaica primarily from Eastern Europe or Morocco. These shops do not take credit cards. Most items are stone-encrusted silver, colored glass, menorahs, and mezuzahs. Walk along Ben Yehuda Street from Ben Gurion south to Allenby. Stop at *Sinai Antiques* (number 52), *Victoriana* (number 54), *Zakar* (number 58), *Mizrani Zim* (number 90), *Abraham* (number 74), and *Antiques Galli* (number 46), *Robert P* (number 84) specializes in prints and antique maps of the Holyland.

Turn left onto Allenby Street for *Menora Antiques* (number 40) and *Stieglitz* (number 71).

If you're a collector of rare books, visit *M. Pollack's* shop at 36 King George Street. Just a few doors down at 42 King George Street, he has another shop which specializes in antique maps and prints.

If you enjoy antiquing and talking about antiques, you'll have a wonderful time. Many shop owners here are old-timers with a million stories to tell.

Archeological Antiques

Antiquarium, 1 Simtat Mazel Taleh, Old Jaffa, has authenticated ceramic pieces—pots, and sculpted animal and human figures—plus ancient coins and glassware. The authentication assures you that the piece is genuine and also permits it to be exported.

Archeological Centre, 7 Simtat Mazel Taleh, Old Jaffa. Items in this shop are dated backed six thousand years to biblical times, from the Roman era and Bar Kochba rebellion, from Jesus' lifetime and the Arab era. Oil lamps, pots, crucibles, and Islamic glass are featured. Here too, all items are certified.

Sports

Tennis

The National Tennis Center in Ramat Aviv has a dozen hard courts, all well maintained. Guests are welcome, on a space-available basis. Call 5447222. Fee is very reasonable; there are additional fees for equipment rental. No space? Call Maccabi Tzafan Tennis Club at Rocheach Avenue. (Ask at hotel desk.)

Squash

Herzliya Squash Club (fifteen minutes by car or public bus) on Shivat Hakochabim Boulevard. Phone (052) 557877.

Swimming

Most hotels have small swimming pools, but if you are a lap swimmer, head to the *Gordon Street Pool* on the beach near Kikar Namir.

Tel Aviv's beaches are very lovely from March through October and my friends tell me that hardy types swim year round. There are lifeguards at the Hilton beach strip, and at the long beach strip from the Carlton Hotel to Trumpeldor Street. (No lifeguard —don't swim!)

Windsurfing/Sailboats

Windsurfers and small sailboats can be rented at the Tel Aviv Marina (on the beach in front of the Hotel Carlton). Lessons are also available. Another rental area is at the southern end, near the Dolphinarium. Rowboats are available at the Yarkon River, northern Tel Aviv.

Sundown to Sunup

Tel Aviv offers visitors many evening options, with most in operation seven nights a week. Whether your taste runs to rock or symphonic music, folk dancing or disco dancing, clubs with shows, piano bars, or cappuccino under the stars, it's all here. Tel Aviv is not a night town like Rio or New York, however, so most

clubs are in full swing by 9 P.M. and start to wind down by 2 A.M..
Nightclubs and discotheques "in" one season can be down and
out the next, but frequently a new club pops up in that space.
Clubs are limited by size and tend to fill up quickly, so if something strikes your fancy, get reservations early.

The *Jerusalem Post*, particularly Friday's edition, is your best
source of entertainment news. It lists clubs, concerts, cinemas,
theaters, and special events. The local tourist office helps by
preparing a monthly list of special events which you can pick up
at their office at 7 Mendele Street (near the Dan Hotel).

Concerts and Theater

The Mann Auditorium   Seating three thousand people, the auditorium is home to the Israel Philharmonic, and host to visiting
orchestras, dance troupes, and international stars. Most seats are
filled by subscription, but there are usually some available at the
box office or through local ticket offices. (See Tel Aviv Potpourri.)

Habima Theater   Plays from Shakespeare to Simon are performed in Hebrew but frequently are simultaneously translated into
English. Again, most seats are filled by subscription or long in advance, but you can try the box office or ticket offices. You might
get lucky. Phone 6919510.

Shalom Aleichem   The shtetls of Europe are brought to life
through the words of the famous Yiddish storyteller, Shalom
Aleichem. English performances at the Diplomat Hotel,
Hayarkon Street, every Wednesday night at 9:30 P.M..

Israel Chamber Orchestra   Classical concerts presented at the
Tel Aviv Museum, 27 Shaul Hamelech Boulevard (phone
261297).

Zafta (Tzavta) Club   30 Ibn Givrol St. (phone 6950156). Shows
with Israeli music—classical, popular, jazz—Hassidic songs, and
dances. No credit cards.

Zoa House   1 Daniel Frisch Street (phone 6959341). The Zionist
Organization of America founded this community center, where
English-language plays are frequently presented. Oneg Shabbat
programs (Friday evenings) include folksinging, lectures,
concerts, and dancing.

Discotheques and Clubs

Herbie Sam's   Yamit Hotel (entrance on Herbert Samuel Promenade). You can gain admittance to this members-only club by flashing your passport. Herbie Sam's—new, sleek, and tasteful—draws Israel's beautiful people, diplomats, and the international jet set. No reservations. Major credit cards.

Liquid Club   117 Solomon (phone 5376814). A raucous club with loud music and revelers. International rock stars and well-known punk and rock groups perform here. Major credit cards.

Byblos   128 Petach Tikva Boulevard (phone 562627). If you like jazz and blues, head to Byblos, where the guests are knowledgeable and the music mellow. It's especially fun on Wednesday evenings when, from 10 P.M. on, musicians drop in for impromptu jam sessions. Other jazz and blue clubs are *Logos* at 14 Nahalat Binyamin (phone 660995) and *Jazz Bar* at 22 Rabbi Akiva (phone 655096). *Jazz Bar* is closed Sundays.

Beit Lessin Club   34 Weitzman Boulevard (phone 216652). Open nightly, Beit Lessin's shows include good jazz bands, flamenco, folk music and singing, rock for listening and dancing. No credit cards.

Soweto Club Tel-Aviv   6 Frishman Street, corner of Hayarkon Street (phone 5240825). Open every night except Sunday. Reggae and African soul are the featured dance tunes at this popular basement club. Murals of Bob Marley, Peter Tosh and other popular Reggae musicians are on the walls and green, red and yellow, the colors of the flags of many African nations, dominate. If you want to dance all night, this is the place to go. *Jamaica Club* at 58 Hamasger Street is another popular Reggae club.

The Sigal Club   73 Hayarkon Street (phone 5103049) is home to the samba, mambo, and lambada musicians of Israel. Latin music for listening and dancing. Guest artists appear frequently. *Harcosit* at 5 Kikar Malchei Israel (phone 242013) combines jazz with Brazilian music.

Pubs and Supper Clubs

Plitz Café   81 Hayarkon Street (phone 652778). Good food, continental style, and dance music of the 1950s and 1960s make the Plitz a congenial spot for Tel Aviv's over-thirty crowd. Music Monday, Thursday, Friday, and Saturday evenings, dinner only other nights. Major credit cards.

The Bell   281 Dizengoff Street (phone 462948). The Bell houses both a French restaurant and a popular pub. Stick to the finger foods, well-mixed drinks, and fine jazz at the pub, which is always crowded. The long bar, a singles meeting spot, is open seven days. Look for the bell over the entrance. Major credit cards.

Hamatmon Pub   3 Yirmayahu Street (phone 457025). Dim lights, good noshing food from an eclectic menu that offers Moroccan cigars and eggrolls, and the best piano players in town keep the Hamatmon at the top of Tel Aviv's nightlife. Major credit cards.

The Saloon   1 Yorde Hasira Street, Little Tel Aviv. A western-style saloon draws a young beer-drinking crowd to munch on burgers, steaks, and chops. Loud, noisy and fun.

Reading Pub   270 Hayarkon Street, Little Tel Aviv (phone 449806). Unusual art-deco design, the long red bar, and an imaginative menu have made Reading Pub one of Tel Aviv's most in spots. Specialties include fondue, the *crouc* (a French-style sandwich), and tempura. Reading is open till 4 A.M. Major credit cards.

Chimney   2 Mendele Street (phone 235215). Dining and drinking choices are overwhelming. The exotic drink list alone is six pages long, and both the wine and beer lists are extensive. Typical pub fare, cheese platters, and Middle Eastern and French specialties grace the menu. Great rock classics provide the background music. Open noon to 3 A.M. Major credit cards accepted.

Jaffa is a nighttime center as well. You can wander from one club to another here, and since restaurants in the area also stay open late, it's a lovely place to be. A few clubs you might enjoy include *Hakochar Ha'adom* at 15 Yefet (phone 9613354), which opens at 8:30 P.M. (except Wednesday and Sunday) for Middle Eastern and Turkish music; and *Mivneh 5* at the Jaffa Port (phone 814770) for Israeli music and dancing, which opens at 9 P.M. and stays open until 2 A.M.. *Sun City Club* at 22 Mazel Arie (836506) draws a young crowd for dining and listening to good music.

Israeli Nightclubs

Michael's Aladdin 5 Mifratz Shlomo, Jaffa (phone 82676). Housed in an old Turkish bath, the Aladdin is a large club, but it fills up on weekends. Shows usually feature a belly dancer and are fun and noisy. Small cover charge on Friday and Saturday evenings. Closed Sunday.

El Hamam 10 Mifratz Shlomo, Jaffa (phone 813261). The high arched windows offer a lovely view of the nearby mosque and the twinkling lights of Tel Aviv's seashore in the distance. Music and dancing nightly, with a show at 10:30 P.M. that frequently features a stripper. Cover charge includes one drink. Major credit cards.

The Cave 14 Kikar Kedumin, Jaffa (phone 829460). You can enjoy dinner, dancing and a show that features Israeli folksingers and dancers here. You can sing along (well, at least hum).

Cinemas

Many cinemas are located within easy walking distance of Hayarkon Street. Films are shown in their original language with Hebrew subtitles, and many theaters offer first-run U.S. films. You can (and should) purchase tickets at the cinema box office early in the day. Most have one showing at 7 P.M. and another at 9:30 P.M.. Check the *Jerusalem Post*. Tel Aviv's Cinematheque, 111 Hayarkon Street, offers classic films in a variety of languages (primarily French).

Piano Bars/Bars

Bernie's Bottle Club 231 Ben Yehuda Street. Bernie, an Israeli who grew up in the U.S., has single-handedly turned his club into a meeting spot for American embassy people and locals. Flags hanging form the ceiling give the place an upbeat look.

M.A.S.H. 275 Dizengoff Street. Sit at one of the sidewalk tables and watch the local action.

Hotel Spots

Piano bars and lounge areas are frequently found in the lobbies of the better hotels, such as the Hilton, the Carlton, and the Dan. The Sheraton has a lovely discotheque as well.

Late-Night Cafés

Late-night imbibers and nibblers have several options. *Herbert Samuel Promenade, the Little Tel Aviv area, Dizengoff Street,* and *Atarim Square* are the best choices. My favorite, particularly in spring and summer, is the beach promenade, where sidewalk cafés are open-air and the smell of the sea is everywhere. *Chaplin's*, behind the Yamit Hotel, is one of the nicest cafés here, and another is the nearby *Café Vienna*, which you'll spot because it has yellow chairs. *Balloons* at the southern end of the promenade (Trumpeldor Street) is a popular spot for the apple-pie-and-ice-cream set. *Atarim Square*, near Ben Gurion Boulevard, circled by outdoor eateries featuring burgers, ice cream, and Italian food, draws a younger, noisier, and far less sophisticated crowd. Blintzes, piroshki, and crêpes can be found at the lovely sidewalk cafés on *Yirmiyahu Street* and in the entire *Little Tel Aviv area*. The *London Konditorei* has fabulous pastry and coffee, while the all-pink *Plintzi* serves wonderful blintzes. *Dizengoff Street*, from Dizengoff Square to Ben Gurion Boulevard, is lined with cafés and fast-food eateries that are open well into the wee hours.

Tel Aviv Potpourri

Beauty Salons   Max, 24 Yirmiyahu Street; Shuki Ziki, 186 Ben Yehuda (near Jabotinsky); Niso, 219 Ben Yehuda (near Yirmiyahu).

Books   For best-sellers, Steimatsky has cornered the market. The store has several-branches, some in major hotels.

The 2 in 1 Bookshop at 203 Dizengoff Street is a trading post for used paperbacks on every topic and from every era.

Phone Area Code   03.

Ticket Agencies   Hadran, 90 Ibn Givrol Street, phone 5279797,
Le'an, 101 Dizengoff Street. Phone 5247373.

Tourist Office   5 Shalom Aleichem Street. Phone 660259. Hours:
Sunday through Thursday 8:30 A.M. to 5 P.M., Friday 8:30 A.M. to 2
P.M.; closed Saturday.

Excursions from Tel Aviv

Caesarea

Set dramatically on the edge of the Mediterranean about midway
between Tel Aviv and Haifa, Caesarea is one of Israel's most attractive archeological sites. Although the area surrounding it has
been developed (it now houses a five-star hotel, the country's
only golf course, a riding stable, and upscale villa-style homes),
Caesarea itself remains tranquil and almost untouched by these
modern intrusions. Its excavated sites include a Roman amphitheater and aqueduct, Byzantine streets, and a spectacular
Crusader city. On our ruins-rating scale, Caesarea is a definite
ten. You can visit the ruins on a half-day excursion from Tel Aviv
or Haifa, but if time permits, stay overnight at the Dan Caesarea,
play a round of golf or trail ride, listen to a concert in the ancient
amphitheater, and love every minute of it.

An Impressive Past

The Phoenicians, who were great seafarers, constructed a small
harbor and trading post here in the third century B.C. Named after
their king, it was known as **Straton's Tower**. The small city was
later incorporated into the Israelite Hasmonean kingdom, which
was shortly thereafter overthrown by the Romans. They granted it
to Herod, a prolific builder who in twelve frenetic years enlarged
and beautified the town. Now a spectacular port, it was named in
honor of Caesar Augustus. Granite from Egypt and marble from
Italy were used to construct the palaces, temple, amphitheater,
hippodrome, and public buildings. Herod also constructed a

top-notch harbor. Inhabited by Jews, Romans, and Gentiles, it was a leading maritime city, a position it retained even after Herod's death.

A Christian community was started here in the first century and was visited by both Peter and Paul. Campaigns against the Jewish community began and thousands died in the amphitheater or were shipped to Rome as slaves. Caesarean Jews led the revolt against Roman rule, which resulted in the razing of Jerusalem. A later revolt, Bar Kochba in the second century, saw over one half million Jews killed and one of the Israelites' greatest scholars, Rabbbi Akiva, was brought here to die.

Barred from Jerusalem, small groups of Jews returned to Caesarea and the community flourished as a center of Jewish thought under Byzantine rule. The Byzantines used materials from Herod's city to build their own. Soon the city housed 100,000 people.

Conquered by the Arabs in A.D. 640, the city fell into disrepair and remained so until the arrival of the Crusaders five hundred years later. Led by Baldwin I, they slaughtered the entire Arab population and started to rebuild the city. They opened the harbor, strengthened the fortifications, and, using the materials they found, started their own city. The city then seesawed between Crusader and Arab rule. Even the mighty fortifications built by Louis IX of France were of no avail; the city fell to the Arabs once more. During the years of Ottoman rule, marble and stone from Caesarea was taken to build parts of Akko (Acre) and the mosque in Jaffa. The city was left to the shifting sands and the sea.

In the early twentieth century, Baron Rothschild drained the swamps which covered much of the area and planted trees and vines. A kibbutz was established in 1940 and many an illegal immigrant waded ashore here, evading the British blockade. Soon after independence, archeological excavations began.

Visiting the Ruins

Caesarea is part of Israel's National Park System. Open daily (except Saturday) from 8 A.M. to 5 P.M., there is a modest entrance fee. The ruins stretch along a two-mile strip of beach. At the southern edge is the Roman amphitheater and bath. The Crusader city is to the north of the amphitheater and just beyond it is the Jewish Quarter and Straton's Tower. The Roman aqueduct is a fifteen-minute walk along the beach. Across the road from the Crusader city (behind a snack bar), you'll see the Byzantine street and further inland is the Hippodrome. The ruins are carefully explained in English and for a few cents you can buy a pamphlet explaining them further. You can enter the ruins at either the amphitheater or the Crusader city. Your ticket is good at both entrances. Bus #921 or #922 (to Or–Akira Junction) will drop you here.

The Roman Amphitheater and Bath

Now restored, the theater is used for concerts. (The first, in 1961, featured Pablo Casals.) Stone seats rise from the floor in a semi-circle and all face the sea. If you miss some of the music because your mind wanders back to the time the central stone floor was the site of gladiators' battles and lion fights, you won't be alone. The bath is nearer to the beach in front of the theater.

The Crusader City

If you walk along the beach, you'll first see the Crusader citadel (near the shops). It was damaged by a 1937 earthquake. A Turkish minaret is nearby. Inland from the citadel, you'll spot the three remaining walls of St. Paul's Cathedral, built by the Crusaders over the site of a Byzantine church that may have housed the Holy Grail. As you stroll along the stone paths, which were grooved to prevent horses from slipping, you see public buildings, Herod's temple, and stone archways connecting one street to another. Notice the massive fortified walls which enclose the city. These were built by Louis IX but failed to protect the city from Arab invaders. The gate-house in the wall (the entrance to the city now) has high stone walls and spectacular vaulted arches. It feels very cool inside. Beyond the walls lies a dry but very deep moat. It's hard to believe now, but the Crusader city is about one third the size of Herod's city and the Byzantine one that followed it.

The Jewish Quarter/Straton's Tower/Aqueduct

On the beach beyond the fortified walls are the remains of the once-flourishing Jewish community. This area was inside the walls when Herod built his city. Straton's Tower nearby was the Phoenician building that was the first structure here. If you continue along the beach, you'll see the aqueduct that was built in the first century. Only a small part has been unearthed—it is actually almost six miles long.

The Byzantine Street

Look for the snack shop across the road from the Crusader city. Just beyond it are the unearthed portions of a Byzantine street which is paved with marble in a mosaic design and holds statues from the Roman period.

The Hippodrome

In a field behind the street, you'll find the partially excavated racetrack which could seat twenty thousand people.

Several small restaurants and souvenir shops have been built on the beachfront near the Crusader city. It's a shame they weren't built across the road. One, the Crusader Inn (*Hazalvanim*), is open for lunch and dinner and serves delicious fish dishes. If you want to dine here before a concert, reserve. Phone (063) 62400.

Dan Caesarea Hotel

A five-star hotel in a gardenlike setting amid manicured lawns, the Dan Caesarea is a self-contained resort. It has a bright, cheery dining room and the food is very good. The pool area is large and there are many planned activities for guests. There is a discotheque on weekends. Deluxe.

Caesarea Golf Club

You are welcome to play at the club but be sure to reserve in advance. Weekends are particularly tight. The eighteen-hole course has a par 73 and is moderately difficult to play and lovely to walk. Greens fees are reasonable and shoes, clubs, and balls are available for rent. The club has changing rooms, a restaurant, and a practice driving range. It is open seven days a week, closing only on Yom Kippur, Holocaust Day (May 6), and Memorial Day (May 13). Call (063) 61174 to reserve a starting time.

Herod's Riding Club

Ezy Shenkar is the manager of Herod's and leader of the riding tours along the beach and to the ruins. The club has twenty horses, gives lessons, and organizes group rides. Weekends are busy, but if you reserve you'll have no problem. Call Ezy at (063) 61181.

Herzliya

One of the signs of having made it in Israel is to live in Herzliya, Tel Aviv's golden suburb, just to the north. No father's boast is prouder than the one that says "my son just bought a new home in Herzliya."

Little did the original settlers, who arrived in 1924 to establish a citrus-growing village, realize that the swamps they cleared would become a ritzy enclave and a barometer of financial success. The original settlement, inland, remained undisturbed amid a growing profusion of orange and tangerine trees until statehood and the completion of a modern highway. Now accessible, the town became an elite haven for wealthy Tel Avivians, politicians and industrialists as well as an ambitious and growing upper-middle class. The city expanded westward toward the beach strip and now houses 63,200 people. Called Herzliya Pituah, the strip has seen the construction of several luxury hotels, exclusive restaurants, and without a doubt, some of the most beautiful villas in Israel. Herzliya, a lovely beach resort, was named for the founder of the political Zionist movement, Dr. Theodor Herzl.

Getting There

If you drive, take *Derekh Haifa* (Haifa Road) from North Tel Aviv and continue on Route 2 (or 4). Signs are highly visible. Egged buses from the Central Bus Station make the trip in twenty-five minutes, with buses leaving every fifteen minutes. Sit near an open window and you'll smell the salt air all the way to town.

Orientation

Shalit Square is the center of activity in the resort area. The better hotels are situated on the beach; moderate-priced hotels are near the square, as are a substantial number of good eating spots.

Where to Stay

If you decide to spend some time here you will enjoy Herzliya's hotels. Three exceptional five-star stops are right on the shore.

DANIEL TOWERS 5★

Herzliya Pituah	Phone (052) 544444
Herzliya 46769	Fax (052) 544675
	Major Credit Cards

The Daniel Tower's five stars are well deserved. All 180 elegantly furnished state-of-the-art rooms in the golden tower feature a view of the sea and overlook a beautiful stretch of beach. A recent major overhaul has forged the Daniel's new reputation as one of the best spa-facility hotels in the country. Extensive activity programs include tennis, horseback riding, wind surfing, and waterskiing at the semiprivate beach called Zeblon. The Daniel has several fine restaurants, which we'll discuss in the Restaurant section. *Deluxe*.

THE DAN ACCADIA 5*

Herzliya Beach 46769

Phone (052) 556677
Fax (052) 571311
Telex 341811
Cables: Accadia
Major Credit Cards

A member of the exemplary Dan Hotel Group, the Accadia is an exceptionally attractive hotel with 192 waterfront rooms, all with balconies. The Accadia is nestled in lovely green gardens and lawns. The Back Door Grill, Sabra Coffee Shop and Terrace, Mediterranean Lounge, and main dining room uniformly serve food of a high standard. The poolside snack bar and summer barbecues will keep you munching at poolside. The hotel offers some convenient services like transportation to and from the airport, guided tours, a car rental, and a synagogue on Sabbath and holidays. There is also a gift shop, a beauty parlor, a jeweler, a boutique, and a barber shop on the main floor. Six tennis courts, petanque (French bowling), minigolf, and a sauna are but a few of the sports and health facilities available. In the evening, the Dan Accadia provides cultural programs, nightly entertainment in the Cabin No.9 Piano Bar, and movies in the cinema club. *Deluxe*.

THE SHARON 5*

Herzliya Beach

Phone (052) 575777
Fax (052) 572448
Major Credit Cards

Not as glamorous as its two neighbors, the Sharon is nonetheless an extremely popular stop here. A 200-room hostelry with two pools, a health club that includes both wet and dry saunas, and an organized water-sports program, the Sharon is a self-contained resort. The Apyrion Bar features music with dancing at night, and the hotel sponsors cocktail parties, lectures, and folklore programs. *Deluxe*.

Restaurants

As you stroll through Herzliya, you will notice a disproportionate number of restaruants for a town this size. But keep in mind that the sea air makes you hungry, Israelis love to eat, and Herzliya is an extremely popular beach destination on weekends. There are plenty of restaurants near Shalit Square and in the hotels, and others pop up in the strangest places.

If you are in the mood for some superb seafood, head for the Paz-Ronit Gas Station on the road between Tel Aviv and Herzliya. That's right, *Ahmed and Salim's*, a terrific restaurant, is on the property of this gas station. Fresh buri and forel and St. Peter's fish are delicious. Moderately priced.

Henry VIII at 35 Havazet Hasharon Street is considered Herzliya's finest by townspeople, as well as by Israelis who come here from afar. Continental specialties. Expensive.

The Safari, Herzliya Beach, serves burgers, steaks, and salads. Inexpensive.

The Zevulon, Herzliya Beach, is an informal spot serving tasty grilled meats, fish, and burgers. Inexpensive.

Sunup to Sundown

If you're staying at one of the luxury hotels here, most of your activity will be centered in, around, and upon the adjoining hotel beach. If you are just passing through and decide to refresh yourself, you pay an entrance fee for your place in the sun. There are shops galore at the mall (Shalit Square) and you can find anything you need. Herzliya is not exactly full of historical or ancient sights, but if you have a car, a bicycle, or a good pair of legs, you can walk to *Tel Arshaf*, which is just one and a quarter miles north of Herzliya. Here, on the coast, you will find the ruins of a port and fort called Rishpona (called *Reshef, Appollonia, Arsur,* and *Arshef* at various times throughout history, depending on the invaders of the moment). The name probably comes from *Resheph* (which means "spark" or "flame"), who was one of Ephraim's sons and whose territory this once was. This ancient port flourished under the Maccabean rule, and the Romans, Arabs, and Crusaders all called it theirs at different times. Remains of a Roman amphitheater and several other structures from the first century A.D. were excavated here about thirty years ago. There is a mosque here called Sidna Ali, which the

Samaritans claim to be the burial place of Eli. Moslems named the mosque in honor of a soldier in Salahalim's army.

Sundown to Sunup

Herzliyans entertain at home frequently and lavish parties are often seen and heard at the villas in town.

The people you find in the hotel bars, nightclubs, and discos, or in Shalit Square's many late-night cafés are usually Tel Avivians away on a weekend jaunt. The hotels are probably the best places for a drink, some tinkling music, and hob-nobbing; if you want to mix it up, do what Herzliyans would rather do—go to a movie or take a nighttime stroll along the beach. Just don't go swimming. The waters here are particularly treacherous and the lifeguards are off-duty at night, so resist any urge to jump into the surf—it's strictly risky business.

From Herzliya, it's a hop to Netanya, the diamond capital of Israel. Along the way you'll pass the Wingate Institute, which is a physical-education and sports-oriented school for young Israelis.

Netanya

In the early 1920s, a young Zionist, Ben Ami, returned to his native Belgium to encourage members of Antwerp's large Jewish community to emigrate to Palestine. Many had been involved in the business of diamond cutting and polishing and had become wealthy and established. For some the comforts of Antwerp were too great to leave, but others heeded Ben Ami's call (thereby un-wittingly saving their lives) and moved Netanya, a coastal town between Tel Aviv and Haifa. A budding diamond industry was es-tablished, which continued to function during the war. After statehood, new immigrants from the east and North Africa flooded the region. They knew nothing about diamonds or the skills required to cut and polish them, which are painstaking and exacting. The Belgian old-timers realized that the only way to keep their industry alive was to train these newcomers. Today, most of the people employed in Netanya's burgeoning diamond industry are Oriental and Sephardic Jews. The skill with which these people handle and craft precious stones is remarkable.

Netanya's greatest natural resource is its lavish Mediterranean beachfront, on which canny businessmen have opened a slew of hotels. While Herzliya is a magnet for wealthy Israelis and foreign visitors, Netanya is a blue-collar resort. Although it has five-star hotels, most are two- and three-star establishments with the majority of the guests British, French, and Australian. Twenty miles north of Tel Aviv, easily accessible by bus, with a relaxed resort atmosphere and showrooms featuring exquisitely cut diamonds, Netanya is a nice stop for those with extra time.

Orientation

Netanya is not a small town (it has 100,000 residents), so pick up a map at the IGTO, which is in Ha'atzmaut Square (Independence), around which most of Netanya's attractions are located. The city's major street, Herzl, leads into the square.

What's Doing in Netanya?

Pick up a monthly activity list at the IGTO. Definitely try to visit the Netanya Diamond Center on Herzl Street; their guided tour is both informative and dazzling. It's a rare opportunity to see a rough stone transformed into a priceless gem. The sell is hard but you are under no obligation to buy. Netanya has a chamber orchestra, art galleries, and cinemas. Its major interest, however, is its championship caliber football (soccer) team, the Maccabees. Try to see a game if you can. A late-afternoon stroll along the seafront promenade is refreshing, as is a delightful ride in a whimsically painted, flower-bedecked horse-drawn carriage.

Restaurants

Netanya's restaurants run the gamut, catering as they do to tourists. Most are Middle Eastern, moderately priced, and informal. There are dozens of falafel and kebab places for a quick, inexpensive meal.

The Cliff Grill Room at the Dan Netanya Hotel is the most elegant eating spot in town.

The Taipei Restaurant, 7 Ha'atzmaut Square, serves nicely spiced, just-hot-enough Thai and Chinese food.

Sesame, 1 Herzl Street, is open twenty-four hours a day, serving fish and dairy specialties.

Casa Mia, 10 Herzl Street, serves ten varieties of pizza and other Italian specialites

Mini-Golf Pub on Nice Boulevard (near the Dan Netanya) has good barbecued food as well as a milk bar with light dairy choices.

Hotels in Netanya

Netanya's hotels are clean and nicely situated on the beach in town or a few kilometers away.

BLUE BAY 4★

37 Hamalchim Street   Phone (053) 623322
                                   Fax (053) 337475

On cliffs overlooking the sea, two miles from Ha'atzmaut Square, Blue Bay has 208 rooms with balconies and sea views. There's a large pool and a sundeck. *Expensive*.

DAN NETANYA 5★

Nice Boulevard   Phone (053) 30044

This ultramodern, seventeen-floor hotel on the beach has landscaped gardens, a fresh-water pool, tennis, and sauna. All 129 rooms have sea views. *Deluxe*.

KING SOLOMON HOTEL 4★

18 Hamaapilim Street   Phone (053) 338444
                                   Fax (053) 611397

The swimming pool here sits on the second floor over the lobby, there is an authentic Finnish sauna, and all ninety-nine rooms have balconies facing the sea. Friendly staff, too. *Expensive*.

Haifa
and
the
North

ise King Solomon, who had a discerning eye for the fairer sex, had one for natural beauty as well. In Song of Songs, Solomon said, "Thine head upon thee is like Carmel—how fair and pleasant art thou." Haifa, Israel's third largest city, which clings to this famed mountain, is indeed fair and pleasant, and its graceful bay is in a class with those of Rio and San Francisco. A view from the summit of Mount Carmel reveals a trilevel city of 266,000 that has clean, wide, tree-lined streets, with many green spots, including the Bahai Shrine, whose garden is the loveliest we've ever seen. Small, neat homes and newly constructed apartment complexes house hard-working, energetic, well-educated people, many of whom are recent immigrants or children of illegal immigrants from the pre-state era. Haifa's exceptional technical school, the Technion, draws Israel's finest students, and the city boasts excellent museums and several concert halls. It has the country's only underground train, which links the three tiers, and its buses run on the Sabbath. Because the city does not have one unique feature or a distinctive beat, it is often overlooked by tourists, a fact that irks Haifa's highly chauvinistic residents. In a country with an overwhelming number of sites and sights, it might be easy to overlook this highly civilized city's quiet appeal, but it would be a mistake. If you have the time, you'll thoroughly enjoy your stay here, and the excursions from Haifa to Akko, Druze villages, and Rosh Hanikra's grottoes are among Israel's most exotic stops.

Orientation

Getting There

Haifa is ninety-seven kilometers from Tel Aviv. Highway 2, a freeway, skirts the sea, passing Herzliya, Netanya, and Caesarea en route. Route 4, further inland, is the older connecting road. Still in good repair, it passes En Hod and Zikhron Ya'akov. Haifa is sixty-four kilometers from Tiberias and fifty-five kilometers from Zefat. Roads in the Galilee are well maintained and scenic. Haifa is serviced by Egged buses from all parts of the country, on frequent schedules. Sheruts run between Haifa, Tel Aviv, and Jerusalem. Haifa and Elat are linked by Arkia Airlines.

Getting Around the City

The Carmelit

Haifa's three tiers are linked by a one-mile, six-station underground train, the Carmelit. Trains run every ten minutes from 5:30 A.M. to midnight, but do not operate on the Sabbath. The six Carmelit stops are: (1) Place de Paris (lowest level); (2) Solel Boneh; (3) Haneviim; (4) Massada; (5) Eliezer Golomb; and (6) Gan Ha-Em(upper level). Stops 1, 3, and 6 are of most importance to you.

Buses

An extensive bus system links all parts of the city and can take you beyond the city limits to Haifa University and the Technion. A limited bus schedule is in effect on Saturday; however, there is no bus service from 6 P.M. Friday to 9 A.M. Saturday. Fares are set by distance traveled, so tell the driver where you are going and pay accordingly.

Sheruts and Taxis

Taxis are plentiful and can be called as well as hailed. Sheruts operate on main streets in Hadar. You pay by the seat and by the distance you travel.

Walking

Walking can get tiring here, for the city is on a hillside. You can walk from one tier to the other (at various points stone steps connect the levels), but as a general rule, this is tiring and time-consuming.

Major Streets and Landmarks

Haifa has interesting sights and activities on all levels; here is a quick rundown on names you should know.

Port Level

The city's lowest tier is tied to the harbor and businesses connected with shipping. Many Arabs live and work here. *Kikar Paris* (square), at the first Carmelit stop, is the center of things. *Derekh Yafo* (Jaffa Road)is the main commercial street. *Bat Galim*, the beach area, has a promenade and good restaurants.

Mid Level

Hadar Ha Carmel(Glory of the Carmel), is the city's middle-class residential district, a busy shopping center, and a commercial area as well. The Haifa Museum is here and so is the city's Municipal Theater. *Kikar Mazaryk*, at the third Carmelit stop, is the heart of this area, and *Herzl Street* and *HaNeviim Street*, which lead from Mazaryk Square, are major thoroughfares.

Nordau Mall, a short walk from Kikar Mazaryk, is a lovely pedestrian-only street lined with restaurants and shops.

Upper Level

Carmel, the city's highest tier, looks like a suburban community. The area's social scene revolves around its hotels and commecial centers. *Central Carmel* is a small arcade near the Carmelit stop. The *Panorama Center* adjoins the Dan Panorama Hotel and has several eateries and upscale shops. The newest center, *Horev Center*, is in the Ahuza section and is not as accessible as the other two.

Carmel has several interesting sections. *French Carmel* and *Ahuza* boast some of the city's finest homes, while *Kababir* is home to Haifa's wealthiest Arabs. The main street here is Hanassi Boulevard. *Yefe Nof* (Panorama Road) is a promenade overlooking the city.

And now to to bed down in Haifa.

Hotels

Haifa has surprisingly few hotels. These are located in the Central Carmel area and in Hadar. There is no high or low season in Haifa, so rates are firm year round. The exceptions are major holidays such as Passover, Rosh Hashana, and Yom Kippur, when many Israelis head to Haifa. Rates rise slightly and a minimum stay is sometimes required. Note: Hotels accept major credit cards except where specifically noted.

DAN CARMEL 5★

87 Hanassi Boulevard	Phone (04) 386211
	Fax (04) 387504

High above the city, the classy Dan Carmel is a resort hotel with lots of open grounds, a large swimming pool, and a health club. Although it has 220 guest rooms, the Dan has so many small hideaways that it seems intimate. Its large lobby has several sitting areas with comfortable club chairs, a cocktail lounge, and a weekend discotheque. A popular dairy coffee shop is on the main floor, and the more formal main dining room is nearby. An elegant French restaurant is on the second floor. The Dan Carmel is aging and, while your room will be large and comfortable, furnishings are well worn. Ask for a room with a view of the bay. It's spectacular. *Deluxe.*

DAN PANORAMA 4★

107 Hanassi Boulevard   Phone (04) 35222
                                            Fax (04) 352235

The Dan Panorama is part of the central Carmel shopping complex, the Panorama Center. A 270-room tower with brightly furnished modern rooms and first-rate facilities, the Panorama is the perfect stop for the business traveler. It is formal where its sister hotel, the Dan Carmel, is resortlike. Conference facilities and special business services are availible. There is a pool, and a health club is being contemplated. The lobby piano bar is a good spot for late-afternoon cocktails. *Deluxe.*

NOF HOTEL 4★

101 Hanassi Boulevard   Phone (04) 354311
                                            Fax (04) 388810

The Nof, next door to the Dan Carmel, is an excellent stop. Its one hundred rooms are large and comfortable with air conditioning and full baths. The lobby is small but comfortable, and there is an entrance into Panorama Road, where the views of the city are special. If the Nof had a pool and some grassy areas, it would be a five-star stop. *Expensive.*

SHULAMIT HOTEL 4★

15 Kiryat Sefer Street   Phone (04) 342811
                                            Fax (04) 255206

The smaller Shulamit, with only eighty rooms, is on the Carmel, but it is in a quiet neighborhood and it's a hike to Central Carmel and the Carmelit.

The rooms are good size, have radio and telephones, and are air-conditioned. Good service and a well-trained staff bring repeat customers here each year. *Moderate.*

DVIR HOTEL 3*

| 124 Yefe Nof Street | Phone (04) 389131 |
| | Fax (04) 381068 |

Yefe Nof is Panorama Road, and the views from the front rooms and stone front porch of the Dvir Hotel are spectacular. Rooms in the Dvir are small and certainly not fancy, but they are carpeted and very clean with watercolor paintings and nice small touches. The Dvir is a training school for employees of the Dan Hotel Chain, and the young staff is always smiling and helpful. This is an excellent choice. *Moderate*

BETH SHALOM GUEST HOUSE 2*

110 Hanassi Boulevard	Phone (04) 377481
	Fax (04) 372443
	No Credit Cards

Managed by a Swiss hotelier, this Protestant guest house is across the road from the Hotel Nof. Rooms are small, but they are carpeted; each has two single beds, a writing desk, and air conditioning. The thirty rooms are off an inner courtyard and the breakfast room is downstairs. A minimum stay of three nights is required. *Inexpensive*

VERED HA CARMEL 2*

| 1 Heinrich Heine Square | Phone (04) 389236 |
| | *No Credit Cards* |

This hotel is on the Carmel but is a healthy walk from the Central Carmel area. The Vered Ha Carmel's twenty-two rooms are small, and all but three have only showers in the bath, but the small private house is modern, and your room will have a TV and air conditioner/heater. Some have small patios, and the hotel has a pretty garden around it. This is only two-star rated, but is not a basic hotel. *Moderate.*

Hotels in Hadar

CARMELIA HOTEL 3★

35 Herzliya Street   Phone (04) 521278
                                       No Credit Cards

The Carmelia's fifty rooms are located in two adjoining rust-colored brick buildings which are brightened up by red-and-white striped awnings. Most of the rooms have baths with shower only, but you'll like the rooms, for they are clean and nicely maintained. The lobby was recently refurbished and the owner is very proud of it. Ask for a room with a balcony. *Moderate.*

ZION HOTEL 3★

5 Baerwald Street   Phone (04) 664311
                                       No Credit Cards

The ninety-four-room Zion has a good location in central Hadar. All except five rooms have full baths. The hotel is often filled with guests attending conferences in the Zion's conference hall. Clean and well-maintained, the Zion is a comfortable choice. *Moderate.*

HAIFA TOWER HOTEL 3★

63 Herzl Street   Phone (04) 677111
                                       Fax (04) 661863

Conveniently located in the heart of Hadar Hacarmel, rooms at the Haifa Tower feature great views of the beautiful Carmel Mountain range or Haifa Bay. All one hundred rooms are carpeted and have private baths and color televisions. There is a comfortable lobby bar and restaurant.

Underground parking, a bank, a post office and shops adjoin the hotel. *Moderate.*

Kibbutz Guest Houses

BEIT OREN 3★

Mount Carmel   Phone (04) 222111

Set in a pine forest on Mount Carmel, Beit Oren (House of Pine) is only six miles south of Haifa. The kibbutz was organized in 1939 as a *nahal* (defense) outpost, and the guest house went into operation three years later, Guests can stay in a large building that has twenty-eight rooms or in smaller stone buildings that have fifty other rooms. All have private baths and air conditioning/heating. The kibbutz has a swimming pool and the large dining room overlooks the Mediterranean. *Moderate.*

NIR ETZION 3★

Mobile Post Hof   Phone (04) 842541
Carmel 30808   Fax (04) 843344

Nir Etzion is the guest house of an Orthodox moshav. The house, with seventy-five rooms in several small stone cottages, opened in 1952. The grounds are particularly well maintained. Nir Etzion guest house is open from April through November. The moshav is extremely proud of its beautiful synagogue. Food here is *glatt* kosher and much of it comes from the moshav's own farms. *Moderate.*

Restaurants

Deciding where to eat in Haifa presents problems, for good dining spots are scattered throughout the city on all three levels. While these restaurants serve top-notch food, and there is a wide variety of cuisine, they are not as posh as eateries in Tel Aviv or Jerusalem. However, it does seem that prices are a bit lower here and good service is commonplace. You will find that many of our choices are attractive and tastefully furnished, some with delightful ocean views and others right on the shore.

Carmel

RONDO GRILL

Dan Carmel Hotel   Phone 386211
                                               Dinner only
                                              (Closed Friday)
                                          Major Credit Cards

Haifa's most elegant eatery, the circular Rondo extends from the hotel for a perfect view of the harbor and city below. The Rondo has wendows around the dining area and tables on two levels, so you should have a lovely view no matter where you sit. The sevice here is rather formal, with a maitre d' and a wine steward. The food is French but kosher, so expect a less rich flavor to the sauces. St. Peter's fish, served whole, is delicious, as is the pepper steak Rondo (it flames) and the tournedos café de Paris (make sure they are rare). A rolling cart materializes with delicious pastries and fresh fruits for dessert. The piano in the background is another delightful touch for an elegant dining experience. Reserve for Saturday night. *Expensive.*

LA TRATTORIA

119 Hanassi Boulevard   Phone 379020
                                           Lunch and Dinner
                                       11:30 A.M.–midnight
                                          Major Credit Cards

La Trattoria is a bilevel restaurant in a small shopping arcade adjoining the Carmelit entrance. The friendly owners, Lisette and Eddy, are always on hand, and Lisette is the French-trained chef. Her specialty is couscous royale, a Middle Eastern stew that combines meats and grains. It's delicious and quite filling. The majority of the dishes are Italian, and lasagna, ravioli, and several other pastas are most frequently ordered. The pizzas, prepared for one or more munchers, come with fourteen different toppings, and you can mix and match what you like. Upstairs is more formal. The sidewalk café is less formal but right on Hanassi Boulevard. *Moderate.*

ENTRECOT

52 Moriah Ave   Phone 372594
Carmel   Lunch & Dinner
                                              Major Credit Cards

An intimate dining choice with a relaxed ambience, Entrecot has a brick façade and a glass-enclosed terrace for dining, as well as an indoor dining room. Thick steaks with a variety of sauces are house specialties, and seafood is also on the menu. Dishes have a French flavor. *Expensive*.

GOAR

120 Yafe Nof (Panorama Road)   Phone 377150
                                                  Dinner Only
                                              Major Credit Cards

Goar is an Armenian restaurant with a lovely view of the harbor and city below.

Specialities include shishliks, dolmas, and Armenian salads. You can sip a cocktail on the terrace before dinner or even just stop by to have a late-night drink and listen to the Armenian, Russian, and Jewish music that livens up the place. *Moderate*.

DA VINCI

131 Moriyya Street   Phone 341994
Ahuza Section, Carmel   *Major Credit Cards*

A small Italian restaurant near the Horev Center, Da Vinci serves al dente pasta dishes with lots of different sauces. They also serve terrific seafood and pasta combinations. Skip dessert here and head next door to *Recital* a small restaurant serving delicious cakes, pastries, and fresh fruit salads. *Moderate*

SEA WAVES

99 Yefe Nof Street   Phone (04) 375602
                                              Major Credit Cards

If you plan to visit *Sea Waves*, try to call ahead and reserve a table near the picture window overlooking the city. The view is magnificent and will be just one of the highlights of your meal. The extensive Chinese menu features many old and new favorites, including fried wontons, beef with pineapple, and chicken with cashew nuts. If you've got a big appetite, start with the special Sea Wave mixed appetizer platter. *Moderate*.

NARGILA

125 Hanassi Avenve

Phone (04) 375959
Open 24 Hours
Major Credit Cards

Part of a fast-growing chain with branches springing up across the country, Nargila specializes in Yemenite cooking.

At any time of the day or night, diners can feast on *malawah*, a special Yemenite pastry served with several toppings, along with a wide variety of European and Middle Eastern dishes. *Inexpensive*.

CHIN LUNG

126 Hanassi Boulevard

Phone 381308
No Credit Cards

If you've walked by number 126 several times and are convinced Chin Lung no longer exists, don't give up. This informal eatery is down a flight of steps through the wrought-iron gate on Hanassi Boulevard. The owners are Taiwanese, and Chin Lung is an engineer on an Israeli ship. That leaves his wife, Hwang, in charge here, and her chefs, who specialize in Szechuan- and Shanghai-style cuisine, are fellow Taiwanese. For authentic flavoring, Hwang imports many spices. Definitely try the spicy shrimp with hot peppers and the garlic fish. Be prepared with breath freshener mints, for you'll need them. With two days' notice, Hwang will prepare the house specialties—shark fins in chicken sauce, or a whole boned duck that has been stuffed and stewed. *Inexpensive*.

THE DELI

100 Hanassi Boulevard at Supersol

Adjoining the Carmelit station, the two-level shopping arcade has two meat restaurants. The one on the lower level is fancier, but the home-style food at the upper level Deli is better. There are only a handful of tables, but you can select from stuffed cabbage, potato pancakes, chopped liver, and other typical Eastern European favorites. Lots of take-out here. *Inexpensive*.

BAGEL NOSH

120 Hanassi Boulevard at Wedgewood 8 A.M.–9 P.M.

No Credit Cards

Such favorites as freshly baked bagels spread thickly with cheese mixtures, tuna, or salmon salad and eggplant with anchovies are served for breakfast, lunch, and midafternoon nosh. Platters are garnished with fresh vegetables and creamy cole slaw. The menu features omelets, quiches, and blintzes too. This is a great lunch stop. Fast service is the key, whether you get your food at the counter or are waited on. Sit at an outdoor table on the terrace and watch the action on Hanassi Boulevard. *Inexpensive*.

PEER COFFEE RESTAURANT

130 Hanassi Boulevard Phone 382333

7 A.M.–midnight

No Credit Cards

The Peer isn't Haifa's most attractive restaurant, but it has loyal customers who enjoy reading the morning paper with their hearty breakfast or kibbitzing with friends over a pizza (several varieties) at lunch. More filling are lunch items such as the lasagna, cannelloni, and other pasta dishes served with thick bread. Skip dinner here, for it's much the same, but it's a great spot for a late-night cup of coffee. *Inexpensive*.

Bat Galim

A small district in the northwest portion of Haifa's lowest tier, Bat Galim is alive on weekends year round and on warm summer evenings when the city's residents throng to the beaches nearby. Bat Galim has a lovely promenade, and many fine restaurants, particularly seafood ones, are in the area.

DOLPHIN

13 Bat Galim Avenue Phone 523837

Lunch and Dinner

Major Credit Cards

An attractive restaurant with gold and brown decor and lots of greenery, the Dolphin is the place for fish in Haifa. The small

Greek salad is delicious, and the herring, not too salty, is served with sliced onion. The two-pound lobster was very meaty and easily enough for two. It was served broiled with a butter sauce. Large shrimp, either fried or with a provençal sauce, were tasty too. Freshly caught trout, sole, snapper, and St. Peter's fish in butter and garlic sauce, poached in lemon and butter, or with a hot and spicy sauce, were all well prepared. Fried pineapple is a light, sweet dessert. Good wines—a nice dining experience. *Moderate*.

MISADAG

Bat Galim Promenade   Phone 524441
                                                       Lunch and Dinner
                                                       Major Credit Cards

Misadag, in a private house on the promenade, has two indoor dining rooms and tables on the sidewalk. The ships' steering wheels and fishermen's nets alert you to the fact that the specialty here is seafood. The menu here is larger and more varied that than of the Dolphin. Hot stuffed mushrooms were excellent and we enjoyed the mezze too. Shrimp Misadag, which had large shrimp in a sauce of cucumbers, mushrooms, and almonds, was fabulous and the sole tunice in a spicy tomato-based sauce was another excellent entrée. Baked lobster was moist and very big. Hannah, the owner, has relatives in Los Angeles and speaks English fluently. Any questions about Haifa? Ask Hannah. *Moderate*.

PAGODA

1 Bat Galim Avenue   Phone 524585
                                                       Lunch and Dinner

Owned by the same hard-working Taiwanese family as Chin Lung (on Carmel), the Pagoda has one small dining room and only a dozen tables. The decor is minimal, with only an occasional Chinese lantern and colorful mobiles. Food's the thing and service may be a bit too fast, so order in a piecemeal fashion to allow digestion to take place. Pagoda prepares Szechuan dishes if you ask for them, but most dishes here are prepared in Cantonese style. The hot and sour soup had chunks of fish in it and was very good. We shared stewed chicken with chestnuts and beef with green peppers and onions (rather like pepper steak); both were very good. The hot dish we tasted was shredded chicken with spicy sauce. It was very hot! Prices here are a shade higher than at Chin Lung. *Moderate*.

NEPTUNE

19 Margolin Street   Phone 535205
Major Credit Cards

Neptune, on the beach promenade, serves both seafood and grilled meats, Middle Eastern style, which does open up the eating options. There is also a serve-yourself salad bar, and the fresh vegetables and mixed salads were exceptionally good. Most people head for the outdoor terrace here, but we found the wooden tables uncomfortable for an entire meal. The indoor dining room is air-conditioned and has hanging plants. You'll find the service slower and more relaxing here. Both meats and fish are prepared on the charcoal grill and if you like that taste, you'll really enjoy eating here. *Moderate*.

Hadar Ha Carmel

Haifa's middle tier is very commercial. Lunch finds restaurants here crowded with businesspeople and shoppers. Dinner is far quieter, but there are few other evening activities in the area to interest you.

The Nordau Street Mall

The social center of Hadar is the pedestrians-only Nordau Street Mall, which is lined with trees and small boutiques, restaurants, and pubs. It is the only part of Hadar that is alive with people at night. The nicest restaurant on the mall is *Voilà* (review follows), and there are many other informal dining spots from which to choose. The *Kapulsky Restaurant* at #6 is one of the nicest looking in the chain. Dairy foods are served, and the salads and sandwich fixings are fresh and tasty. *The Ritz* and *Prego* are also good stops for light meals. Slightly more upscale, *Nameus* at #20 is a vegetarian restaurant that also serves fresh seafood.

Voilà

21a Nordau Street	Phone (04) 664529
	Noon to 12:30 A.M.
	Open 7 days a week

A piece of Switzerland has made its way to Haifa in the form of a lovely Swiss garden chalet, alias Voilà. The food and ambience of this delightful eatery will make it one of your best memories of Haifa. The French-Swiss cuisine is unforgettable—deliciously light crêpes, fondues, fresh fish, and salads. Don't pass on dessert. The homemade ice cream is terrific with apple strudel. *Moderate.*

Pizzeria Rimini

20 Ha-Niviim Street	Open 7 days a week
	Till midnight
	MasterCard, Visa.

You can stop in at Rimini for a slice of sizzling pizza and carry it to one of the small tables nearby, To sample other Italian specialties or share a whole pie, head to the second floor dining room. It is large and its many windows make it bright and airy. *Moderate.*

Mataamin

24 Herzl Street	Phone 336295
	Closed for Sabbath
	No Credit Cards

The larger front room has a dozen tables and looks like a cafeteria. The nicer dining area is upstairs at the back of the restaurant; it is air-conditioned and there are cloths on the tables. Mataamin has a huge menu. Swedish meatballs were good but not exactly Swedish meatballs as we know them, while the fried kreplach were authentic and delicious. We shared a goulash that had enormous beef and potato chunks in a thick sauce. These dishes were filling and we skipped dessert. Recommended only for lunch. *Inexpensive.*

Port Area

La Chaumire

40 Ben Gurion Avenue   Phone 538563
Lunch & Dinner
Closed Fridays and Saturday lunch
Major Credit Cards

La Chaumire is a French restaurant in a two-story stone house in the German Colony overlooking the port. The husband and wife that own La Chaumire are both chefs, and the food is more traditionally French than that at the Rondo Grill. The pâtés are terrific, and so is the chateaubriand with green pepper sauce. Don't skip the chocolate mousse—you can walk off the extra calories in hilly Haifa. *Expensive*

Daliya

22 Ben Gurion Boulevard   Phone 522157
(Closed Saturday)
No Credit Cards

Daliya is a very pretty spot. It looks like a greenhouse, with a garden around the glass-enclosed dining room. Specialties here are Middle Eastern and nicely prepared. Stuffed cabbage, chopped liver, goulash, and skewered meats are what draw diners here. *Moderate*

Lunch Choices

There is little reason to be in the port area after dark since the streets are rather deserted. But, if you are exploring the area during the daytime hours, you can eat really well and really inexpensively. Head to the city market on Eliyahir Ha-Navi Street near the Paris Square Carmelit station. There are several choices for Middle Eastern foods here but the two most popular (read "standing room only") are *Naim's* and *Abu Hani*. Each serves falafels, hearty soups, lamb and beef shishliks, and delicious vegetable salads.

Light Fare—Falafel Row

If you prefer to eat lunch quickly, Hadar has several fast-food shops and an entire falafel street. Head downhill from Mazaryk Square to the corner of HaNeviim and Hehalutz Streets (about two blocks). On your right, lining both sidewalks, are at least a dozen falafel stands and each has a crowd in front. The counter is filled with huge bowls of sauces and vegetables—sliced tomatoes, onions, radishes, shredded cabbage, lettuce, sliced cucumbers and turnips, olives, and many others. Take as much as you like of what you like, douse it with tehina sauce and voilà a delicious, healthy, inexpensive lunch or afternoon snack.

Pancake Herzl, 35 Herzl Street, serves them with raisins, walnuts, apples, or berries. Good syrup. Crêpes as well.

Snir Konditorei, at Herzl and Biâlik Street (near IGTO), has a take-out ice cream parlor up front and a luncheon restaurant in the back. Pizzas, quiches, big bowls of soup, and a variety of over-stuffed dairy sandwiches are on the menu. Fast service.

Milky Pinky,HaNeviim Street (uphill from Carmelit), has outdoor tables shaded by red-and-white umbrellas and serves light fare.

Newsstands often have large vats of boiling water filled with corn on the cob. Eat as you walk!

Mac David is in Central Carmel.

Sunup to Sundown

The three tiers make a walking tour of Haifa impractical. Instead we will describe the city's most interesting sights, grouping them so you can plan your visit. But before you visit these specific sights, you should have a sense of what Haifa is like as an entity. The best way to do that is to hop on the Carmelit and explore. Note:Haifa doesn't get too many tourists, and signs are often in Hebrew only. However, many people do speak some English, so don't be shy about asking.

Stop #1, Paris Square (Lower Level)

This is the port area and much of it is on landfill. Look for *Ha'atzmaut Road*, which was once on the waterfront. Now a mélange of old and new buildings, it is the local red-light district. *Jaffa Road* is filled with Arab shops selling inexpensive handicrafts and with cafés and small businesses. If interested, stop at the *Dagon Silo*, a huge grain elevator with a museum explaining the history of grain storage and handling. If you'd like to see *Germantown*, follow Jaffa Road to Ben Gurion Boulevard (three blocks) and turn left onto Ben Gurion. Here you'll notice the gardens in front of the red tile-roofed houses—many of them are now home to restaurants. Looking ahead on Ben Gurion, you'll see the magnificent Bahai Shrine. If you are in great shape, you can walk it.

Stop #3, HaNeviim Street

This is on the Hadar Ha Carmel level and you emerge from the Carmelit in *Kikar Mazaryk. Herzl Street*, to your right, is a major commercial center, and *HaNeviim*, in front of you, is another busy street. The IGTO is at 20 Herzl Street. (Hours are 8 A.M. to 4 P.M. daily; Friday 8 A.M. to 2 P.M. Closed Saturday.) Pick up a city map and a list of monthly events. Hadar is the blue-collar part of the city. Lots of shops, theaters, cafés, and the Haifa Museum are in this area.

If you head downhill on HaNeviim Street for two blocks, you will see Falafel Row, a street lined with a dozen or more falafel stands. The Haifa Museum, at 26 Shabatai Tzvi Street (left of Mazaryk Square), houses the museums of Ancient and Modern Art, Music, and Ethnology. Your entrance ticket here is also good for the National Maritime Museum, Tikotin Museum of Japanese Art, Mane Katz Museum, and the Stekelis Museum of Prehistory. The ancient-art exhibit (third floor) consists of six rooms with artifacts found locally, and the final room on the left has a terrific exhibit that explains how food was grown and stored in the fourth through the sixth centuries. The music and ethnology exhibits share the first floor, and the native clothes worn by Jews of the Diaspora are on exhibit. Not as interesting as the exhibit in the Israel Museum, but it is attractive. Hours are 10 A.M. to 1 P.M.

Sunday through Saturday, there are evening hours 5 to 9 P.M. Monday through Thursday and Saturdays.

Walk back to Mazaryk Square and continue along Herzl Street till you come to an intersection where three streets meet (look for Arlosorov Street). Turn right to *Nordau Street* which is a pedestrian-only mall; the shops here are nicer than on Herzl Street. Nearby you'll see Haifa's *Municipal Theater* and *Central Synagogue*. If interested, you can follow Balfour Street(near IGTO) uphill to the Old Technion Building, which was the first building constructed in Hadar. Now that the Technion has a new building, this one houses the National Museum of Science and Technology.

Stop #6, Carmel

Since most hotels are on this level, you are probably most familiar with the commercial area here, *Central Carmel*. The large park alongside the Carmelit entrance is *Gan Ha'Em*(Mothers' Park). It has a children's zoo, playgrounds, outdoor cafés, and the *Museum of Prehistory* (early archeological finds from the Carmel). Hours are Sunday through Thursday 8 A.M. 3 P.M.; Saturday from 10 A.M. to 2 P.M. Buses #21, #22, #23, #28, and #37 will also get you here.

The *Panorama Center*, a two-story shopping arcade, is to the left of the Carmelit, and the *Haifa Auditorium* is to the right. While Hanassi Boulevard is a commercial street, much of Carmel is residential and looks rather suburban. *Yefe Nof* (Panorama Road) follows the ridge of the hill and offers wonderful views from its park benches. Make sure to come here at night (it's absolutely safe).

Along Hanassi Boulevard you'll find two small museums. The *Tikotin Museum of Japanese Art*, 89 Hanassi Boulevard, is unique in Israel, with over seven thousand items that illustrate both ancient and modern Japanese tradition including paintings, woodblock prints, lacquer, metal and ceramics. This was Felix Tikotin's private collection. Open Sunday through Thursday 10 A.M. to 5 P.M.; Saturday 10 A.M. to 2 P.M. Buses #22, and #23 will also get you here.

Next door, the *Mane Katz Museum* at 89 Yefe Nof Street is a collection of works by this well-known Israeli artist, and the furnishings of the house are museum pieces as well. Open Sunday through Thursday 10 A.M. to 4 P.M., and Friday and Saturday 10 A.M. to 1 P.M.

Specific Sights

Most specific sights are historical, so first a bit of Haifa lore is in order.

A Capsule History

Although Haifa is not mentioned in the Bible, it would seem from artifacts found in caves in Carmel that the area was inhabited in prehistoric times. The city, whose name means "beautiful coast," is mentioned in the Talmud and by the eleventh century was known as a shipbuilding community with a Jewish majority. The Crusaders lay siege to the city for six months and when it finally fell, they slaughtered most of the remaining Jews. During the Crusader period, a Carmelite monastery was erected atop the mountain. The city languished under a host of invaders, and the monastery was destroyed.

In the early eighteenth century, Dahir el Umar conquered the Galilee. He started a new settlement in Haifa (still visible near Paris Square)and developed the harbor. His successor, Ahmed Jazzar, permitted the Carmelite order to rebuild their monastery near Elijah's Grotto, and he built a lighthouse nearby. (These are both still there today.)

Two events followed that influenced Haifa's development. The steam engine was perfected, which forced larger ships to dock in Haifa's deeper harbor rather than in nearby Akko, and the Turks decided to sell large parcels of land outside their settlement to a German religious organization called the Templars. These hardworking people laid out wide streets, planted gardens, and built one-family, red-tile-roofed houses just like those in their native Wurtemburg. This area, which lines Ben Gurion Boulevard, looks much the same today. Their cemetery is nearby on Jaffa Street. When the Templars tried to expand their colony up the mountainside, they ran into opposition from the French Carmelites at the monastery. The Carmelites went so far as to build a wall on the mountain's edge. This area is known as French Carmel today. By the way, the German community prospered under Turkish rule but the Templars were forced to evacuate during the Second World War.

With the completion of a railroad line linking Damascus with Haifa, the city started to prosper as trade increased. The old city started to expand and small settlements opened near Germantown. Arabs, Christians, and Jews moved to these areas.

In 1918, the British took control of the city and the rate of growth expanded. The Hadar Ha Carmel area was founded in 1920, the Ahuza neighborhood in 1921, and Bat Galim in 1922. Most of these new areas were Jewish, and this left the lower port level primarily Arab, which it still is today.

The period that changed Haifa and made it a name in newspaper headlines started in the 1930s. All during that decade, small shiploads of Jewish immigrants arrived in Haifa from Europe. As it became obvious that a war was brewing and that Jews would be persecuted by Hitler's Nazis, increasing numbers of Eastern European Jews sought refuge in Palestine via ships to Haifa. Suddenly in 1939, Britain, in an effort to mollify oil-rich Arab states, issued a white paper which limited Jewish immigration to Palestine and would not permit Jews to purchase land there. This paper signaled to world Jewry that Britain was reneging on the Balfour Declaration (to create a Jewish homeland) and it closed a major escape route for the Jews trapped in Eastern Europe.

Underground fighters stepped up their efforts to bring in refugees, even if it was illegal. Leon Uris's book, *Exodus*, was the story of one ship that was actually turned back. Small boats, overcrowded and in disrepair, tried to evade the British warships by dropping refugees at beaches from Tel Aviv to Haifa. Often they were caught and towed to Haifa, and the refugees were sent to detention camps on Mauritius or Cyprus. One ship, the *Patria*, was blown up in the harbor by the underground to prevent its leaving, and 250 passengers drowned. One of these blockade runners, an American carrier, the *Af-al-pi-khen*, serves as the centerpiece in the Clandestine Immigration and Maritime Museum, where the story of these events is told in photos and the words of the people who lived it. Don't miss it; this museum tells the story of Haifa's finest hours.

Stella Maris French Carmelite Monastery and Church

The monastery and church are on Stella Maris Road, Carmel. Drive from Hanassi Avenue to Tchernikovsky Street. The monastery will be on your right soon after the turn. When Napoleon attempted to establish an Eastern empire, he lay siege to nearby Akko. Forced to retreat, he left his wounded in the care of the Carmelites at this monastery. As soon as he set sail, the Moslems attacked the monastery and killed all the soldiers there. At the edge of the cliff stands the Carmelite Church, built over Elijah's Cave. You can visit the church from 8:30 A.M. to 1:30 P.M. and 3 to 6 P.M. daily.

Cable Car

Haifa's cable car leaves from the nearby cliffiside. Each car has three separate compartments that hold five people. It whisks you down to Bat Galim (beach area) and the city's most interesting museum, the Clandestine Immigration and Maritime Museum. The cable car operates from Sunday through Thursday and on Saturday, 10 A.M. till 6 P.M. (till 11 P.M. in the summer) and on Friday from 10 A.M. till 6 P.M. Take bus #25, #26, #27, #30, #31, #41, or #42.

The Clandestine Museum

From 1934 to 1948, Jews struggled to emigrate to Israel, but the British restricted their immigration, leading to a clandestine movement. In those years, 122,000 refugees from Europe arrived in Israel—108,000 by sea on 116 different ships, some little larger than tugboats, on 141 trips. Those who were admitted under the British quota landed at Haifa harbor, but most landed illegally on the beaches along the coast. Many were caught and towed back to Haifa, where they were sent back to Europe or placed in detention camps on Mauritius or Cyprus.

The centerpiece of the museum that recounts the victories and defeats of those exciting times is the *Af-al-pi-khen*, one of the ships that successfully evaded the blockade several times until September 27, 1947, when it was caught with 437 people on board. Other ships and people were less fortunate. The *Patria* was sunk in the harbor (by Jewish commandos) with tremendous loss of life. The heartbreaking and triumphant story of the refugees and those who tried to bring them to freedom is recounted in photos, in newspaper headlines, and in the words of the survivors themselves. This museum is Haifa's "must" stop. It is located at 204 Allenby Road (near Bat Galim). Open Sunday through Thursday 9 A.M to 4 P.M., Friday 9 A.M. to 1 P.M.; closed Saturday. Take bus #3, #5, #43, or #44.

Elijah's Cave

Across the road from the Clandestine Museum is Elijah's Cave, which is beneath the Carmelite church. In the fourth century A.D., the Byzantines identified this cave as the one in which Elijah found refuge from King Ahab and his Phoenician wife, Jezebel, who had reintroduced pagan cults to the people of Israel. The cave has intact chalky walls, and people come here to light candles and pray. Elijah had challenged the pagan priests of Baal to a duel by fire. Each erected an altar and slaughtered an ox upon it. Each then appealed to their God to reply by fire. The priests chanted for hours—to no avail —but Elijah's prayers were immediately answered.

Christians, Jews, and Moslems all revere this site, for another legend says that Jesus and his family stayed in this cave on their return from Egypt. Oriental Jews pray here on Tisha Bav, asking for a better year. Hours are Sunday through Thursday 8 A.M. to 4 P.M. Friday 8 A.M. to noon; closed Saturday.

If you have further interest in Elijah, visit the Carmelite monastery at Mukhraka (near the Druze village, Daliyat el-Carmel), where the confrontation is said to have taken place.

The National Maritime Museum

Nearby, at 198 Allenby Road, the National Maritime Museum, presents the history and evolution of shipbuilding and seafaring.

Founded in 1955, the museum has a collection of ships (in scale models) that covers five thousand years of history. King Solomon's Tarshish ships and Phoenician and Roman crafts are on display, as are an interesting collection of water deities on coins and ancient oil lamps. Open Sunday through Thursday 10 A.M. to 4 P.M., Saturday 10 A.M. to 1 P.M., closed Friday. Take bus #3, #5, #43, #44, or #45.

Bahai Shrine and Gardens

Haifa is the international headquarters of the Bahai faith, which started in Persia. The massive golden dome of the shrine, visible from all parts of the city, is Haifa's best-known landmark. In 1844, a Persian, Mirsa Ali Mohammed, declared that he was Bab, the "gateway to God." He was killed by firing squad in 1850, along with many of his followers. His successor, Musa Hussen Ali, took the name Bah-Ullah. Forced to flee, he went to Palestine, where he was kept under house arrest by the Turks for twenty-four years. He did much of his spiritual writing here and died a natural death in 1892. He was buried in a shrine near Akko, called Bahje House. (It is near Kibbutz Shamerat.) His disciples arranged for the remains of the Bab to be brought from Persia, and in 1909 they buried the remains on this hillside of Haifa. The dome over the tomb was completed in 1953. The gardens surrounding the tomb are as beautiful as any we've ever seen. The pebbled walkways are outlined by palm trees and perfectly manicured towering cypress trees. Inside, the Bab's tomb itself is very simple. The tomb is all carpeted, and chandeliers are at its head and foot. Wear modest dress and remove your shoes before you enter. No photographs may be taken.

The Bahai adherents who watch over the tomb or work in the nearby archives and library are delighted to explain their faith, which they say has three million followers worldwide. The Bahais believe in the brotherhood of all people and in a common world language and a unity of religion. They believe that Christ, Moses, Mohammed, and Buddha were sent by God as teachers to lead the world at various times in history. They also believe that Bab-Ullah is the latest teacher sent by God. Very gentle people, they welcome the curious and their own pilgrims with open arms. You can walk here from Yefe Nof in Carmel or come by bus #25 from Hadar or #22 from the lower level. The shrine is open daily from 9 A.M. until noon and the gardens from 8 A.M. to 5 P.M.

The Technion

The Israel Institute of Technology, always called Technion, was originally located on Hadar Ha Carmel. Now, ensconced in a magnificent campus on Mount Carmel, it draws Israel's ablest students to its schools of engineering, architecture, and medicine. With over one hundred buildings on a three-hundred-acre campus, it is Israel's largest research center.

The Coler California Visitors' Center is the place to start your visit. A short film, narrated by Kirk Douglas, explains what Technion is, and exhibits throughout the building explain the various aspects of research carried out here.

In the Jack Lemmon Auditorium you can see a slide presentation of what results the research carried out here have achieved over the years. The Coler Center is open Sunday through Thursday 8 A.M. to 2 P.M.; closed Friday and Saturday. Bus #17 or #19 from central Carmel will take you there.

Sports

Swimming   Haifa has several lovely beaches. Bathing is permitted when lifeguards are on duty, from May through October. The municipal beaches are Dado, Carmel, and Bat Galim. All are free. Carmel and Bat Galim also have swimming pools, while Dado has a water slide and windsurfers.

Squash   There is a squash club at Kfar Zamir. Call regarding free time: 539160.

Tennis   There are several tennis centers in Haifa. Try the Israel Tennis Center at Kfar Zamir, phone 522721, or the Maccabi Club at Bikkurim Street, phone 86028.

Picnics

Atop Mount Carmel is Israel's largest national park, with more than 25,000 acres for picnics and relaxing.

Sundown to Sunup

Haifa is not a late-night town, but there are some places you might enjoy. Don't forget to pick up the *Listing of Events in Haifa* from IGTO.

The Haifa Auditorium, 138 Hanassi Boulevard, has concerts, operas, and visiting international companies. Check at the box office or in the *Jerusalem Post*. Phone 380013.

The James Rothschild Cultural Center (Beit Rothschild) is next door to the Auditorium at number 142 and has smaller-scale concerts, dance companies, exhibits, and lectures (some times in English). Phone 382749.

Cinematheque is next door to the Center. This theater has classic films in many languages.

Pubs and Discotheques

Chaplin Club, in the basement of the Dan Panorama Hotel (Carmel), is a lively disco that is open every night. Patrons are thirty-something and the music is laid-back. There is a minimum on Friday night, when you should have a reservation. Phone 352222.

Palache's Pub, in the Dan Carmel Hotel Lobby, is open Friday and Saturday nights.

Butterfly Disco, at 137 Hanassi Boulevard, is "in" at this writing. Dark and frenetic. Closed Sunday and Monday.

Little Haifa Club, at 4 Sha'ar Halevanon Street (near the Carmelit entrance) in Carmel, draws a young singles crowd.

Yefe Nof (Panorama Road) has several night spots. Check out *Hitchcock*, a disco near the Dvir Hotel, and two pubs, *Hamizpor* at #115 and *Delet Ahorit* at #120.

Bat Galim Promenade has several late night options as well. *Pan-ass Boded*, a pub and piano bar, is crowded on summer evenings, as is *Hasfinah*, a lively disco.

The Pub and *Mash* are pubs with music located on Nordau Mall (Hadar).

Haifa Potpourri

Haifa Events   Phone (04)374253 for an English summary of events, tours, and other goings-on.

IGTO   18 Herzl Street,phone 666521.

IGTO Free Walking Tour of Carmel   Starts at Yefe Nof at Sha'ar Halevanon Street (near Panorama Center), Saturday at 10 A.M., with an English-speaking guide.

Municipal Tourist Offices

Municipal Tourist Offices are located at the Central Bus Terminal, Port Level, and at 106 Hanassi Avenue, Carmel, phone 374010.

Mosque

The El Iskital Mosque at Faisal Square is open 8 A.M. to 1 P.M.

Churches

There is a Greek Orthodox Church at 23 Ein Dor Street (phone 523012) and a Roman Catholic Church at 80 Hameginim Street (phone 524346).

Synagogues

The Central Synagogue is located at 60 Herzl Street.

The Progressive Congregation is located at Hadash at Beit Rothschild, 142 Hanassi Street.

The Sephardic Synagogue, Heichal Netanel, is located at 43 Herzl Street.

Excursions from Haifa

The excursions from Haifa are among the country's most exciting. To the north, Akko has an exotic walled city and subterranean Crusader city and, beyond it on the Lebanese border, Rosh Hanikra has grottoes which are reached by cable car. To the southeast, Druze villages, an artists' colony, and Israel's largest wine cellars can be visited on a half-day excursion.

Akko

The old city of Akko is one of my favorite stops in Israel. Only twenty-six kilometers north of twentieth-century Haifa and on the same stunning bay, Akko looks like the setting of *Ali Baba and the Forty Thieves*. Enclosed by thick fortified sea walls on three sides, the inner city is a maze of narrow medieval streets. Densely populated (almost eight thousand Arabs live in this small inner city area), the city is always alive and active. As you wander through the lively Oriental market and Turkish bazaar, you'll feel yourself gently pushed along through the crowds of haggling shoppers. The ancient citadel, which now houses a military museum, was used as a prison by the British, and the town museum is in an old Turkish bath. The aged khans still stand, and the Ahmed Jazzar Mosque is one of the country's loveliest. But the pièce de résistance of a visit to Akko is the Subterranean Crusader City, which you enter through Turkish gates. A wondrous site beneath high vaulted ceilings, the Knights Halls and the Crypt (not a burial site) are cool and hushed. You can follow the secret tunnel the Crusaders built from one part of Crusader City to another. It took the National Park Service twelve years to clear Crusader City, for over the years the Turks had used it as a khan, a sewer, and a defensive position. Concerts and plays now take place in the halls where King Richard the Lion-Hearted supped. You can sup there too, for there are several small cafés inside the city. Old Akko has an active marina and there are several excellent restaurants in the port area. You'll need at least half a day to wander through Old Akko. It is one of Israel's most exotic stops. You can take bus #271 to get there.

A Capsule History

Once again we find a city that dates back to ancient times, but the fascination here is that Akko, because of its strategic position on a harbor, has been continuously occupied for thousands of years. For many of those years it was Palestine's major port.

Early excavations would indicate hat the Canaanite city originally stood one and a half kilometers to the east at Tel es Fukhar (now being excavated). captured by pharaohs, Persians, and Phoenicians, it was never captured by the ancient Israelites, who attacked it several times. Often Akko was used as a base from which to attack other parts of the country. The Arabs used it as a supply port, but in 1104 the Crusaders, led by Baldwin I, captured the city and renamed it St. Jean d'Acre. They built their city here and made it headquarters for the religious chivalric order, the Knights of St. John. Taken for the Arabs by Sultan Saladin, it was retaken by King Richard, who made it the capital of the Crusader kingdom. It is believed that fifty thousand people (Arabs, Jews, and Christians) lived here. The Crusaders' brutal treatment of the Arabs of Akko was repaid in full when the city was razed by the Mamelukes. That ended the Crusader state, which had lasted less than two hundred years. The city lay in ruins till the Ottomans arrived in the fourteenth century. They started to rebuild and expand it (hence the Arab city around the Crusader one). In 1775, Ahmed Jazzar, called "the butcher," became pasha. Ruling till 1805, he left his mark on the city. He rebuilt the outer walls and built the mosque that bears his name, as well as the citadel and Turkish baths.

Napoleon's attempt to establish himself in the east failed when he lay seige to Akko for two months (from a hill outside the walls), but was unable to capture the city. As the nineteenth century came to an end, Akko lost its prominence as a port to its neighbor, Haifa, which has a deeper harbor. In 1918, when the British took the city from the Turks, only eight thousand people lived in it. The British used Akko's citadel as a prison for captured underground fighters, including Ze'ev Jabotinsky. Several were hanged here as well. The citadel was stormed by Jewish commandos in 1947, and many prisoners escaped. Israel took

Akko in 1948, and the city expanded with residential areas constructed to the north and east. Now a city of thirty-nine thousand, Akko has the country's only steel mill, as well as iron works and chemical plants.

Orientation

When you arrive in Akko, the old city will be on the water to your left. Look for the glittering domes, minarets, and colorful flags. There are also signs. Look for Rehov Weizman and park your car in the lot.

When to Visit

Try to avoid a Friday visit to Akko. Friday is the Moslem Sabbath and many shops are closed. It is also unlikely that you will be allowed into the mosque. By afternoon, all the Jewish-owned shops and the museums will be closed for the Jewish Sabbath.

A Walk Through Old Akko

As you cross the street from the parking lot, you'll see the *Mosque of Ahmed Jazzar* on your left. Built in the eighteenth century by Pasha Ahmed Jazzar, the mosque is very beautiful inside. The surrounding courtyard, with a sundial in one corner, is dominated by an octagonal fountain that is used for ritual cleansing before prayer. Five times each day a devout Moslem washes his face, neck, hands, and feet before entering the mosque, where he prays (facing Mecca) on thick carpets. The mosque, built over the ruins of a Catholic church and a Crusader fortress, has a small room upstairs with several hairs of Mohammed's beard. These are shown only on the twenty-seventh day of the feast of Ramadan. The tombs of Jazzar and his son are also in the garden.

Lining the street here is the *Turkish Bazaar*, which is fun to shop at. As you cross Rehov el Jazzar, which is crowded with shoppers, look for the thick wrought gate that marks the entrance to the *Subterranean Crusader City*. As soon as you enter you will be aware of the drop in temperature. As you buy your ticket (also good for museum entrance), look for the columns from the original Crusader structure. This entrance is actually a Turkish building. The Crusader City was the administrative headquarters for the chivalric order of the Knights of St. John, as well as a hospital.

As you leave the entrance chamber, you will find yourself in a large courtyard. Look up and you'll see the Citadel, used by the British as a prison. Head to the Knights' Halls (everything is well marked), which are virtually intact after seven hundred years. Notice that these rooms are massive; you can visualize the long wooden tables at which the Crusaders ate. These rooms were filled with rubble by the Turks for defensive purposes and, in fact, when the Crusader kingdom fell, the entire city was covered by mounds of dirt. Other structures, including the Citadel, were built over it, which made clearing it very difficult. During the British Mandate period, Jewish prisoners tunneled out of the Citadel, landing in the Knights' Halls. With no way out, they went back to their cells. A concrete patch on the ceiling marks their futile effort. The rooms now house a collection of modern sculptures, and concerts are held here.

Cross the courtyard to the Grand Manoir, which was the administrative section. The architecture here, very different from that of the Knights' halls, would indicate that these halls were built at another time. Parts of the Grand Manoir have not been excavated. Here too we find massive rooms with high ceilings.

The entrance from this massive area to the Crypt, the lowest level of the city, is very narrow. Not a burial site, the Crypt was given its name because of its depth, and was actually the guest and dining halls. The Crypt could be entered from three sides, and it is believed that Marco Polo was entertained here on a stopover on his journey to China. Look carefully at the stones near the entrances and you'll see a faint fleur de lis, the emblem of French royalty.

From the Crypt you can follow a low, narrow underground tunnel which has several paths. In ancient times, it led to the port area and various parts of the city wall and was probably built for defensive purposes. It now leads to *The Post*, a six-hall complex, a good distance (sixty-five meters) from the Crypt. The post may have been the hospital or it may have been a khan for pilgrims. Many of the artifacts found in the Crusader City are on display in the nearby museum. The city is often used for concerts and shows. Check with the local IGTO. There are several cafés inside too.

The Municipal Museum is housed in Pasha Jazzar's bath house (Haman el Pasha), which functioned as a Turkish bath till 1947. You can see the marble floors and the benches where the bathers sat. Exhibits in the museum besides those from Crusader City include Islamic art and folklore, as well as an interesting collection of ancient weapons.

Retrace your steps to the mosque, then turn right on Rehov Weizman for just a few feet. Turn left and you'll find yourself in the *souk*—noisy, smelly, crowded, and wonderful. Sacks of aromatic, colorful spices, fly-encrusted meat, slippery fish, ceramic plates, clothing, and brass line the sidewalks, and the Arab merchants, beads in hand, sit serenely as you are gently moved along by the crowd.

Old Akko has three ancient khans (most have been torn down) and the one facing you, *Khan el-Shawarda*, is the least interesting. Site of a Franciscan sisters' convent, it was overrun by the Mamelukes in 1291, causing the sisters to commit suicide. Beyond the khan you'll see *Burj es-Sultan*, one of the fortresses guarding the city. At the western tip of the city, it is fortified and you can walk to it if you like.

The next large structure is *Khan el-Franj*, which was known as the European khan. Built in 1600, it is on a Crusader site that was a nunnery founded by St. Francis of Assisi. The nuns here disfigured themselves rather than be taken by the Mamelukes.

Look up and find the dome of a mosque. Beside it stands *Khan el-Umdan*, called Inn of the Pillars for the columns that support it. It is the most beautiful khan here, and is home to the IGTO. The first story was the stable; the guest rooms were upstairs. In 1906, a clock tower was added to the khan (the clock is now gone).

At this point, you are in the marina area, which is still an active fishing port and private dock. You can take a boat ride around the harbor from here (it goes several times a day), and there is also an active diving center. You can rent equipment or join a day diving trip if you are certified; phone (04) 918990. In the bay, you'll see the breakwater and watchtower built by the Crusaders. Nearby, the *Abu Christo Restaurant* is on a terrace overlooking the bay. Serving excellent seafood and Middle Eastern cuisine, this is one of Akko's best dining spots.

At this point you can walk on the walls that lead to the lighthouse in the city's southwest corner. You'll soon pass *St John's Church*, which was built over the Crusader Church of St. Andrew. Part of the wall was destroyed by an 1837 earthquake. This is a residential area, and you will notice small children playng soccer, laundry drying, and women carrying food. Just before you reach the northwest point of the wall where Burj Kurajim (a Turkish fortress) stands, leave the wall and follow Rehov Hagona to the *Citadel,* the *Museum of Heroism.* The citadel, built over part of the Crusader City, was used as a top-security prison by the British. Here they kept Jewish underground fighters, and you can see the room where several were hung. You can visit the cells, which now house posters, newspapers, and articles from the pre-state era that describe the struggle against the British. A daring jailbreak occurred in 1947 when commandos stormed the prison. Open 8 A.M. to 4:30 P.M. daily (8 A.M. to 1 P.M. Friday).

Now is the time to wander through the market and shop for some memorabilia or foodstuffs. Some of the shops here are exceptionally nice.

If you stay for a concert, head to *Oudah Brothers* restaurant in the market for Middle Eastern food, several dining rooms, and a very authentic flavor. Stays open late too.

If you are hot and sticky after your walk, you can take a dip at nearby *Hof Argamen*, which is open from May through September. Walk through the land gate on the far side of the parking lot.

If you are still game, you can drive to Nahariya and Rosh Hanikra, on the Lebanese border, to see the wonderful grottoes.

Rosh Hanikra

As beautiful as the grottoes of Capri, these little-known caves have been carved out of the cliff by the sea. The white cliff overlooks the sea, and from its summit you can see Haifa and Mount Carmel forty-four kilometers away. The grottoes at the foot of the cliff can be reached by cable car daily from 8:30 A.M. to

4 P.M. You can enter the limestone caves; you'll hear the water rushing in and see it splash off the sides, forming pools of sea water. It's cool and salty and a lot of fun. The beach has some of Israel's best reefs.

On your return to Haifa, you might stop for lunch in Nahariya, a resort community with good beaches and windsurfing, which is a favorite Israeli honeymoon destination.

Zikhron Ya'akov

In 1882, a group of Eastern European Jews arrived in these hills overlooking Caesarea and the Mediterranean. It was one of the first modern Jewish settlements in Palestine, but it would never have succeeded without the intervention of Baron Edmond de Rothschild. He offered financial assistance and purchased the community's first winepress. The village now houses Israel's largest winery, *Carmel Oriental*. You can visit the cellars and taste the grapes and the wine on guided tours conducted each day from 9 A.M. till 3 P.M. (till 1 P.M. on Friday; closed Saturday). The village has a lovely view of the beach, and from here Rothschild spied the swamps near Caesarea and determined to create the Israeli Riviera. Also nearby is the *Aaronson Museum*, which tells the story of the short but effective role played by the Nili spy ring during the First World War. The museum is open Sunday through Thursday 8:30 A.M. to 1 P.M.. You can stop at Zikhron Ya'akov on your way to Haifa. It is thirty-three kilometers away on Route 4. You can combine a stop here with one at En Hod and the Druze villages, descriptions of which follow.

En Hod Artists Village

En Hod, a cooperative artists' colony, is a unique village, nestled in the Carmel Mountains with a panoramic view of the Mediterranean. The village, run by a council of elders, was built in the early 1950s on the site of a deserted Arab village. After the War of Independence, the village was slated to be razed but Marcel Janco, a well-known artist, convinced the government that it was the perfect spot for a village of craftsmen. With the aid of Haifa tourist officials, the village took form. The old buildings were repaired or converted into workshops. A gallery, an outdoor theater, and a small restaurant were built. The village now houses painters, sculptors, ceramicists, potters, and weavers. Dancers, musicians, and writers also live here. The town is picturesque, rough hewn, and earthy. En Hod's museum is worth a visit; it houses a permanent exhibit of the works of Janco, who was a leader of the Dada movement. Rotating exhibits on the lower floors are often the works of rising artists. The Janco-Dada Museum is open every day from 9:30 A.M. to 4 P.M. Adjoining the museum is the village gallery, where the works of resident and guest artists are displayed and sold. The works range from religious and traditional to avant-garde. A small entrance fee is charged to aid in the upkeep of the gallery, and works are competitively priced. The village is tiny, and a ten-minute stroll will suffice. A soft drink on the restaurant terrace comes with a view of the sea and a Crusader castle, Athlit, which is used by the Israel military and is therefore off-limits. Daily buses travel to the village from Haifa.

Isfiya and Daliyat el-Carmel (Druze Villages)

For a peek at one of Israel's most interesting minorities, spend a half day at the villages of Isfiya and Daliyat el-Carmel.

High in the Carmel Mountains, sixteen kilometers southeast of Haifa, overlooking the Jezreel Valley, are villages inhabited by Druze, an Arabic people who are neither Moslem nor Christian. The Druze religion is a secret one, but one of their prophets, Jethro, was the father-in-law of Moses. Druze serve in the Israeli Army and are represented in the Knesset.

The Carmel range is stunning and as the road climbs into the hills, you'll see the Mediterranean on your left and neatly terraced farms in the valley below on your right. Isfiya, the smaller of the two villages, has boxy one-family homes and several shops. You'll see Druze men, easily identifiable by their white caps and bushy mustaches, sitting outside cafés sipping thick black coffee or working in the fields. The women wear white head scarves, and often long black dresses; however, the younger ones wear western-style clothes and the traditional scarf.

Three miles away, larger Daliyat el-Carmel has a real town center which is filled with small cafés and shops. Druze handicrafts look much like those in the markets of Jaffa and Jerusalem, but prices here are somewhat lower and bargaining is definitely in. An interesting item is a saddle blanket woven in thick, colorful braided cotton. It makes a terrific wall hanging. Lots of straw, wicker, and ceramics, too.

Sheruts from Haifa make this trip, as do local buses. Driving? Leave Haifa through the Ahuza section and head to Route 4. Pick up road signs here. Combine a visit to these villages with one to En Hod and Zikhron Ya'akov.

Bet She'arim Burial Caves

The Bet She'arim Burial Caves are only part of an excavation that is located nineteen kilometers from Haifa. This historical site is in a park overlooking the Yizre'el Valley. Josephus Flavius mentioned Bet She'arim, which was part of an estate owned by the great-granddaughter of Herod, Berenice. Later, it became the center of the Sanhedrin(ancient Israel's Supreme Court). Rabbi Yehuda Hanassi, who was responsible for the Mishnah, was the chief of the Sanhedrin in the second century A.D. and was buried here along with other Jewish scholars and clerics of the period. Excavations started in 1956 and revealed sites that had been forgotten since the fourth century A.D., when the Romans destroyed Bet She'arim. A Byzantine church was a major find, but most impressive were the twenty or so burial chambers, which are richly decorated and contain sarcophagi that bear inscriptions and Hebraic symbols, and the ram's horns and menorahs. Interestingly, some of the inscriptions (in Hebrew and Greek) on the wooden or lead coffins have been deciphered and prove that certain of these coffins came from distant places such as Babylon and Yemen. Thus Bet She'arim was the burial place of Jews from different lands (probably because Jerusalem was prohibited to Jews for any purposes by the third century A.D.).

Bet She'arim has well-tended grounds and facilities, including a small outdoor restaurant. Hours are: April through September, 8 A.M. to 5 P.M. (Friday until 3 P.M.); October through March, 8 A.M. to 4 P.M. (Friday until 3 P.M.). Phone (04) 931643. Buses #74, #75, and #338 run here.

The Galilee Region– Part I

Tiberias and the Lower Galilee

his land means many things to many people. As Israel, it is a state, the political affirmation of a cherished dream and a chance for people of the Jewish faith to live in relative peace and harmony in a twentieth-century democracy. As the Holy Land, it symbolizes for many the root of their beliefs, the place where their faith took form in the image of Jesus Christ. It is in the small towns that lie quietly around the circumference of Lake Kinneret (Sea of Galilee) that the passion and pain of Jesus' life are most keenly felt. The history of Capernaum, Tabgha, and the Mount of Beatitudes reveal much about Jesus and his times. Groups and individuals alike are drawn to this area from distances far and near. These modern-day pilgrims on tour buses, hymn books clutched in their hands, have come to see the places they've visualized since their childhoods. It is not uncommon to be in a courtyard in one of the towns when suddenly a choir of voices is raised in prayer.

The entire Galilee region is physically stunning as well. The northern part of the country is the antithesis of the south; almost every Galilee acre is green and fertile. It was the major area of Zionist settlement during the early years of *aliyah*. The lush rural atmosphere attracted many immigrants (mainly Eastern Europeans) who started kibbutzim on the shores of Lake Kinneret. These later spread throughout the countryside. Deganya, at the lake's southern edge, was Israel's first kibbutz. Founded by Russian settlers in 1909, it was the birthplace of Moshe Dayan, one of Israel's brightest sons.

The intense efforts of Jewish immigrants to populate and farm the Galilee brought a hostile reaction from the Arabs who had for centuries lived in communities throughout the region. Bedouins and Druze also had settled here, and all supported themselves through agricultural work. A small group of ultraorthodox Jews had lived unobtrusively in the northern Galilee (Zefat) in poverty for centuries. The influx of new settlers and an increasing number of kibbutzim and moshavim provoked Arab attacks during which the kibbutzim served as the first line of defense. Today, Arab, Jewish, and Druze villages exist side by side and everyday life here is peaceful. Many of the Arabs are converts to Christianity, divided between the Roman Catholic and Greek Orthodox sects. To get a real sense of Arab life in the Galilee, we suggest a visit to Nazareth (see Excursions from Tiberias).

The area remains pastoral, and as you drive through these lower foothills of the Galilee Mountains, you'll still see small towns built on the slopes of the hills looking peacefully down upon tidy irrigated plots of fruit, grains, and vegetables. But the landscape is changing rapidly. In just the few years between the first and second editions of this guide, scores of housing complexes have been erected. Others are under construction.

The Lower Galilee is dominated by the Yizre'el Valley, known to most Israelis simply as *Ha-Emeq*, the Valley. In antiquity, the valley was green and alive and it became a highly coveted piece of real estate. Great powers such as Egypt and Mesopotamia claimed it, as did Assyrians, Persians, and Romans. However, by the late-nineteenth century, the area had decayed to the point that it was an uninhabitable swamp infested by malaria-carrying mosquitoes. Groups of Eastern European Jews cleared the swamp, determined to reclaim the land. The carefully planted and tilled soil and irrigated fields you see today, rife with waving grasses, orange groves, fruit arbors, vineyards, and flowers, are the results of their labors. This vast land-reclamation project opened the area for farms and settlements which produce such an abundance and variety of crops that they not only feed Israel but are exported as well. The next time you savor a Jaffa orange or slice a Carmel tomato or a Hula Valley avocado, you'll remember your drive through the Galilee.

Your base for exploring the Lower Galilee is Tiberias, a delightful resort on the western shore of Lake Kinneret. From its promenade you can gaze at the moon's reflection in the placid water and see the shimmering lights of a tiny village on the far shore. Here a lone rowboat and fisherman send ripples across the surface, and if you are quick you'll see the silver fish leap, splash, and disappear. One of Judaism's four holiest cities and only a stone's throw from Capernaum, Tabgha, and other pilgrimage sites, Tiberias has rich cultural and religious interests. But don't lose sight of the fact that even without these interests, Tiberias would be a highly recommended destination. It is a charming lakeside resort with exceptional hotels, two first-rate spa facilities, and distinctive restaurants, and the lake supports an active program of water sports. You can trail ride at Vered Hagalil, a dude ranch nearby owned by former Chicagoan Yehuda Avni, or you can play on the curvy water slides at Luna Gal Park.

Tiberias is a more sedate getaway than Elat in the south. The people here are more traditional, with many able to trace their roots back through the centuries. They are proud of this Galilean heritage and eager to talk about the area, and you immediately sense how deeply they love it. To many a visitor, Tiberias is a picturesque place to recharge and to have a good time. We suggest you balance your time here by combining visits to the religious sites with stops at the recreational facilities.

Before you orient yourself in Tiberias, a bit of information about the lake which is such an integral part of the area seems in order.

The Sea of Galilee, like the Dead Sea, is a misnomer. It's not a sea at all. Both bodies of water are in fact lakes in the truest sense of the word. The Sea of Galilee is now known as Lake Kinneret, a name which is derived from the Hebrew word *kinnor*, meaning "lute." The people likened the lake to a lute because of its shape and the gentle music of its lapping waves. It's the largest freshwater lake in Israel and teems with an abundant variety of fish: mullet, sardine, and the delicious St. Peter's fish. This last fish is named in honor of that disciple, who cast his nets upon the water–unsuccessfully at first. At Jesus' behest, Peter recast his empty net and hauled in a quantity of fish that was beyond anything imaginable. You can still make a fine dinner out of this lake fish which, except for its many bones, is extremely tasty either broiled or fried.

The lake sits seven hundred feet below sea level, and the surrounding green valley is dotted with picturesque villages and drowsy settlements that still possess a biblical aura, with their groves of silvery knotted olive trees and citrus. Miracles are said to have occurred on and around this lake; poets and artists have been drawn to its loveliness. You will be attracted by its duality as a holy site of pilgrimage and a resort where motorboats, water amusements, and floating discotheques jolt the reverie into the active present.

Orientation

Getting There

You can drive to Tiberias from Tel Aviv or Haifa. Roads here are quick but scenic, and you can select a route that goes through Nazareth or you can bypass it and return for a longer visit. We suggest you visit on a day trip from Tiberias, but if time is short, definitely stop for a few hours. The roads from Jerusalem (Route 1 to Jericho and then north on route 90 to Bet Shean) go through the West Bank. At this writing, it is not advisable for you to drive through the West Bank. The best route is to drive to the coast and then north. Please check with the IGTO for the most current information.

Major Streets

Tiberias is a small town and the part of most interest to you is the old city, which hugs the lakeshore. The best hotels and restaurants are in this area and most of the historical in-town sights are within walking distance, while the view of the lake is a natural high. *Kikar Ha'atzmaut* is the main square; adjoining it, *Ha Yarden Street*, filled with falafel stands, runs from the shore to the bus station. *Ha Galil Street*, which parallels the shore, houses some fine hotels, good restaurants, and shops. The shore line drive heading north of town becomes the *Rosh Pinna Road*. In town, called *Gdud Barak*, it has several small hotels and beach facilities. Heading south around the lake, the shoreline drive,

Sederot Eliezar Kaplan, takes you to Hammat and the Tiberias Hot Springs.

North of the old city and in the hills that overlook the lake is the residential district, *Qiryat Shmuel*. City Hall is here, as are a number of budget hotels, cinemas, and discotheques.

Hotels

Tiberias has a great number of hotels but only a handful are top-notch. Many are three-star-rated and located on the hills above the old city. These are fine if you have a car. In the old city, you will see several hotels not listed here. These one- and two-star-rated stops are not equipped with the facilities a Tiberias stay deserves. The city's three five-star hotels are exceptional, and there are also a handful of excellent four-star stops available. Since the climate in Tiberias is mild in the winter, hotels are often fully booked. Prices do rise at this time and also at Passover and the Jewish High Holy Days (in autumn). Reserve here in advance. Note: Hotels accept major credit cards, except where specifically noted.

Hotels in the Old City

MORIAH PLAZA HOTEL 5★

Habanim Street	Phone (06) 792233
Tiberias 14100	Fax (06) 792320
	USA 800-462-7442

This deluxe 272-room establishment has recently been bought by the Moriah chain and it is really special. Modern and imposing, it dominates the Promenade and the tourist complex nearby. Stunning inside, its spacious expanse of marble floor is filled with comfortable lounge areas and a small piano bar. Often when the pianist leaves, a guest will play his or her nation's top tunes as friends sing along. The hotel has several restaurants, with one on the Promenade. The pool is good-sized, there are comfortable lounge chairs, and towels are provided. Parking is free. Make sure to request a room facing the lake. *Deluxe*.

THE GALEI KINNERET HOTEL 5★

1 Eliezer Kaplan Street	Phone (06) 792331
Box 90	Fax (06) 790260
Tiberias 14100	

In direct contrast with the Moriah Plaza, the five-star Galei Kinneret is Old World where the Moriah is modern. On the lake, its 125 rooms have balconies, televisions, and direct-dial telephones. A sweeping blossom-lined driveway leads to the villa-style building with awnings over each window. The Panorama breakfast room, the Golan dining room, the cocktail bar, and the poolside snack bar offer fine meals plus friendly service. The hotel has its own beach and a grassy sundeck. A delightful low-key choice. *Deluxe*.

TIBERIAS CAESAR HOTEL 5★

Box 275	Phone (06) 723333
Tiberias 14100	Fax (06) 791013

If you're active and enjoy water sports, consider the Caesar, the newest five-star hotel on the shores of Lake Kinneret. Taking full advantage of its beachfront location, guests at the Caesar enjoy windsurfing, sailing, waterskiing, and fishing, as well as swimming in the hotel's indoor and outdoor pools. On dry land, the Hercules Fitness Center features a fully equipped gym with accredited instructors, reflexology massage, and a Finnish sauna. Fine dining, evening entertainment, and elegant accommodations are also part of a stay at the two-hundred-room Tiberias Caesar. *Deluxe*.

JORDAN RIVER HOTEL 4★

Habanim Street	Phone (06) 721111
Tiberias 14201	Fax (06) 721111

The Jordan River has a devoted clientele who insist that this is *the* place to stay in Tiberias. With a wonderful location on the main street of the old city, and with special amenities such as a private marina and a large pool with an enormous sundeck and nearby snack bar, the Jordan is indeed a great choice. As an added attraction, the Jordan River has glass panoramic elevators from which you can see across the lake. A perfect stop for the business traveler, the hotel has an executive floor, seminar rooms, and access to bilingual secretaries and translators. The Jordan Restaurant is informal, while the Marina is more romantic and intimate. A nice touch is the pub, located in an ancient Crusader building; there is also a terrific disco. *Expensive.*

THE HOTEL GANEI HAMAT 4★

Habanim Street   Phone (06) 724443
Box 22, Tiberias 14101   Fax (06) 724443
(adjoining Tiberias Hot Springs)

The four-star Ganei Hamat, a ten-minute walk from the old city downtown, has a private beach and beautiful grounds. A large white building with shooting fountains in the lobby, the hotel sits in a garden surrounded by flowering trees and stone walkways. There are tennis courts, but no swimming pool, although a full water-sports program is available at the beach and the Ganei has special arrangements with the adjacent spas. *Expensive.*

Hotels in Qiryat Shmuel Section

WASHINGTON HOTEL 4★

13 Zeidel Street   Phone (06) 791861

Another popular stop, the Washington is frequently filled with groups who've come to Tiberias as pilgrims. It is a bright, comfortable choice with careful service and a friendly staff. Rooms are good-size and all but three of the 111 rooms have baths with full tubs. You can be quite comfortable here. *Expensive.*

THE GOLAN HOTEL 4★

14 Achad Ha'am Street   Phone (06) 791901
                                                   Fax (06) 721905

The four-star Golan overlooks Lake Kinneret, and what it lacks in ultramodern sophistication, it makes up for with caring service.

It's true that the hotel exterior looks a bit like an institutional block, but inside, the rooms are clean, with built-in furnishings and beds with white-and-black accents and full baths. You will experience an at-home feeling whether you're in the red-and-navy-blue bar (dark and comfortable), in the kosher dining room with the pristine white tablecloths, or sunning on the large patio deck beside the pool. The hotel's seventy-two rooms are all air-conditioned, with telephones and radio. *Expensive*.

THE HARTMAN HOTEL TIBERIAS 4★

3 Achad Ha'am Street   Phone (06) 791555

The four-star Hartman is the kind of hotel your uncle might have; in fact, there's a Hartman behind the scenes–Yaakov–who makes certain that things are just right. The seventy rooms are all air-conditioned and have telephones, radios, and bathrooms with tubs. You can rent a TV if you like. The pool is small but pleasant with a sauna and a sundeck. Make sure you ask for a room with a view of the lake. *Moderate*.

HOTEL TIBERIAS 3★

19 Ohel Yaakov Street   Phone (06) 792270
                                        No Credit Cards

The seventy-two rooms at the Tiberias are pleasant, spacious, carpeted, and fully air-conditioned, with telephones, radios, and full baths in all. There are two TV rooms and a card/game room as well as a piano bar. Amenities include a sauna, Jacuzzi, and gym. *Moderate*.

PEER HOTEL 3★

2 Ohel Yaakov Street   Phone (06) 91641

The newly renovated lobby and public rooms make the three-star Peer look nifty, but the rooms are in need of redecoration and are drab. A small hotel with only sixty-six rooms, the Peer has one of the city's liveliest discotheques. *Inexpensive*.

RON HOTEL 2*

12 Achad Ha'am Street   Phone (06) 790829
                                                 No Credit Cards

The 48-room Ron, near the larger Golan Hotel, is rated two stars,
but the amenities are equal to those three-star stops we saw. The
view of the lake is five-star and makes a stay here comfortable if
not luxurious. Modern furnishings and air conditioning/heating.
Inexpensive.

THE ASTORIA HOTEL 3*

13 Ohel Ya'akov Street   Phone (06) 722351
                                                   Fax (06) 722352

The Astoria is a good value, considering it has earned three stars–
the fifty-seven rooms are clean and all have telephones, air conditioning, bathrooms (most of these have showers), and balconies. The location is good if a bit busy and there is a dining terrace
on the roof of the hotel. *Moderate*.

EDEN HOTEL 3*

4 Ohei Ya'akov Street   Qiryat Shmuel
                                                Phone (06) 790070
                                                 No Credit Cards

The Eden is a well-run hotel with eighty-two spacious air-
conditioned rooms and a kosher kitchen. The food is good and
the dining room is pleasant; the guest rooms all have private
bathrooms (most of these have showers), radios, and telephones.
Moderate.

Hotels on the Shore

RON BEACH HOTEL 3*

Box 173   Phone (06) 791350
Gdud Barak Street   Telex 6711
                                                   Fax (06) 791351
                                                 No Credit Cards

The Ron Beach is not pretentious–it really can't be; it has
no pool, is humbly furnished, and doesn't need to compete

with its glitzier neighbors. The Ron is a comfortable hotel, the rooms are spacious and carpeted, all have dressing tables, and the beds are restful. The Ron is only two floors high and it has a wonderful spot at lakeside with delightful grounds. The Ron Beach Fish Restaurant is a popular place for dinner. The dining room, coffee shop, bar, and souvenir shop, plus the rooms, which all have balconies, contribute to make the Ron a pleasing place. *Inexpensive.*

THE QUIET BEACH HOTEL 3★

Box 175   Phone (06) 790125
Gdud Barak Street   Fax (06) 790261
                                                  Major Credit Cards

The Quiet Beach is not luxurious, and sometimes it's not even quiet, but its terrific location on Lake Kinneret makes up for that. The all-around feeling is bright, with flower boxes on the balconies and well-tended grounds. The seventy-six rooms have telephones, radios, and full bathrooms. A large pool is just a couple of feet away from the shore, and equipment for water activities is available here. There are a dairy bar and a kosher restaurant on the premises. *Inexpensive.*

GAI BEACH HOTEL 3★

Derech Hamerchatzaot   Phone (06) 790790
                                                      Fax (06) 792776
                                              USA Phone 800-345-8569
                                                    or 718-651-8777
                                                  or Fax 718-429-5764

The 120-room Gai Beach is a lovely yet unpretentious two-story hotel on the shores of Lake Kinneret. The lobby, complete with waterfall, is tastefully decorated in light woods with pale marbleized floors. There is a small coffee shop in the hotel and plenty of open space for strolling. *Moderate.*

A Nearby Kibbutz Guest House

NOF GINOSAR KIBBUTZ GUEST HOUSE 4*

Kibbutz Ginosar	Phone (06) 792161
14980 Israel	Telex 6668
	Fax (06) 792170

The kibbutz was established in 1937; the four-star guest house opened its doors in 1964. The kibbutz grows bananas, grapefruit, mangos, avocados, and cotton, in addition to raising poultry and dairy cattle. The hotel offers a private lakeside beach with kayaks, wind surfers, and sailboats for rent. You can fish, play tennis, and join in a guided tour of the grounds. The hotel is set on lovely manicured, parklike grounds, and its 170 rooms are clean, spacious, and attractive. Facilities include a souvenir shop, a coffee shop, a bar for snacks and drinks, a TV video room, and a sunshine-filled lobby. Conference and meeting rooms are available. The kosher dining room serves generous meals, the self-service buffet is dairy, the meat and fish sections are real sit-down affairs, and the Israeli breakfast is monumental. The Museum of Galilee and the Yigal Alon Memorial Center are under construction. *Expensive.*

Restaurants

Restaurants in Tiberias, always an erratic lot, run the gamut from charming and imaginative to highly predictable and uninteresting. However, a spate of new dining choices have opened recently and these have made an impact. Keep in mind that informality is the byword here and even our top-rated restaurants are very casual, offering picturesque surroundings rather than elegant ones. Fish, especially St. Peter's and forel, which are caught in the lake, are nearly always delicious. Dairy products, including locally made ice cream, and fruits and vegetables garnered from nearby kibbutzim are always fresh and therefore salads are top-notch. In-town restaurants tend to cluster on the promenade, on Donna Gracia Street nearby, and around Mosque Square. This square is crowded with sidewalk cafés and fast-food stops. We'll also mention the better restaurants at nearby kibbutzim. Because there are so few restaurants, rather than list them by type of food, we've listed them in the order they pleased our taste buds.

THE HOUSE RESTAURANT

Gdud Barak Road   Phone (06) 792353
1 to 3 P.M., 6 P.M. to midnight
Chinese/Thai
Major Credit Cards

Set in an Oriental-style garden, complete with a tiny bridge spanning an even tinier stream, this stone house with beautiful vaulted windows is an eclectically furnished triplex with a relaxed bar downstairs and two floors of dining rooms. The Oriental theme is achieved with large Chinese fans and parasols decorating the walls and ceiling; there is a cozy fireplace in the bar. Upstairs the rooms are all bright and airy. Wonderful food like shrimp sesame seed (as an appetizer), black bean calamari, chicken in oyster sauce, and fried apples have earned the restaurant kudos from the world press. One review states: "One of the best Chinese restaurants in the world." The House pays homage to its special location on Lake Kinneret with sweet and sour St. Peter's fish that not only a disciple would love. A great place to eat. Open seven days a week in the summer, Fridays and Saturdays only at other times. *Moderate*.

PAGODA RESTAURANT

Lido Beach   Phone (06) 792564
12:30 to 11:30 P.M.
Kosher
Major Credit Cards

Kosher Chinese and Thai cuisine is served at this beautiful Oriental style restaurant right on the water. You can dine à la carte, choosing from a number of selections including vegetarian Thai salad, chicken curry, duck Thai style, numerous fish dishes and chow meins, or, if you're with a companion, try one of the special dinners for two which include soup, egg rolls, main course, dessert and tea. The Pagoda has the same owners as The House. *Moderate.*

TANDOORI

Moriah Plaza Hotel   Phone 724939
Dinner Only
Major Credit Cards

Part of the national chain of Indian restaurants, each in a fine hotel, Tandoori is on the promenade level of the Moriah Plaza Hotel. You can enter from the promenade or from the lobby. The foods served here are typical of Northern India and therefore not terribly hot or spicy. Dip the thin crisp bread into any or all of the sauces served with it. Then try one of the curries or the typical Tandoori chicken which is baked until it is bright red. A traditional dancer performs on the small stage at intervals during the evening. *Moderate.*

THE PINERY

Donna Gracia Street   Phone 790242
Lunch 12:30 to 3 P.M.,
Dinner 6 P.M. to midnight
(closed for Sabbath)
Major Credit Cards

Attractively decorated, The Pinery has bright red tablecloths and napkins which contrast with the green placemats and green plants throughout. Hanging lanterns complete the Chinese decor. The covered terrace adjoins the main dining room. The Pinery has a huge menu that includes dishes using beef, lamb, duck, and chicken. *Moderate.*

On the Promenade

The seafront promenade has several eating spots. Virtually identical, with small indoor dining rooms and tables on the promenade itself, these small places specialize in fish, particularly those found in Lake Kinneret: forel and St. Peter's fish.

THE NOF KINNERET

Tiberias Promenade   Phone (06) 720733
Middle Eastern/Fish
Visa

This is the nicest of the promenade cafés. They all have the same great location but Nof is more tasteful by a long shot. The open terrace has wicker armchairs and enormous planters with trees sprouting up in the center, forming a green canopy–it's all very languid. The food is more or less familiar–trout, mullet, and St. Peter's fish, fried, grilled, or baked in spicy sauces, are always on the menu, as are mixed and Oriental salads. Skip the Bavarian cream for dessert and go directly to the fresh strawberries (Israel has big juicy ones) with vanilla ice cream. *Moderate*.

KARAMBA

Tiberias Promenade   Phone (06) 791546

This large outdoor garden restaurant directly on the promenade is hard to miss. Fish and vegetarian dishes dominate the lengthy menu. For a light meal try the soup tartare–an interesting combination of yogurt, cucumber, olive oil and herbs—followed by the smoked salmon, or Mushroom Magic–crêpes stuffed with mushrooms, tomato sauce, and cheese. Also recommended are the potato pockets, potatoes stuffed with vegetables, and the St. Peter's Fish, which together make for a fairly substantial meal. Save some room for dessert: warm apple pie à la mode. *Moderate*.

Ha-Kishon Street

A small street, running only one block, Ha-Kishon fronts the Jordan River Hotel. Restaurants and pubs line both sides of the street. They stay open later than other eateries, and have a casual, laid-back atmosphere.

AVI'S RESTAURANT

Ha-Kishon Street   Phone 79197
                                                    Noon to 1 A.M.
                                                    Visa, MasterCard

Avi's has two floors and even some outdoor tables. Avi is always there–just ask for him. The varied menu includes steak and fish as well as Middle Eastern staples such as hummus, eggplant and tehina, and tempting pastries and crêpes. *Moderate.*

The Garden nearby also serves Middle Eastern foods. The sausages are served with a variety of vegetable salads, as is the St. Peter's fish. *Moderate.*

LITTLE TIBERIAS PUB RESTAURANT

Ha-Kishon Street   6 P.M. to ?
                                                    No Credit Cards

This pub is a popular spot for light, inexpensive fare like kebabs and shishlik. They serve a selection of grilled meats with the sauce of your choice, tender steak filets, Italian entrées, and seafood specialties. Draught beer and an extensive wine list. *Inexpensive.*

Eating Near Mosque Square

The area around Mosque Square has changed dramatically since the first edition of this guide. While there are still many fast-food places here, including MacDavid and Burger Ranch, lots of newer restaurants line Midrachov Street adjoining the square. Each restaurant has an indoor dining area, but most popular are the outdoor tables on the promenade. This area is crowded with young families during the day and with young singles after dark.

EL GAUCHO RESTAURANT

Mosque Square   **Kosher**

Part of a chain, El Gaucho is an Argentinean-style restaurant both in decor and in menu. The open charcoal grill is front and center while the restaurant itself is decorated with gaucho hats and wagon wheels; the waiters are in gaucho attire. Start with the tomato and onion salad or any of the cold vegetable salads, then move on to a thick, juicy steak, lamb chops, or assorted innards. *Moderate*.

KAPULSKY

Midrachov Pedestrian Mall   **Phone (06) 720341**
8 A.M. to 2 A.M.
Major Credit Cards

Part of a national chain based in Haifa, Kapulsky is best known for delicious cakes and pastries. You can also get a complete meal here. Blintzes, pizza, pasta, assorted quiche, stuffed baked potatoes, and filling salads are on the menu. Breakfast is especially good here–their fruit shakes and waffles are a personal favorite. *Inexpensive*.

SESAME VEGETARIAN

Midrachov Pedestrian Mall   **Phone (06) 720038**
Kosher

Indirect lighting, simple wooden tables and wicker chairs, small prints dotting the walls, and dried flowers throughout create a very casual atmosphere that is made all the more delightful by the good food served here. Soups are all homemade and delicious and together with a salad make a perfect light meal. Pizza, seafood, crêpes, and blintzes are also on the menu. *Inexpensive*.

DOLPHIN FISH RESTAURANT

Mosque Square   *Major Credit Cards*

This is one of the better fish places in town. The dining room is filled with nice wooden tables and the food is simple–shrimps in cheese sauce, fried calamari, kebabs, hamburgers, and what you should come here for: St. Peter's locous, forel, buri–fish, prepared any way you like it. Later, take a stroll around Mosque Square and go for one of those fresh hot waffle cones filled to overflowing with excellent ice cream. *Imexpensive*.

CHERRY'S

Midrachov Pedestrian Mall   8 A.M. to 2 A.M.
Major Credit Cards

Bright and colorful, Cherry's is another dairy vegetarian eatery on the mall. Its tables adjoin those of Kapulsky and its menu is similar. Best choice here is pizza which comes with all the usual toppings (olives, mushrooms and anchovies) and such popular dishes as spinach lasagna and blintzes. *Inexpensive*.

Other Dining Options

THE HABIKTA RESTAURANT

Eliezer Kaplan Street   Phone (06) 791222
near Ganei Hamat,   10 A.M. to 4 P.M.
facing Guy Beach   6 P.M. to midnight
Kosher-Middle Eastern
No Credit Cards

An unassuming bungalow, this is a pleasant summery place to enjoy excellent grilled specialties. It has proven to be so popular that it is enlarging its two dining rooms, which are wood paneled with French doors and rattan chairs bedecked with tropical print cushions. Sit on the terrace and hear the gentle break of the waves. Good burgers, shishlik, skewered liver, and Oriental salads. Trying to keep your weight down? Your best bet is the forel, freshwater fish from the lake. It's grilled and very moist. *Inexpensive*.

THE YEMENITE RESTAURANT

Ha-Galil Street   Oriental Kosher
No Credit Cards

The only Yemenite restaurant in Tiberias is keeping itself a secret, and it shouldn't. It's an extremely pretty place, cavelike, with vaulted alcoves and stone walls. Simple Yemen cuisine, which is slightly different from the typical Middle Eastern fare in that it combines unusual meat and vegetables and relies more on stews and casseroles than on grilled meats. *Inexpensive.*

LIDO KINNERET RESTAURANT

On Lido Beach   Noon to 3 P.M.,
6 P.M. to midnight
No Credit Cards

It's big, it's airy, and its brown-and-white interior is inviting. The Lido may not be much of a beach, but the boats here are for rent and the sailing here is fine, as is this simple restaurant, which offers a fixed menu at a low price (good value). You should order the Chicken Ha-Galil (a break from St. Peter's fish–although that's on the menu, of course). Price includes salad, rolls, and beverage. Wine is served as well. *Inexpensive.*

THE QUIET BEACH RESTAURANT

Gdud Barak Street   Noon to 11 P.M.
No Credit Cards

This restaurant is located on the ground floor of the hotel but is privately run. The restaurant does a lot of things with fish and serves up a moist roast chicken and wiener schnitzel (all come with choice of salad and fruit) for a fixed price. The atmosphere inside is nothing special, but the location right on the lake is. The hotel has a disco which, if we were to measure its popularity by decibels, is a busy place, indeed. *Inexpensive.*

THE BLUE BEACH RESTAURANT

At Blue Beach   *No Credit Cards*

Another fish-oriented place that's as casual as they come–but it's the nicest among the restaurants lining this northern stretch of the shore. Blue Beach has a small pool and lots of deck chairs. A word about the beaches here–don't imagine a fine, white expanse of sand; the beaches are tiny and the sand is more like coarse black gravel and nothing to write home about. Blue Beach is pleasant, though, and operates a discotheque in the evening. *Inexpensive.*

HELL BEACH FISH RESTAURANT

Between Lido and   *No Credit Cards*
Shell Beach

Was the name originally Shell Beach Fish Restaurant–and the *S* fell off–or was it intentional? The staff refused to commit themselves. There is nothing hellish about this place–it's in a circular stone turret with mosaic fish and shells inlaid in the stone. The porthole windows and the restaurants' interior (nets and nautical details everywhere) make this one of the most unusual looking spots in town. There's a small dance floor in one of the two indoor dining rooms and a disco on Friday and Saturday nights. *Inexpensive.*

Falafel Row

Ha-Yarden Street, near the Egged Bus Station, is more interesting than Mosque Square, for here you sense what Tiberias was like before progress set in. The street is made all the more narrow because multitoned kiosks clog the sidewalk, selling souvenirs, gum, newspapers, and falafel. The locals call it Falafel Row and here you get to be the chef, for you can add as many or as few of the salad fixings as you like. The street smells delicious except when you wander past the fishmonger stalls. This street and the smaller strip facing Ha'atzmaut Square is as close as Tiberias comes to a bazaar and it's the best place to watch the locals gather and kibbitz about the weather. On Ha-Yarden Street, you sense what it's like to be in a city in transition from a sleepy town to a modern resort.

Out-of-Town Dining

THE LOAVES & FISHES RESTAURANT

Tabgha; Capernaum   9 A.M. to 11 P.M. daily
                                                         No Credit Cards

It's right behind the Greek Orthodox Church, minutes from the Heptagon, but you may need to ask someone at Tabgha where this restaurant is (it's the only one around, so that shouldn't be a puzzler). It's in a bucolic setting, isolated from the hubbub of Tiberias, and the people who come here are, more often than not, hungry pilgrims who took a detour. The Arab family who owns the place can't do enough for you and the food here is basic home cooking at its best. The *mjaddarah* is as authentic an Arabic dish as you'll find. It's simply a think lentil and rice soup—sort of a national dish. The fried kubbeh with pine seeds and delicious *labaneh* (soft, tangy curd cheese) are great starters—order them together. Skip the baked fish and try the *senia*, which is a ground-meat patty in tehina sauce. Nice salads. A nice lunch stop. *Inexpensive*.

EN GEV BEACH RESTAURANT

En Gev Kibbutz	Phone (06) 758035
Lake Kinneret	*No Credit Cards*
Eastern Shore	

Founded in 1937 by German and Czech immigrants, this kibbutz sponsors popular music festivals (classical) twice each year. It also runs this restaurant, which is at dockside on the beach. With a huge indoor dining room and a smaller outdoor terrace, it can serve a lot of people. Unfortunately, it is often crowded with diners who've come on the boat from Tiberias just to eat here and with people on bus tours of the Galilee. The service then slips and your St. Peter's fish, omelet, or salad can be hastily prepared. If you are here at an off-hour; give it a try, because the St. Peter's fish is wonderful—but skip it if it's crowded. *Moderate*.

VERED HAGALIL

Korazim	Phone (06) 935785
	Noon to 4 P.M., 5 to 8 P.M.
	No Credit Cards
	Reserve for Saturday Lunch

The western-style restaurant at this dude ranch, Vered Hagalil, only nine and a half miles north of Tiberias (on the Rosh Pinna-Zefat road), is a *mitzvah* (blessing) for homesick American palates. Owned by Yehuda Avni (Eddie Stone in his Chicago youth), the comfortable, relaxed dining room features crisp southern fried chicken, thick juicy burgers, freshly baked apple and lemon pies, and chunky chicken salad plates. Under the supervision of his wife, Yonah, the restaurant is often crowded, especially for lunch, with locals and tourists.

Kibbutz Restaurants

Generally, it makes sense to eat in a kibbutz only if hunger pangs set in when you are in the vicinity. However, there are two kibbutzim in the area that have good dining facilities.

NOF GINOSAR GUEST HOUSE RESTAURANT

10 kilometers north of Tiberias   Phone (06) 792161
                                                  2:30, 6:45 to 8:30 P.M.
                                                  Major Credit Cards

On the second floor, the restaurant here overlooks the lake and is exceptionally clean and well maintained. Since Nof Ginosar is kosher, there are separate areas for meat and dairy. Fruit and vegetables are grown nearby, so you might opt for a freshly harvested salad. Fried eggplant, cheese or fruit blintzes, and light spongecake with peach topping are all perfect choices for lunch. Meats run to stews, potted beef, and chicken.

KIBBUTZ LAVI

On the Nazareth-Tiberias Road   Phone (06) 799450
                                                11:30 A.M. to 7 P.M.

Since this is glatt kosher, there is the strictest observance of the dietary laws. Here too we recommend dairy, and you can eat outdoors or in. Closed on the Sabbath. About a 15-minute drive from Tiberias.

Sunup to Sundown

Tiberias has a long and fascinating history. Founded in A.D. 17 by Herod Antipas, who ruled here at the time of Jesus, the town was built on the site of an ancient pagan cemetery; therefore, Orthodox Jews considered it unclean. Jesus, whose life and ministry were so intimately associated with the Lower Galilee, could therefore never have entered this city. In the second century, Rabbi Simon Bar Jochai declared the city clean and it became a center of Jewish cultural and spiritual activity and one of Judaism's holy cities. It became the seat of the Sanhedrin (the high court), the Mishnah and Jerusalem Talmud were completed here, and renowned religious scholars lived and taught here.

A great preview to your travels in Galilee is the *Galilee Experience*, a half-hour slide show that presents an interesting overview of the historical and spiritual significance of the Galilee Region. It is offered every hour from 8 A.M. to 10 P.M., except Friday evening and Saturday during the day, in the new Marina building on the promenade. For more information, you can call the Galilee Experience at (06) 723-620.

Your daylight hours in Tiberias will be busy ones, particularly if you combine historical sightseeing with visits to the exceptional spas nearby, take part in the water-sports activities on the lake, or take a horseback tour of Israel's loveliest region. To get a feel for the city, we suggest a walk through it.

And Now on Your Feet

Start your walk in the center of town, at *Ha'atzmaut Square*. This is where national holidays are celebrated with bands and street dancing. Habanim Street, which fronts the square, has some small falafel stands, as does Ha-Yarden Street, which adjoins the plaza. This area is Tiberias' commercial center and you might like to walk around here for a bit. When you are ready to move on, follow *Ha-Yarden Street* toward the lake. Just beyond Hagalil Street, on your left, you will see an uphill road behind the Youth Hostel. This is *Donna Gracia Street* and it is the most interesting street in town. It was named for the mother-in-law of Don Yosef Nasi, a Zionist who tried to encourage Jews to return to Tiberias after it was destroyed. Donna Gracia Street is actually part of the old city wall and here you will see the remains of a great Crusader castle and fortress. No one is sure if this complex of black basalt structures, called the Northern Citadel, is actually from the Crusader period or is really an eighteenth-century Ottoman building. In any case, much care has been taken to restore it, and it now houses a restaurant complex and Rivka's Art Gallery. From Donna Gracia, descend the stone steps bordered by flowers to *Gdud Barak Road*. Turning right (back to town) you'll see the imposing Church of Scotland. As you approach the new tourist complex, you will see the *Great Mosque*. Looking slightly out of place, surrounded by supermarkets and outdoor cafés, the mosque is no longer in use. It was built by Daher el Omar in the eighteenth century, and part of the money for its construction came from a Sephardic rabbi from Turkey in the ecumenical spirit of cooperation.

Behind the Great Mosque on the promenade is *St. Peter's Church* (Terra Sancta). This Franciscan church commemorates the miracle of the catch of vast numbers of fish by Jesus' disciples. Built by the Crusaders in 1150, it became a mosque and finally a church again. The interior (rebuilt in 1944) features a nave shaped like a boat. The monument in the courtyard was erected by Polish soldiers who lived in the hospice during the Second World War. Nearby are ruins of three Sephardic synagogues, *Ohel Yaakov, Rambam*, and *Senor*, which date to the mid-eighteenth century. No reconstruction has taken place. The smaller mosque in the complex is Jani El Bahr, used as an archeological museum. Recently renovated, the museum has some old artifacts you'll enjoy. Continue to follow the promenade south and soon you'll find yourself at the *Greek Orthodox Monastery*. This, one of Tiberias' oldest structures, was built during the Byzantine period in the third century. It has been destroyed and rebuilt repeatedly. The present building, completed in 1975, has a high-walled garden that leads to four chapels. One chapel is dedicated to St. Paul, one to the twelve apostles, one to Mary Magdalene, and the one in the round tower to St. Nicholas. Since the promenade ends here, head inland one block and continue on *Eliezar Kaplan Boulevard*, which skirts the lake. You will soon pass the Jewish cemetery, some beach areas, and the Ganei Hammat Hotel. Just beyond the hotel you'll see two imposing modern buildings which are part of the Hot Springs of Tiberias' spa (more about the spa later).

The ancient city of *Hammat* is even older than Tiberias, and its springs, renowned even in antiquity, were the reason Herod

Antipas chose this area to build a city. Alas, all that is left of Hammat is one synagogue, but it is a beautiful one. Enclosed in a museum, the tiny structure is notable for the beautifully preserved mosaic floor that dates from the fourth century. The floor has three sections that depict astrological symbols and there is another that illustrates the Ark of the Convenant. It would appear that the synagogue was destroyed and rebuilt, for various Greco-Roman mythological figures from the fifth and sixth centuries were also unearthed in 1961. The synagogue museum is open from 8 to 5 P.M. (till 4 P.M. on Friday). Moderate fee.

The road curves uphill in front of the synagogue and atop the hill in a park-like enclosure is the tomb of Rabbi Meir, the Illuminator. There are actually two adjoining tombs on the spot; the earlier one was built in 1873 by the Sephardim and the latter in 1898 by the Ashkenazim. Both sects revere this great rabbi, who was a pupil of Rabbi Akiva and himself a wise scholar and teacher. Devout Jews pray at these tombs, kissing their tallis and touching the tomb for good fortune. Little is known about the deeds attributed to Rabbi Meir, but legends say he vowed not to lie down until the time the Messiah came and was therefore buried in a sitting position.

At this point you may be tiring, so take a break at the spa coffee shop or a swim at Hammat's beach before retracing your steps to town.

Three other rabbinical tombs (those of Maimonides, Rabbi Ben Zakkai, and Rabbi Akiva) are located in Tiberias. You can continue your walk to see them at this time or see them at another point in your stay.

The first tomb, that of Maimonides, is reached by walking along Hayarden Street to Ben Zakkai Street. Two blocks away and on your right you'll spy a black wrought-iron gate leading into a garden. This is the entrance to Rambam's tomb (the name comes from his full name, Rabbi Moses ben Maimon) and it is enclosed by a high stone wall. The twelfth-century scholar was born in Spain and for a time served as a physician to Saladin's court in Egypt. He is considered the Jewish world's greatest religious scholar. He died in Egypt, but his wish was to be buried in the Holy Land and so his remains were strapped to a camel. The journey was long and arduous and legend has it that the poor beast collapsed at this very spot.

Nearby (uphill) are the remains of Rabbi Yohanan Ben Zakkai, who is credited with salvaging Jewish learning after the fall of Jerusalem. Ben Zakkai begged to be allowed to leave, and he was carried out of the dying city in a coffin. He settled in the coastal town of Yavne; the school he started there assured the continuation of Jewish life and learning in the Holy Land.

The last resting place on this walk is farther out, in a section called Ramat Menasche. Rabbi Akiva's tomb is located on a hillside. Walk directly to the west from Rambam's tomb, crossing Yehuda Halevi Street; you'll soon see a white-domed cave tomb overlooking the town. Rabbi Akiva had an interesting life. Born poor, he tended sheep for a living. His employer was a rich Jerusalemite who tried to help the illiterate boy. The man had a beautiful daughter, Rachel, who fell in love with the shepherd. They married and with her encouragement, he educated himself. He become a great scholar and nationalist. His was the spiritual strength that fueled the Bar Kochba Revolt. He was skinned alive in Caesarea at the hands of the Romans in 135. He is revered as one of Judaism's greatest martyrs.

Now that you have seen Tiberias' most important sights, you are ready to visit the small towns, some religious and ancient, some modern and activity-oriented, that border Lake Kinneret. Make certain to be modestly dressed for this trip, but be sure to pack a bathing suit and a towel too.

Touring Lake Kinneret

Tiberias, on the lake's western shore, is the perfect base for exploring the tiny towns spread around the sea. Many, particularly those on the northern shore, relate directly to the life of Jesus, and nowhere in Israel is his presence felt more than here. In a single day, centuries of turbulent history will make their mark on your imagination forever. As always in Israel, the old and the new walk hand in hand. This is most clear as you depart from a revered town which now contains but a few ruins and a nearly buried past and immediately enter a futuristic water-amusement park. En route you'll pass productive kibbutzim and holiday villages on stunning beaches. If you desire, you can visit an ostrich farm and an alligator farm at a huge spa adjoining the Jordanian border. This day may be one of your finest in Israel.

You can circle the sea in either direction, but because the important historical sites are north of Tiberias, we will move in that direction. No car? No problem! Egged Bus Minus #200 will take you on this run (it goes four times each day), and you can stay at a particular stop till the next bus passes. (Details at the end of this section.)

Follow *Gdud Barak Road*, which becomes Route 90 (to Rosh Pinna) and as you leave Tiberias behind, you will find yourself circling the lake. Just beyond the lake, on your right, you'll spot a small white dome. Pull over if you can, for this is the home of *Mary Magdalene*, branded throughout eternity by Christians as a fallen woman. Actually the Bible merely states tht Jesus cast out seven demons from her repentent soul and she then became one of his most devout followers. Just beyond, you will pass a turnoff (left) to *Arbel*, which was the bastion of the Jewish Zealots who lived in caves in the cliffs here. The canyon below Arbel is *Wadi Haman*. In this canyon is the tomb of Nabi Shueib (Jethro, Moses' father-in-law), the most important shrine of Israel's Druze community. Each year a grand festival is held at the site. The town of Migdal, birthplace of Mary Magdalene,is today a farming community and of little interest.

As you continue along Route 90, you will pass *Nof Ginosar Kibbutz* and see the irrigated fields of the kibbutz on either side of the road. The road climbs a bit (there is an electric power plant) and now you are faced with two options:you can bear left here and visit the Mount of Beatitudes and ancient Korazim (approximately nine miles) or you can bear right (around the lake) and proceed directly to Tabgha and Capernaum.

We will take the left road and visit the *Mount of Beatitudes*, which is only a five-minute ride with sweeping views of the Galilee all the way up.

Mount of Beatitudes

This tranquil spot set on a high hill is where Jesus uttered one of his most touching and exalted sermons, words that have for centuries given strength and solace to so many: "Blessed are the poor in spirit, for theirs is the Kingom of Heaven ...." The Beatitudes contain eight verses, all of which begin with the words

"Blessed are ..." and stress the spiritual riches that will come from practicing the qualities of meekness, gentleness, and humility.

The Church of Beatitudes was constructed by a world-famous Italian church architect, Antonio Barluzzi. Completed in 1938, the church is built of basalt in an octagonal shape, commemorating the Eight Beatitudes. Antonio Barluzzi also designed the Church of All Nations in Jerusalem's Garden of Gethsemane. The Beatitude Church is copper-domed and features unusual windows with passages from the Bible in Latin beneath them. The interior walls are of dark-veined marble, and there are geometric mosaic designs on the floor. The gallery surrounding the church is shady and lovely.

The Franciscans started to excavate here in 1935 and found the remains of a Byzantine church, as well as a mosaic-paved fore court and an apse of bare rock. These have been dated at the fourth century A.D., but were damaged by Arab conquerors in the sixth century. Today, the Italian Order of Franciscan Sisters is housed in a lovely hospice erected in 1912. The Italian nuns care for the church and maintain the twenty-four spotlessly clean rooms, where you can stay for reasonable rates. The hospice address is 12365 Doarna Hevel, Korazim.

Korazim

From the Mount of Beatitudes, a ten-mimute drive will take you to Korazim. En route you will pass Vered Hagalil Dude Ranch. The town of *Korazim* was substantial during Roman times; the large Jewish community there was engaged primarily in agriculture. Like nearby Capernaum and Bethsaida, Korazim incurred God's wrath because it refused to allow Jesus to preach his message. This accursed village grew in population after the second revolt against Rome in Jerusalem had failed. Wealthy Jerusalemites funded the building of a great synagogue, which resembled the one at Capernaum. The black basalt structure, excavated in 1905, had three huge portals, or entries, that opened out to the south toward Jerusalem. The remaining stone columns and lintels are elaborately carved with snakes, fruits, flowers, and vegetation (traditional Jewish symbols), as well as with animal and human figures. By looking at the friezes, capitals, and cornices that remain, you can appreciate the grandeur of the Korazim Synagogue. There was a thriving town here once, and traces of dwellings, streets, and ritual baths can still be detected, but little has actually been excavated so far. There are varying reports on habitation in Korazim. Some texts date the last community at the eighth century A.D., while others claim the sixteenth century as the last period of occupation. The former date is believed to be the more plausible one.

Return along the Rosh Pinna Road to the turnoff for Capernaum on Route 87. Turn left here (if you bypass Mount of Beatitudes and Korazim, it will be a right turn.) *Tabgha* will be on your right. There is a parking lot and a snack/souvenir shop.

Tabgha (Heptapegon)

In the days before Israel's resurgence, Tabgha was an extension of the malarial swamps that covered much of the Galilee area. The German settlers who sold the land to Jewish groups and Christian orders in the 1800s had no idea of its importance. The Franciscans, being among the most active of the Christian orders, excavated the land around Tabgha as if by divine inspiration. What they discovered was the most concrete evidence of Jesus' life and ministry. It was an illuminating time for Christianity and Judaism when restoration began on the Church of the Loaves and Fishes and the Church of the Primacy nearby. Heptapegon means "seven springs," and *Tabgha* is the Arabic corruption of the word. Christian tradition has placed three episodes in Jesus' life around the immediate area: the miracle of the multiplication of the loaves and fishes, the post-resurrection appearance where Jesus conferred the role of leadership on Peter for the continuation of the ministry, and the Sermon on the Mount (of Beatitudes).

The miracle of the loaves and fishes is beautifully commemorated at Heptapegon by an exquisite Byzantine mosaic from the sixth century. This mosaic covers the spot where Jesus placed the abundant food and which became the altar site for the churches that were erected here. Archeologists have verified the existence of a church at this same location as early as A.D. 381. Documents written by an early pilgrim to the Holy Land, a woman called Etheria, would seem to confirm this too. The original church consisted of a small nave and very simply designed mosaic floors, which can be viewed today beneath the wooden trapdoors in the floor of the present structure. Later on in the fifth century, the church was enlarged to almost double its size and the floors were redesigned, only this time in an ornate and highly artistic style. Mosaics in the transept part of the church depict lovely flora and fauna; water-birds standing on and amidst exotic foliage, partridges, and flamingos doing battle with a serpent are incorporated into the design. It is interesting to note that some of the flowers and plants (like the bell-shaped lotus) depicted are not indigenous to this part of the Middle East; rather they are a holdover of the Egyptian or Nilotic style prevalent during the Roman and Hellenistic periods. The round tower with gradations on it (the Greek letters are the numbers six through ten) on the right transept section of the floor resembles those found in the Nile River to measure the water level during floods, graphic proof of the Egyptian influence here. But most significant of all the motifs is the renowned mosaic of two fish bordering a basket of loaves.

The structure that encloses the area was built in 1936 merely as a protective covering for the mosaic floors. The wings that provide shelter for the Benedictines who take care of this site were erected in 1956. Hours for the church are from 7 A.M. to 5 P.M.

Nearby, but entered through a private gate (parking off the road here), is the *Church of the Primacy of Peter*. The gate is flanked on either side by entrepreneurs with rosary beads, olive-wood carvings of Jesus and Mary, crosses and postcards.

Once through the gate, however, all is serene as you approach a humble black basalt stone chapel built by the Franciscan order and completed in 1934. This church or sanctuary, also known as *Mensa Christi* (the "Table of Christ"), is bordered by a eucalyptus grove on one side and the still waters of Galilee on the other. The church is perched so close to the edge that its full reflection shimmers in the mirror of the water. The modern structure emulates previous churches built at this site, which were even more basic. Portions of the fourth century A.D. church, noted by the pilgrim Etheria, can be seen at the end that is farthest from the altar and at the base of the walls. This ancient church survived quite well and was even used during the Arab and Crusader periods. There is a Crusader structure beside the church as well as two water towers dating from the Byzantine period.

Right at this spot on the shore Jesus directed his disciples to recast their nets into the water, after they had had no luck on previous attempts. If you know your Bible, you will remember that the nets could barely be hauled in, because they were so full of fish. After the meal, which was eaten on the flat rock inside the church, Jesus instructed Peter to "Feed my lambs... Feed my sheep" and asked him three times, "Simon, son of Jonah, dost thou love me?" Peter went on to become the Bishop of Rome, the first Pope. The tradition of primacy being passed on from one generation to the next is what the Papacy bases its legitimacy on. Below, at the foot of the church and partially covered with water, are six heart-shaped stones whose purpose is shrouded in supposition—perhaps they once supported a wooden stage, or were taken from other structures by believers and placed there to symbolize the twelve Apostles. (They are double stones, thus twelve.) The rock-cut steps that lead down from the church to the lake look extremely old. Perhaps they date from the second or third century, when this area was used as a limestone quarry (the method in which they were chiseled gives credence to this theory).

The church is open from 8:30 A.M. to 4 P.M. and a small donation is appeciated. The Franciscans have put in a pretty flower garden and there is a contemporary statue of Jesus in the center of it, looking out onto the lake.

Capernaum

From Tabgha, continue moving eastward and just two miles away you will see Capernaum. In Capernaum, *Kefar Nahum* in Hebrew, we see a mixture of Judeo-Christian interests. Its history begins in the second century B.C. A substantial and predominantly Jewish town during Roman times, Capernaum was the birthplace of several of Jesus' disciples: Simon Peter, his brother Andrew, James, and his brother John. The town's industries were mainly fishing and trading, and it was here among these fishermen that Jesus made his ideology bear fruit. In Capernaum he felt free to teach and so the town became the headquarters of his three year ministry in the Galilee.

In Capernaum, Jesus preached in the synagogue and many of his miracles were performed near here. Nonetheless, the citizens rejected him, causing him to curse them and vow that they would go to hell.

The large building with the pinkish dome that you see as you approach Capernaum is a Greek Orthodox Church, but the ancient ruins are on the grounds of a Franciscan Monastery. The most amazing example of an early Galilean synagogue (third or fourth century B.C.) is here, as well as the House of St. Peter and a group of basalt buildings that date from the first to the sixth century A.D. As you enter the archeological site, look for the open-air museum on your right. Here you'll see some really interesting carved stones, made of rare limestone rather than the cruder-looking black basalt that was, and still is, so plentiful in the region. There are finely executed designs on the stones depicting grapes, figs, palm trees, lions and what might have been an artist's impression of the Ark of the Covenant on one lintel. There is an inscribed stone in Aramaic, dedicated to one of the synagogue's benefactors.

A few steps beyond, you will see the House of St. Peter, who was also known as Simon Peter. The house sits among a grouping of primitive-looking basalt dwellings which were occupied from the first to sixth centuries A.D. This particular dwelling is different in that the floor seems to have been built upon earlier floors and is strewn with crushed limestone rather than dirt or basalt pebbles. The walls still bear traces of fresco work, but are too badly damaged to interpret. Archeologists believe that this spot, venerated by Christians since the first century A.D., was partitioned off from the rest of the dwellings. By the fourth century, it had a sturdier roof and two additional rooms on either side (built perhaps by Joseph of Tiberias, a devout Christian convert). A century later, an octagonal church was built over the holy room, and a mosaic floor, very similar to that in the Church of Multiplication of the Loaves and Fishes, was installed. The church was destroyed by the Arabs in A.D. 700. The ruined dwellings that surround this site housed nearly one hundred people. Compare their crudity with the magnificence of the Synagogue at Capernaum. This synagogue couldn't have been the one where

Jesus delivered his sermons, for it clearly resembles other synagogues (at Korazim) of the early Galilean period. Built sometime during the second or third century A.D. the synagogue's doors faced in the direction of Jerusalem, which was in the Jewish tradition. A hoard of coins, unearthed by the Franciscans during the major excavations, were dated mostly from the fourth century A.D., which means that the synagogue probably dates from that period. What is evident about the structure is the grandeur of it — it bears a striking resemblance to a classical Roman temple where the outward appearance was always more important than the interior. Based on archeological finds, the temple had a second level and the stone benches inside retain the truest meaning of the word *synagogue* (a congregated assembly of people, as opposed to a house of worship). Whenever it was built, this imposing temple is one of the most impressive sights in Israel.

Upon leaving Capernaum, continue east on Route 87; two miles later you will cross the muddy rivulet that is the Jordan River. At this point, the lake is not in view, so watch carefully for the second turnoff (a right) to Route 92. This road leads south along the lake's eastern shore. There will be several roads here that lead into the Golan Heights, which dominate the skyline on your left. The first leads to Gamla, an ancient Jewish town with little of interest today, and the second leads to a holiday village, Ramot. If you haven't tired of ancient ruins, you can follow the third (Route 789) to the town of Kursi.

Kursi

Kursi lies close to the mouth of the Zemakh, or Samak, River, which flows down from the Golan Heights. In the gospels it bears the name *Gadaral*. Kursi in later years was an Arab village, but in biblical times it was the site of one of Jesus' miracles. Here Jesus performed the miracle of the Gadarene swine, casting the demons out of two possessed men. The demons entered a herd of swine, who waded into the lake and drowned. The ruins of a sixth-century Byzantine church were uncovered at Kursi when a road was being cleared following the Six Day War. This discovery unveiled what is still today the largest monastic Byzantine complex in Israel. The ruins at this site date from the middle of the fifth century A.D., and have some fascinating features. The basilica sits in the midst of a plaster wall enclosure whose interior sides had been decorated. The church floor (72 feet by 135 feet) is covered entirely with mosaics of simple geometric design and some floral and animal motifs. Additional structural remains include those of a baptistry and rooms that run the length of the basilica.

The most significant sight at Kursi is a room that you enter through a stone trapdoor, which is at the entrance to one of the outer chapels. Here you'll see a stunningly preserved underground crypt that was the monks' burial chamber. The anteroom and the long barrel-vaulted ceiling room contain six stone troughs, and a number of male skeletons were discovered here.

Luna Gal Beach

Want a change of pace? Head to Golan Beach (next on Route 92) and its unique water-amusement center, Luna Gal, which is the largest water-amusement recreation center outside the United States. An entrance ticket allows you unlimited use of rides and facilities; the Wild Rapids innertube water course, Typhoon water run, Kamikaze slide, Hurricane slide, Bump-em boats, and other "disastrous" laugh-producing activities are within the Luna Gal center.

There are also changing facilities and fast-food emporiums within the center. When you tire of the slides, head across the path to the beach. Golan Beach has thick white sand and the Yamiah Center can rent you just about any water-sport equipment you can think of. Waterskiing is the most expensive but you can windsurf, pedal-boat, kayak, or speedboat, or you can just sack out on the beach and swim. There are picnic tables and a variety of eating spots nearby. At night, the Luna Gal Pub and Disco round out the fun. The park is open from 9 A.M. to 5:30 P.M. most of the year; the discotheque operates only in the summer months. Bus #22 from Tiberias stops at Golan Beach, as does the Minus #200 Line.

En Gev

Continuing south along Route 92, you'll soon see the sign for *En Gev*, a multifaceted kibbutz that gives a special flavor to the eastern shore. The daily ferry from Tiberias stops here, as do tour buses. The kibbutz's popularity is twofold. It has a busy fish restaurant (see Restaurants) and it hosts music festivals and other cultural events in its concert hall-amphitheater. If you contact the IGTO, they will alert you to the concert dates at En Gev. You must reserve long in advance, for they are always solidly booked. The kibbutz grows dates and bananas; in its garden you'll find a touching sculpture by Chana Orloff of a mother and child. En Gev also operates a holiday village that offers campsites and mobile homes. You can call the kibbutz for information at (06) 758027.

Susita

Across the highway from *En Gev*, a footpath leads to the ancient city of Susita, or Hippos, as it was known to the Greeks. Settled by the Seleucids (Greek rulers of Syria) during Alexander the Great's conquest of the region, Susita was at first a Jewish city, but it reached its height during the Byzantine era when it became a purely Christian one. Its fine public buildings and four churches (it even had a bishop) attest to its status and population. Susita's former glory can be glimpsed through the hundreds of stone columns, pillars, watchtowers, pools, paved streets, and mosaic work that remain at the site. One of the churches has a mosaic floor with strategically placed sockets (probably for a chancel screen). A baptistry built in 591 is inscribed with the date and a framed dedicatory inscription to the Saints Damian and Cosmas. Other significant ruined structures include three churches, a Roman nymphaeum (west of the cathedral), and a Byzantine bath. Water was supplied via an underground cistern that was fed from a pipe that channeled the water from the Golan plateau. Susita was destroyed in the seventh century and has remained uninhabited.

The newest attraction on the lake is the ostrich farm at Kibbutz Ha'on. The land here was once owned by the Bahais, who leased it to Arab tenants who then worked the land for them. The kibbutz is the largest ostrich-breeding farm in Israel (only South Africa has larger ones), and if you are interested you can observe the entire life cycle of an ostrich.

Kibbutz Ma'agan, still further south, is located on the lake's most beautiful beach. The kibbutz operates a holiday village consisting of sixty-five mobile homes. The lakefront rental facility has surfers, pedal boats, and fishing equipment. Phone (06) 753753.

Kibbutz Ma'agan is near the turnoff for Hammat Gader Spa. You can visit it on this round-the-lake tour, although it is slightly off the route, or you can come back on another day (it is only twelve miles from Tiberias). We will discuss Hamat Gader later in this section.

The Southern Shore

You are now on the lake's southern shore, the last leg of your trip. Soon you will recross the Jordan River. As you do so, look for a low stone wall on the lake side of the road (your right). This is *Ohalo*, the cemetery that provides a tranquil final resting place for several prominent Jewish figures. Berl Katznelson, the Zionist labor leader, and Rachel, the poetess of Kinneret, are buried here. Rachel "Hameshoreret" was one of Israel's leading poets—she led a solitary life and wrote many of her poems under a large tree which stands to the right of the cemetery. A monument to Theodor Herzl has been created in the center of this peaceful garden.

On the left side of the highway, you will see *Deganya*, founded in 1909 by a freethinker and staunch Zionist, A.D. Gordon. It is the country's oldest kibbutz (it later branched out to Deganya A and B) and produced some of modern Israel's most individualistic leaders. A good reason to stop at Deganya is to see the *Bet Gordon Museum* (06) 750040. The very next stop, *Yardenit*, is near Kibbutz Kinneret, which began as a sister kibbutz to Deganya. The kibbutz has cleared a site at the point where Lake Kinneret becomes the River Jordan. Here the water is clear and the setting is beautiful. Pilgrims can come to this spot for ritual baptism (showers, snack bar, and wheelchair access for the disabled are available). Was Jesus really baptized at this spot? The answer is probably not; all indications point to a part of the Jordan River nearer to Jericho.

In just a few minutes you will be in Hammat Tiberias and then in Tiberias itself, just in time for a refreshing cocktail or a late-afternoon swim.

Touring Information

Get an early start on this trip so you do not have to hurry and you can relax at the beach of Luna Gal or Ma'agen. There is a comfortable and convenient way to take this tour via the Egged Bus Service. The Minus #200 Line is a special route around the lake, which takes you to the major spots like Tabgha, Capernaum, En Gev, and Hammat Gader. Buses are air-conditioned and will pick you up at a number of stations (Tiberias Hotel, Galei Kinneret, Egged Bus Station, to name a few). A one-day ticket entitles you to ride all day long and to get on and off at points along the way and a 25-percent discount in restaurants and attractions is part of the deal. Buses leave four times a day; for time information call Egged Tours at (06) 720474. Egged also offers tours from Tiberias. A one-day tour will take you to Upper Galilee and the Golan Heights—towns included are Qatzrin, the Druze village of Massada, the ancient Crusader fortress at Nimrod, Banias, and the Tel Dan Nature Reserve. Buses return via Qiryat Shmoneh and depart at 8:30 A.M. on Tuesday, Thursday, and Saturday.

Spa Facilities

Hammat Gader Hot Springs

Route 90 South will take you to Hammat Gader, twelve miles from Tiberias, through what used to be very precarious territory —Syrian-planted land mines were commonplace here. Rest assured, the Yarmuk Valley is 100 percent detonated and safe. The traces of battle remain; you'll see barbed-wire fences, sentries, patrol trucks, and notices that read "Do Not Enter." The Yarmuk River forms Israel's border with Jordan at this point.

The area was inhabited five thousand years ago, when these hot sulphur springs rivaled those at Hammat Tiberias. The

Roman baths here are regarded as the finest ever found. They had three pools: the Frigidarium was the cold-water pool; the Tepidarium's waters were maintained at room temperature; those in the Caldarium were kept very hot. Roman genius is evident in the systems that were devised to produce these environments—pipelines, a drainage and sewer system, and cooling and heating installations.

Today, you can bathe in an open-air mineral pool in a parklike setting. The natural water contains sulphur, chloride, calcium, and magnesium. The temperature is 107.6 °F year round. There are also a covered pool, twelve water-massage installations, and a bathhouse that has showers and changing rooms.

An added attraction here is the alligator farm. In 1981, 120 alligators were air-lifted from Florida and now reside here. You can watch them, but they seem quite immobile much of the time. The Reptilarium is fascinating, for here a baby might hatch as you watch.

There is regular bus service from Tiberias weekdays (check for schedule at Egged or IGTO). Hammat Gader is open from 8 A.M. to 4 P.M., including Saturdays; however, it closes at 2:30 P.M. on Friday and holiday eves.

Tiberias Hot Springs (Hammat Tiberias)

The Tiberias Hot Springs may be the oldest in the world, for even the ancients were aware of the highly curative powers of these sulphur- and mineral-rich waters. So highly regarded were these baths that in the time of Rabbis Akiva and Meir, Orthodox Jews were permitted to cleanse themselves in them—even on the Sabbath. Herod built baths here, but the ones that survived were built by the Turks in the eighteenth century. The Lion's Pool was built during the rule of Sultan Ibrahim Pasha, and the modern spa complex sits parallel to this pool. This, the older of the two facilities here, was built in the 1950s and is called the Tiberias Care and Health Center. Each day hundreds of visitors enjoy thermal dips, massages, and mud-pack treatments. The baths here have a temperature of 140 °F and contain twelve different salts.

The newer building, built in 1978 on the lake side, has the latest in spa facilities, including indoor and outdoor mineral pools, hydrothermal treatments, electrotherapy, and physiotherapy for people suffering rheumatic ailments. For detailed information about treatment, write to Tiberias Hot Springs Company, Tiberias, or call (06) 791967. You can walk to the facility from Tiberias or take bus #2 or #5.

A Galilee Dude Ranch

VERED HA GALIL DUDE RANCH

Mobile Post Korazim   Phone (06) 935785
Tiberias—Rosh Pinna Road

The name means "Rose of the Galilee" and indeed there are beautiful roses growing in Vered's gardens. Owners Yehuda and Yonah Avni have spent twenty years turning their dream of a fine riding establishment into reality on this once-barren piece of land. Vered's stone cottages are comfortable and rustic, its pool is inviting, and its restaurant is renowned for its American-style food, but it is the horses, many of them Arabian stallions, and the professional riding program that draws visitors here.

Yehuda's (he was Eddie Stone when he grew up in Chicago) enthusiasm is contagious and before you know it, even if you are a neophyte, you will be off on an hour's trail ride. You might follow cow paths to an Arab village or ride through a wadi to a Bedouin encampment. The hour is over before you know it. Experienced riders can join groups on a full day's ride, and frequently groups are organized for a full week's ride to the upper Galilee and as far afield as Jerusalem. All rides are led by experienced guides.

Serious riders might like to stay in one of Vered's cottages. Since all the guests have a common interest, evenings at Vered Ha Galil are spent swapping riding tales and adventures. Bet you can't top Yehuda's stories! Vered Ha Galil is a fun stop, and if you have any interest in riding, write or call for information.

Boat Rides

A bilevel ferry makes a daily crossing from Tiberias dock (near the Great Mosque) to En Gev Kibbutz. It runs more frequently in summer. The thirty-five-minute ride is very peaceful and relaxing, buy tickets at Kinneret Sailing Company on the dock. Phone (06) 721831.

The Gamla, a large sailboat, leaves from this dock several times a day for an hour's sail around the lake. The trip is lovely and you see several of the biblical towns on shore, but avoid windy days, when the lake seems more like the North Atlantic.

Lido Beach (just north of town) also operates round-the-lake cruises. Schedules are not firm, so stop by for information or call (06) 721538.

Beach Areas

The beach areas noth of Tiberias (Lido, Shell, Quiet, Blue) are disappointing; they have narrow strips and dark sand. You pay a modest fee to enter and use the facilities.

Those to the south of town are more appealing, with wider strips and nicer facilities.

Sironit Beach, the Municipal Beach, and Valley Beach are on the stretch of seashore between Tiberias and Hammat. Sironit has a water slide. Guy Beach, at the Galei Kinneret Hotel, is closest to town; the Ganei Hamat Beach is farthest.

We've already discussed Golan Beach (with Luna Gal Amusement Park) and Ma'agan Beach on the lake's eastern shore. Hof Tsemach, near Kibbutz Kinneret on the lake's southern shore, also has a water-amusement park (on a smaller scale) and equipment rentals. It's a ten-minute drive from Tiberias.

RIVKA'S FORTRESS

Crusader Tower	Phone (07) 721375
Donna Gracia Street	9 A.M. to noon; 5 to 9 P.M.

Visiting this aerie, high above Tiberias, is not just a matter of seeing Rivka Ganon's artwork, which is delicate and re-creates the lovely vistas of her native town; it is to experience a labor of love. Avram Ganon has spent the last fourteen years reconstructing and rebuilding the crumbling interior of this tower room. What his hard work has wrought is a miracle in itself. The beamed ceilings and exquisite stained-glass windows Avram has installed are worthy of a cathedral—the golden light that filters through onto the shiny glass-polished floors is mesmerizing. Avram dates the castle back about eight hundred years. Rivka, his wife, is the tireless, prolific woman who works in various media. She sculpts, paints in oil and watercolors, and has created some stunning mosaics. Both Avram and Rivka are Tiberian-born. Even if you don't intend to purchase art, stop in to say hello and to admire this gorgeous renovation of a Crusader castle. Avram loves to practice his English. A recent addition to the gallery is a small café serving cake, coffee and liqueurs.

Sundown to Sunup

The IGTO on Habanim Street (near Big Ben Pub) has a prepared monthly list of special events in Tiberias. It will alert you to open-air concerts, folk-dance shows, and English lectures in town.

The Moriah Plaza's piano bar and lobby lounge stay open late and are classy and friendly. You'll want to join in the infectious camaraderie that occurs at the baby grand when the professional pianist leaves. The Galei Kinneret also has an inviting lounge.

The Tower and Tiberias Eyes at the Tiberias Restaurant complex have a piano bar and a folksinging duo in the outdoor restaurant. Open late.

Tiberias has several discotheques. The loudest and liveliest is the Pub on the Promenade near the Greek Orthodox Church. The Jordan River, Moriah Plaza, and Tiberias Caesar hotels all have weekend discos. In Qiryat Shmuel, head to the Peer Hotel discotheque or its neighbor at the Eden Hotel.

At night (summer evenings primarily) the ferry is bedecked with colored lights, a disc jockey clambers aboard, and voilá! Instant floating disco. The crowd it attracts is often quite young, so check it out first. Ask at Kinneret Sailing Company on the dock.

The Nof Kinneret Restaurant on the promenade has music under the stars.

Big Ben Pub in Mosque Square is wood-paneled and very British-looking. It's where the singles of Tiberias meet.

The Hard Rock Pub in the marina building on the promenade features outdoor tables right on the lake and is another popular meeting place. Petra Pub Restaurant in the Lake Castle is very popular with young Tiberians and features a disco every night after midnight. The waterfront Pirate Pub in the Tiberias Caesar Hotel is also very popular.

Blue Beach (Gdud Barak) has a discotheque in the evening.

Tiberias has several movie theaters and United States films are most popular. The Aviv Cinema is in Qiryat Shmuel on Bialik Street. The Gil Cinema is the most centrally located for those of you staying in the old town; it's right off Ha-Yarden Street in Kikar Ha'atzmaut.

Sporting events are often held at Tiberias' Municipal Stadium, which is in the northwest end of town (Sheknunat Ahuzzat Kinneret section). It's directly behind the Heichal Dor building. Soccer, or football, as it's called in Israel, is probably the most popular sport here; basketball is also a competitive sport.

Shoppng in Tiberias

There's not a lot to tell about shopping here. Tiberias does not have a typical craft or item that is linked with it. There are, however, many good shops and several mall-type shopping centers, so if you require anything at all, you'll find it easily.

Excursions from Tiberias

To Nazareth

The mere mention of the name *Nazareth* strikes a sympathetic chord in devout Christians everywhere. It is a special place whose very name gives rise to non-Christians' definition of those people who follow the teachings of the holiest Nazarene. The Israelites called the Christians *notzrim* and many people even today call those of Christian faith the Nazarenes. Nazareth in the days of Jesus was just another small village, surviving as best it could off the land. It was never mentioned by the prophets of the Old Testament or by the historians of that time. The town did not stir the public awareness in any way until the period of Jesus' life that has come down to succeeding generations through the New Testament. Nazareth, then a Jewish settlement, was home to many of the Virgin Mary's family members. It was here that the Annunciation took place, when the Archangel Gabriel appeared to the young Jewish virgin, telling her that soon she would bear a son named Jesus. Those were the days of Herod and his crazed edicts, and Mary and her husband, Joseph, and the child fled to Egypt in fear. As the danger subsided, they returned to Nazareth, where Jesus spent most of his life and formed the ideologies that led to his subsequent veneration. At the time, however, his ideas were not greatly appreciated. When he attempted to express his beliefs in the synagogue, he was cast out and ridiculed, whereupon he left Nazareth for Capernaum. Here his ministry would blossom.

Four centuries elapsed until a church was erected in Nazareth to honor its most famous son. A convert to Christianity, the former Jew, Joseph of Tiberias, is said to have built the first church here, over the house of Joseph and Mary–but the remains are lost to the dust. The Byzantines built churches here, but they were destroyed by the Jews and Persians of the town. When the Byzantines returned and saw the vandalism, they proceeded to destroy Nazareth. Succeeding centuries found an Arabization of Nazareth, but when the Crusaders conquered the town, they erected Christian religious structures. These were destroyed in turn by the troops of Saladin. The years between 1200 and 1700 saw a ritual tug-of-war between Arab, Druze, and Christian participants for the control of Nazareth. It was in the mid-1700s that Nazareth became a point of pilgrimage open to Christian individuals and institutions. Napoleon was one of the most illustrious pilgrims of that century, staying at the Casa Nova for the duration.

In the modern era, from the First World War to the present, Nazareth has weathered Turkish, German, and British occupation; Arab insurrectionist and terrorist groups; a large resettlement of Christians in the area; and, in 1948, the War of Independence, which has proven a positive stabilizing force on the town.

The 1950s saw a lot of changes here. In the years following statehood, the Arab population of Nazareth grew steadily to its present size of forty thousand, half of which is Christian and the other half Muslim. In 1957, Jews settled a hilly area east of town and called it *Nazerat Illit* or "New Nazareth." (One main industry is the Elite Chocolate factory.) They live a peaceful if separate coexistence wih their neighbors down in the following sections.

Orientation

Getting into and around Nazareth isn't complicated. No matter how you enter the town, you will soon find yourself on Paulus VI Street, the main thoroughfare. Park your car (or get off the bus) and walk along Paulus VI Street to the point where it intersects Casa Nova Street. This is the hub of town; most religious sites, hotels, hospices, shops, and restaurants are located in this vicinity. You'll need a detailed map of town, so head to the Tourist Information Office on Casa Nova Street, which is open 10 A.M. to 5 P.M. daily and closed Saturday. Many of the Christian holy places and religious institutions, the most splended being the Church of the Annunciation, are within the town center and will be described fully in the following section.

Hotels in Nazareth

Most visitors are content to spend a day in Nazareth as an excursion from Tiberias or Haifa, where they have a greater choice in hotel accommodatons. If you are a traveler to whom a visit to the Holy Land means a deep immersion into the spiritual, you can easily spend two or three days in Nazareth.

Nazareth does have hotels for those who choose to stay here and they are listed below.

There are no four-star hotels, but the three-star hotels in town all share a common feature, Arabic hospitality. You will be treated like an honored guest in Nazareth by people who are anxious to please. We have included a religious hospice with the hotels. It is probably much more minimal than you're accustomed to, but it offers a flavor of what Nazareth must have been like for the pilgrims of years gone by.

The Grand New Hotel 3★

St. Joseph at Ring Road   Phone (06) 573325
Fax (06) 576281
Major Credit Cards

This is one of the best choices for a brief sojourn in Nazareth. The ninety-two rooms are fully air-conditioned, clean, and modern. All have phones and bathrooms with tubs, and there is a pleasant restaurant and a bar/lounge. Rooms have nice views of Nazareth. Janet, at the reception desk, is friendly and helpful. *Inexpensive*.

The Galilee Hotel 3★

Paulus VI Street,   Phone (06) 571311
near the Church of the Annunciation   *Major Credit Cards*

Much more central with slightly less atmosphere, but clean and within walking distance of everything, this hotel has ninety rooms with bathrooms (showers only). It's cool and quiet inside, with a spacious lobby and sitting area. The Galilee Souvenir Shop next door really has everything—Hebron glass, carved olivewood, brassware, stamps, pretty stone necklaces, and tea samovar and cup sets. *Inexpensive*.

The Nazareth Hotel 3★

Paulus VI Street   Phone (06) 577777 or 554502
Box 291   Fax (06) 578511
Nazareth 16000   *Major Credit Cards*

The Nazareth's eighty-eight rooms are air-conditioned and have bathrooms (with tubs) and telephones. This is a good choice, for it has ample parking, a more-than-adequate Middle Eastern restaurant, and a quiet location on Paulus VI Street (on the road to Haifa). All rooms have private balconies. *Inexpensive*.

Casa Nova Pilgrims House

Across the street from the Church   Phone (06) 571367
of the Annunciation   *No Credit Cards*

Don't expect deluxe accommodations, but the price per day includes breakfast. This hospice has long been a favorite of pilgrims and Franciscan brothers passing through. Its forty-three rooms are clean, airy, and comfortable. The staff at the Casa Nova is young and eager to assist you. The place is usually booked solid, but if you'd like to try, call a month or two ahead of time to ensure your room. *Very inexpensive.*

Restaurants in Nazareth

There is a good deal to see in Nazareth and chances are that you will get hungry sometime during the day. Most restaurants are in the Casa Nova/Paulus VI area. We've found several that are clean and efficient and serve some interesting dishes.

THE ASTORIA RESTAURANT

Casa Nova Street and Paulus VI Street   Phone (06) 577965
8:30 A.M. to 9 P.M.
Middle Eastern
No Credit Cards

You'll love the Astoria! It is so plain, clean, and down to earth, with the hoi polloi of Nazareth constantly streaming past the large windows and the occasional donkey kicking up a cloud of dust outside. Inside you should focus on the food—freshly prepared, plentiful, and reasonably priced. Select a dish that includes lamb or grilled meats, or choose from a wide assortment of salads. Good selection of desserts and cold drinks.

AL JENEENAH RESTAURANT

Paulus VI Street   Middle Eastern
No Credit Cards

Al Jeneenah is a real family-run place; Mom and Dad are in the kitchen and the kids are waiting tables. This simple restaurant, with the large open terrace and the pavilion outside, is a favorite of Nazareth wedding parties. Specialties include some unusual variations like *sfeeha* (small pita breads with a highly savory meat stuffing, which make a terrific appetizer), *siniya* (essentially lamb kebabs in a tehina sauce); and that fabulous dessert *kenafa* (a "pie" made with a light cream cheese–type filling, topped with jam and eaten warm from the oven, its spicy scent redolent of cinnamon and cloves).

THE HOLYLAND RESTAURANT

Across the street from
the Galilee Hotel

Lunch and Dinner
Italian
No Credit Cards

It's a bit mysterious finding out when this place is open—hours are erratic—but if you happen to be in the vicinity of the Holyland and find the gates are open, head inside and enjoy their surprisingly good Italian fare—basic southern-style pastas and casseroles.

ABU-NASSER'S RESTAURANT

Casa Nova Street

Lunch and Dinner
Middle Eastern
No Credit Cards

Yet another shishlik and hummus emporium—one of the better ones. Offered here just in case the Astoria is packed to the rafters with hordes of hungry pilgrims.

Also in the area and worth trying are the Omar El-Khayam and the Riviera.

Sunup to Sundown

Virtually all there is to do in Nazareth is done by the light of day. Travelers looking for evening activities here are searching for a needle in the proverbial haystack. The young locals hie off to nearby Tiberias or Haifa when they want some action. The charm and significance of Nazareth lies in the testaments to faith that are all around this picturesque town—the churches and mosques that form a heavenly skyline, a walk through the Arab market, or *souk*, and a side trip to Mount Tabor sum up the sights here.

Start your walk on Casa Nova Street, at the *Basilica of the Annunciation*, which is the likeliest symbol of Nazareth, considering its importance. The boldly modern structure is built over the hallowed place where the Angel Gabriel is believed to have brought the news of Jesus' birth to Mary. There were other, earlier structures built between the years 1730 and 1877 to protect this venerated spot. The crypt or cave where Mary sat and received Gabriel can be seen today. The remains of a Byzantine church and a Crusader church have been uncovered after exhaustive archeological work. Most awe-inspiring, however, is the modern basilica, which was built and completed in 1966, and is under the care of the Franciscans. This two-level church (the lower level houses the Grotto of the Annunciation) is justly renowned for the upper level, which serves as the public place of worship. The entrance is through a portico on the western side of the church. The arcades, stairways, pulpits, and an impressive cupola with a copper overlay which rises to a height of 195 feet are all examples of innovative and successful blending of religion and modern architecture, the old and the new. The most controversial and notable features of the church interior are the murals that line the nave and come from nations all over the world. The Virgin and the Christ Child are depicted in diverse styles and media—sometimes reverent, sometimes brashly bold, but always original. These murals, contributed by Christian denominations, display the unique and interpretive ways different cultures view the Holy Family. Pay special attention to the murals from the United States, Japan, the Cameroons, Mexico, and Spain—each tells a story and illustrates national perceptions of Christianity and what it means to them—boldness, delicacy, pageantry, passion, and pain. Hours are 8:30 to 11:45 A.M. and 2 to 5 P.M.(until 6 P.M. in summer), closed on Sunday mornings, unless you are attending Mass.

Proceed along Barclay's Bank Road past the Terra Sancta Monastery to *St. Joseph's Church*. St. Joseph's Church (just north of the basilica) was built in 1914 on the site that is believed to have been the location of Joseph's workshop. You may find it interesting that the Bible never describes Joseph as being a carpenter. The word used for his vocation was *teknon* which means "skill" or "work," a more general term than commonly accepted. The church was built on top of the site, which can be entered by descending a flight of stone-cut stairs and a narrow passage. There are a number of silos at the lower level which date from the pre-Byzantine period. A winepress and parts of Byzantine mosaic floors are quite interesting.

Near the El-Abyad Mosque is the *Synagogue Church* (it's near the Arab bazaar). This church, under the auspices of the Greek

Catholics, is the synagogue where Jesus, according to tradition, preached his first sermon as a young man.

From here, walk along Route 403 (slightly northwest) to the *Franciscan Mensa Christi Church*. This small chapel was built in 1861. The church was erected around a slab of limestone, which it is believed was the table at which Jesus and his disciples sat and dined following his resurrection.

Retrace your steps to the Synagogue Church and continue southward till you reach the *Sisters of Nazareth Convent*, which lies parallel to the Anglican Church. The convent is not open to visitors unless a previous appointment has been made. The most interesting aspect of the convent is what lies beneath it—an ancient Jewish necropolis, including a tomb sealed with a rolling stone. There are also traces of a Crusader monastery on the site.

This short walk is self-contained and two hours is the minimum time needed to appreciate everything. If you can stay longer, there are several other sites that you will enjoy.

An extension to the previous walk includes two special sites: *St. Gabriel's Greek Orthodox Church* and *Mary's Well*. To reach the Rum (Greek Orthodox) Quarter where they are located, walk up(northward) to Paulus VI Street and the Es-Salam Mosque. This mosque is new (built in 1965) and impressive, a reminder of the enduring Moslem presence in Nazareth. The mosque is built on a pedestal that resembles the base of the Taj Mahal. There are Coptic and Baptist churches right behind the mosque; bypass these until you reach the site of Mary's Well. The water that flows into this well springs from a source within St. Gabriel's Church. The well, with its rough stone arched wall, is the place where Mary and the women of Nazareth drew water, and where the Archangel Gabriel first appeared to Mary.

The Galilee Region–Part II

Zefat, the Upper Galilee, and Golan

efat, a town of nearly seventeen thousand inhabitants, encircled by Israel's highest peaks and greenest valleys, is always referred to in mystical terms as if a divine spirit hovers over it. This mystical connotation stems from the fifteenth and sixteenth centuries, when Zefat (often spelled *Safed* and pronounced Tzfat) was one of Judaism's four holy cities and attracted brilliant Sephardic scholars, whose interpretations of the Talmud and ethical writings remain guidelines for orthodoxy even today. It was here that great universities and Talmudic centers flourished and the first Hebrew printing press was introduced in 1563. But that was four hunded years ago, and if you are picturing a place rather like Brigadoon, then you are mistaken.

Twentieth-century Zefat, a picturesque town built on several levels, has retained its mystical flavor and honors its past but has moved beyond it. Most inhabitants are "newcomers," having settled here since 1948. Only in the old city will you find people who trace their roots back to those vibrant times. It is true, however, that even the newcomers are extremely devout and to arrive in Zefat on the Sabbath is to enter a virtual ghost town.

Israel's highest town, 2,790 feet above the Jordan Valley, with cool, crisp, mountain air and very cold winters, Zafed has become a favorite summer retreat for Israelis trying to escape the often oppressive heat of the coastal plain. Interestingly enough, the town has also attracted a large number of artists, who have established a thriving colony in the part of the old city that was the Arab Quarter until 1948.

Some of the towns in the Northern Galilee have that ancient, lived-in look, while others are modern and obviously recent additions. Using sophisticated irrigation techniques, the energetic Israelis of the kibbutzim and moshavim of the Upper Galilee, who love this land with a nearly fanatical passion, have forged an agricultural wonderland. Avocados, bananas, melons, and oranges seem to grow bigger and better here than anywhere else in the country, and the nearby Hula Valley is the most fertile growing area in Israel. Of course, nature has done its share as well.

Using Zefat as your base, a two- or three-day stay in the Northern Galilee will give you the opportunity to visit some stunning natural areas such as the Baniyas Waterfall and the Hula Nature Reserve, the ancient tel at Hazor, a Crusader castle, and a quaint town where Jews have lived uninterruptedly for eighteen centuries. Weather permitting, you can schuss down one of Mount Hermon's slopes or enjoy a refreshing ride on the non-skier lift.

Here, as elsewhere in Israel, the ancient and the modern blend and mesh to offer a variety of experiences.

Orientation

Getting There

Route 90 from Tiberias snakes through the Galilee Range and each curve brings a more stunning view of the valley below and shimmering Lake Kinneret in the distance. Just forty-five minutes later, you will find yourself in the small town *(moshava) Rosh Pinna*, on the slopes of Mount Canaan. This, the first modern Jewish settlement in the Galilee, was established in 1882. A local airport nearby links this region with Israel's large cities. Here the road splits and you turn left onto Route 89, which immediately starts to climb on its way to Zefat. En route you will see a monument to the first Jew hanged during the British Mandate period, which looks rather like a Black Power salute, a raised clenched fist. The area is also an observation point. As you approach the town limits, Route 89 becomes Ha Galil Road.

Major Areas and Landmarks

Zefat is built on three adjoining hilltops. The first, on your right (east of town) is *Mount Canaan*. It has one major street which is lined with hotels and little else. If you select a hotel here, you can take a local bus into town, a five-minute ride.

At the next intersection, make a sharp left onto *Rehov Ha'atzmaut*, which heads down into the valley before climbing to the main part of town. Be careful, for if you miss this turn, you are on your way to Akko.

The main part of town, *Gan Hametzuda*, is residential and has hotels, restaurants, and shops. Focal points in this area are the old city, the Artists' Quarter, and the *Ofer* and *Ma'or Haim Quarter*, which houses the ancient synagogues.

The main street in town is circular Rehov Yerushalayim (Jerusalem Street). The local IGTO, at 50 Jerusalem Street, is open from 8:30 A.M. to 1 P.M. and 4 to 6 P.M. Sunday through Thursday with an early closing on Friday and no Saturday hours.

The third hilltop is *South Zefat*. which leads to the town's industrial quarter, but there is little of interest for you here. Actually the best way to see Zefat is to wander around the main area; the more lost you get on the narrow old streets, the more fun you'll have.

Hotels

Zefat's hotels are found on Mount Canaan and in the area around Jerusalem Street. Local Buses (#1, #3, #1/3, and #1/4) link the two areas, but if possible stay in town, for there is little of interest outside this area. Since Israelis flock here in the dog days of summer and for Passover and the High Holy Days, hotel space at those times is hard to come by. Rates rise accordingly (about 20 percent) and some hotels insist that you take full board. Since there are few restaurants in town, that is not a major problem. There are no five-star hotels here, but some very comfortable four- and three-star choices are available. Hotels are very small—none have more than fifty rooms—so reservations make sense.

Fortunately, the Northern Galilee has several kibbutz guest houses for you to consider as well.

RIMON INN 4*

Artists' Colony   Phone(06) 920665
Quryat Haomanim
Zefat

The loveliest stop in Zefat is the four-star Rimon Inn in the Artists' Colony. Each of the thirty-six rooms is decorated differently, but all have air conditioning, heating, and telephones. Ask for a room with a balcony—half have them. The main building is over three hundred years old, and was originally a Turkish khan. The dining room was once a stable and the metal hitching bars are still visible. Views of the surrounding hills, arbors, pomegranate trees, and honey-suckle vines, plus a good-size swimming pool (June through October) add to the allure of the Rimon Inn. *Expensive*.

THE RON HOTEL 4*

Hativat Yiftah Street   Phone (06) 972590/1/2
Zefat 13110

The fifty-room Ron, the largest hostelry in town, is another solid choice. Hativat Yiftah Street is near HaMetzuda Park. A sleek, modern building, well cared for by management, it has a large, airy lobby decorated with art (for sale) by local artists. A good dining room, a triangular pool, and a garden densely planted with flowering bushes make the Ron an enjoyable stop. *Expensive*.

THE CENTRAL HOTEL 3*

37 Jerusalem Street   Phone (06) 927366
                                                   Major Credit Cards

The Central is just that—central. It's right in the heart of things. Nothing fancy, the fifty rooms are clean, with air conditioning and heating but without phones. Half the rooms have tubs, the other half have showers only. There's a bar, a coffee shop, and a large kosher dining room. *Moderate*.

THE BERINSON HOUSE 3ᴬ

Ridbaz Street
Phone (06) 972555
Major Credit Cards

Also called the Hotel Tel Aviv, the Berinson is in a narrow lane off 24 Jerusalem Street. Its thirty-eight rooms, in a stately stone building, are clean and have full baths. A quiet location. *Moderate*.

THE CARMEL HOTEL 2⋆

8 Javitz Street
Phone (06) 920053
Zefat, 13208
No Credit Cards

In a narrow lane behind 14 Jerusalem Street stands a *pension*-like hotel. The Carmel, managed by Zaid Shlomo, who lives here with his family, is a refurbished old mansion. The upstairs rooms (ten) have balconies and all have showers only and are not air-conditioned. Breakfast, included in your rate, is served on a terrace surrounded by a magnificient grape arbor. *Inexpensive*.

Hotels on Mount Canaan

THE RUCKENSTEIN 3⋆

Mount Canaan
Phone (06) 920060
Zefat

A family-style hotel, the Ruckenstein reminded us of our summers at camp—accommodations are in rustic cabins. They are well maintained, and there is a bar and a coffeeshop. The Ruckenstein's kosher dining rooms are considered the best in town. Typically large portions of Eastern European, *haimishe* food—meat or dairy—are served on the terrace. Orthodox owners. *Moderate*.

THE NOF HA-GALIL 3⋆

Mount Canaan
Phone (06) 921595
Fax (06) 973116
Major Credit Cards

A solid stop, the Nof Ha-Galil has thirty-four rooms, all with lovely views of the surrounding hills and valleys. Ask for a room with a bath (ten have only showers). The owners are friendly here. *Moderate*.

THE DAVID HOTEL 3★

Mount Canaan   Phone (06) 920062
Zefat

The David is a standard three-star choice, with a white stucco exterior and forty-two bright, airy rooms. All have full baths, but they aren't all air-conditioned. *Moderate*.

Two other hotels on Mount Canaan, somewhat less attractive, are the Pisgah (06) 930105 and the Hotel/Motel Zefat (06) 930914. You can try them if you are shut out elsewhere.

Unusual Choices

HOTEL BEIT YOSEF 3★

Jerusalem Street near Tourist Office   Phone (06) 730012
No Credit Cards

Look for a sign reading "Israhai Tours and Seminars." Inside the well-kept garden and courtyard, which were once part of the British High Commissioner's residence, is Hotel and Restaurant Beit Yosef. The hotel has eighty-five rooms scattered over two buildings. Half the rooms have full baths. Not a luxurious stop, Beit Yosef is actually rather basic, but the dynamic duo who run this enterprise, Chaim Sidor and Yisrael Shalem, offer more than a place to rest your weary head. They know as much about Zefat and the Upper Galilee as humanly possible and they like nothing better than to tell you about the many facets of the region. The programs include audiovisual shows, walking tours, and lectures (see Sunup activities). Drop in even if you stay elsewhere. *Moderate*.

SEAVIEW HOTEL 3★

Rosh Pinna–Zefat Road (Route 89)   Phone (06) 937014
Box 27   *No Credit Cards*
Rosh Pinna 12000

On the highway, the Seaview has twenty-four rooms and all have phones and full baths. An organic farm, a restaurant, and a shop are part of the complex, as are a gym, a solarium, a pool, a Finnish sauna, and a massage parlor (legitimate, if you please). Nice healthy-looking staff. *Moderate*.

Kibbutz Guest Houses

The Upper Galilee has several guest houses you might consider. All are north of Zefat and in areas you will want to visit during your stay here.

KFAR GILADI 3★

Upper Galilee 12210   Phone (06) 941414

Telex 6610

Major Credit Cards

Just south of Metulla, Israel's northernmost town, and the Lebanese border, Kfar Giladi is the oldest kibbutz in the Northern Galilee and one of the largest too. The guest house, opened in 1942, has 134 rooms, which are in a variety of buildings. All rooms are air-conditioned and heated, and the kibbutz has a large swimming pool, tennis and basketball courts, and a vast library (multiple languages). The Beit Hashomer Museum here is a tribute to the *shomrim*, the watchmen of the early settlements, who formed the basis of the Haganah. *Moderate*.

HAGOSHRIM 3★

Mobile Post   Phone (06) 956231
Upper Galilee 12225

Founded in 1948 by Turkish Jews, Hagoshrim's guest house is separated from the kibbutz grounds by the Dan River, one of the tributaries of the Jordan. Guest rooms, 121 of them, are in a large central area with one-, two-, and four-story buildings. Rooms are large, carpeted, and air-conditioned. The main building of the kibbutz, built over an Arab sheikh's house, has a terrific gift shop that sells Persian rugs and archeological artifacts. Hagoshrim has a pool. *Moderate*.

KFAR BLUM 3*

Upper Galilee 12150   Phone (06) 943666

The "American" kibbutz, Kfar Blum was organized in 1943 by American, Canadian, and British Jews. English is certainly a strong second language here. With sixty-six rooms (twenty more are in the planning stage), Kfar Blum is proud of its Olympic- size swimming pool and sauna. Looking at the tall cypress trees and green lawns, it is hard to believe that this area, the Hula Valley, was a swamp just forty years ago. *Moderate.*

AYELET HASHACHAR 4*

Upper Galilee 12200   Phone (06) 932611

Ayelet Hashachar, or "Morning Star," one of the two four-star kibbutz guest houses in the country, is actually luxurious. The guest house, which started in 1947, has sixteen two-story buildings arranged in neat rows and encircled by lawns, trees, and flowers. Each house has the name of a woman from the Bible and there are 144 rooms in all. Near Tel Hazor (the museum is on the kibbutz grounds), Ayelet Hashachar has a pool, tennis courts, and a soccer field. *Expensive.*

Restaurants

Zefat is primarily an Israeli vacation destination and most Israelis eat in their hotels, taking either full or half board. Out-of-hotel restaurants have a tough time making it and there are only a few we can recommend to you. With that in mind, we still urge you to eat in some of our choices, for it's the best way to meet local Zefatis and the ambience is often worth seeing.

THE HA MIFGASH

75 Jerusalem Street   Phone (06) 920510
Middle Eastern, Kosher
Noon to 4 P.M., 6 P.M. to midnight
No Credit Cards

Big, informal, a noisy television blasting away, old brass cooking utensils hanging from the rafters, and a quieter, vaulted-stone dining alcove toward the back — this is IIa Mifgash, which means "the meeting place" — and if you like people, this is the spot. Portions are enormous and there are specialties like stuffed chicken, charcoal steak filets, kubbeh, and memulaim (stuffed vegetables). Try a baked apple or homemade fruit pie. *Moderate*.

THE PINATI

81 Jerusalem Street

Phone (06) 920855
Noon to 4 P.M., 6 P.M. to midnight
Closed Saturday
Middle Eastern
Diner's Club, Visa

A friendly scene and plentiful food make Pinati one of Zefat's few long-time eateries. All the salads are fresh, the grilled meats and fish are tasty, and sandwiches are filling. But the best part about Pinati is watching the locals drift in for a Macabee, a game of shesh-besh, and some kibbitzing. It's the local "joint." *Moderate*.

THE CALIFORNIA FALAFEL

At the walkover where
Jerusalem and Arlosorov
Streets intersect

Middle Eastern
No Credit Cards

In the never-ending quest for the "King of Falafel" Zefatis in the know wind up here. This is the do-it-yourself falafel, with little dishes of assorted goodies within arm's reach; you create the masterpiece. The place is big, bright, and always full—a very good sign. *Inexpensive*.

CAFE BAGHDAD

Jerusalem Street Mall

Phone (06) 974-0657
7 A.M. to midnight
(Closed Saturday)

A delightful choice for breakfast or a light meal, the Cafe Baghdad features delicious omelets, fresh bagels, sandwiches, soups, and salads. Windows throughout provide some great views of the valley. Palermo Pizza nearby is a great spot for pizza —whole pies or by the slice.

DUBI'S

Hotel Ruckenstein

Phone (06) 920060
Lunch and Dinner
(Closed for Sabbath)

Dine indoors or outside on the terrace at this fine kosher restaurant, one of the town's finest. Bagels with lox and cream cheese, smoked trout, cheese fondue and homemade ice cream are just a few of the favorites served here.

CAFÉ ANAT

Jerusalem Street Mall

Café Anat has a great view of the city and the surrounding countryside from its perch on the hillside. It serves dairy foods and is open for all three meals. Soups, salads, omelettes and freshly baked breads and cakes are all popular.

PALERMO PIZZA

Jerusalem Street Mall

Thin, crisp pizza served by the slice and by the pie are on the menu here. Pick up your food and take it to one of the two covered outdoor eating areas.

THE SEAVIEW VEGETARIAN RESTAURANT

Rosh Pina–Zefat Road

Phone (06) 937014

For a nice change of pace, if you have a car, head to the Seaview, which is part of a hotel. Strictly kosher, the Seaview grows and serves organically grown fruit and vegetables and the variety of preparation makes for enjoyable light eating. *Inexpensive.*

Sunup to Sundown

Zefat is really a daytime town. Most of its splendors, both the hidden and the obvious ones, are best viewed in the light of day.

Sightseeing here can be deceptive; looking at a map with all the sights nicely numbered in sequence, you may think that Zefat is worth but a few hours of your time. But that is a major faux-pas. Discovering Zefat means finding your own little medieval alleyway or a abandoned stone synagogue. This is an amateur archeologist's playground. The maze of streets, cobblestoned and dropping down many levels to the valleys below, conceal the nerve center of an important sector of Jewish society—and, if you're up to the challenge, it's all waiting to be revealed. The town must be traversed on foot—don't try driving along those slivers of streets. There are three distinct areas of town that you'll want to explore: the center-of-town Citadel area, the old city, and finally the Artists' Quarter. We will guide you through them, but first a few words about the history of Zefat, a stronghold of Judaic tradition.

Capsule History

Zefat speaks in whispers of faith and devotion to the Torah; its word is an absolute. Zefat's pride in its roots as one of the four holy cities of Judaic tradition is very obvious.

When the Babylonians conquered the Holy Land and destroyed the Temple in A.D. 66, there was a mass exodus of the Jews from Jerusalem. Many headed to Zefat, which became a peaceful haven for these banished souls. The armies of the Crusade, when they arrived, erected a fortress, allocating the area to the Knights Templar, who subsequently killed or expelled the Jews. By 1170, there were no Jews left in Zefat.

In A.D. 1219, Saladin's armies reduced the Crusader fortress to rubble, but the stalwart Crusaders rebuilt it in grand fashion. Invading armies of Mongols, Mamelukes, and Turks tried with varying results to take the citadel, but it remains today at the core of town. Amazingly enough, Jews returned to Zefat during these years of turmoil and each time they came with a renewed vigor.

The Jewish Renaissance started with the rebuilding of Zefat's first synagogue (today called the *Air-Sephardi*). In the fourteenth and fifteenth centuries, Zefat's Jewish population received a boost when thousands of Sephardic Jews fled the atrocities of the Inquisition. By the early 1500s Zefat had become the center of Jewish learning in the Galilee.

Among the new arrivals were several great rabbis who were attracted to the region because of its proximity to the tomb of Rabbi Shimon Bar Yokhai. Rabbi Shimon wrote the *Zohar*, a commentary on the Five Books of Moses, which theorized that the words had mystical and higher meanings. These rabbis studied and taught and published works of their own, using the country's first Hebrew printing press.

Among the most revered scholars were Yosef Caro, whose work *Shulkhan Arukh* was a guide for Jewish life, and the poet Solomon Alkabets, who wrote the Sabbath hymn "Lecha Dodi." Among those who devoted their lives to the study of the Cabbala, the greatest was Rabbi Isaac Luria, known as the Ha'Ari (the lion). The Rav arrived from Egypt in 1569 and died of plague three years later, but he left a system of Cabbala known as the Lurianic system.

Plagues and earthquakes struck the town and Jewish life settled into a holding pattern for several centuries.

During the War of Independence, the city was encircled by hostile Arab forces. Both Orthodox and secular residents built fortifications and fought–even on the Sabbath. One amusing anecdote tells of the defender's secret weapon, the *Davidka*, a homemade cannon (on display on Jerusalem Street) which was virtually nonoperational, but made such a horrendous noise when fired that the Arab forces fled in fear. Zefat is now a totally Jewish town.

Walking Through Zefat

Although we will address the three areas of town in separate walks, you can easily do them in sequence and on the same day. Zefat is a small town.

Walk #1, The Citadel Area

Start at the Post Office on Jerusalem Street. Here you will spot the unmistakable homemade cannon, the *Davidka*, on the right. This humble but effective little weapon sits opposite the Ministry of the Interior and the British Police Station. Look for the sign that says "Metzuda" and climb a flight of crumbling steps leading up into a high ridge above the town called Hativat Yiftach Street. On either side you will see the *Citadel Hill* (Givat Ha Metzuda) and the remains of the castle wall. These ruins date from Crusader times, although archeologists believe that the Jewish inhabitants of Zefat had, during the Roman period, built a fortress here. The park area is cool, shady, and so peaceful that it's really difficult to imagine the booming sounds of war and soldiers falling in battle. Those brave men of the Palmach defenders are touchingly remembered. A winding walkway takes you to the top of the hill, where you will see the memorial dedicated to the fighting men who defended Zefat against the Arab forces during the War of Independence. This monument to the fallen of 1948 is set in a tranquil, pastoral spot with benches and lovely flowers. This fortress which, because of its exceptional strategic position, was fortified over generations by Jews, Crusaders, and Mamelukes, affords you a spectacular view of Mount Meron, Mount Tabor, and, on a clear day, the entire Galilee region. In Citadel Hill Park, up near the top of the hill, you'll see a giant beached whale. This is in the *Metzuda*, which is the only place for outdoor dancing in town. What a view—the stars above and the twinkling lights of the Galilee below. Coming down on the western slope of the hill, you'll see a stately old mansion surrounded by a courtyard and palm trees. This building houses the *Israel Bible Museum*, once called the Glickenstein Municipal Museum. Lovingly renovated by a talented group of Zefat builders, this 120-year-old building was once the Turkish governor's house.

The museum has been reborn, and a vital, spirited American named Philip Ratner has been and remains the catalyst here. Mr. Ratner, whose works have been exhibited at the Smithsonian and will be featured in a permanent exhibit at the new museum on Ellis Island, brings all his fire and spark to this venture. It's the only museum in the world dedicated to biblical art and to the telling of the Bible story, through the means of mixed media. The artwork is arranged on the three floors of the building and follows a sequence from the creation of Adam and Eve to the books of the prophets. Mr. Ratner plans to turn this mountaintop into a Bible center where Christian and Jewish groups can meet and focus on the true essence of the Bible. This bicoastal genie (Washington, D.C.–Zefat) is a natural resource.

You're in luck if he's around, but if he's not, Steve Ornstein carries on admirably and ably in his stead. You must visit the Israel Bible Museum and say hello. Hours are from 10 A.M. to 6 P.M. Sunday through Thursday 10 A.M. to 2 P.M. on Saturday; closed Friday. Admission is free.

Descending the steps from the museum to Jerusalem Street will place you near Bar Ilan University and the War Memorial right across the street. You will be walking toward *Javitz Street*, where the Institute of the Cabbala and Ascent (another Cabbalistic-oriented religious institute) are located. These are particularly interesting to Jewish travelers, since most of the programs are intense immersions in the Jewish experience. Ascent conducts seminars on Jewish mysticism, the Cabbala, and Hassidism. They function as educational centers with the largest English reading library on Torah subjects in Northern Israel. Even if you aren't Jewish, the sight of the serious and dark-clad men scurrying to and from a rabbi's lecture makes you feel as if you've spied on another century.

Walk #2, The Old City

Start from the IGTO on Jerusalem. Bear left on Bar Yochai Street, which will lead you to *Kikar Hamaginim* (Charcoal Square), the start of the old city. You will notice the difference immediately. The streets are, more often than not, nooks and alleys with no names at all. Cobblestoned, they are lined with low, oddly shaped houses. Many houses have balconies and on these you'll see the old city dwellers. Devout, bearded, and black-clad men pray inaudibly in Hebrew while speaking aloud—almost shouting—in Yiddish. Young women, heads covered with kerchiefs, wearing ankle-length dresses, shepherd their younger siblings home from school. The ancient synagogues nearby are interesting to see, but even more interesting is walking in this quarter. Don't forget your camera.

Turn right at the steps, and to the right you'll see the H'Ari-Ashkenazi Synagogue on Rehov Najara. It might add to your appreciation of the various synagogues if you understand the function of those features which are common to most of them. The

Aron Ha Kodesh is the Ark in which the Torah scrolls are stored. They are found on the southwestern wall of Zefat's synagogues, since Jerusalem lies southwest of the town and Jews traditionally pray in the direction of that holy city. The Bima, or platform, occupies a central elevated position in the temple and seating is arranged around it. This necessitates that the worshipers look up to the Torah, symbolizing respect. Crosses never appear, not even accidentally, in traditional synagogues. Even tiles have to be laid ingeniously on the floor, so as not to form right angles. The Geniza is a storing place, usually found in the back of the synagogue. It resembles a cabinet with glass doors and serves to protect the holy books which are old or damaged and thus can no longer be used. Holy books are never thrown away—if the Geniza is full to capacity, the older books are given a dignified burial.

The Cabbala

It will be helpful to have at least an inkling of what the Cabbala is all about before you go any further. The Cabbala is a complicated philosophical approach to interpreting the Torah. Cabbalists claim that this abstract method of reading the Bible dates back to the days of Abraham's sojourn in the Sinai—but the evidence for this is vague. The Cabbala gained a foothold in the sixth and seventh centuries and reached a peak during the period of the expulsion of the Jews from Spain and Portugal. Sephardic Jewry was receptive to this discipline, in which the Scripture was believed to hold a hidden meaning, revealed only to a select few with enlightened consciousness. There was an element of magic in all this and it allowed for a great many interpretations. It was left to the great sages to make the mystical Cabbala more accessible to the masses. The H'Ari-Ashkenazi was built after the death of Rabbi Issac Luria (the Ari). The Ari is supposed to have originated the Friday-evening service to welcome the Sabbath at this spot. Typical of Sephardic synagogue design is the vaulted ceiling and the gaily painted columns within.

The H'Ari-Ashkenazi has a finely carved bima, or pulpit, and the Ark, made of olivewood, is one hundred years old and took ten years to carve. It is extremely beautiful and ornately wrought.

There are three Torah scrolls inside which are notable: the one from Persia is two hundred years old, the one from Iraq is three hundred years old, and the one from Spain is five hundred years old.

Other Synagogues

Down on Alkabets Street (where it meets Beit Yosef) is the famous *Yosef Caro Synagogue*. The brilliant cerulean-blue walls are a common sight in Zefat; blue is supposed to ward off the evil eye, and it looks pretty besides. The architectural simplicity in the small dome room beneath the synagogue marks the spot where an angel, in the guise of an itinerant preacher, appeared to Rabbi Caro. The visitation inspired Caro to write *A Preacher of Uprightness*, the Magid Mesharim. The synagogue sits atop the site of the ancient yeshiva where the rabbi taught. Inside, notice the Oriental-style seating arrangement—a low, cushioned bench that runs along the walls.

The *Abohav Synagogue* is just one block away. The original building dates from the 1490s, erected according to Cabbalistic outlines given by the Rabbi Abohav himself. Interesting to note are the crowns on the dome, the pictures of the tribes of Israel, musical instruments, and the painting of the Dome of the Rock. The earthquake of 1837 leveled it, except for the wall containing the Ark and the Torah scroll written by the rabbi. The synagogue is also in early Sephardic style, painted in light blue, with an impressive wooden pulpit and a whimsically painted ceiling. The ten windows represent the Ten Commandments; the partitioned area to the left is for the women. The *Ora Gallery* on Beit Yosef Street features the works of Hassidim and other religious artists and artisans from throughout Israel.

Still farther down, past Edeii and Ha-Sephardim Street, is the *Bannai Synagogue*—the burial place of the Mishnaic sage, Rabbi Yosef Bannai, called Ha Lavan (the "white one"). Local legend has it that a cruel Arab governor ordered the Jews of Zefat to bring him a large number of white chickens. The people prayed at Rabbi Bannai's grave, and all the chickens in Zefat turned white. The synagogue houses an ancient Torah scroll, which is carried to Mount Meron every Lag B'Omer.

Down at the lowest tier of the old city and overlooking the Jewish cemetery is the second synagogue named in the honor of Ha'Ari, the Rabbi Isaac Luria. The *Ari-Sephardi* Synagogue, built on the site where the Ari actually prayed, is Zefat's most famous synagogue. It has finely carved wooden doors, and a small dark niche where he prayed and studied. During the War of Independence it served as a Haganah headquarters.

From the Ari-Sephardi, you can descend into the valley beyond and visit the town cemeteries—old, new, and military. The old cemetery contains the tombs of many of the most highly revered Cabbalists; Isaac Luria, Yosef Caro, and Moshe Cordevero are all laid to their eternal rest here. The new cemetery holds an especially tragic association—the twenty-four teenagers who were massacred at Ma'Alot are interred on this spot. The military cemetery contains the graves of many of the Palmach commandos and the soldiers who fought during Liberation. East of the cemetery is the *Ari Mikveh*, an ancient natural-spring ritual bath. Near the mikveh is a high, wide staircase called the *Ma'Alot Olei Hagardom*, "Martyrs' Staircase," built by the British in order to separate the Jewish and Arab sections of town after the Arab massacre of the Jews in 1929. The name is a memorial to the Jews hanged by the British in 1947–48. When you reach the top, turn left on Chatam Sofer Street (it's just before Jerusalem Street). You may find it interesting to visit *Chabad House*. An attractive new building, it houses the Lubavitch headquarters in Zefat. Exhibits relating to religious (primarily Hassidic) themes are planned weekly; a gift shop and an extensive library are available to interested people. The little *Tschernoble Synagogue* nearby was started a hundred years ago by a group of Hassidim from the unfortunate town that has become a household word because of a devastating nuclear accident in 1986.

Walk #3, The Artists' Quarter

The Artists' Quarter lies east of the old city and was the Arab Quarter before Independence. Whether you enter from Jerusalem Street or from the Jewish Quarter, the place to start is at the *Ma'Alot Olei Hagardom* staircase. Halfway up (or down) the steps, on the Jewish Quarter side, is the Ethiopian Folk

Center. (Zefat has absorbed a large number of Ethiopian Jews.) This is a place where they can showcase their skill at handicrafts —weaving, carving, and sculpting. Bright, primary-colored carpets and vests and an assortment of trinkets make this an excellent place to pick up a little gift for someone back home. The center also has special programs and the people there are only too pleased to answer any questions you may have about the special concerns of Ethiopian Jewry. On to Arlosorov Street; down the first flight of steps you will see a sign that says "General Exhibition"—here you can saturate yourself with Zefatian art. If you walk on a little farther you'll see small studios dotting the corners and the cul-de-sacs of the quarter. Over ninety self-proclaimed artists make their homes here, although most of them disappear during the winter. Almost all of these studios and, of course, the General Exhibition are open to view with free admission or a small fee that allows you entry into everything. A lot of the art is of the "Fiddler on the Roof" variety—lots of bearded sages and samovars—but here and there are traces of a budding Chagall or Chana Orloff. Shalom of Safed is a town legend, and if you find an authentic work by this artist you've lucked out; they are considered collectible. More likely you'll find a signed lithograph or poster. Colorful, they look great when you frame them back home. Galleries are open from 9 A.M. to 6 P.M. Fridays, and from 10 A.M. to 2 P.M. Saturdays. Studio hours seven days a week are 10 A.M. to 1 P.M. and 4 to 9 P.M.

The Museum of the Art of Printing is at the eastern end of the quarter. Exhibitions of Jewish folklore and five hundred years of printing and art are on display (also called the Zvi Assaf Printing Museum). Hours are 10 A.M. to noon and 4 to 6 P.M., Fridays and Saturdays from 10 A.M. to noon. Admission is free.

The Rimon Inn, Rimonim Street, is worth a look if you are not already staying there. It is the most charming spot in Zefat. The hotel, formerly the old Austrian Post Office, was built by the Turks two hundred years ago in a distinctly Ottoman style. The three tiered gardens dipping down into the hillside provide a most enchanting place to take in the panoramic view. Nearby, Milo is the house of an artist and a coffee shop/art gallery. You'll find it at the entry to the Artists' Quarter, and it's a good place to trade art news with the creative locals who frequent the place. You can return to Arlosorov Street, where you will see the town's only traffic light! It's on the right of the street. On the other side of the walkover is the Cave of Shem Ve Ever (near the bridge on Ha Palmach). This is one of several holy caves in and around Zefat. Tradition has it that Noah's son and grandson, Shem and Ever, studied the Torah here.

Other Activities in Zefat

Daytime activities with less emphasis on walking are plentiful. You can take a swim at the *Emek Hatchelet* pool. This is a recreation center that offers a miniature golf course, a children's and adult's pool, a cheery restaurant-snack bar, and a children's playground. The pool is located in the valley at the entrance to Zefat. It has a sports field and charges a small admission fee. Buses #1 and #3 will take you there from the town center.

There are two Community Centers—the Blum Center, near the Rassin Center, features a health club on its premises (phone 930052) and the Wolfson Center in the old Turkish Government House (on the far eastern side of town) on Ha Palmach Street near the market, schedules a variety of musical and cultural events.

Beit Gesher, situated atop Mount Canaan, is an educational center for the study of Judaism for youth from Israel and abroad. They offer lectures, seminars, and visits to historical sights. The phone number is 930297.

One of the most satisfying and memorable activities is the planting of your own personal tree in Biriyya Forest. Your holiday may come to an end, but your spirit will live on forever if you take part in the greening of the Holy Land. It's a real privilege; you can obtain all the details and information by contacting the IGTO at 50 Jerusalem Street (phone 9230633).

If the link with the Cabbala is what draws you to Zefat, you may want to chat with Rabbi Noach Hefitz at the Institute of the Heritage of Zefat in Halacha and Caballa (phone 972946, 930559). This spry and persuasive man will explain even the most circuitous mystical problem in a crystal-clear and exciting way.

Beit Yosef organizes special events that deal mainly with the historical and religious facets of Zefat: audiovisual programs, lectures, walks. For a look into Zefat's future, ask Chaim Sidor and Yisrael Shalem at Beit Yosef about the "To Build and To Be Built" program. This three- month work/study program is geared primarily toward Jewish youth from western countries. These young people, who come from the U.S.A., the U.K., and Australia, spend every morning in a rigorous program of reconstructing many of the old neglected buildings in Zefat. The work they do is admirable and it's not at all unusual for them to sink a shovel in the ground and come up with some valuable artifacts. Zefat is sitting on a lot of centuries.

Shopping

Do you have a good eye? If you do, you'll probably go home with some real treasures. Obviously, the Artists' Quarter is the best place to go on a scavenger hunt. Be wary, however, of some of the outdoor stalls that sell shoddy prints and sloppy "original"— these are destined to become the dust collectors of tomorrow. Those of you who collect Judaica (tallisim, Hannukiahs) will find some lovely one-of-a-kind pieces here.

Sundown to Sunup

You will not be astonished to learn that Zefat is not a night town —but we did find one or two things for you to do before you turn out the lights.

The Wolfson Center holds concerts several times a year, usually chamber music. Check with the IGTO for dates.

The Rimon Inn, the Ron Hotel, and the Ruckinstein Hotel on Mount Canaan have bars and sometimes music in high season.

The Yard Tea House has a piano bar with live music and folksingers.

Check with Israhai Tours and Seminars at Beit Yosef. Chaim and Yisrael conduct in-depth, custom-made tours to suit different personalities—and some are held at night. These include:

Information tours focus on architecture, history, and Zefat lore. These tours can be arranged for days and evenings and usually meet at a hotel in the town center.

Nature orientation tours are expertly guided tours of the north of the country or what is called the Upper Galilee, going as far up as "The Good Fence" area near Metulla.

Mixed programs (or *kef*, meaning "fun and good times") are tours that offer a light overview of the attractions in Zefat and culminate in an evening stroll through the town. These tours are a good idea if you're interested in the deeper aspect of the town and enjoy the company of a group (usually about twenty people).

Excursions from Zefat

Using Zefat as your base, you can explore the Upper Galilee and the Golan Heights area. Nearby, you'll want to visit Meron (a town which has housed Jews for 1,800 years) and Bar'am, with a well-preserved second-century synagogue.

Meron and Bar'am

Meron, a very religious town and site of exuberant celebration on the festival of Lag b'Omer, is only five miles west of Zefat, on Route 89. Jews have lived in the area continuously for 1,800 years, but it is the tomb of Rabbi Shimon Bar Yochai that draws thousands of young and old Hassidim here each Lag b'Omer. This holiday, which falls thirty-three days after Passover eve (usually in May), is an occasion of wild celebration. Rabbi Shimon, a second-century scholar, lived in a nearby cave to escape Roman persecution.

Promising God that the Torah would never be forgotten, he wrote the *Zohar*, "Book of Splendor," which is the mystical Cabbalists' most precious book. On Lag b'Omer thousands of Hassidim arrive from all parts of Israel (and from the U.S.) and with candles lighting the way, amid chanting, fervent singing, and dancing, pay homage to their sage by marching from town to his tomb atop Mount Meron. Obviously, this is the time to be here, but if you aren't you can always make the climb to the tomb (several other sages' tombs are also here, as is an excavated synagogue) and a rock called Messiah's Chair. Legend holds that on the day he arrives, the Messiah will sit here while Elijah's trumpet sounds to herald his arrival.

Return to Route 89 (there's a gas station here) and follow signs to Sasa on your left. Sasa is a kibbutz founded by Americans and Canadians in the early days of statehood. Just beyond the kibbutz, quite near the Lebanese border, is Bar'am, which has the country's best-preserved Galilean synagogue. It dates from the second century and its main façade still stands. There are three stone lintels. The central one, decorated with grape leaves and grapes, is guarded on either side with carved lions. Because it is one of the earliest synagogues found, it has been studied for clues into the nature of early houses of worship. Part of the National Park System. Open 9 A.M. to 5 P.M. daily, 9 A.M. to 1 P.M. Friday. Modest fee.

Into the Northern Galilee

Heading north from Rosh Pinna on Route 90 to Metulla (Israel's northernmost settlement), you can explore ancient tels, relax in the beautiful nature reserves in this very green, fertile area, and visit sites of interest in the Golan Heights—including a ski resort. Tip: Restaurants are virtually nonexistent here and your choices will be limited to kibbutz guest house dining rooms and nature park cafeterias. Pack a picnic lunch and eat at one of the nature reserves. There are picnic tables at each and they are lovely places to eat.

Tel Hazor

Six miles north of Rosh Pinna, Tel Hazor is the country's largest tel, covering two hundred acres. Hazor was a large and important city in ancient times, for it sat on the Via Maris, a major trading route. It is mentioned as far back as 19 B.C. The tel has two areas; the larger is a huge mound called Upper City, while the plateau below it is called Lower City. Twenty-one different levels have been unearthed in digs starting in 1938. The major work was done in 1955 by Yigael Yadin, who excavated the Massada some years later. A cemetery from the Middle Bronze Age, a temple from the Late Bronze Age, and a fabulous water system from the ninth century are all part of the ruins. By the way, diagrams and explanations are clear and informative. Artifacts from the tel are

In a small museum at Kibbutz Ayelet Hashahar, across the road
Part of the National Park System. Open 9 A.M. to 5 P.M. daily, till 1
P.M. on Friday. Small admission charge.

The Hula Valley Nature Reserve

The Hula Valley was once a vast marshland around a lake fed by
the waters of the Jordan. Its acres, spread as far as the eye could
see, contained fantastic wildlife, including water buffalo, wild
boars, and exotic birds migrating from Europe and Asia to Africa.
The flora included papyrus reeds.

When Israel became a state, it needed these fertile acres and,
with water scarce in the southern part of the nation, it was
necessary to drain the marsh by creating a vast canal system that
crisscrosses the 775 acres. The valley is now agricultural, the
most fertile area in the nation. Avocados, citrus, and tomatoes are
grown there.

Striving to maintain the area's wildlife, a nature park was
created that occupies one part of the valley. Here you can see a
bird sanctuary, fish ponds, reed ponds with water buffalo wall-
owing in the mud, and a small swamp area.

You can get an overview of the area from the Heights of Naftali
(the next left off the highway), where a British fortress stands.
The Arab name for it is *Nebi Yesha*, the Hebrew *Metzudat
Ko'ach*. *Ko'ach* means "twenty-eight"; the fortress was named
for twenty-eight soldiers who were killed here during the War of
Independence.

Qiryat Shemona/Tel Hai

Qiryat Shemona "Town of the Eight," the largest town in the Upper Galilee, nineteen miles north of Rosh Pinna, was named in
memory of the eight heroic defenders of Tel Hai, a settlement
one mile north that was established in 1917. The pioneers here,
attempting to establish an agricultural community, lived in a
small building that was on the land when it was purchased from
the Arab owner. The tiny settlement was constantly raided by
Arabs but gamely fought them off till one day in 1920 when their
luck ran out. Six men and two women died that day—among
them Josef Trumpeldor, the Israeli's Nathan Hale.

Born in Russia, where he lost an arm fighting for the Czar, Trumpeldor organized the Hehalutz, the Russian Zionist organization. Arriving in Palestine in 1912, he settled in Tel Hai and soon died here in defense of this land. On his grave stands a roaring lion of Judah and his last words, "It is good to die for our country." Also buried here are his fallen comrades, those of the *Hashomer*, the prestate defense force, and soldiers who died in the War of Independence.

The Arabs staging the murderous attack on Tel Hai had come from a nearby town, Halsa, the site on which Qiryat Shemona stands today.

From here you can continue to Metulla, the country's northernmost settlement, on the Lebanese border. There's not much to see in town, which is small and orderly, but of interest nearby is the *Nahal Iyon Nature Reserve* (between Qiryat Shemona and Metulla). The best time to visit here is in the spring when there is the most water flowing over the reserve's four waterfalls. The lowest but most beautiful is *Tanur* Waterfall ("the oven") which resembles an old Arab oven. You can see Tanur from the road, but it's a twenty-minute hike to the others from the parking lot. Because Hurshat Tal is not far away, if you are pressed for time, bypass Metulla and Nahal Iyon and head east to the Golan Heights.

To the Golan

Route 99 leads east from Qiryat Shemona to the Golan. Sightseeing in this area is only practical by car or rental cab. Although buses run from Qiryat Shemona to some sites, timing makes this impractical.

Hurshat Tal National Park

Three miles east of Qiryat Shemona, Hurshat Tal National Park was built to preserve the ancient Tabor oak trees that have existed here for centuries—some may date to the time of Jesus. It is astonishing to think that they have escaped the axes of countless invaders, local woodcutters, and nomads, but here they stand and they are quite impressive. Surrounded now by lovely green lawns, picnic areas, and campgrounds, they make a delightful place for a picnic lunch, although there is a small restaurant here and Kibbutz HaGoshcrim is next door. The Dan River, one of the Jordan's tributaries, goes through the park and forms pools where you can swim. Beware—the water is very cold. Hurshat Tal Park is open 8 A.M. to 4 P.M. daily and there is a small admission charge. The park is closed from November through March.

Tel Dan Nature Reserve

Another nature reserve has been established around Tel Dan and the springs formed by the Dan River. This large tel, covered with trees and shrubs, marks the site of the ancient city of Leshem, later changed to Dan when captured by that Israelite tribe. During the First Temple period it was a center for cult worship, and graven images, including a golden calf, were worshiped here. Excavations have uncovered ritual sites, ramparts, a magnificent tomb, and ancient building stones—but not the golden calf. There are marked walking trails through the reserve (the green is a half-hour hike and the yellow twice that) and picnic areas. The flora and fauna of the entire Hula Valley and Upper Galilee are fascinating to see. As you drive through this area you will really enjoy the clean air and delicious aromas of the plant life. If you want to attach names to them, stop at *Ussishkin House* (near Kibbutz Dan), which is a small nature museum. Hours are 9 A.M. to 4 P.M. Sunday through Thursday, 9 A.M. to 3 P.M. on Friday, 10 A.M. to 4 P.M. on Saturday. Small admission charge. Tel Dan Nature Reserve closes from November through March.

When you pass Kibbutz Dan, you enter the *Golan Heights*, a bulge in the shape of the country and an area that was controlled by Syria till 1967. The Syrians used their positions atop the Golan to shell Israeli settlements until the Six Day War when, after fierce fighting, the area was captured. Although it was annexed to Israel in 1982, Israel and Syria are negotiating the status of the Golan Heights as part of a hoped-for peace treaty. The Golan now has several Israeli kibbutzim and moshavim, but the majority of the inhabitants are Druze, caught in the political crossfire. Fearful of accepting Israeli citizenship as their comrades near Haifa have done, they remain Syrians abroad.

Note: Stick to major tourist routes here and don't go wandering off near the fortifications except the ones marked ''for tour buses." The Israelis continue to sweep the Golan for mines, as the barbed-wire fences and yellow and red signs indicate.

Banias Waterfall and Springs

Your first stop in the Golan, about a mile into the area, is Banias. Stop first at the waterfall, which you can hear from the parking lot. It's wide and high and the spray is freezing, for this water is coming from snowcapped Mount Hermon. It rushes quickly along through thick underbrush on its way to Lake Kinneret. About a half-mile farther east, make the left turn (Route 989) to Banias Springs, part of the National Park System. This is where the icy water from Mount Hermon settles before it reaches the falls. You can swim here, but beware of frostbite.

In ancient times, this was a center for the worship of the goat-footed Greek god, Pan. In the cliff beyond the spring, you'll notice curved niches that were probably shrines. An ancient Greek temple stood here till it was destroyed by an earthquake. During the Greek era, it was called Paneas; Banias is the Arab mispronounciation. The Christian chapel to St. George was converted into a shrine to the Prophet Elijah by the Moslems. It still stands and the view from it is lovely.

Nimrod Castle

A mile from Banias (Route 989) stands the well-preserved ruin of this Crusader castle, built between 1130 and 1140. Long and narrow to fit the natural terrain, it commanded the route from Damascus to Lebanon and the sea. Notice the vertical slits in the wall, which were made for archers. Nimrod was not badly damaged in the 1967 fighting, although it was a Syrian mortar position. The views in every direction are stunning. You can see Qiryat Shemona (twenty kilometers away), the Hula Valley, and, of course, Mount Hermon, snowcapped in winter with traces even in spring. Its summit (nine thousand feet) is in Syrian territory, but its southern slopes have been turned into a ski resort.

Skiing Mount Hermon

Even if you are a neophyte and only make one run, how can you miss the opportunity to ski in the Golan Heights? If you have never skied, take the nonskier lift to the observation point at 6,600 feet, where there is a cafeteria. Try to ski during the week, for weekends are very crowded. The season is a short one, starting in December and lasting through March. If you must come on a weekend, come very early; the lot holds only eight hundred cars and there is not an abundance of ski equipment to rent.

There are four trails; the longest is fairly difficult at one and a half miles, with the others far less demanding. Not Aspen or St. Moritz, Mount Hermon is just good fun. Open from 8:30 A.M. to 3:30 P.M. daily; you can call to check on conditions. The slopes are managed by nearby Moshav Neve Ativ Holiday Village, phone (06) 981337. You can stay here (in a member's home) and eat in the guest dining room, which resembles a ski lodge, complete with fireplace. Moderate rates here include meals, ski lift, and entrance fees.

This has been a long day and although the distance you've driven hasn't been great, you are probably anxious to get back to Zefat and a nice hot bath. You have the option now to visit several Druze villages, which are also on the slopes of Mount Hermon. The Druze, an Arabic people, follow a secret religion that started about a thousand years ago. There are four villages here, but the two largest are *Majdal Shams* and *Massada*. Majdal Shams ("Tower of the Sun"), at 2,200 feet above sea level, was strafed by Syrian airplanes during the 1973 Yom Kippur War. The Druze are content to till the soil and mind their own business. They are, however, very courageous when forced to fight. Near these two communities is a large reservoir (Birkhet Ram) and a restaurant—a real rarity in the Golan area.

Retrace your route to Route 99 to Qiryat Shemona, where you can pick up Route 90 south to Rosh Pinna and 89 to Zefat. Sweet dreams!

Appendix A

Israel's Campsites

From the North (Galilee) to the South (Elat)

1. *Tal*—Box 464 Kiryat Shemona. Phone (06) 740400. Open year round. (It is quite cold here in winter.)
2. *En Gev*—Kibbutz En Gev, Mobile Post En Gev. Phone (06) 7582027. Open year round; on a lovely beach.
3. *Ha-On*—Ha-on Mobile Post, Jordan Valley. Phone (06) 752460. Open April–Oct.
4. *Ma'agan*—Mobile Post Jordan Valley. Phone (06) 753753. Mobile homes, on a terrific beach. Open April—November.
5. *Akhziv*—Mobile Post Western Galilee. Phone (04) 824263. Near Nahariya and Haifa. Open April–November.
6. *Hof Dor*—Mobile Post, Hof Ha Carmel. Phone (06) 399018. South of Haifa, has cottages.
7. *Newe Yam*—Mobile Post Hof Ha Carmel. Phone (04) 942240. Near Caesarea and on the sea. Open year round.
8. *Beh Zayit*—Mobile Post Harei Yehuda. Phone (02) 537717. Near Jerusalem. Open year round.
9. *Ramat Rachel*—Box 98, Jerusalem. Only 1.5 kilometers from Jerusalem. Cottages. Open year round.
10. *En Gedi*—Mobile Post, Dead Sea. Phone (05) 784342. Open year-round near an oasis and sulphur springs.
11. *Neve Zohr*—Mobile Post, Sodom. Phone (05) 784306. On the Dead Sea. Open year round.
12. *Eilat*—Sunday, P.O.B. 96. Phone (05) 973105. In the heart of the Arava Desert, near the resort Elat.

Appendix B

Israel's National Parks

Israel's national parks are as varied as the country itself. At this writing there are forty parks from northern Galilee to the tip near Elat. Wonderfully maintained by the National Parks Authority, with access roads, restaurants, lavatories, and informative signs, they include restored historic sites, ruins and recreation areas. Several have already been discussed in depth in this guide.

Hours: April through September, 8 A.M. to 5 P.M.

October through March, 8 A.M. to 4 P.M.

Sites close one hour earlier on Fridays, two hours earlier on holiday eves and are closed on Yom Kippur. The National Parks Authority publishes explanatory brochures to each site. Their office is at 4 Makleff Street, Hakiryah Tel Aviv 61070. Phone (03) 695-2281. Fax (03) 267643. Parks are listed from north to south.

1. *Nimrod's Fortress* (historic site), on Mount Hermon, Highway 989. Phone: (06) 942360. Beautiful fortress from Crusader and Marmeluke periods. Commands views of Northern Huleh Valley into Syria.

2. *Hurshat Tal* (recreation area), in Northern Huleh Valley, Highway 99. Phone (06) 942440. A picnic and camping area popular with fishermen. Lakes and rivers.

3. *Bar'am* (historic site), in Upper Galilee, Highway 899. Phone (06) 989301. One of Israel's most beautiful and best-preserved synagogues, from the second or third century A.D.

4. *Tel-Hazor* (historic site), in the Huleh Valley, Highway 90. Phone (06) 934855. Large, important tel, site of the biblical

Hazor. Remains of fortified cities with walls and temples from the Canaanite and Israelite periods. Archeological museum nearby.

5.   *Achziv* (historic and recreation site), on the Mediterranean, Highway 4. Phone (04) 824263. Impressive remains of ancient settlements. Lawns, picnic areas, restaurant, and swimming.

6.   *Yehiam Fortress* (historic site), in Western Galilee, Highway 8833. Phone (04) 924809. Restored Crusader Fortress from the twelve century located on the grounds of Kibbutz Yehiam.

7.   *Korazim* (historic site), in Eastern Galilee near the Sea of Galilee, at the side of Highway 90. Phone (06) 934982. Remains of the ancient Jewish city mentioned in the Talmud and the New Testament and best known for its grains. Footpath through the remains (25 acres), sanitary facilities, parking.

8.   *Kursi* (historic site), on the eastern shore of the Sea of Galilee, at the side of Highway 92. Phone (06) 731983. Second-Temple-period Jewish town, the traditional site of Jesus' Miracle of the Gaderene Swine. Reconstructed Byzantine church and chapel.

9.   *Hammath Tiberias* (historic site), on the shores of the Sea of Galilee, at the side of Highway 90. Ruins of ancient Jewish City beside the Tiberias Hot Springs. Exquisite mosaics in fourth century A.D. synagogue. The Ernest Lehman Museum of the History of the Baths of Tiberias is nearby.

10.   *Belvoir* (Kochav Hayarden), (historic site), in eastern Lower Galilee, Highway 717. Phone (06) 587000. Restored twelfth century A.D. Crusader Fortress on a promontory overlooking the Jordan Valley. Snack bar at the site.

11.   *Bet She'an* (historic site), in the Bet She'an Valley, near Highways 71 and 90. Phone (06) 585200. One of Israel's most important ancient sites, with ruins spanning twenty layers of civilization dating from the fourth millenium B.C. Impressive partially restored six-thousand-seat Roman the-

ater and amphitheater are among the ruins. Footpath through the site.

12. *Gan Hashelosha (Sachne)*, (recreation site), in the Bet She'an Valley at the foot of Mount Gilboa, Highway 669. Phone (06) 586219. A wonderfully landscaped park with a spring-fed swimming pool, grassy lawns, and shady trees. Indoor heated pool, dressing rooms, restaurant and snack bar, and an archeological museum of the Mediterranean.

13. *Bet Alpha Synagogue (HeftziBah)*, (historic site), in the Harod Valley, Highway 669. Phone (06) 531400. Sixth-century A.D. synagogue built to serve the Jews of Bet Alpha. Colorful mosaic floor is one of the largest and best-preserved in Israel. Park and snack bar.

14. *Maayan Harod* (recreation site), in the Harod Valley at the base of Mount Gilboa, near Highway 71. Phone (06) 532211. Site where the biblical judge Gideon, in order to select the fittest of his men to fight against the Midianites, tested them in the famous "trial by water." Lawns, wooded areas, swimming pool, dressing rooms, parking, camping, and restaurant.

15. *Tel Megiddo* (historic site), at the edge of the Jezreel Valley, Highway 66. Phone (04) 891100. One of the most important archeological mounds in Israel, remains of historic Megiddo, a fortified city on the ancient coastal road. Archeological-historic exhibit, restaurant.

16. *Bet She'arm* (historic site), in the Tivon Hills near Kiryat Tivon, near Highways 75, 722. Phone (04) 831643. An intricate network of rock-hewn catacombs uncovered during excavation of this ancient Jewish city which flourished during the Mishnaic-Talmudic period. Footpath with informative signs, a museum and snack bar.

17. *Carmel Park* (recreation site), at the top of Mount Carmel, near highways 2, 4, 70. Phone (04) 228983. Lush natural park with magnificent views, churches, monasteries, ruins of Canaanite, Jewish, and Samaritan settlements, and caves used by prehistoric man. Information stations, picnic grounds, footpaths, paved roads, and parking.

18. *Caesarea* (historic site), on the Mediterranean Coast, near Highways 2 and 4. Phone (06) 361358. Ancient port city built by Herod the Great. Restored Crusader fortifications, a Byzantine Street, and a Roman theater. Restaurants, galleries, and swimming.

19. *Samaria* (Sebaste), (historic site) on Mount Samaria, near Highways 57 and 60. Former capital of the Israelite kingdom, destroyed by the Assyrians and rebuilt by Herod the Great.

20. *Afek (Antipatris)*, (recreation and historic site), near Petah Tikva, near Highway 444. Park alongside the Yarkon River incorporating the ruins of the ancient city of Afek-Antipatris. Landscaped gardens and sports facilities.

21. *Ein Hemed (Aqua Bella)*, (recreation site and historic site), west of Jerusalem, near Highway 1. Phone (02) 344200. Group of springs called "Beautiful Waters" by the Crusaders, ruins of a fortified agricultural farm.

22. *Castel* (national memorial) at the entrance to Jerusalem, near Highway 1. Phone (02) 330037. Site of many important battles during the War of Independence. Model of the battles with explanations, rest areas.

23. *Jerusalem Walls National Park*. Seven-hundred-fifty-acre park encircling the walls of the Old City. Archeological sites.

24. *Herodion* (historic site) at the edge of the Judean Desert, near Highway 356. Fortified mountain palace built by Herod the Great; includes a luxurious palace, impressive buildings, bathhouse and pools. Impressive view of the Judean desert from the mountaintop observation post.

25. *Tel Jericho* (historic site) in the Jericho Valley, near Highway 90. Phone (02) 922909. Site of biblical Jericho and, according to the Bible, the first city captured by the Children of Israel after arriving in Canaan. Ruins from the Neolithic through the Persian periods.

26. *Jericho Synagogue* (historic site), in the city of Jericho near Highway 90. These are the remains of an ancient sixth-century A.D. synagogue.

27. *Hisham's Palace (Jericho)*, (historic site), north of Jericho, near Highway 90. Phone (02) 922522. Remains of the magnificent winter palace built by Caliph Hisham of the Omayyad Dynasty. Royal buildings, mosque, square with a fountain, and an impressive mosaic floor.

28. *Qumran* (historic site), on the northern shores of the Dead Sea, Highway 90. Phone (02) 942235. Home of the Dead Sea Cult as early as the eighth century B.C. Archeological finds—houses, ritual baths, a pottery workshop, and large hall with stone tables and inkstands used for writing the Dead Sea Scrolls.

29. *Massada* (historic site), in the Judean desert, near Highway 90. Phone (057) 584207. Solitary mountain refuge with remains of luxurious palaces, mosaic floors, frescoes, a synagogue and biblican scrolls, human skeletons, and pot shards with Hebrew inscriptions. Cable car, sound and light shows in the summer, snack bar, restaurant.

30. *Bet Guvrin* (historic and recreation site), on the Judean Plains at the side of Highway 35. Phone (051) 811020. Ancient city of Bet Guvrin containing antiquities and unique man-made caves. Footpaths with informative signs, sanitary facilities, parking, snack bar.

31. *Ashkelon* (historic and recreation site) on the Mediterranean Coast near Highway 4. Phone (051) 36444. One of the oldest and most important cities of Israel. Shoreside park with landscaped grounds and the remains of ancient fortifications.

32. *Yad-Mordechai* (national memorial), on the Southern Coastal Plain, Highway 4. Phone (051) 20528. Site of a major battle during the War of Independence, a memorial to courage and determination. Reconstructions of the battle and a museum dedicated to Jewish Heroism in the Holocaust and during the War of Independence.

33. *Eshkol* (recreation site), in the northwestern Negev, Highway 241. Phone (057) 985110. One-thousand-acre park on the banks of the Besor River with ruins from the Canaanite

to the Byzantine periods. Man-made; recreation and sports facilities, swimming pool, and footpaths.

34. *Tel Arad* (historic site), in the northeastern Negev, near Arad, near Highway 31. Ancient mound containing the reconstructed ruins of a five-thousand-year-old Canaanite city.

35. *Mamshit (Kurnub)*, (historic site) in the eastern Negev Mountains, near Highway 25. Ruins of the ancient Nabatean city, conquered by the Romans, prosperous during the Byzantine Period, and defeat by the Muslims in 636 A.D. Residential areas, public buildings, churches, and bathhouses.

36. *Shivta* (historic site), in the western Negev mountains, near Highway 211. Partially reconstructed ancient Negev city established by the Nabateans and abandoned in approximately 900 A.D. A reconstructed ancient agricultural farm is adjacent to the ruins.

37. *Ben-Gurion's Burial Place* (national memorial), in the Central Negev Mountains, near Highway 40. Phone (057) 555684. Final resting place of Israel's first prime minister, David Ben-Gurion, and his wife Paula. Lovely views of the surrounding countryside.

38. *En Avdit* (recreation site), in the Central Negev Mountains, near Highway 40. Canyon just north of Avdat. Spring waters flow into natural pools. River flora, poplars, and flocks of ibex (wild goats).

39. *Avdat* (historic site) in the Central Negev Mountains, near Highway 40. Phone (057) 550954. Extensively excavated and reconstructed Negev city on the Beer-sheva-Yerucham-Mizpe Ramon Highway. Built by the Nabateans as a caravan station on the road from Petra to Elat.

40. *Nahal Alexander* (bathing beach and recreation site), near Yannai Interchange, Highway 2. Phone (053) 666230. A terrific vacation spot with natural flora and wooded areas, a shore of craggy cliffs and sand dunes, and plenty of swimming. Shade huts and parking. Recreational facilities are to

be constructed along the banks of the Alexander River at the center of the park.